MW01009146

Destiny
A Chronicle of Deaths Foretold

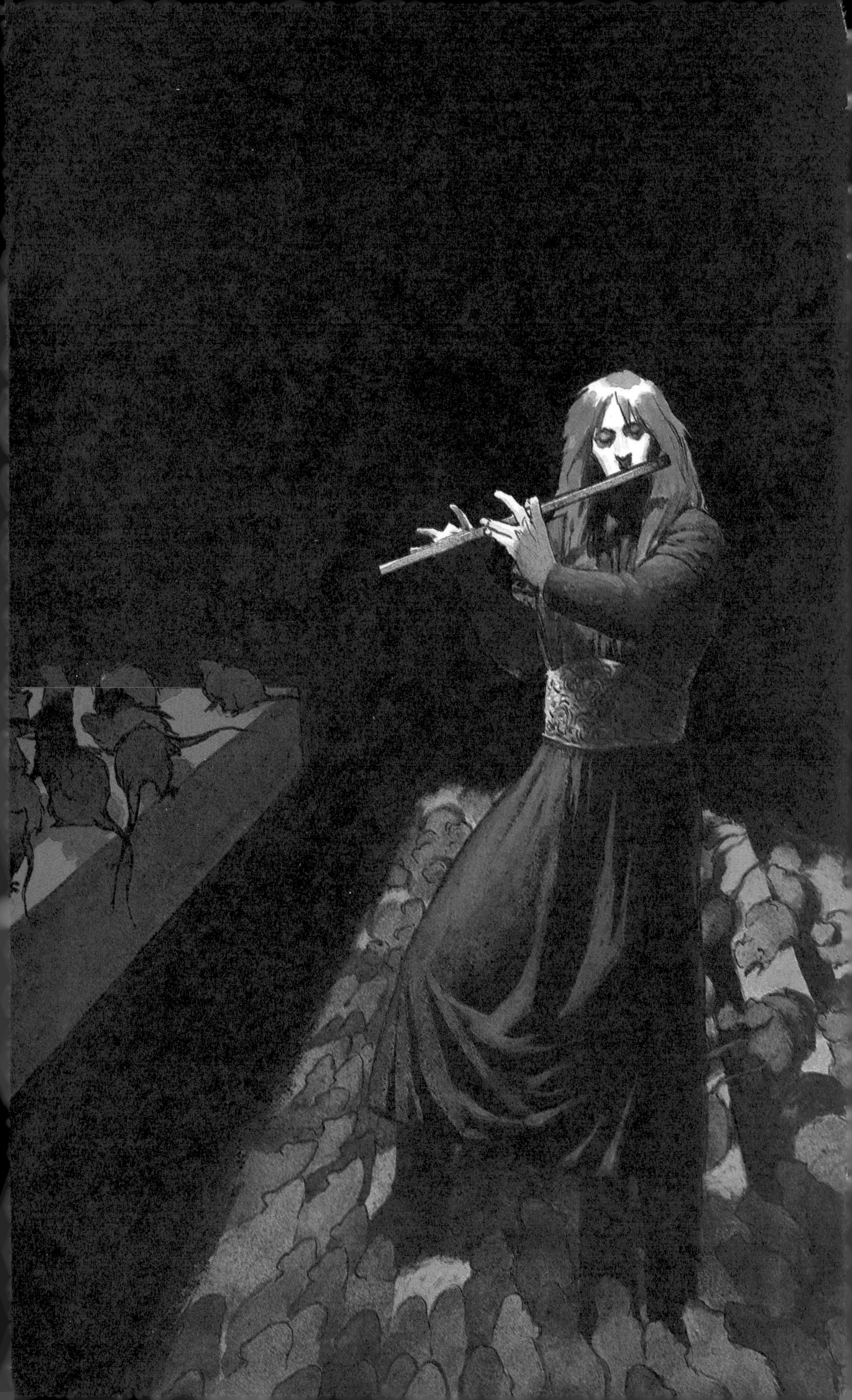

Destiny
A Chronicle of Deaths Foretold

Alisa Kwitney
Writer

Kent Williams　**Michael Zulli**
Scott Hampton　**Rebecca Guay**
Artists

Sherilyn Van Valkenburgh
Color Artist
(pp. 20-52)

Todd Klein
Letterer

To Mark, whom I plague every day. —Alisa Kwitney

✳

Jenette Kahn
President & Editor-in-Chief

Paul Levitz
Executive Vice President & Publisher

Karen Berger
Executive Editor

Dale Crain
Editor-collected edition

Joan Hilty
Associate Editor-original series

Michael Wright
Assistant Editor-collected edition

Georg Brewer
Design Director

Robbin Brosterman
Art Director

Richard Bruning
VP-Creative Director

Patrick Caldon
VP-Finance & Operations

Dorothy Crouch
VP-Licensed Publishing

Terri Cunningham
VP-Managing Editor

Joel Ehrlich
Senior VP-Advertising & Promotions

Alison Gill
Exec. Director-Manufacturing

Lillian Laserson
VP & General Counsel

Jim Lee
Editorial Director-WildStorm

John Nee
VP & General Manager-WildStorm

Bob Wayne
VP-Direct Sales

DESTINY: A CHRONICLE OF

DEATHS FORETOLD

Published by DC Comics.

Cover, introduction and compilation

copyright © 2000 DC Comics.

All Rights Reserved.

Originally published in single magazine

form as DESTINY: A CHRONICLE

OF DEATHS FORETOLD 1-3.

Copyright © 1997 DC Comics.

All Rights Reserved. All characters,

their distinctive likenesses and related

indicia featured in this publication are

trademarks of DC Comics.

The stories, characters, and incidents

featured in this publication are

entirely fictional.

DC Comics, 1700 Broadway,

New York, NY 10019

A division of Warner Bros. - A Time

Warner Entertainment Company

Printed in Canada. First Printing.

ISBN: 1-56389-505-6

Cover illustration by Kent Williams.

Cover design by Addie Blaustein.

Chronicles of a Hypochondriac Thrice Told

First, a warning: You have to be a little bit of a hypochondriac to fully appreciate this story. If you've never stared at that little brown mole on your thigh and wondered if it was melanoma, or considered the possibility of contracting antibiotic-resistant tuberculosis from that guy hacking his lungs out on the subway, then you probably don't feel the way I do about the Plague.

But then, you've also probably never been pregnant.

Just about everyone becomes a hypochondriac when pregnant. It's the side effect no one talks about, right up there with nausea and fatigue. Most obsess about the health of the baby, or the possibility of eclampsia and dying on the delivery table, but in 1995 I discovered something that made all my other fears subside.

Ebola.

As my stomach swelled with new life, and as other expectant mothers pored over the pages of *What to Expect When You're Expecting*, I devoured the nonfiction medical thriller *The Hot Zone* and Laurie Garrett's 620-page doomsday tome, *The Coming Plague*. Creating my own little Ph.D. program in Advanced Germ Phobia, I carried on with McNeill's seminal study of disease and history, perused Gottfried's work on Natural and Human Disaster in Medieval Europe, and half-memorized Ziegler's more macabre account.

My friends asked what names I was thinking of for the baby. I recited other names: Marburg, Ebola, Hanta virus, and the great-granddaddy of them all, Bubonic plague. Coming soon, on an airplane, to a person near you.

My friends, oddly enough, did not seem to want to hear all the many fascinating bits of esoterica I had picked up about plagues in general and The Plague in particular: the three variants (bubonic, septicemic, and pneumonic, each more virulent than the last): the permanent reservoirs of *Y. pestis* bacteria in central Asia, Siberia, east Africa, the Arabian Peninsula,and the southwest United States: the patron saint (St. Roch, often depicted with the dog who, it is said, licked his buboe and cured him).

Then Destiny appeared, in the form of Karen Berger, asking me write something about Destiny, the eldest of the Endless. (Destiny is so old, in fact, that he used to appear in old DC horror titles, as a host not unlike Cain, Abel, the Three Witches and Judge Gallows.)

"You and your plagues, Kwitney," she said. "Write me a proposal."

And so I did, pouring into it all my delicious paranoid fear of disease, my pleasure in adding to the legend of the guy who casts no shadow, and my long-thwarted desire to write something I absolutely and positively did not know.

Ever since ninth grade, when my English teacher rather snidely handed back my story about the death throes of Cleopatra, I had wanted to write great, big, overheated historicals, the kind where you start out with the hero on the verge of manhood, watch him narrowly escape castration, and then follow him through various battles and love affairs until he steps off the page into legend. My model for this was Frank Yerby, the most erudite author to ever pen such "soul-searing, wide-ranging, gut-wrenching, heart-rending" fare. (I quote from one of his reviews, of course.)

I had never done anything of the sort before, and if the plot seems to behave at times like a demented golden retriever, I can only promise that it does, finally, wind up where it was supposed to go.

Along the way, I can promise you a hell of a view: glorious art from Kent Williams, who captures something oddly and perfectly Gothic in his very modern figures; stunningly byzantine drawings from Michael Zulli; the exquisite romance of Scott Hampton's Middle Ages; and the sensual pageantry of Rebecca's Guay's doomed lovers.

Much of the story is true or, at least, it is historical. Procopius's highly prurient accounts of the Empress Theodora, the sad fate of Princess Joanna, even Emmot Siddall — I didn't have to make up a bit of it. As for the antibiotic-resistant strain of bubonic plague, it was reported in *The New York Times* some months after the miniseries was first published.

There. See how easy it is to become a hypochondriac? Now, go. Suffer. Enjoy yourself.

Alisa Kwitney

Alisa Kwitney has also written THE DREAMING, PHANTOM STRANGER, SECRET FILES, the novel *Till the Fat Lady Sings* published by HarperCollins, and *Vertigo Visions* published by Watson-Guptill.

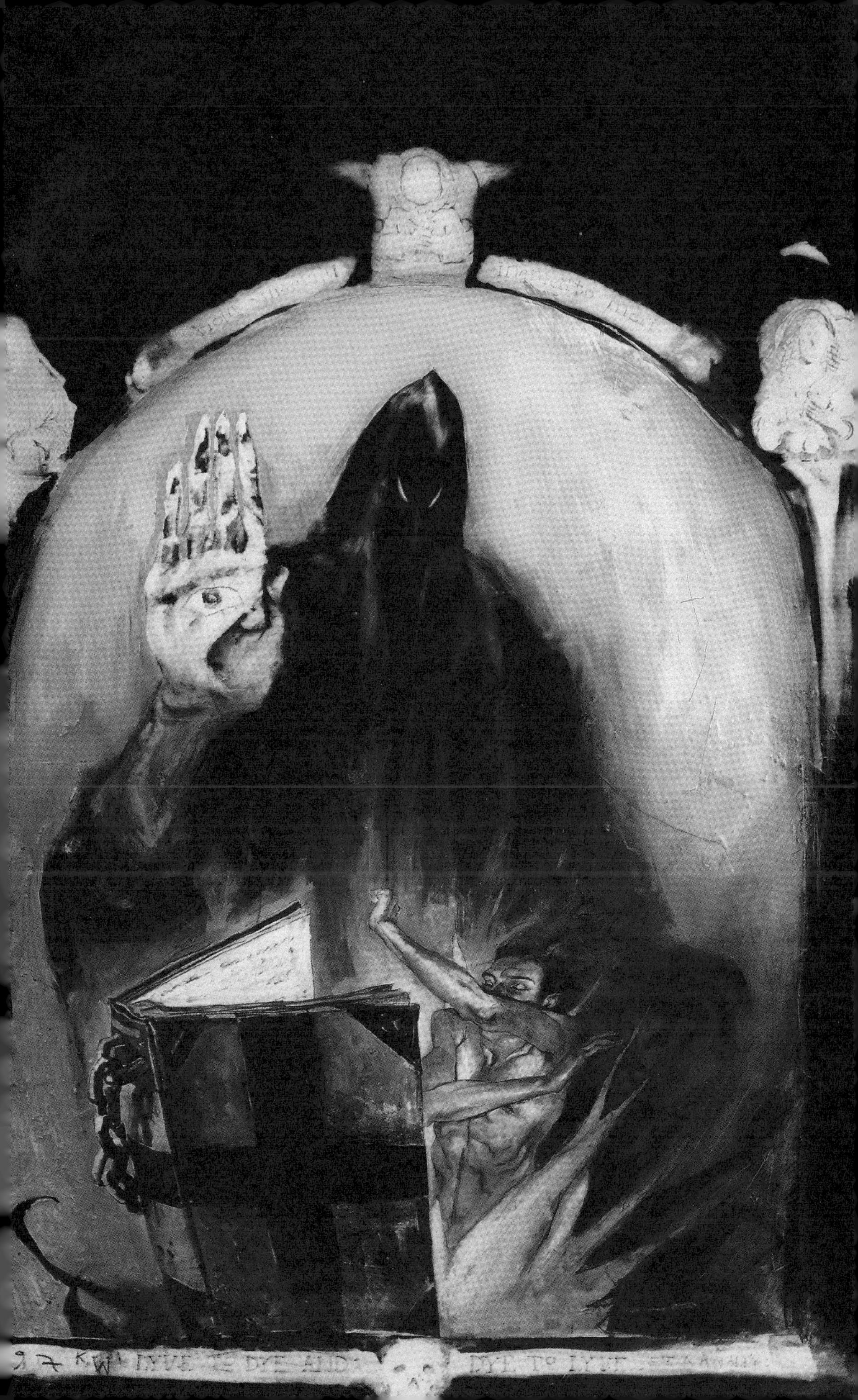
LYVE TO DYE AND
DYE TO LYVE

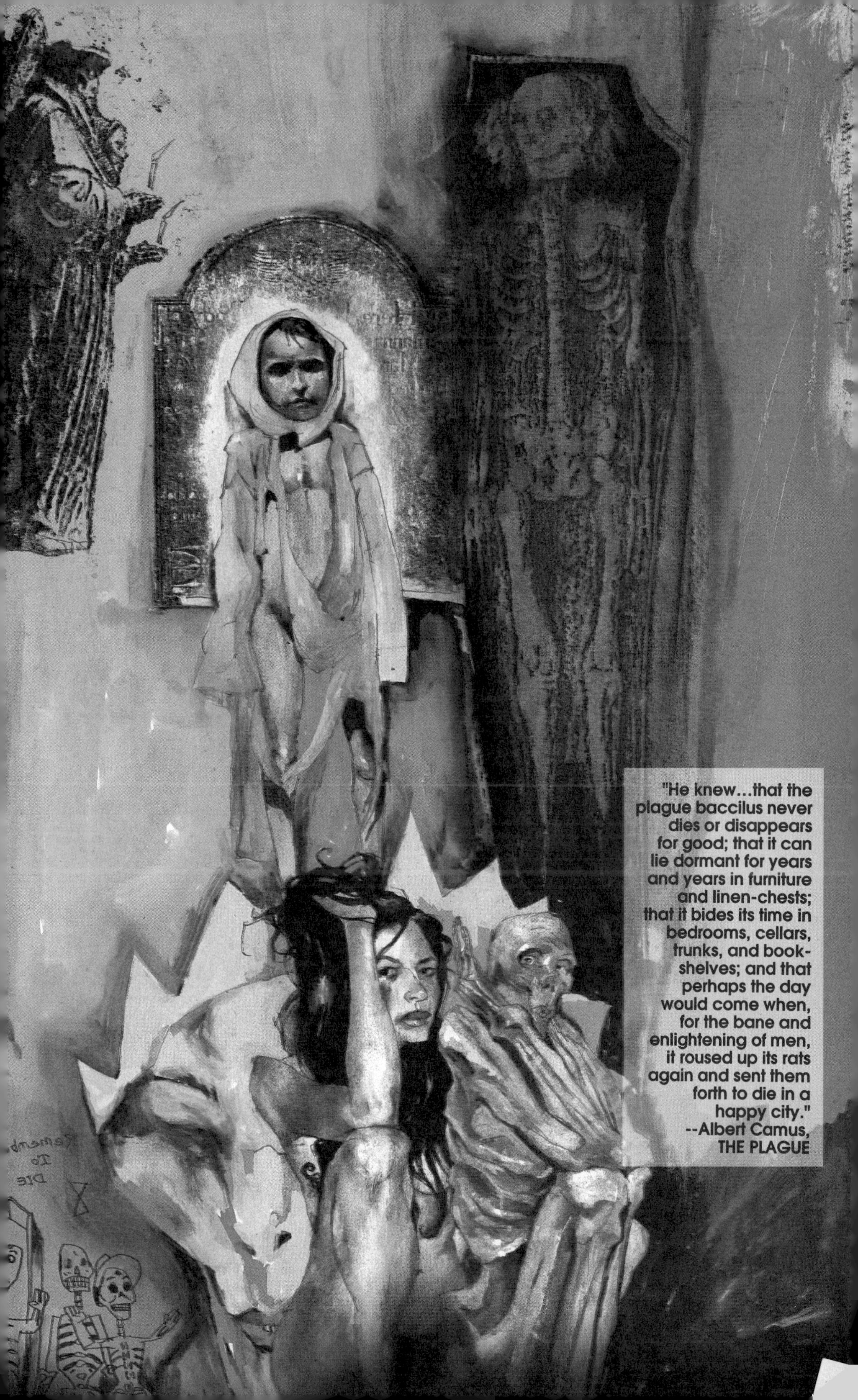
"He knew...that the plague baccilus never dies or disappears for good; that it can lie dormant for years and years in furniture and linen-chests; that it bides its time in bedrooms, cellars, trunks, and book-shelves; and that perhaps the day would come when, for the bane and enlightening of men, it roused up its rats again and sent them forth to die in a happy city."
--Albert Camus,
THE PLAGUE

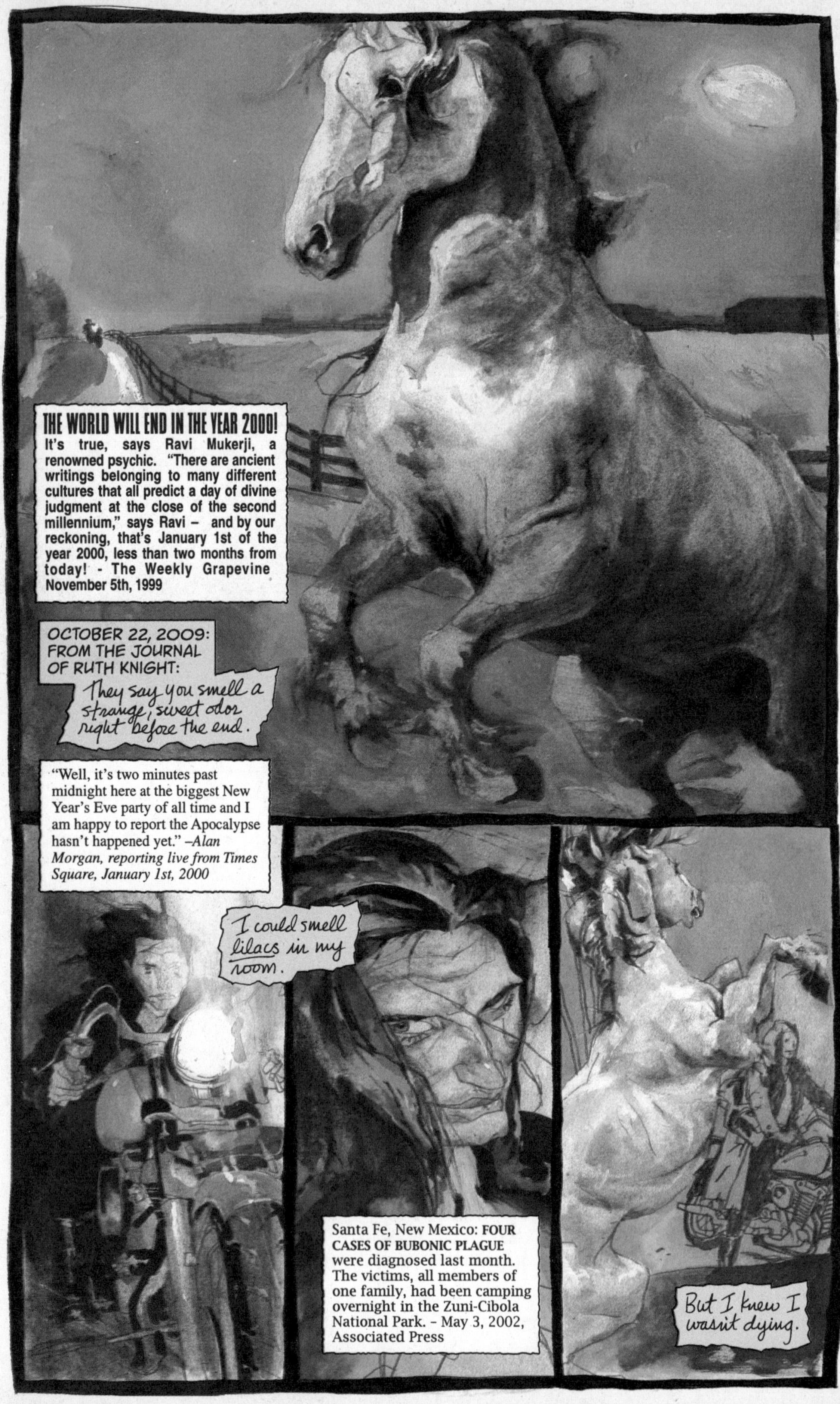
THE WORLD WILL END IN THE YEAR 2000!
It's true, says Ravi Mukerji, a renowned psychic. "There are ancient writings belonging to many different cultures that all predict a day of divine judgment at the close of the second millennium," says Ravi – and by our reckoning, that's January 1st of the year 2000, less than two months from today! - The Weekly Grapevine November 5th, 1999
OCTOBER 22, 2009: FROM THE JOURNAL OF RUTH KNIGHT:
They say you smell a strange, sweet odor right before the end.
"Well, it's two minutes past midnight here at the biggest New Year's Eve party of all time and I am happy to report the Apocalypse hasn't happened yet." –Alan Morgan, reporting live from Times Square, January 1st, 2000
I could smell lilacs in my room.
Santa Fe, New Mexico: FOUR CASES OF BUBONIC PLAGUE were diagnosed last month. The victims, all members of one family, had been camping overnight in the Zuni-Cibola National Park. – May 3, 2002, Associated Press
But I knew I wasn't dying.

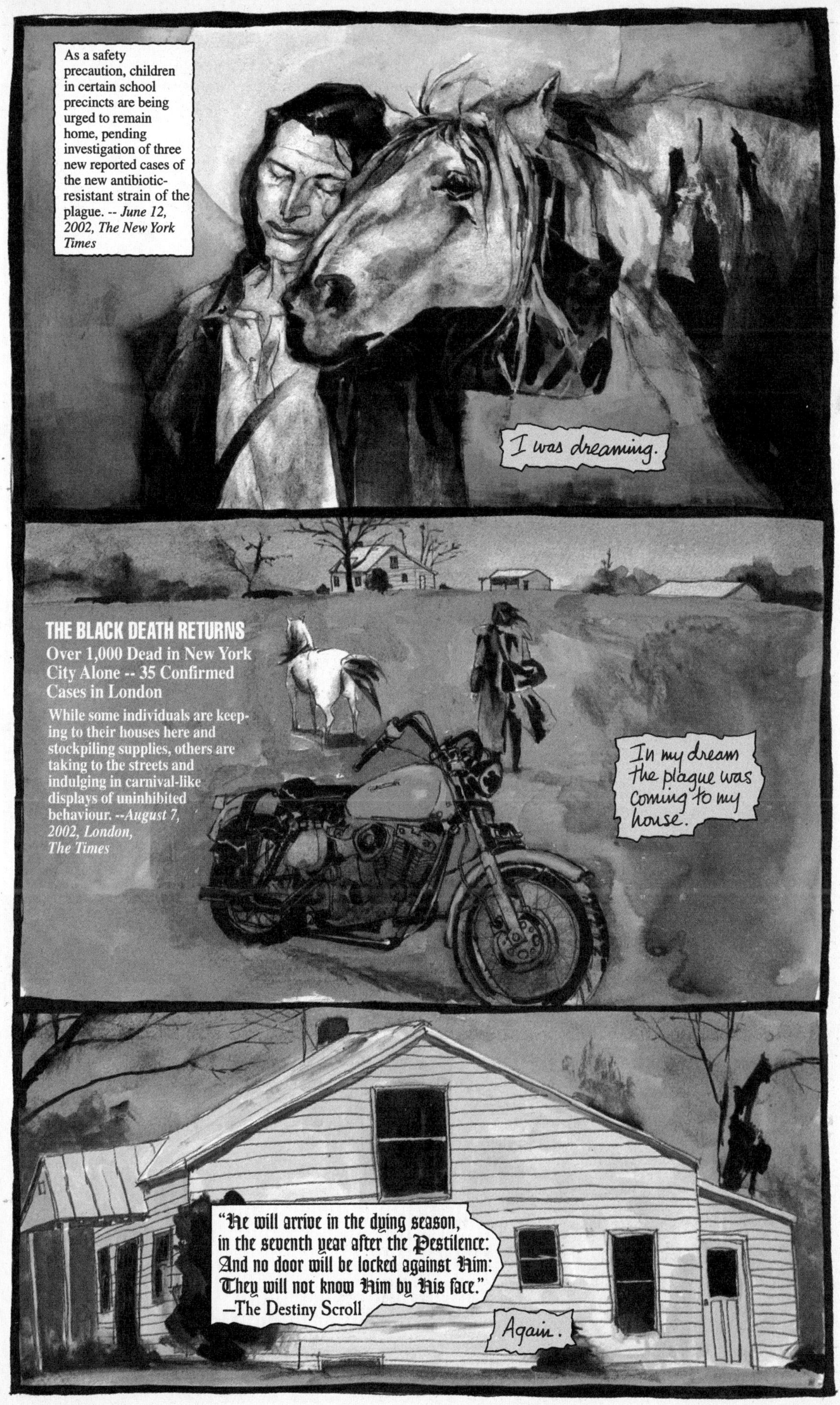
As a safety precaution, children in certain school precincts are being urged to remain home, pending investigation of three new reported cases of the new antibiotic-resistant strain of the plague. -- *June 12, 2002, The New York Times*
I was dreaming.
THE BLACK DEATH RETURNS
Over 1,000 Dead in New York City Alone -- 35 Confirmed Cases in London
While some individuals are keeping to their houses here and stockpiling supplies, others are taking to the streets and indulging in carnival-like displays of uninhibited behaviour. --*August 7, 2002, London, The Times*
In my dream the plague was coming to my house.
"He will arrive in the dying season, in the seventh year after the Pestilence: And no door will be locked against Him: They will not know Him by His face." —The Destiny Scroll
Again.

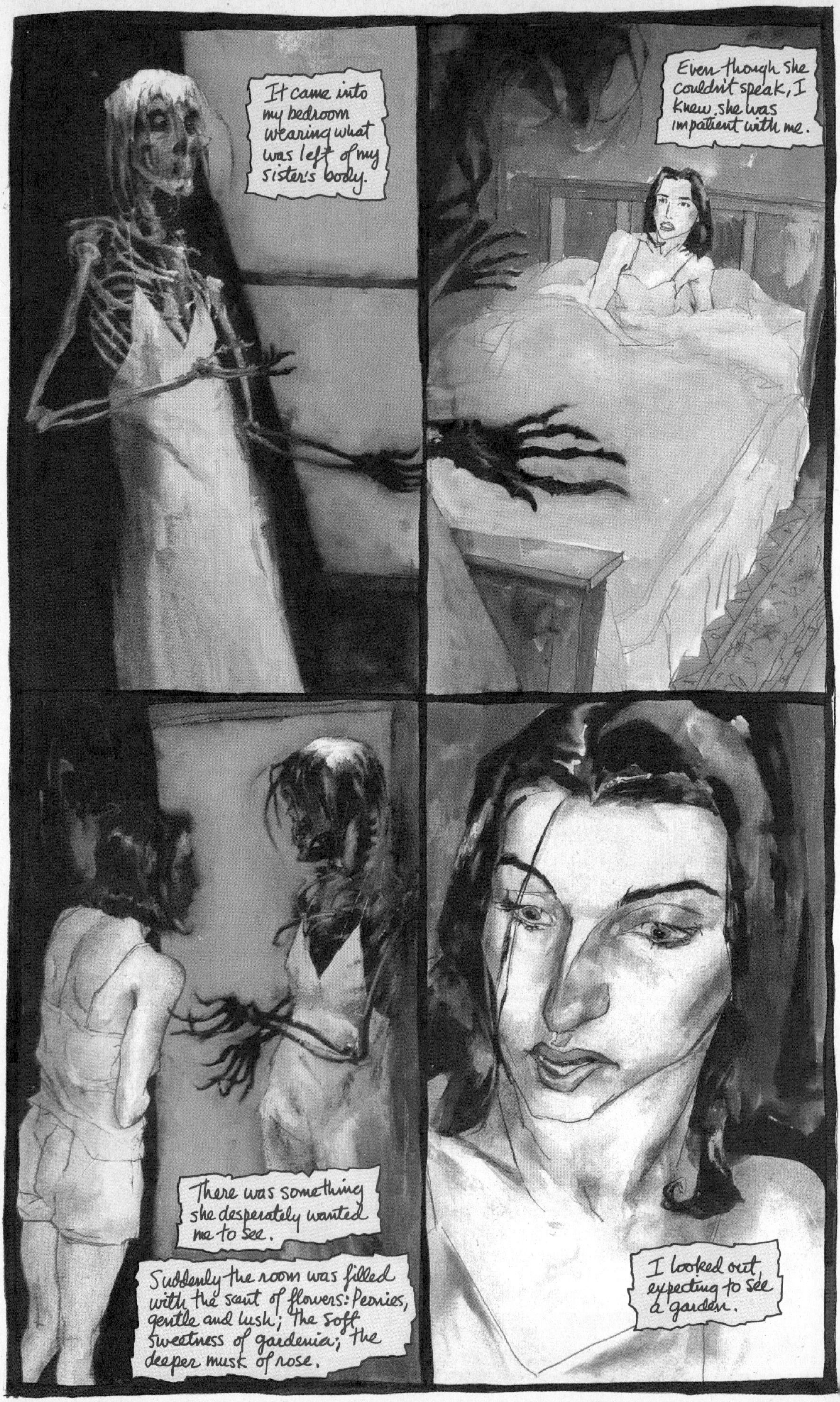
It came into my bedroom wearing what was left of my sister's body.
Even though she couldn't speak, I knew she was impatient with me.
There was something she desperately wanted me to see.
Suddenly the room was filled with the scent of flowers: Peonies, gentle and lush; the soft sweetness of gardenia; the deeper musk of rose.
I looked out, expecting to see a garden.

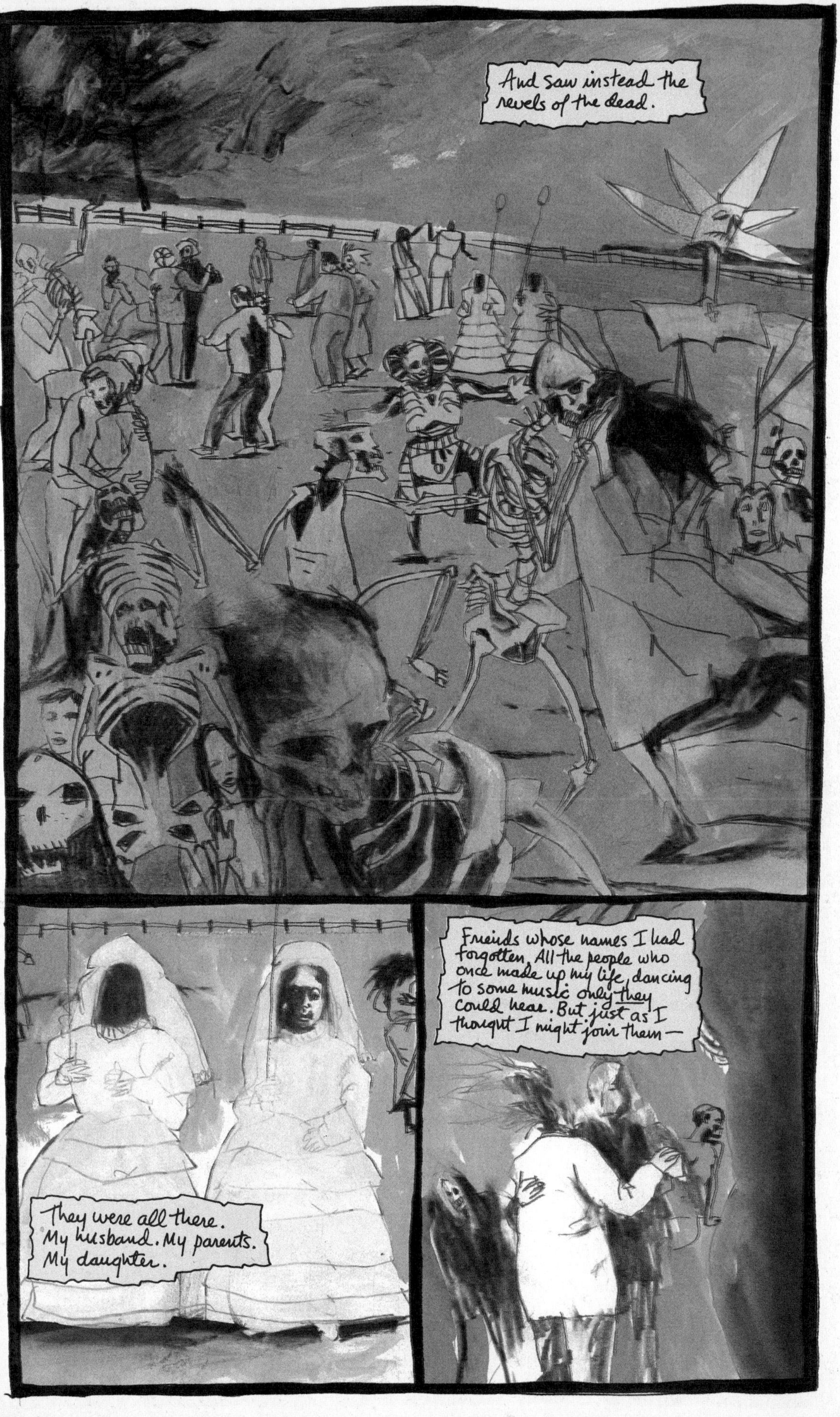
And saw instead the revels of the dead.
They were all there. My husband. My parents. My daughter.
Friends whose names I had forgotten. All the people who once made up my life, dancing to some music only they could hear. But just as I thought I might join them—

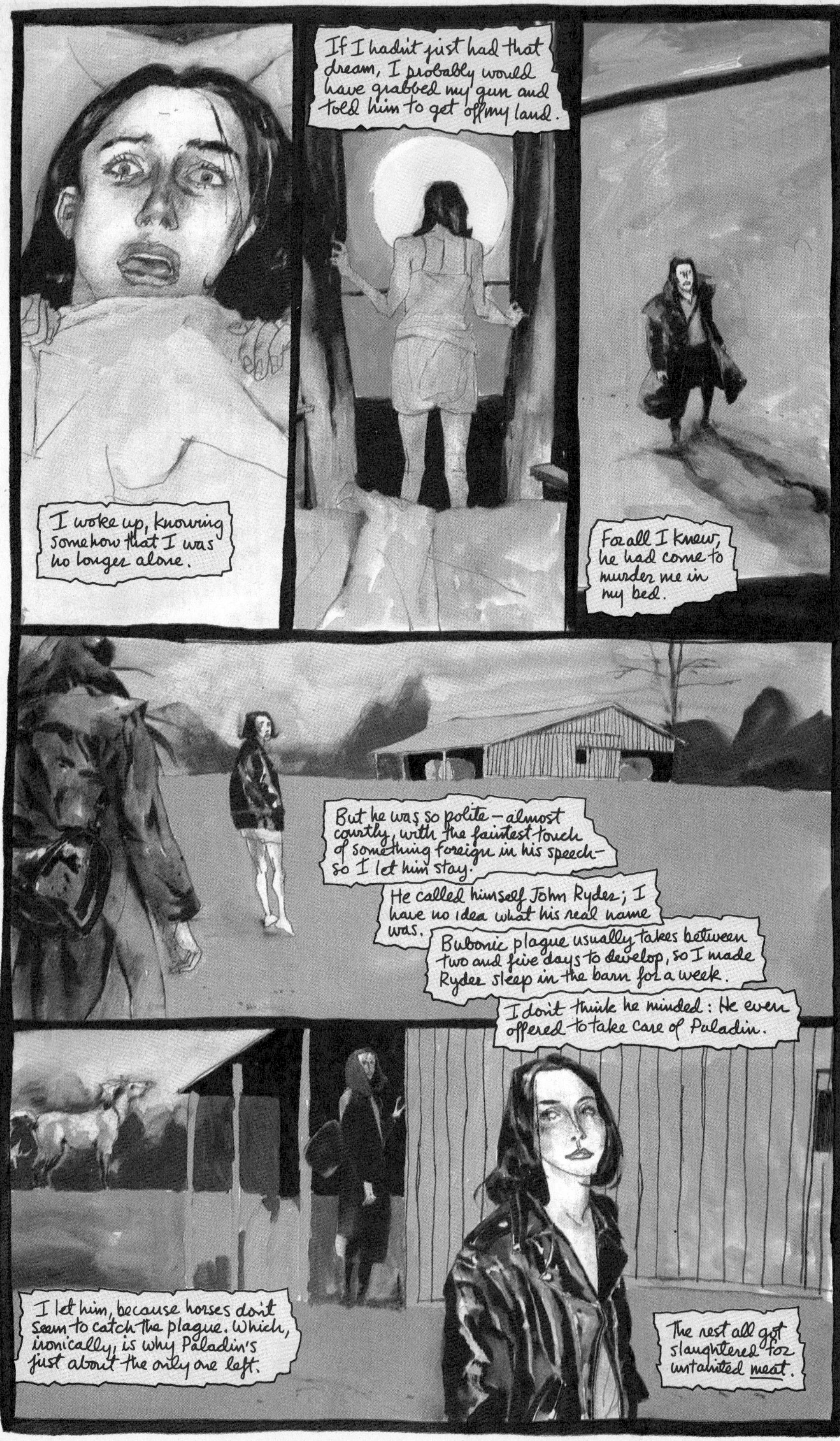
I woke up, knowing somehow that I was no longer alone.
If I hadn't just had that dream, I probably would have grabbed my gun and told him to get off my land.
For all I knew, he had come to murder me in my bed.
But he was so polite — almost courtly, with the faintest touch of something foreign in his speech — so I let him stay.
He called himself John Ryder; I have no idea what his real name was.
Bubonic plague usually takes between two and five days to develop, so I made Ryder sleep in the barn for a week.
I don't think he minded: He even offered to take care of Paladin.
I let him, because horses don't seem to catch the plague. Which, ironically, is why Paladin's just about the only one left.
The rest all got slaughtered for untainted meat.

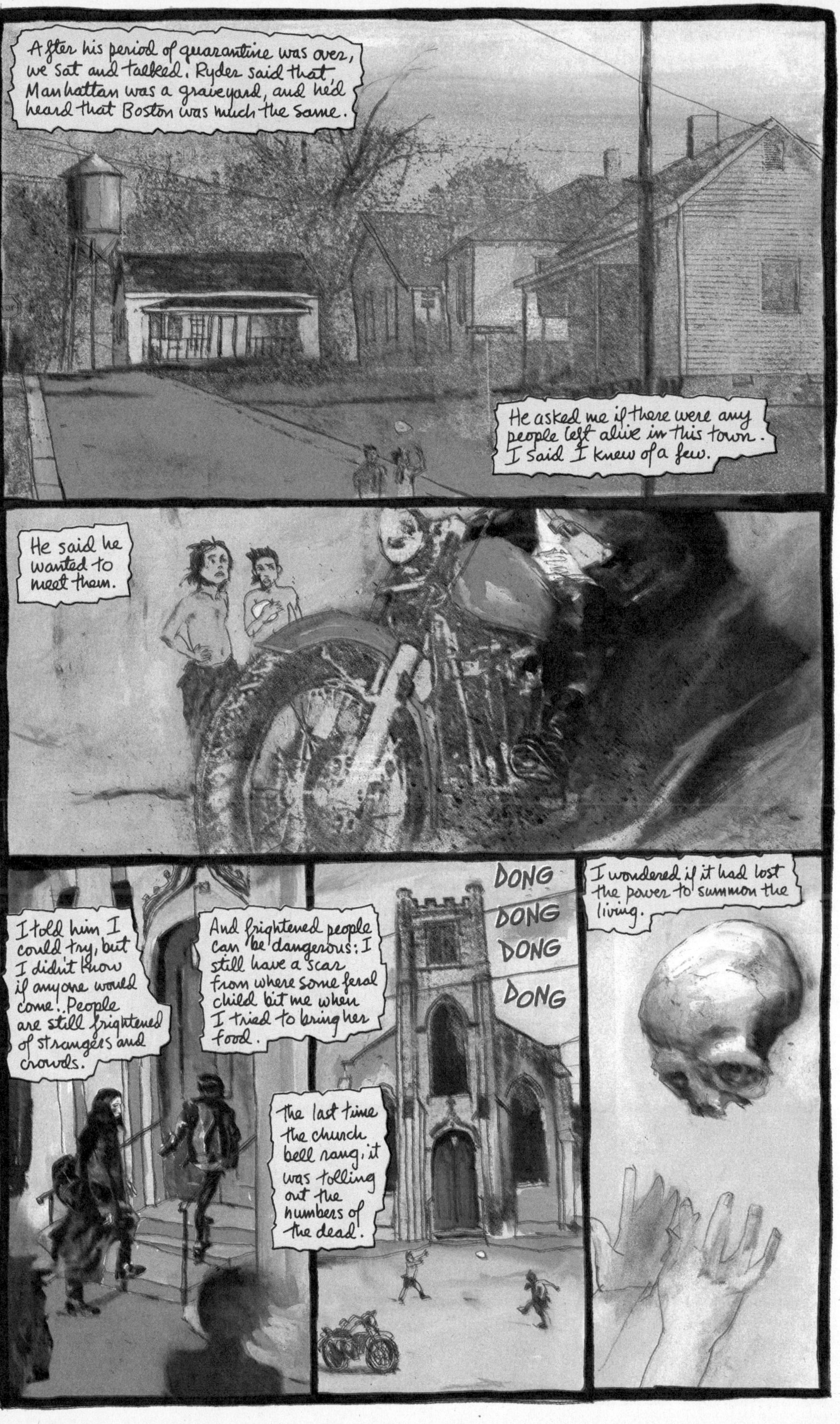
After his period of quarantine was over, we sat and talked. Ryder said that, Manhattan was a graveyard, and he'd heard that Boston was much the same.
He asked me if there were any people left alive in this town. I said I knew of a few.
He said he wanted to meet them.
I told him I could try, but I didn't know if anyone would come. People are still frightened of strangers and crowds.
And frightened people can be dangerous: I still have a scar from where some feral child bit me when I tried to bring her food.
DONG
DONG
DONG
DONG
The last time the church bell rang, it was tolling out the numbers of the dead.
I wondered if it had lost the power to summon the living.

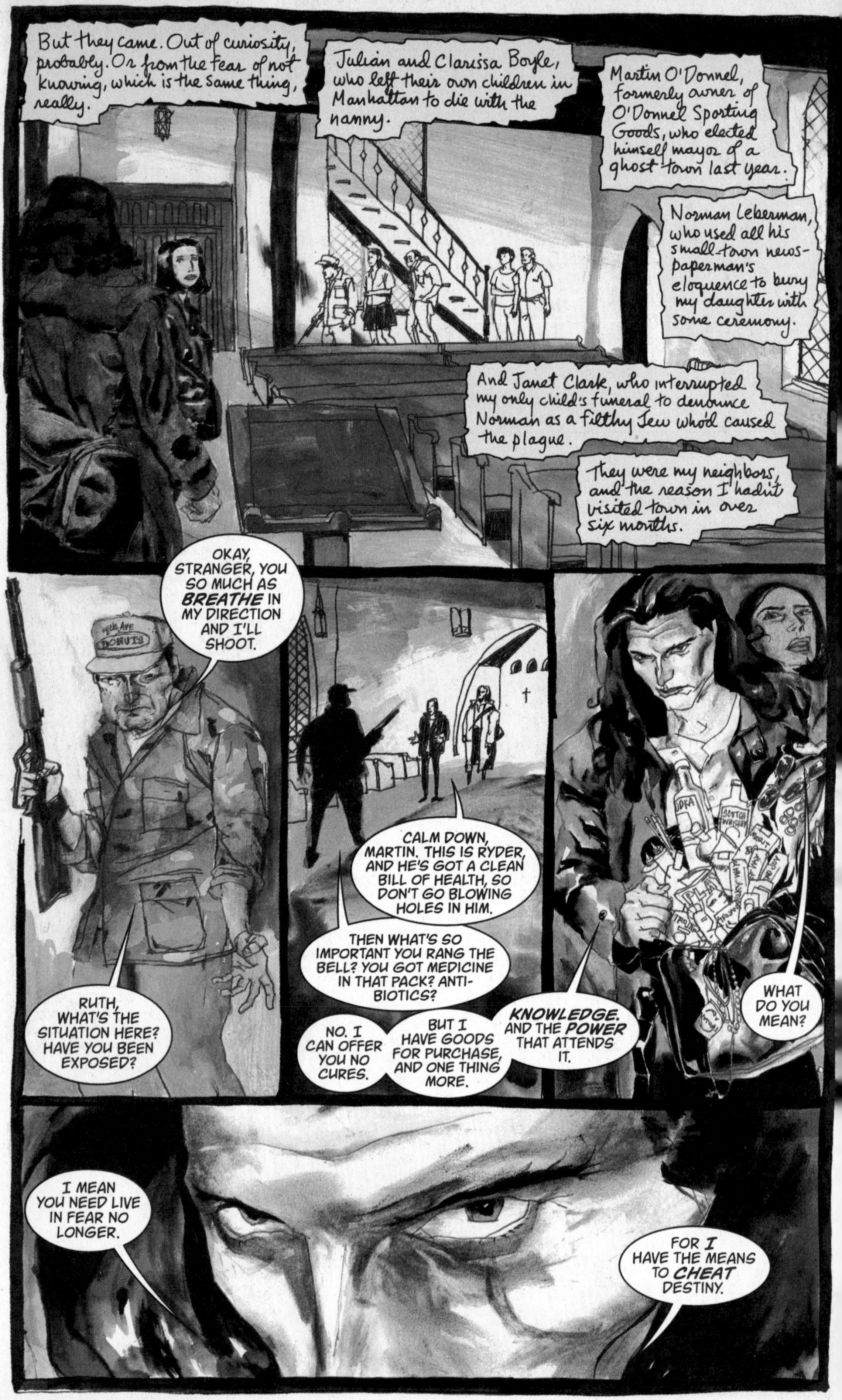
But they came. Out of curiosity, probably. Or from the fear of not knowing, which is the same thing, really.
Julian and Clarissa Boyle, who left their own children in Manhattan to die with the nanny.
Martin O'Donnel, formerly owner of O'Donnel Sporting Goods, who elected himself mayor of a ghost town last year.
Norman Leberman, who used all his small-town newspaperman's eloquence to bury my daughter with some ceremony.
And Janet Clark, who interrupted my only child's funeral to denounce Norman as a filthy Jew who'd caused the plague.
They were my neighbors, and the reason I hadn't visited town in over six months.
OKAY, STRANGER, YOU SO MUCH AS *BREATHE* IN MY DIRECTION AND I'LL SHOOT.
RUTH, WHAT'S THE SITUATION HERE? HAVE YOU BEEN EXPOSED?
CALM DOWN, MARTIN. THIS IS RYDER, AND HE'S GOT A CLEAN BILL OF HEALTH, SO DON'T GO BLOWING HOLES IN HIM.
THEN WHAT'S SO IMPORTANT YOU RANG THE BELL? YOU GOT MEDICINE IN THAT PACK? ANTIBIOTICS?
NO. I CAN OFFER YOU NO CURES.
BUT I HAVE GOODS FOR PURCHASE, AND ONE THING MORE.
KNOWLEDGE. AND THE *POWER* THAT ATTENDS IT.
WHAT DO YOU MEAN?
I MEAN YOU NEED LIVE IN FEAR NO LONGER.
FOR *I* HAVE THE MEANS TO *CHEAT* DESTINY.

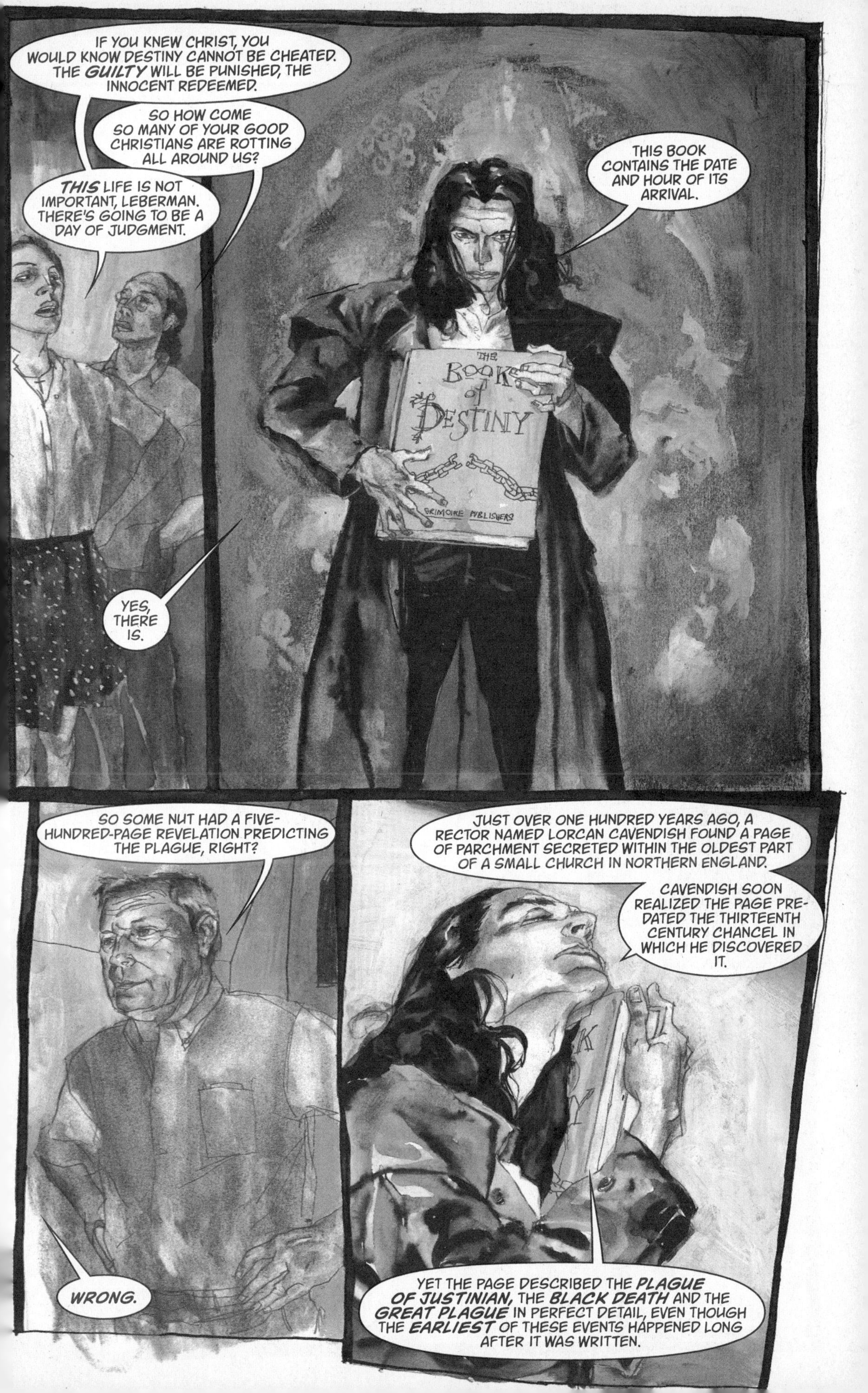
IF YOU KNEW CHRIST, YOU WOULD KNOW DESTINY CANNOT BE CHEATED. THE GUILTY WILL BE PUNISHED, THE INNOCENT REDEEMED.
SO HOW COME SO MANY OF YOUR GOOD CHRISTIANS ARE ROTTING ALL AROUND US?
THIS LIFE IS NOT IMPORTANT, LEBERMAN. THERE'S GOING TO BE A DAY OF JUDGMENT.
YES, THERE IS.
THIS BOOK CONTAINS THE DATE AND HOUR OF ITS ARRIVAL.
THE BOOK of DESTINY
GRIMOIRE PUBLISHERS
SO SOME NUT HAD A FIVE-HUNDRED-PAGE REVELATION PREDICTING THE PLAGUE, RIGHT?
WRONG.
JUST OVER ONE HUNDRED YEARS AGO, A RECTOR NAMED LORCAN CAVENDISH FOUND A PAGE OF PARCHMENT SECRETED WITHIN THE OLDEST PART OF A SMALL CHURCH IN NORTHERN ENGLAND.
CAVENDISH SOON REALIZED THE PAGE PRE-DATED THE THIRTEENTH CENTURY CHANCEL IN WHICH HE DISCOVERED IT.
YET THE PAGE DESCRIBED THE PLAGUE OF JUSTINIAN, THE BLACK DEATH AND THE GREAT PLAGUE IN PERFECT DETAIL, EVEN THOUGH THE EARLIEST OF THESE EVENTS HAPPENED LONG AFTER IT WAS WRITTEN.

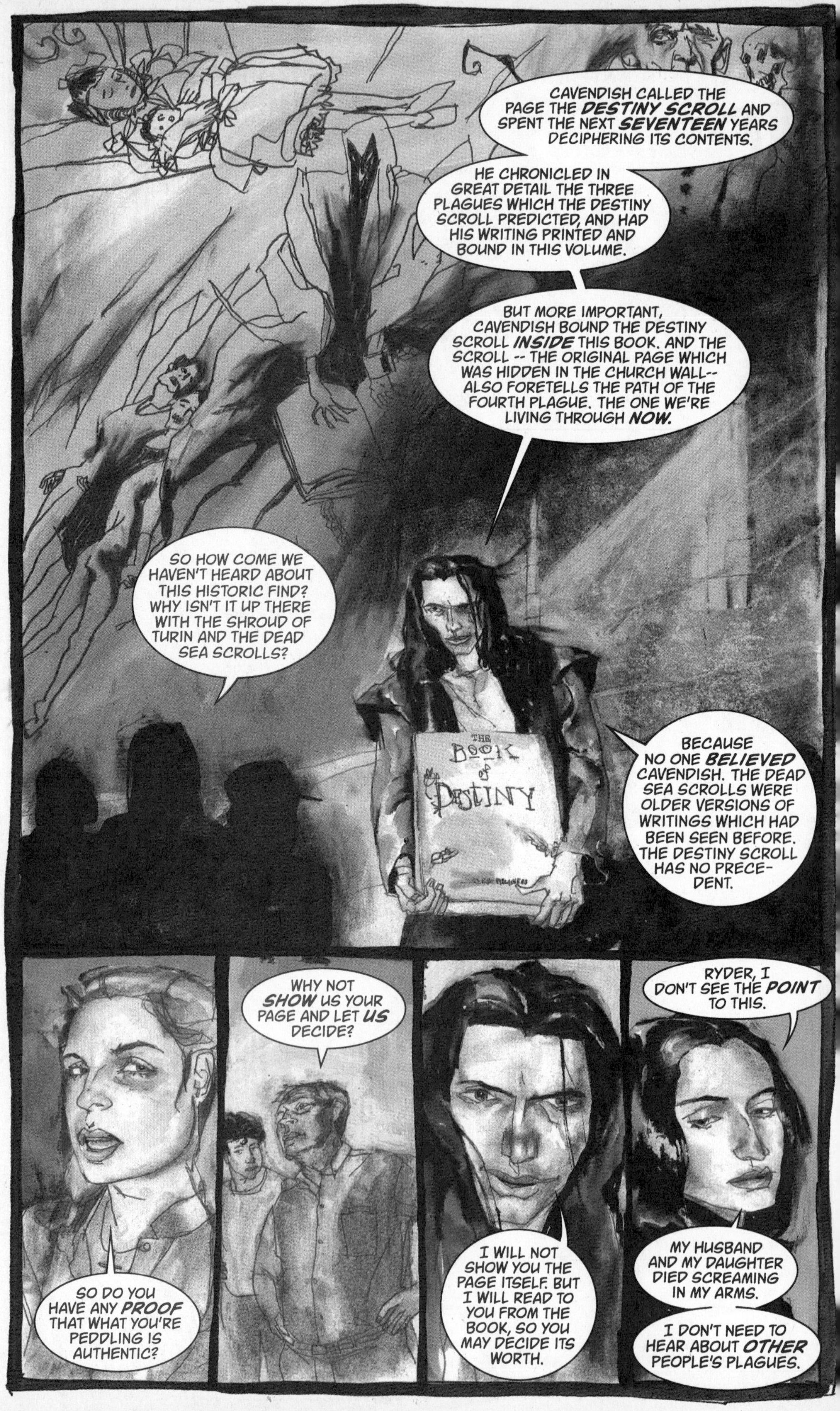
CAVENDISH CALLED THE PAGE THE DESTINY SCROLL AND SPENT THE NEXT SEVENTEEN YEARS DECIPHERING ITS CONTENTS.
HE CHRONICLED IN GREAT DETAIL THE THREE PLAGUES WHICH THE DESTINY SCROLL PREDICTED, AND HAD HIS WRITING PRINTED AND BOUND IN THIS VOLUME.
BUT MORE IMPORTANT, CAVENDISH BOUND THE DESTINY SCROLL INSIDE THIS BOOK. AND THE SCROLL -- THE ORIGINAL PAGE WHICH WAS HIDDEN IN THE CHURCH WALL-- ALSO FORETELLS THE PATH OF THE FOURTH PLAGUE. THE ONE WE'RE LIVING THROUGH NOW.
SO HOW COME WE HAVEN'T HEARD ABOUT THIS HISTORIC FIND? WHY ISN'T IT UP THERE WITH THE SHROUD OF TURIN AND THE DEAD SEA SCROLLS?
THE BOOK OF DESTINY
BECAUSE NO ONE BELIEVED CAVENDISH. THE DEAD SEA SCROLLS WERE OLDER VERSIONS OF WRITINGS WHICH HAD BEEN SEEN BEFORE. THE DESTINY SCROLL HAS NO PRECE-DENT.
SO DO YOU HAVE ANY PROOF THAT WHAT YOU'RE PEDDLING IS AUTHENTIC?
WHY NOT SHOW US YOUR PAGE AND LET US DECIDE?
I WILL NOT SHOW YOU THE PAGE ITSELF. BUT I WILL READ TO YOU FROM THE BOOK, SO YOU MAY DECIDE ITS WORTH.
RYDER, I DON'T SEE THE POINT TO THIS.
MY HUSBAND AND MY DAUGHTER DIED SCREAMING IN MY ARMS.
I DON'T NEED TO HEAR ABOUT OTHER PEOPLE'S PLAGUES.

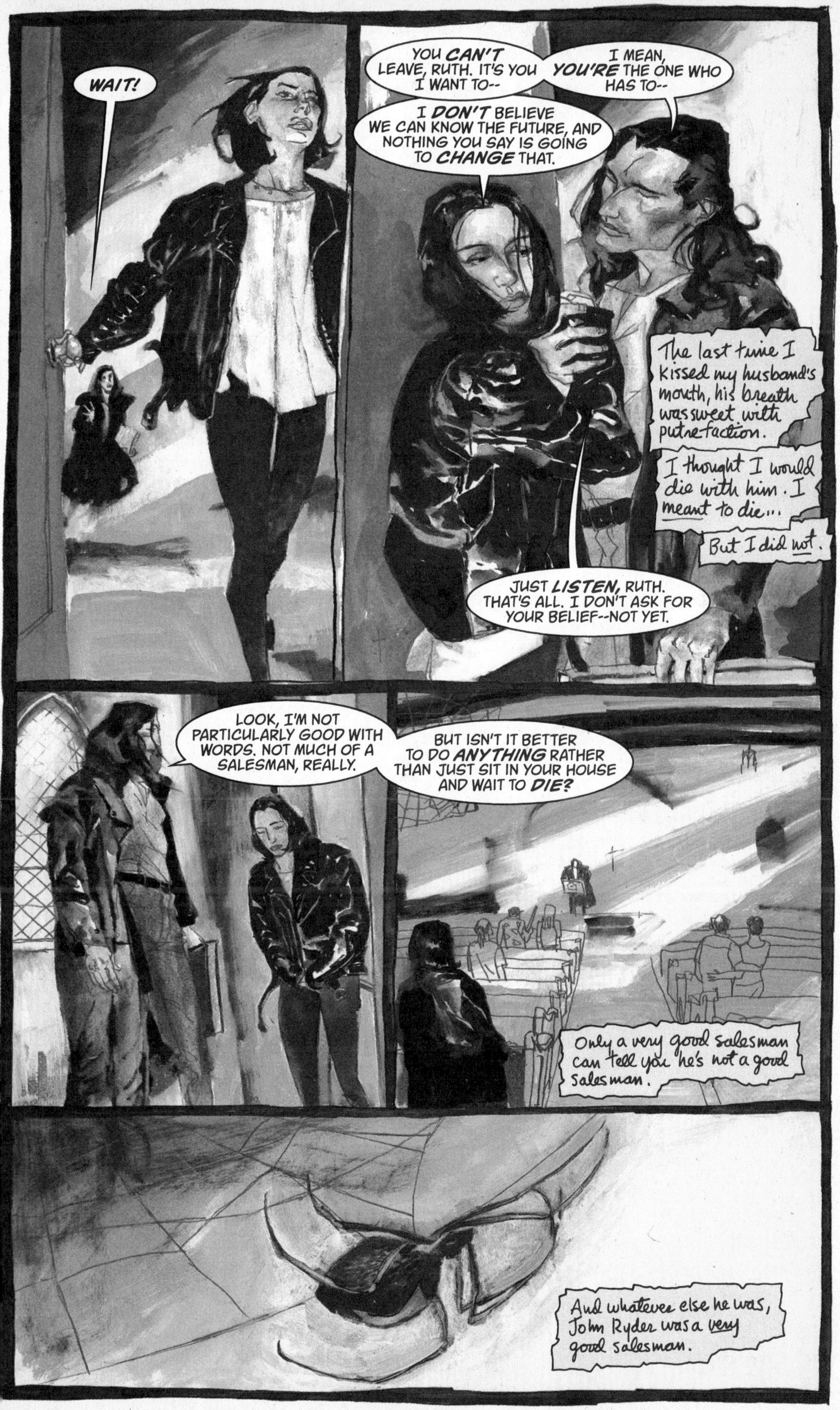
WAIT!
YOU CAN'T LEAVE, RUTH. IT'S YOU I WANT TO--
I MEAN, YOU'RE THE ONE WHO HAS TO--
I DON'T BELIEVE WE CAN KNOW THE FUTURE, AND NOTHING YOU SAY IS GOING TO CHANGE THAT.
The last time I kissed my husband's mouth, his breath was sweet with putre-faction.
I thought I would die with him. I meant to die...
But I did not.
JUST LISTEN, RUTH. THAT'S ALL. I DON'T ASK FOR YOUR BELIEF--NOT YET.
LOOK, I'M NOT PARTICULARLY GOOD WITH WORDS. NOT MUCH OF A SALESMAN, REALLY.
BUT ISN'T IT BETTER TO DO ANYTHING RATHER THAN JUST SIT IN YOUR HOUSE AND WAIT TO DIE?
Only a very good salesman can tell you he's not a good salesman.
And whatever else he was, John Ryder was a very good salesman.

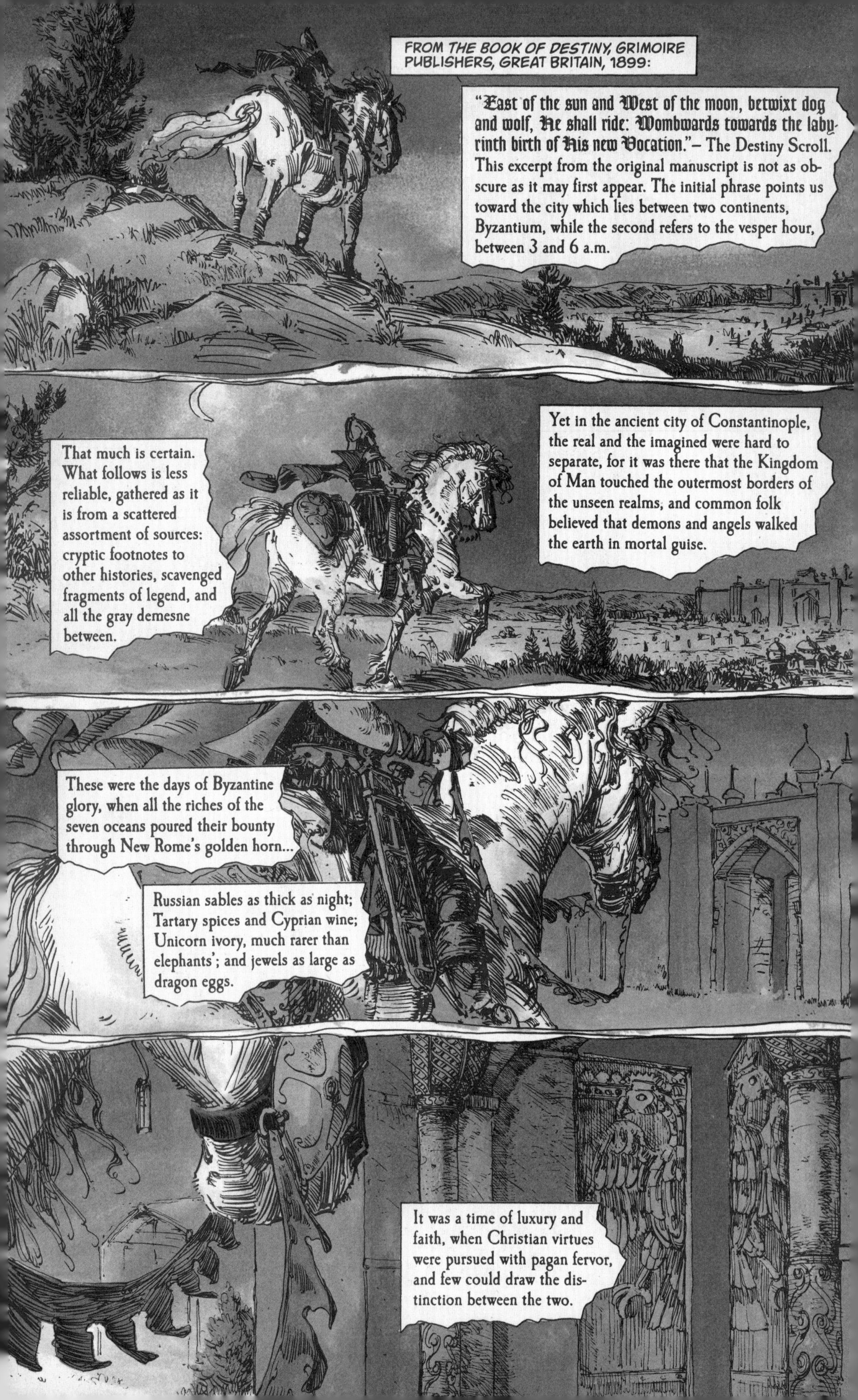
FROM THE BOOK OF DESTINY, GRIMOIRE PUBLISHERS, GREAT BRITAIN, 1899:
"East of the sun and West of the moon, betwixt dog and wolf, He shall ride: Wombwards towards the labyrinth birth of His new Vocation."– The Destiny Scroll. This excerpt from the original manuscript is not as obscure as it may first appear. The initial phrase points us toward the city which lies between two continents, Byzantium, while the second refers to the vesper hour, between 3 and 6 a.m.
That much is certain. What follows is less reliable, gathered as it is from a scattered assortment of sources: cryptic footnotes to other histories, scavenged fragments of legend, and all the gray demesne between.
Yet in the ancient city of Constantinople, the real and the imagined were hard to separate, for it was there that the Kingdom of Man touched the outermost borders of the unseen realms, and common folk believed that demons and angels walked the earth in mortal guise.
These were the days of Byzantine glory, when all the riches of the seven oceans poured their bounty through New Rome's golden horn...
Russian sables as thick as night; Tartary spices and Cyprian wine; Unicorn ivory, much rarer than elephants'; and jewels as large as dragon eggs.
It was a time of luxury and faith, when Christian virtues were pursued with pagan fervor, and few could draw the distinction between the two.

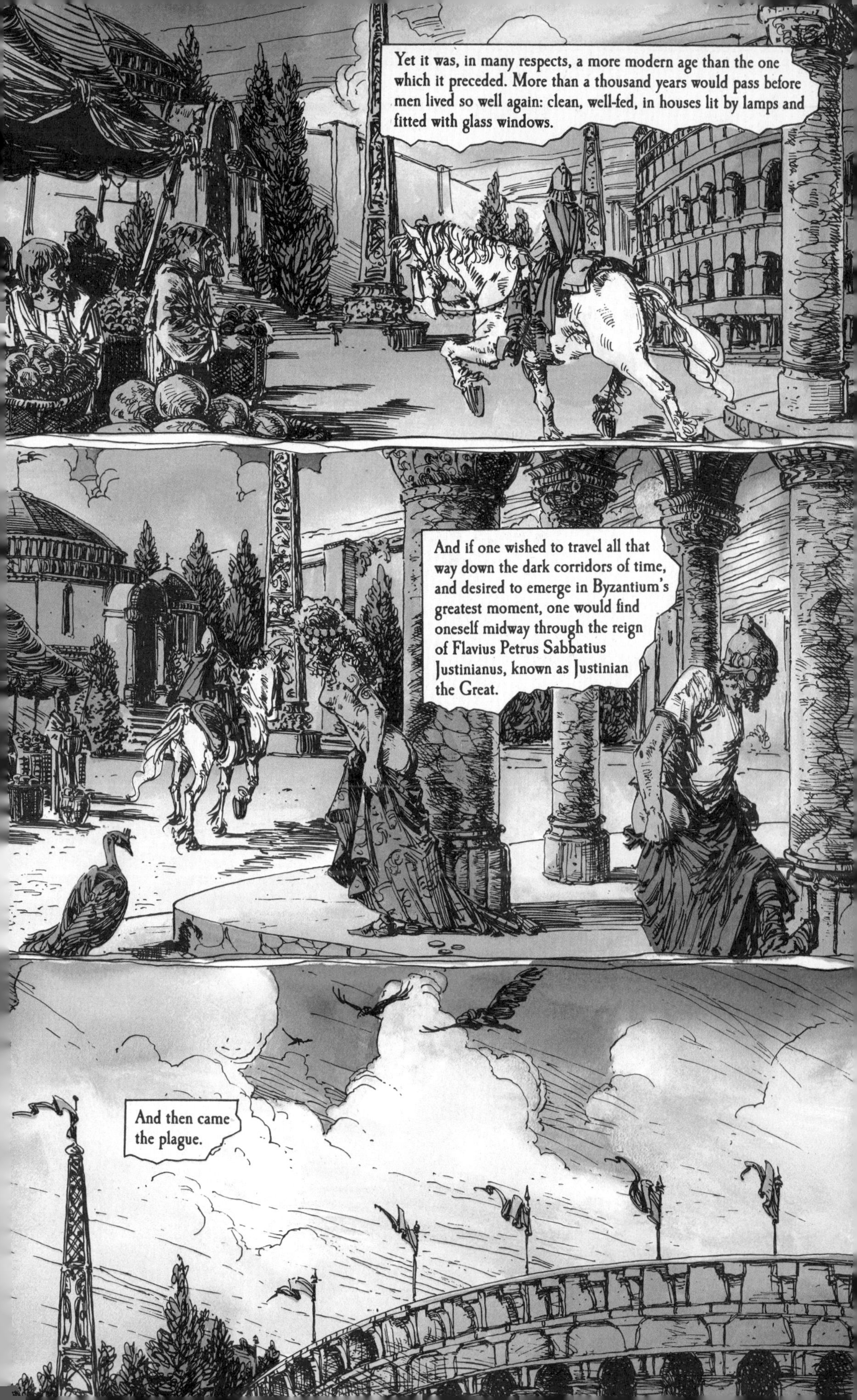
Yet it was, in many respects, a more modern age than the one which it preceded. More than a thousand years would pass before men lived so well again: clean, well-fed, in houses lit by lamps and fitted with glass windows.
And if one wished to travel all that way down the dark corridors of time, and desired to emerge in Byzantium's greatest moment, one would find oneself midway through the reign of Flavius Petrus Sabbatius Justinianus, known as Justinian the Great.
And then came the plague.

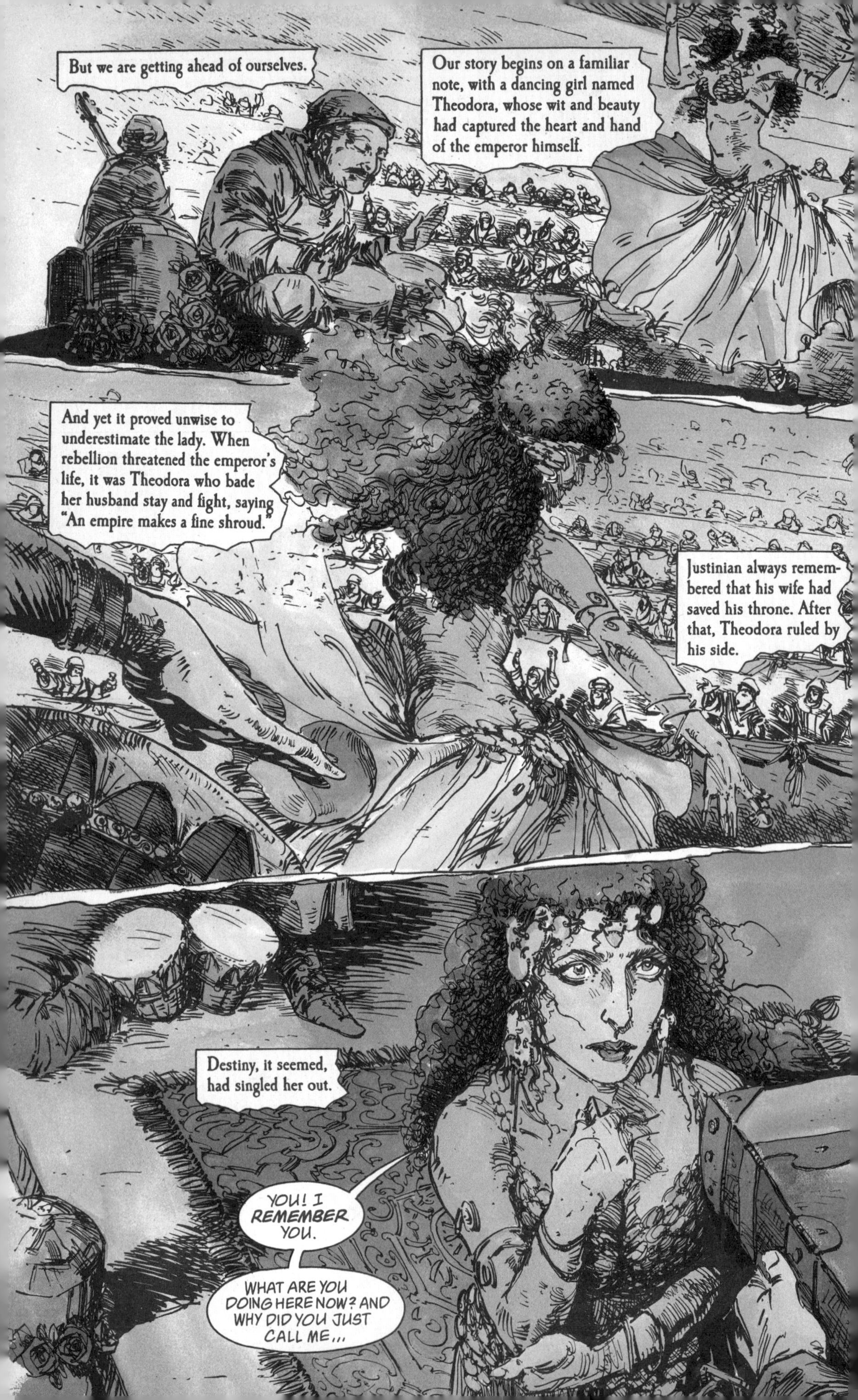
But we are getting ahead of ourselves.
Our story begins on a familiar note, with a dancing girl named Theodora, whose wit and beauty had captured the heart and hand of the emperor himself.
And yet it proved unwise to underestimate the lady. When rebellion threatened the emperor's life, it was Theodora who bade her husband stay and fight, saying "An empire makes a fine shroud."
Justinian always remembered that his wife had saved his throne. After that, Theodora ruled by his side.
Destiny, it seemed, had singled her out.
YOU! I REMEMBER YOU.
WHAT ARE YOU DOING HERE NOW? AND WHY DID YOU JUST CALL ME...

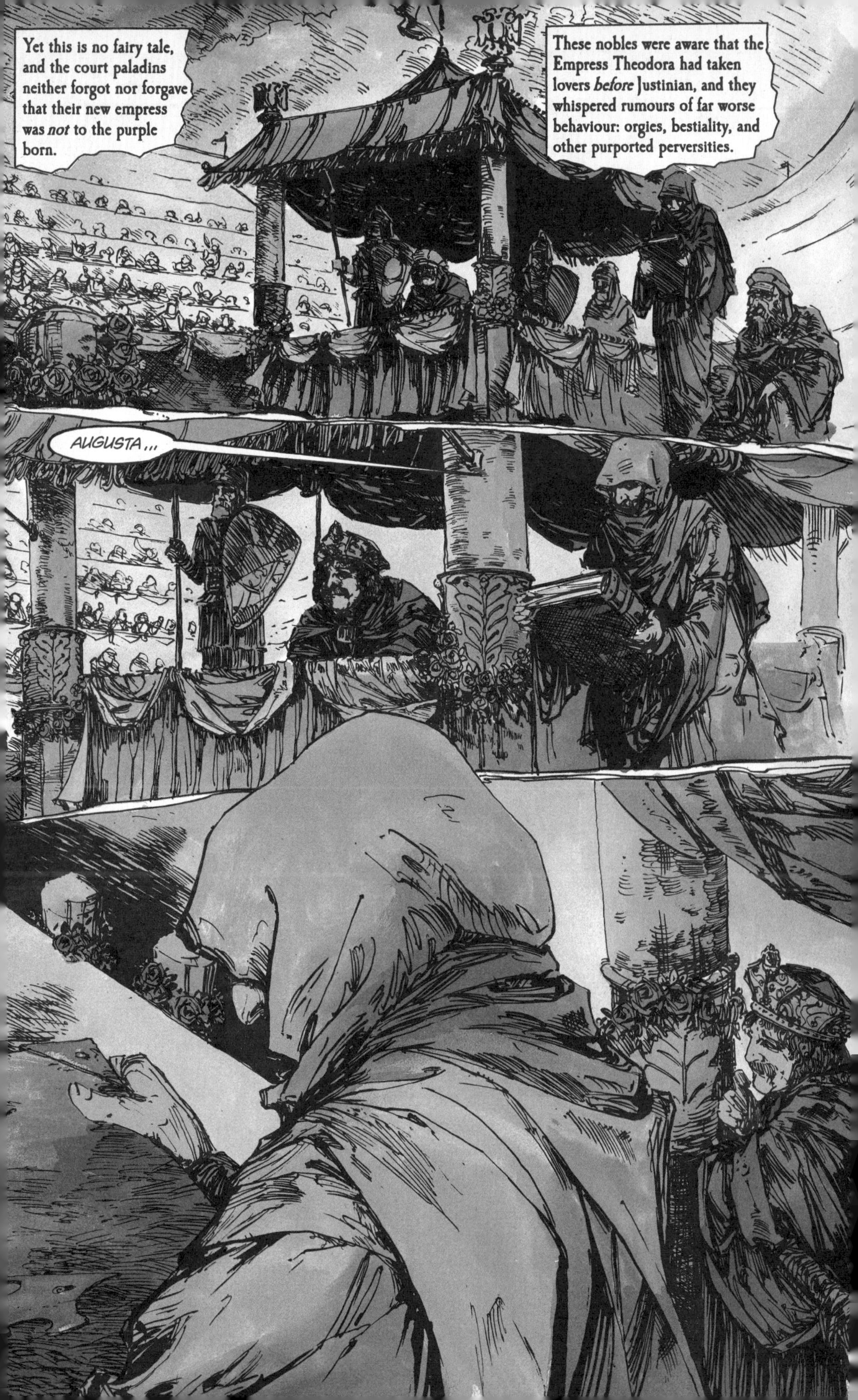

Yet this is no fairy tale, and the court paladins neither forgot nor forgave that their new empress was *not* to the purple born.
These nobles were aware that the Empress Theodora had taken lovers *before* Justinian, and they whispered rumours of far worse behaviour: orgies, bestiality, and other purported perversities.
AUGUSTA...

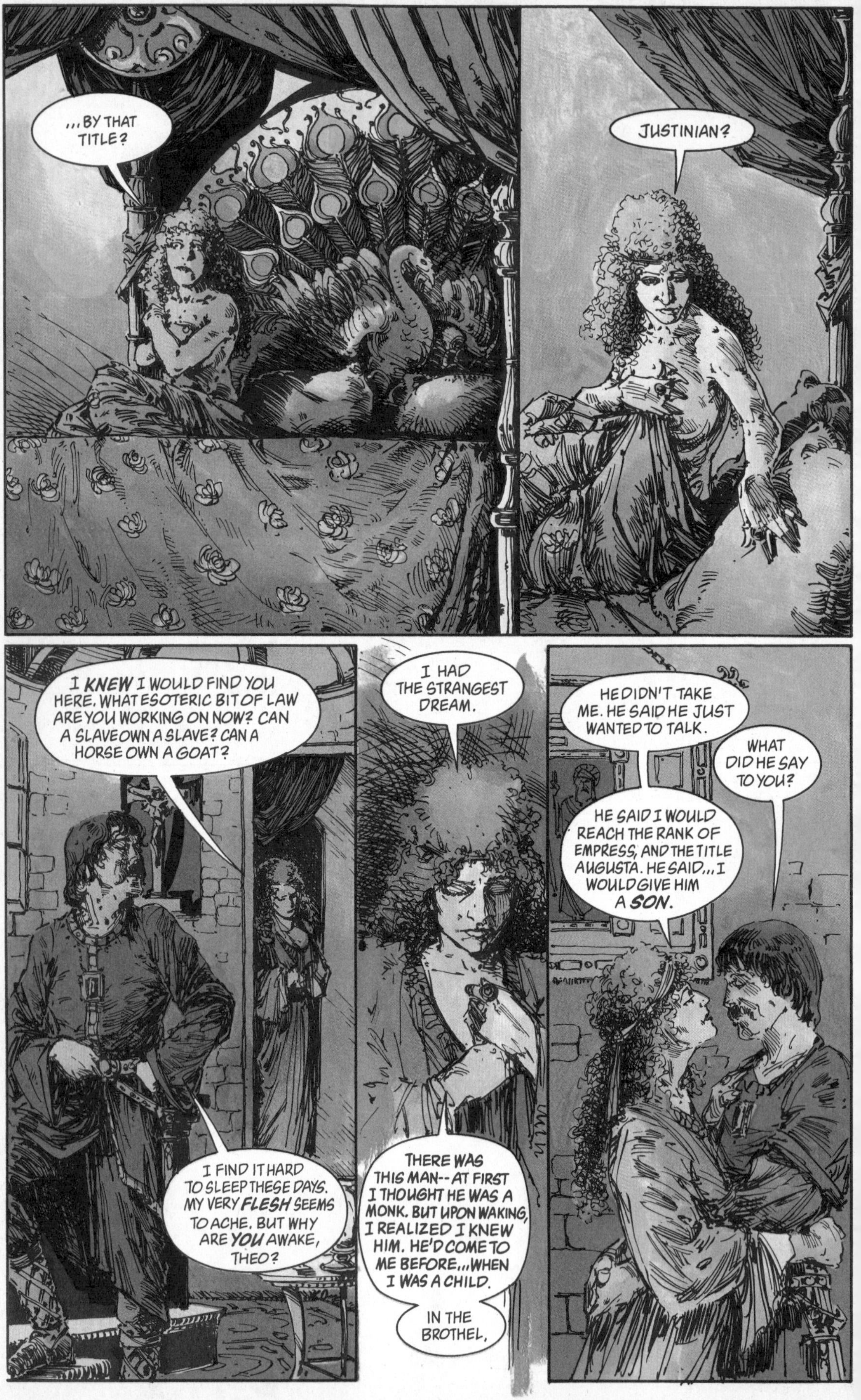
...BY THAT TITLE?
JUSTINIAN?
I KNEW I WOULD FIND YOU HERE. WHAT ESOTERIC BIT OF LAW ARE YOU WORKING ON NOW? CAN A SLAVE OWN A SLAVE? CAN A HORSE OWN A GOAT?
I FIND IT HARD TO SLEEP THESE DAYS. MY VERY FLESH SEEMS TO ACHE. BUT WHY ARE YOU AWAKE, THEO?
I HAD THE STRANGEST DREAM.
THERE WAS THIS MAN-- AT FIRST I THOUGHT HE WAS A MONK. BUT UPON WAKING, I REALIZED I KNEW HIM. HE'D COME TO ME BEFORE... WHEN I WAS A CHILD.
IN THE BROTHEL.
HE DIDN'T TAKE ME. HE SAID HE JUST WANTED TO TALK.
WHAT DID HE SAY TO YOU?
HE SAID I WOULD REACH THE RANK OF EMPRESS, AND THE TITLE AUGUSTA. HE SAID... I WOULD GIVE HIM A SON.

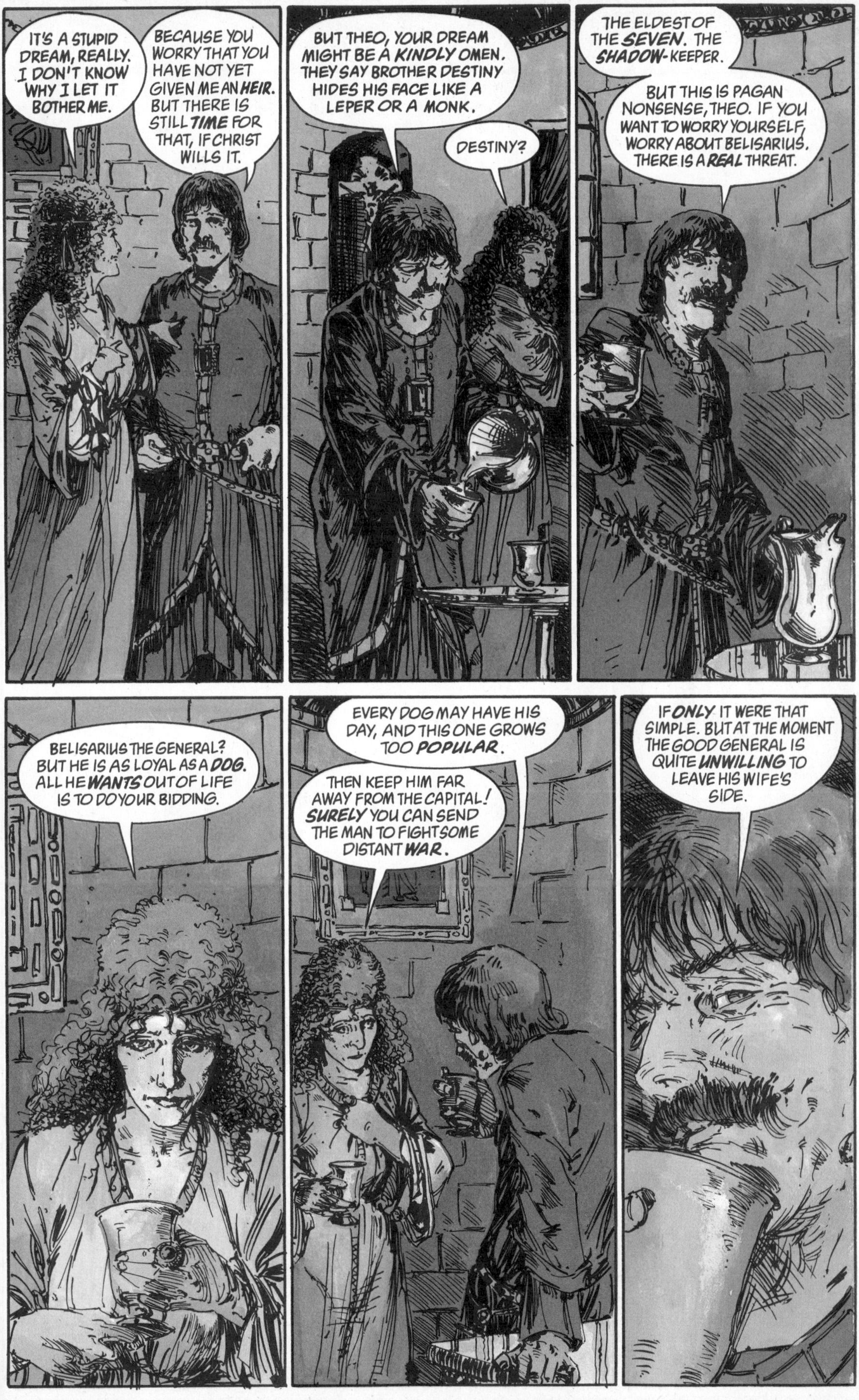
IT'S A STUPID DREAM, REALLY. I DON'T KNOW WHY I LET IT BOTHER ME.
BECAUSE YOU WORRY THAT YOU HAVE NOT YET GIVEN ME AN HEIR. BUT THERE IS STILL TIME FOR THAT, IF CHRIST WILLS IT.
BUT THEO, YOUR DREAM MIGHT BE A KINDLY OMEN. THEY SAY BROTHER DESTINY HIDES HIS FACE LIKE A LEPER OR A MONK.
DESTINY?
THE ELDEST OF THE SEVEN. THE SHADOW-KEEPER.
BUT THIS IS PAGAN NONSENSE, THEO. IF YOU WANT TO WORRY YOURSELF, WORRY ABOUT BELISARIUS. THERE IS A REAL THREAT.
BELISARIUS THE GENERAL? BUT HE IS AS LOYAL AS A DOG. ALL HE WANTS OUT OF LIFE IS TO DO YOUR BIDDING.
EVERY DOG MAY HAVE HIS DAY, AND THIS ONE GROWS TOO POPULAR.
THEN KEEP HIM FAR AWAY FROM THE CAPITAL! SURELY YOU CAN SEND THE MAN TO FIGHT SOME DISTANT WAR.
IF ONLY IT WERE THAT SIMPLE. BUT AT THE MOMENT THE GOOD GENERAL IS QUITE UNWILLING TO LEAVE HIS WIFE'S SIDE.

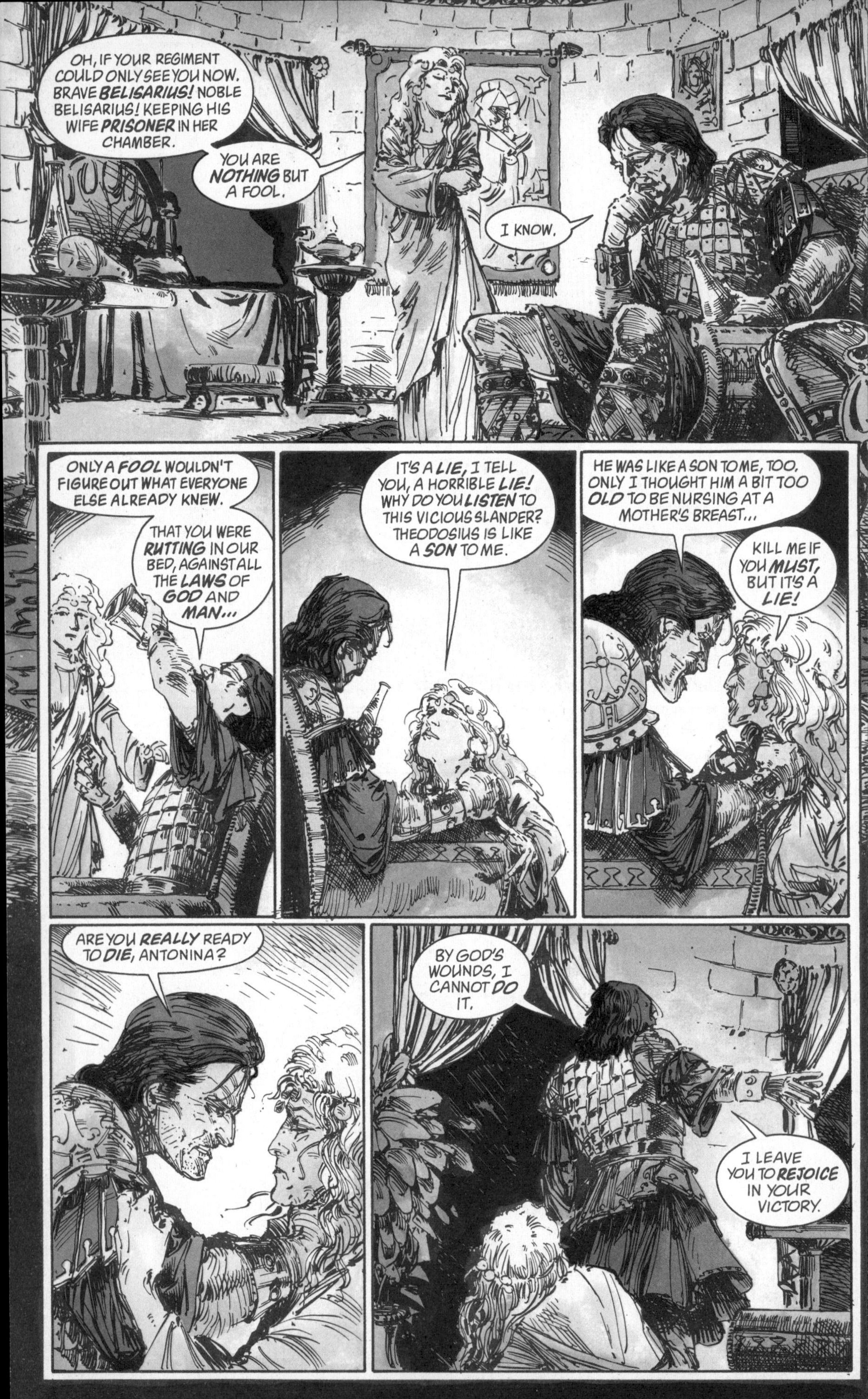
OH, IF YOUR REGIMENT COULD ONLY SEE YOU NOW. BRAVE BELISARIUS! NOBLE BELISARIUS! KEEPING HIS WIFE PRISONER IN HER CHAMBER.
YOU ARE NOTHING BUT A FOOL.
I KNOW.
ONLY A FOOL WOULDN'T FIGURE OUT WHAT EVERYONE ELSE ALREADY KNEW.
THAT YOU WERE RUTTING IN OUR BED, AGAINST ALL THE LAWS OF GOD AND MAN...
IT'S A LIE, I TELL YOU, A HORRIBLE LIE! WHY DO YOU LISTEN TO THIS VICIOUS SLANDER? THEODOSIUS IS LIKE A SON TO ME.
HE WAS LIKE A SON TO ME, TOO, ONLY I THOUGHT HIM A BIT TOO OLD TO BE NURSING AT A MOTHER'S BREAST...
KILL ME IF YOU MUST, BUT IT'S A LIE!
ARE YOU REALLY READY TO DIE, ANTONINA?
BY GOD'S WOUNDS, I CANNOT DO IT.
I LEAVE YOU TO REJOICE IN YOUR VICTORY.

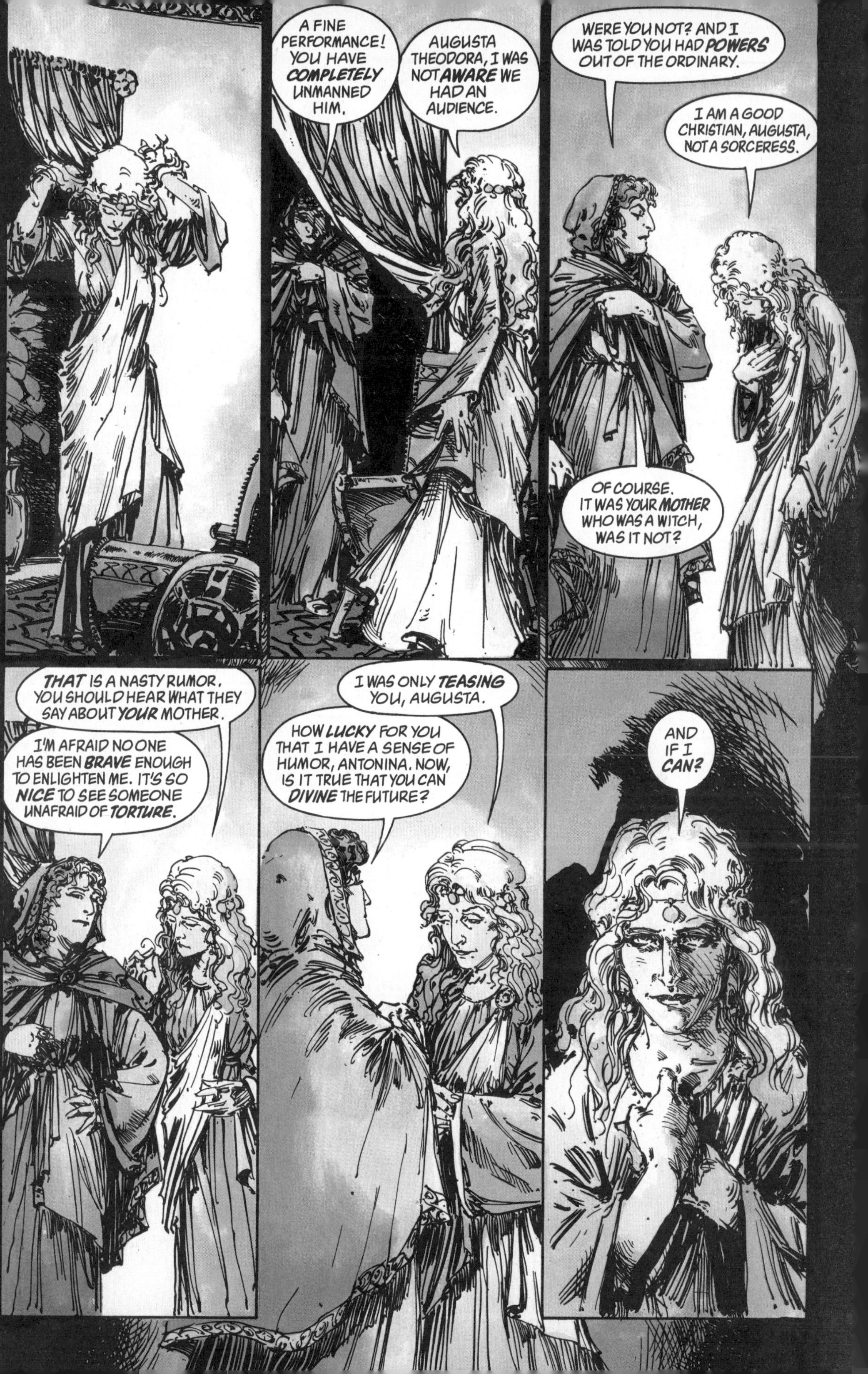
A FINE PERFORMANCE! YOU HAVE COMPLETELY UNMANNED HIM.
AUGUSTA THEODORA, I WAS NOT AWARE WE HAD AN AUDIENCE.
WERE YOU NOT? AND I WAS TOLD YOU HAD POWERS OUT OF THE ORDINARY.
I AM A GOOD CHRISTIAN, AUGUSTA, NOT A SORCERESS.
OF COURSE. IT WAS YOUR MOTHER WHO WAS A WITCH, WAS IT NOT?
THAT IS A NASTY RUMOR. YOU SHOULD HEAR WHAT THEY SAY ABOUT YOUR MOTHER.
I'M AFRAID NO ONE HAS BEEN BRAVE ENOUGH TO ENLIGHTEN ME. IT'S SO NICE TO SEE SOMEONE UNAFRAID OF TORTURE.
I WAS ONLY TEASING YOU, AUGUSTA.
HOW LUCKY FOR YOU THAT I HAVE A SENSE OF HUMOR, ANTONINA. NOW, IS IT TRUE THAT YOU CAN DIVINE THE FUTURE?
AND IF I CAN?

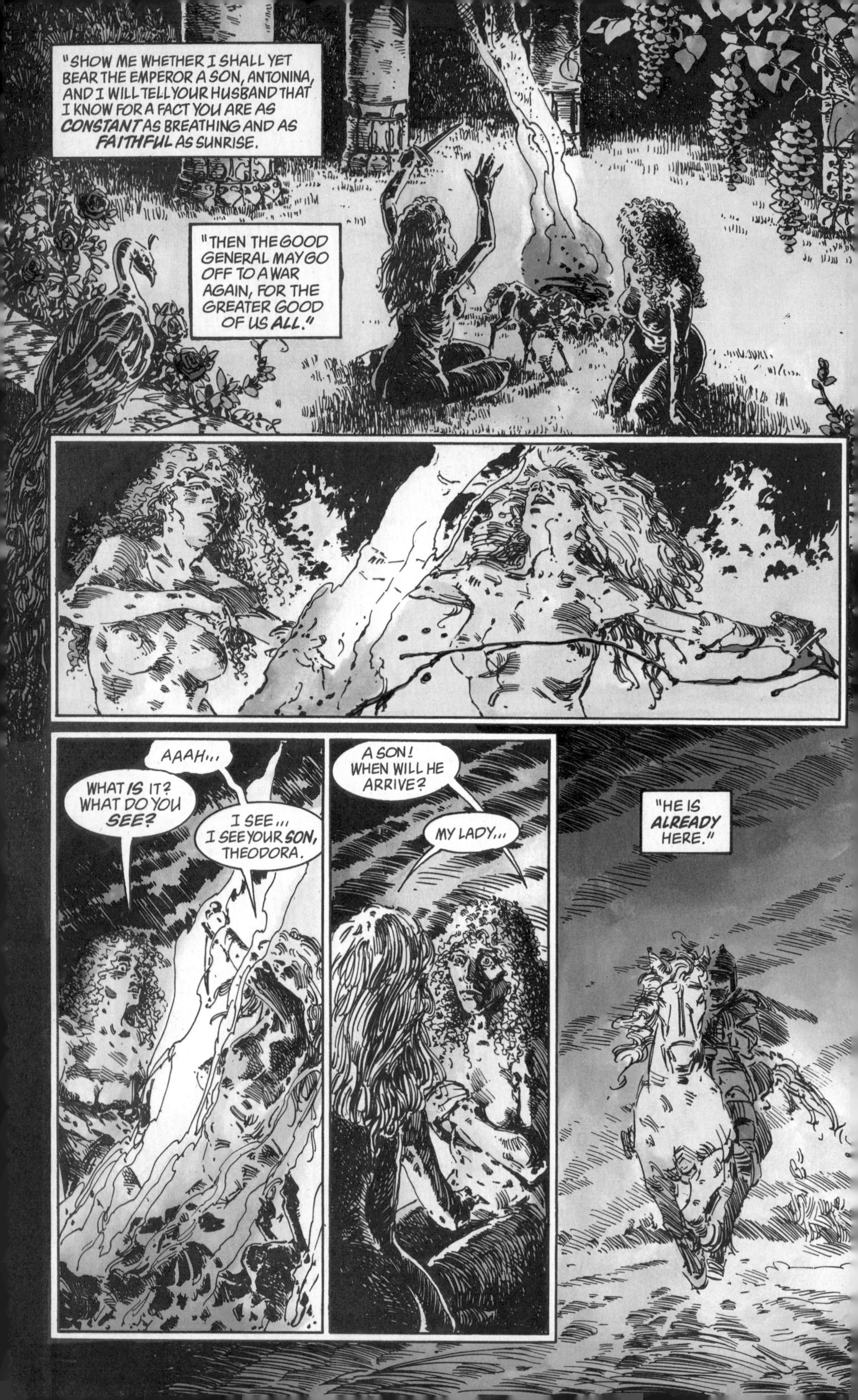
"SHOW ME WHETHER I SHALL YET BEAR THE EMPEROR A SON, ANTONINA, AND I WILL TELL YOUR HUSBAND THAT I KNOW FOR A FACT YOU ARE AS CONSTANT AS BREATHING AND AS FAITHFUL AS SUNRISE.
"THEN THE GOOD GENERAL MAY GO OFF TO A WAR AGAIN, FOR THE GREATER GOOD OF US ALL."
AAAH...
WHAT IS IT? WHAT DO YOU SEE?
I SEE... I SEE YOUR SON, THEODORA.
A SON! WHEN WILL HE ARRIVE?
MY LADY...
"HE IS ALREADY HERE."

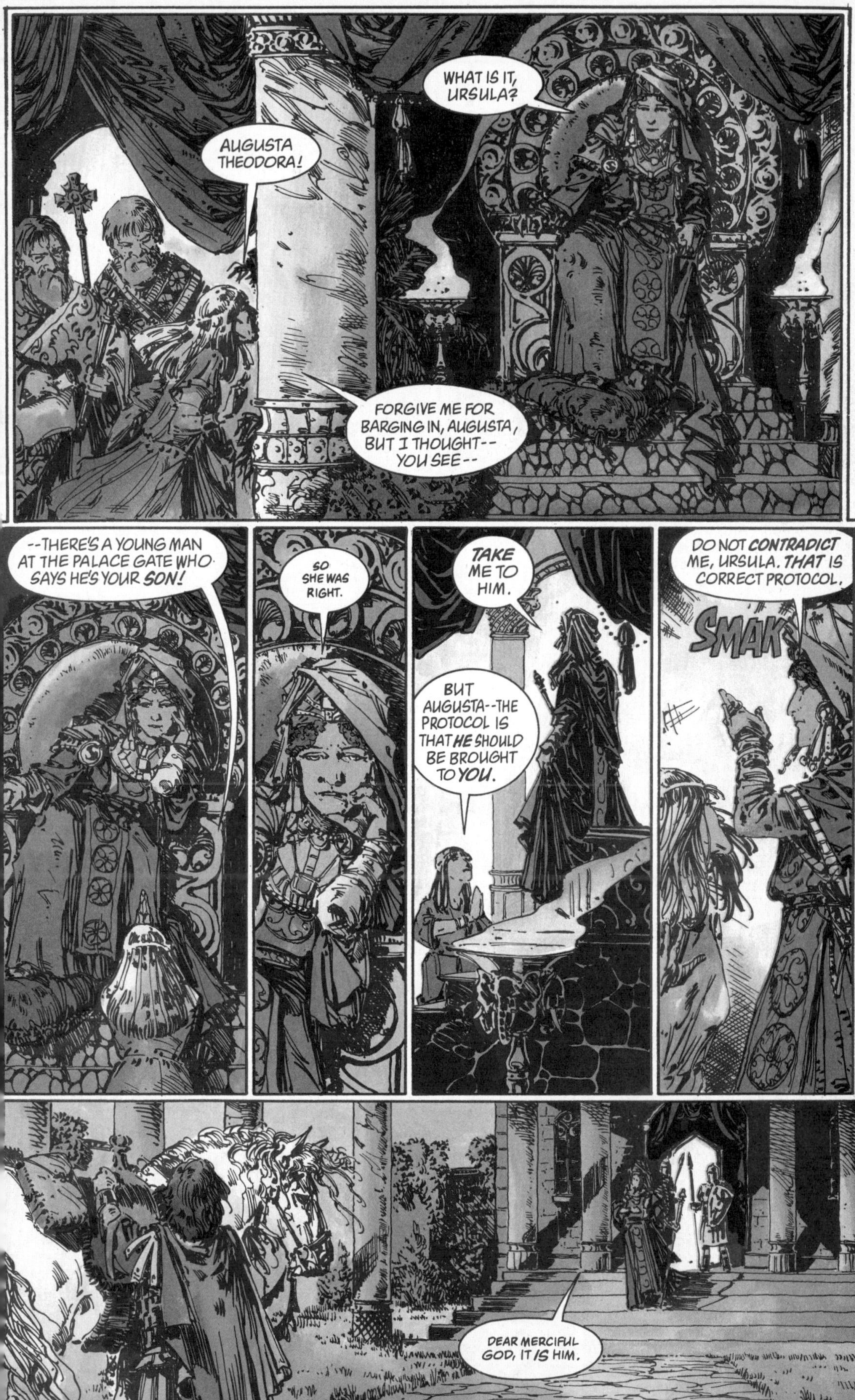
AUGUSTA THEODORA!
WHAT IS IT, URSULA?
FORGIVE ME FOR BARGING IN, AUGUSTA, BUT I THOUGHT-- YOU SEE--
--THERE'S A YOUNG MAN AT THE PALACE GATE WHO SAYS HE'S YOUR SON!
SO SHE WAS RIGHT.
TAKE ME TO HIM.
BUT AUGUSTA--THE PROTOCOL IS THAT HE SHOULD BE BROUGHT TO YOU.
DO NOT CONTRADICT ME, URSULA. THAT IS CORRECT PROTOCOL.
SMAK
DEAR MERCIFUL GOD, IT IS HIM.

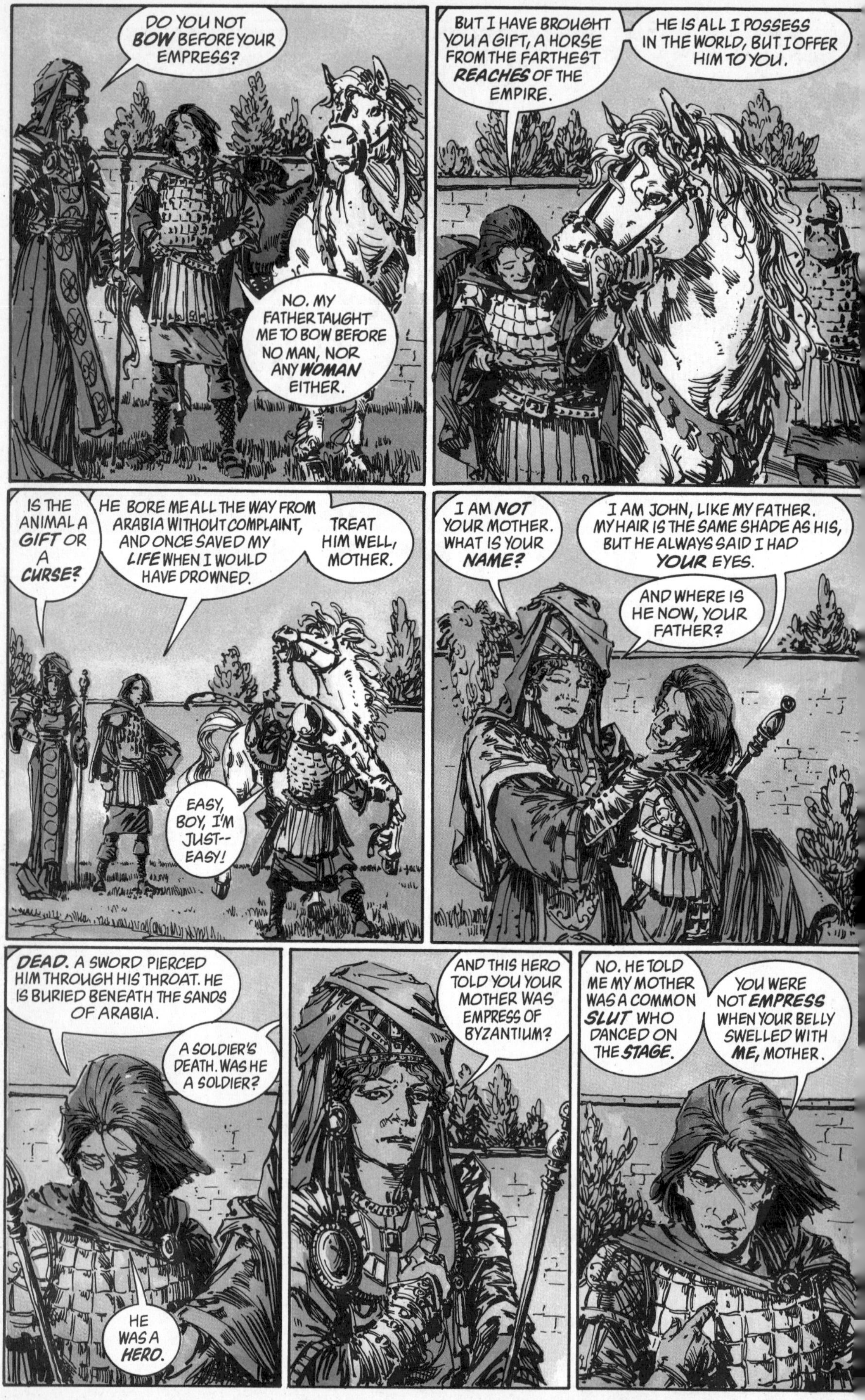
DO YOU NOT BOW BEFORE YOUR EMPRESS?
NO. MY FATHER TAUGHT ME TO BOW BEFORE NO MAN, NOR ANY WOMAN EITHER.
BUT I HAVE BROUGHT YOU A GIFT, A HORSE FROM THE FARTHEST REACHES OF THE EMPIRE.
HE IS ALL I POSSESS IN THE WORLD, BUT I OFFER HIM TO YOU.
IS THE ANIMAL A GIFT OR A CURSE?
HE BORE ME ALL THE WAY FROM ARABIA WITHOUT COMPLAINT, AND ONCE SAVED MY LIFE WHEN I WOULD HAVE DROWNED.
TREAT HIM WELL, MOTHER.
EASY, BOY, I'M JUST-- EASY!
I AM NOT YOUR MOTHER. WHAT IS YOUR NAME?
I AM JOHN, LIKE MY FATHER. MY HAIR IS THE SAME SHADE AS HIS, BUT HE ALWAYS SAID I HAD YOUR EYES.
AND WHERE IS HE NOW, YOUR FATHER?
DEAD. A SWORD PIERCED HIM THROUGH HIS THROAT. HE IS BURIED BENEATH THE SANDS OF ARABIA.
A SOLDIER'S DEATH. WAS HE A SOLDIER?
HE WAS A HERO.
AND THIS HERO TOLD YOU YOUR MOTHER WAS EMPRESS OF BYZANTIUM?
NO. HE TOLD ME MY MOTHER WAS A COMMON SLUT WHO DANCED ON THE STAGE.
YOU WERE NOT EMPRESS WHEN YOUR BELLY SWELLED WITH ME, MOTHER.

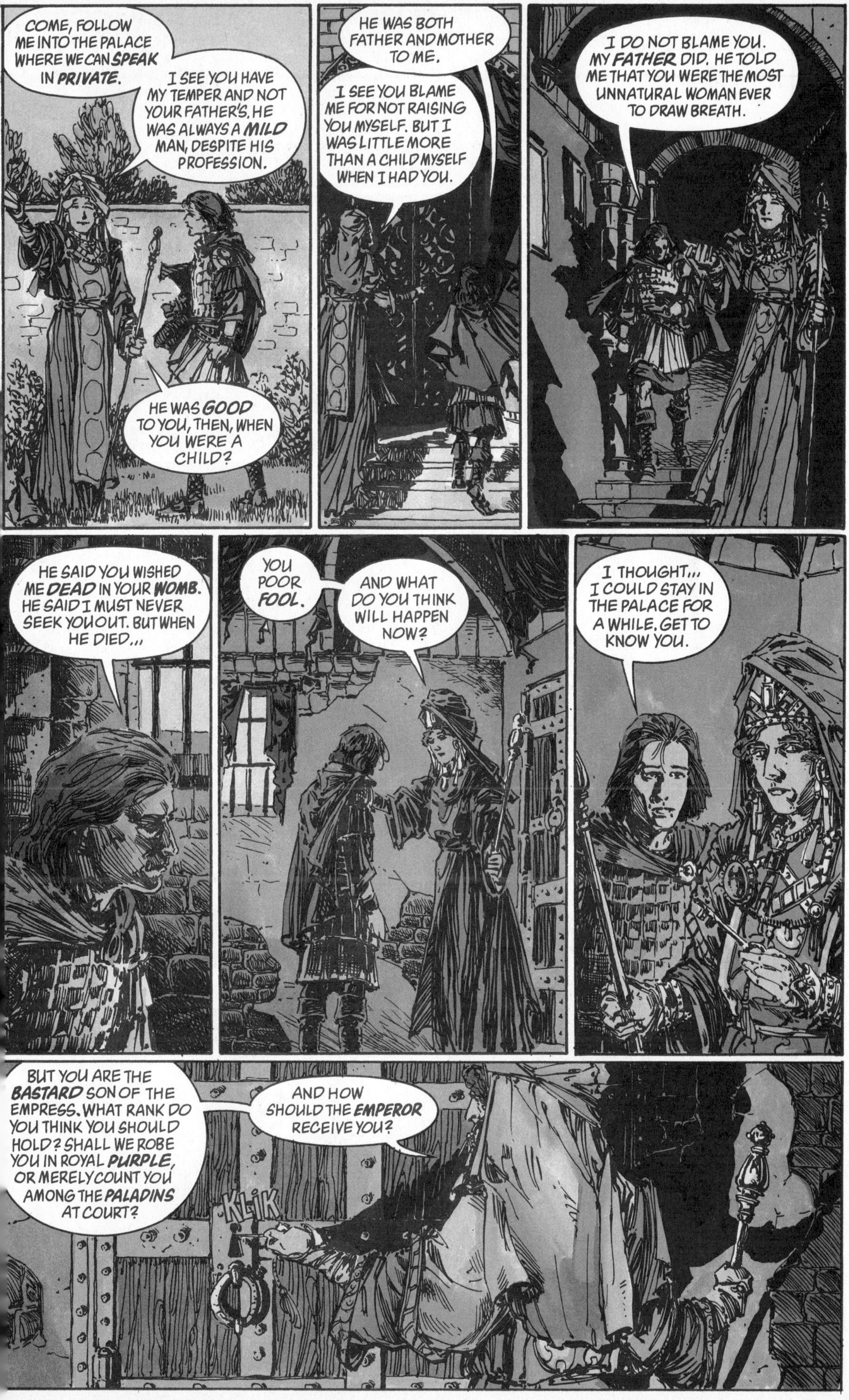
COME, FOLLOW ME INTO THE PALACE WHERE WE CAN SPEAK IN PRIVATE.
I SEE YOU HAVE MY TEMPER AND NOT YOUR FATHER'S. HE WAS ALWAYS A MILD MAN, DESPITE HIS PROFESSION.
HE WAS GOOD TO YOU, THEN, WHEN YOU WERE A CHILD?
HE WAS BOTH FATHER AND MOTHER TO ME.
I SEE YOU BLAME ME FOR NOT RAISING YOU MYSELF. BUT I WAS LITTLE MORE THAN A CHILD MYSELF WHEN I HAD YOU.
I DO NOT BLAME YOU. MY FATHER DID. HE TOLD ME THAT YOU WERE THE MOST UNNATURAL WOMAN EVER TO DRAW BREATH.
HE SAID YOU WISHED ME DEAD IN YOUR WOMB. HE SAID I MUST NEVER SEEK YOU OUT. BUT WHEN HE DIED...
YOU POOR FOOL.
AND WHAT DO YOU THINK WILL HAPPEN NOW?
I THOUGHT... I COULD STAY IN THE PALACE FOR A WHILE. GET TO KNOW YOU.
BUT YOU ARE THE BASTARD SON OF THE EMPRESS. WHAT RANK DO YOU THINK YOU SHOULD HOLD? SHALL WE ROBE YOU IN ROYAL PURPLE, OR MERELY COUNT YOU AMONG THE PALADINS AT COURT?
AND HOW SHOULD THE EMPEROR RECEIVE YOU?
KLIK

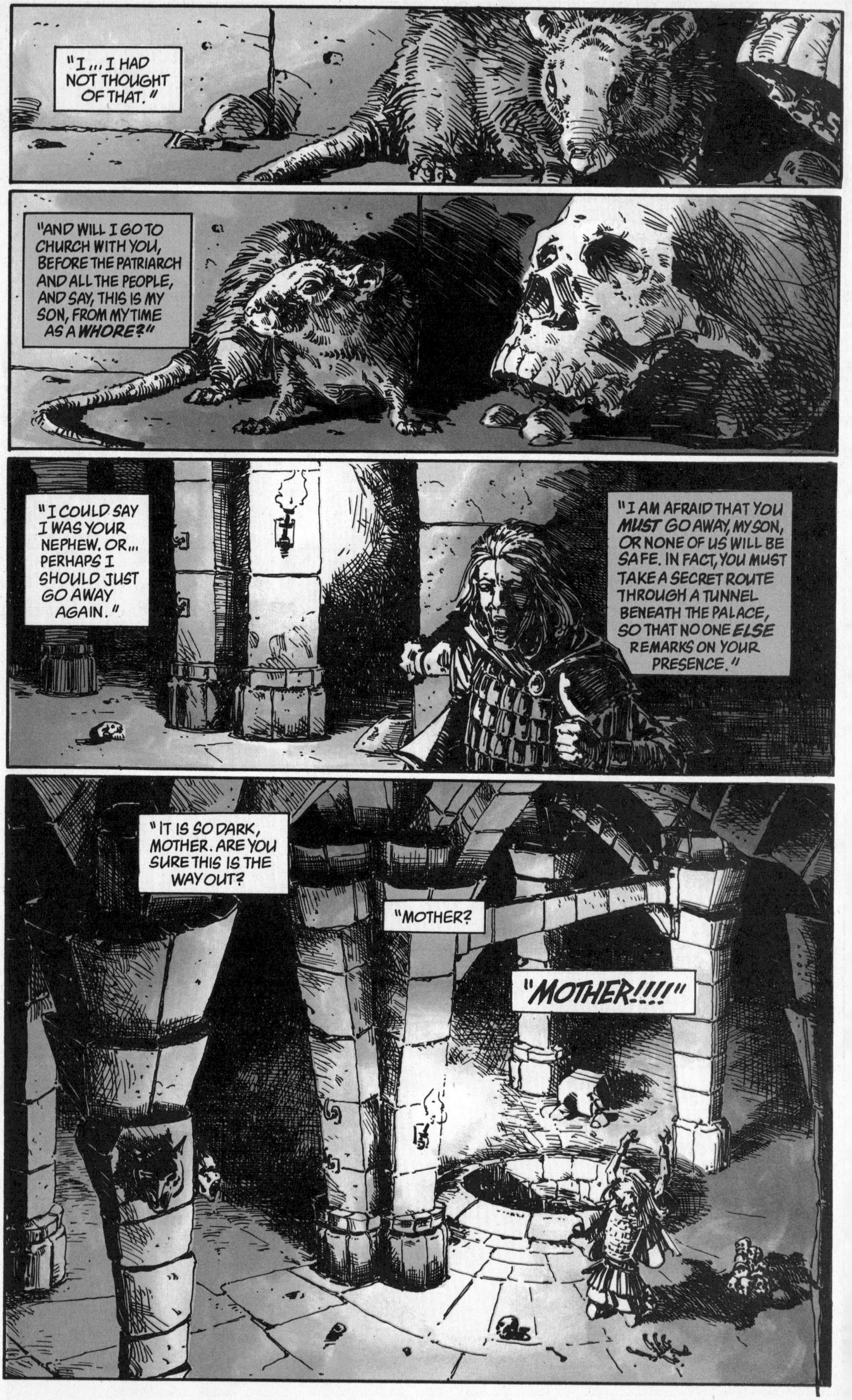
"I... I HAD NOT THOUGHT OF THAT."
"AND WILL I GO TO CHURCH WITH YOU, BEFORE THE PATRIARCH AND ALL THE PEOPLE, AND SAY, THIS IS MY SON, FROM MY TIME AS A *WHORE*?"
"I COULD SAY I WAS YOUR NEPHEW. OR... PERHAPS I SHOULD JUST GO AWAY AGAIN."
"I AM AFRAID THAT YOU *MUST* GO AWAY, MY SON, OR NONE OF US WILL BE SAFE. IN FACT, YOU MUST TAKE A SECRET ROUTE THROUGH A TUNNEL BENEATH THE PALACE, SO THAT NO ONE *ELSE* REMARKS ON YOUR PRESENCE."
"IT IS SO DARK, MOTHER. ARE YOU SURE THIS IS THE WAY OUT?
"MOTHER?
"MOTHER!!!!"

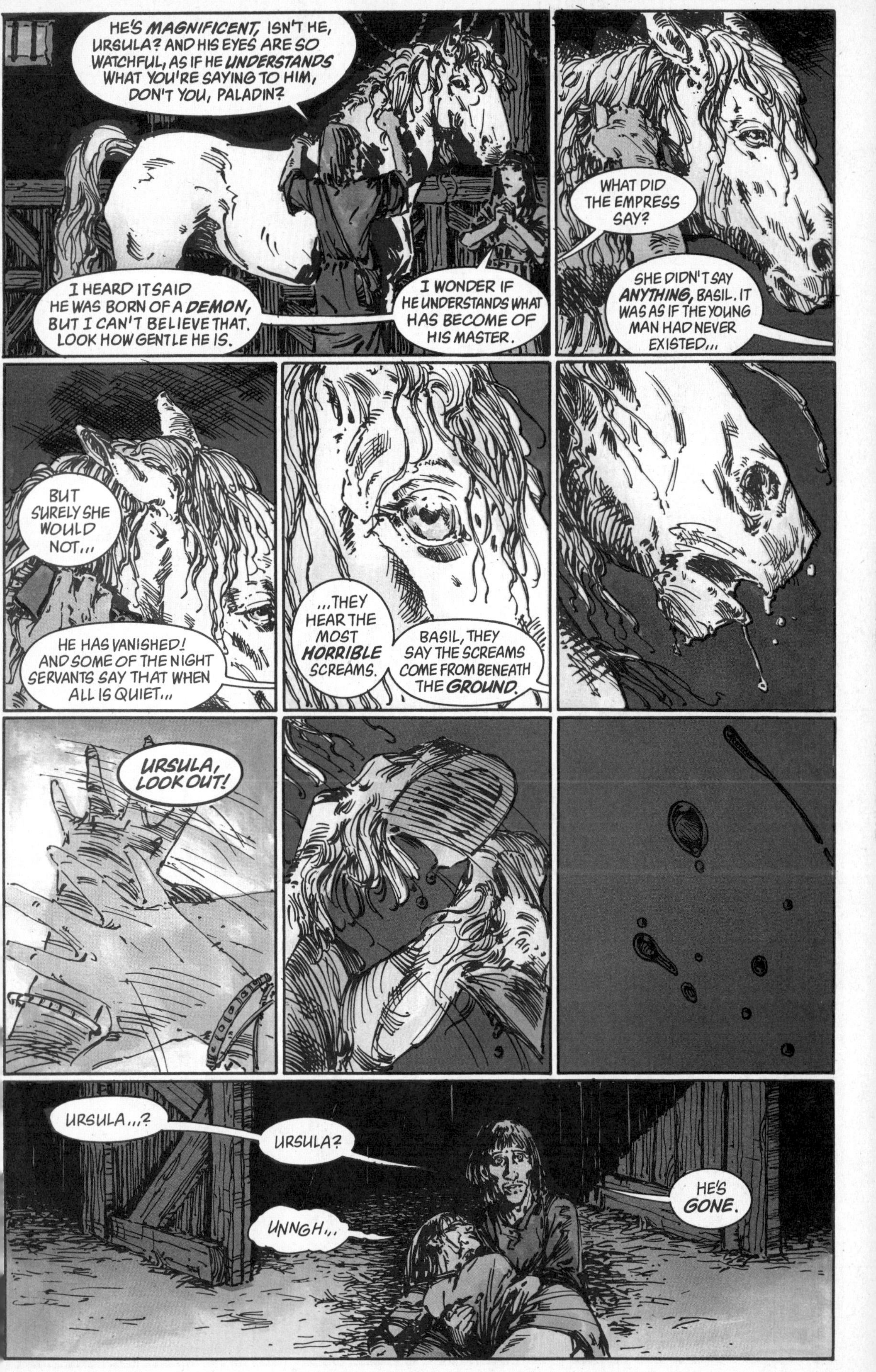

HE'S MAGNIFICENT, ISN'T HE, URSULA? AND HIS EYES ARE SO WATCHFUL, AS IF HE UNDERSTANDS WHAT YOU'RE SAYING TO HIM, DON'T YOU, PALADIN?
I HEARD IT SAID HE WAS BORN OF A DEMON, BUT I CAN'T BELIEVE THAT. LOOK HOW GENTLE HE IS.
I WONDER IF HE UNDERSTANDS WHAT HAS BECOME OF HIS MASTER.
WHAT DID THE EMPRESS SAY?
SHE DIDN'T SAY ANYTHING, BASIL. IT WAS AS IF THE YOUNG MAN HAD NEVER EXISTED...
BUT SURELY SHE WOULD NOT...
HE HAS VANISHED! AND SOME OF THE NIGHT SERVANTS SAY THAT WHEN ALL IS QUIET...
...THEY HEAR THE MOST HORRIBLE SCREAMS.
BASIL, THEY SAY THE SCREAMS COME FROM BENEATH THE GROUND.
URSULA, LOOK OUT!
URSULA...?
URSULA?
UNNGH...
HE'S GONE.

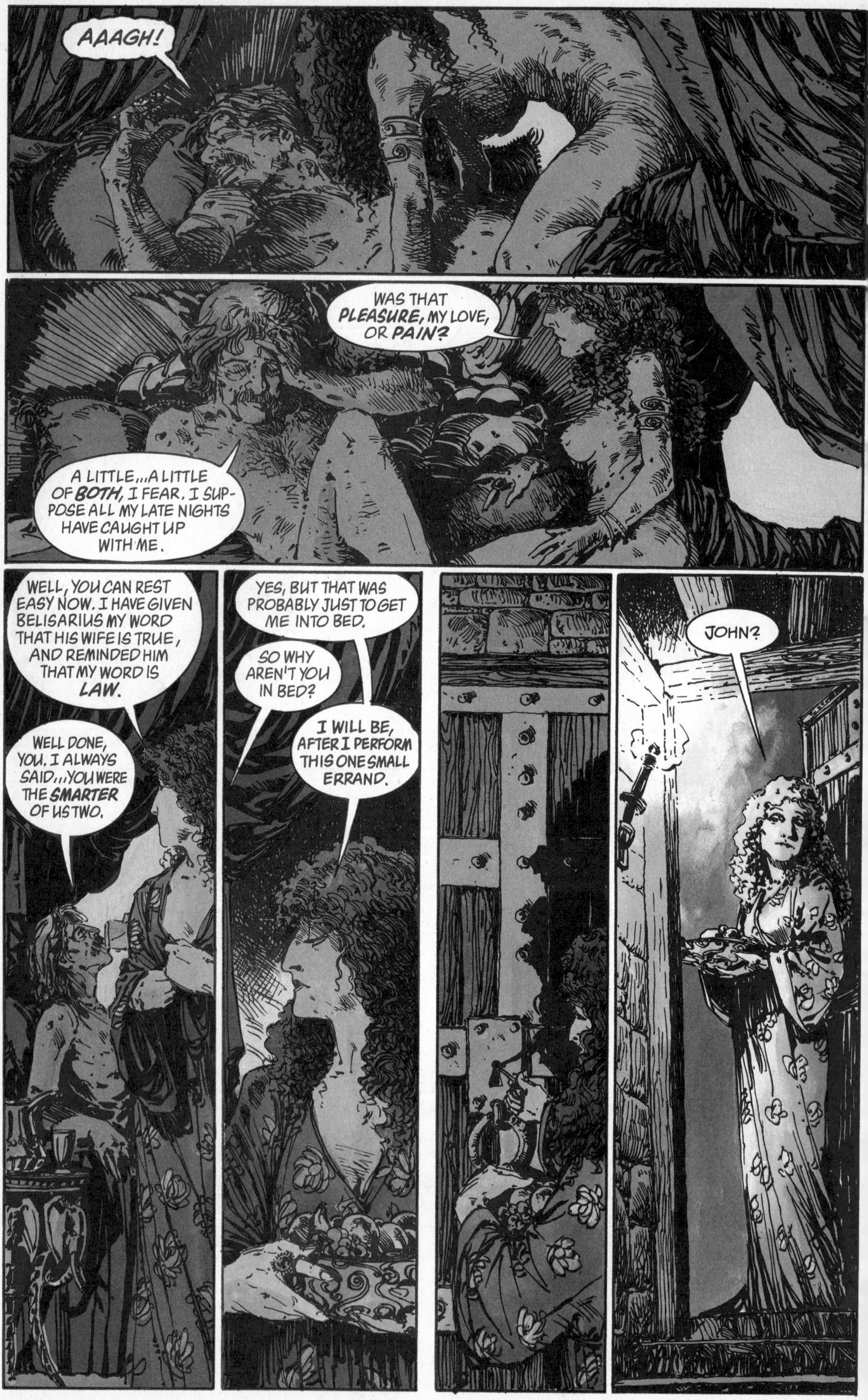
AAAGH!
WAS THAT PLEASURE, MY LOVE, OR PAIN?
A LITTLE...A LITTLE OF BOTH, I FEAR. I SUPPOSE ALL MY LATE NIGHTS HAVE CAUGHT UP WITH ME.
WELL, YOU CAN REST EASY NOW. I HAVE GIVEN BELISARIUS MY WORD THAT HIS WIFE IS TRUE, AND REMINDED HIM THAT MY WORD IS LAW.
WELL DONE, YOU. I ALWAYS SAID...YOU WERE THE SMARTER OF US TWO.
YES, BUT THAT WAS PROBABLY JUST TO GET ME INTO BED.
SO WHY AREN'T YOU IN BED?
I WILL BE, AFTER I PERFORM THIS ONE SMALL ERRAND.
JOHN?

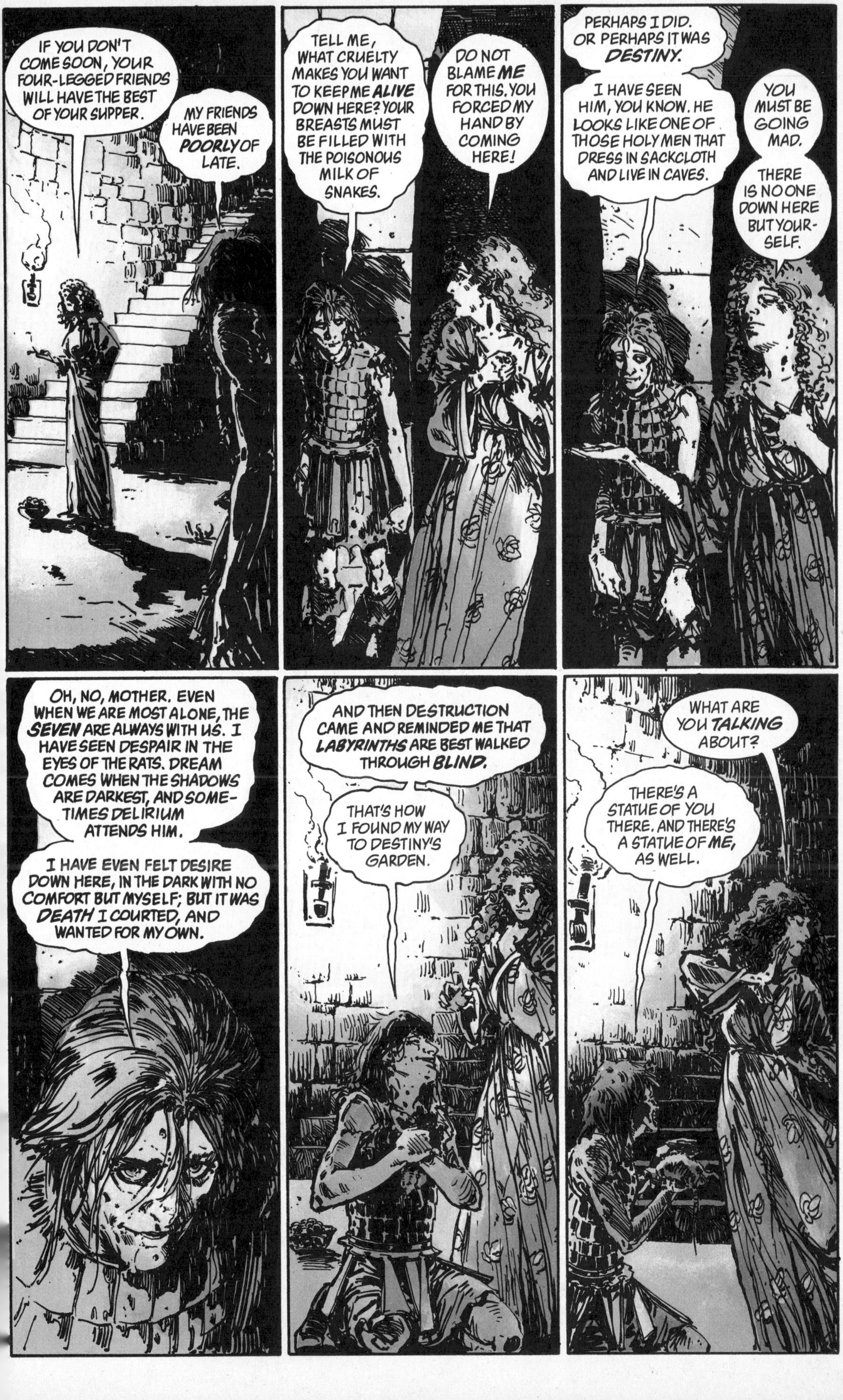
IF YOU DON'T COME SOON, YOUR FOUR-LEGGED FRIENDS WILL HAVE THE BEST OF YOUR SUPPER.
MY FRIENDS HAVE BEEN POORLY OF LATE.
TELL ME, WHAT CRUELTY MAKES YOU WANT TO KEEP ME ALIVE DOWN HERE? YOUR BREASTS MUST BE FILLED WITH THE POISONOUS MILK OF SNAKES.
DO NOT BLAME ME FOR THIS. YOU FORCED MY HAND BY COMING HERE!
PERHAPS I DID. OR PERHAPS IT WAS DESTINY.
I HAVE SEEN HIM, YOU KNOW. HE LOOKS LIKE ONE OF THOSE HOLY MEN THAT DRESS IN SACKCLOTH AND LIVE IN CAVES.
YOU MUST BE GOING MAD.
THERE IS NO ONE DOWN HERE BUT YOURSELF.
OH, NO, MOTHER. EVEN WHEN WE ARE MOST ALONE, THE SEVEN ARE ALWAYS WITH US. I HAVE SEEN DESPAIR IN THE EYES OF THE RATS. DREAM COMES WHEN THE SHADOWS ARE DARKEST, AND SOMETIMES DELIRIUM ATTENDS HIM.
I HAVE EVEN FELT DESIRE DOWN HERE, IN THE DARK WITH NO COMFORT BUT MYSELF; BUT IT WAS DEATH I COURTED, AND WANTED FOR MY OWN.
AND THEN DESTRUCTION CAME AND REMINDED ME THAT LABYRINTHS ARE BEST WALKED THROUGH BLIND.
THAT'S HOW I FOUND MY WAY TO DESTINY'S GARDEN.
WHAT ARE YOU TALKING ABOUT?
THERE'S A STATUE OF YOU THERE. AND THERE'S A STATUE OF ME, AS WELL.

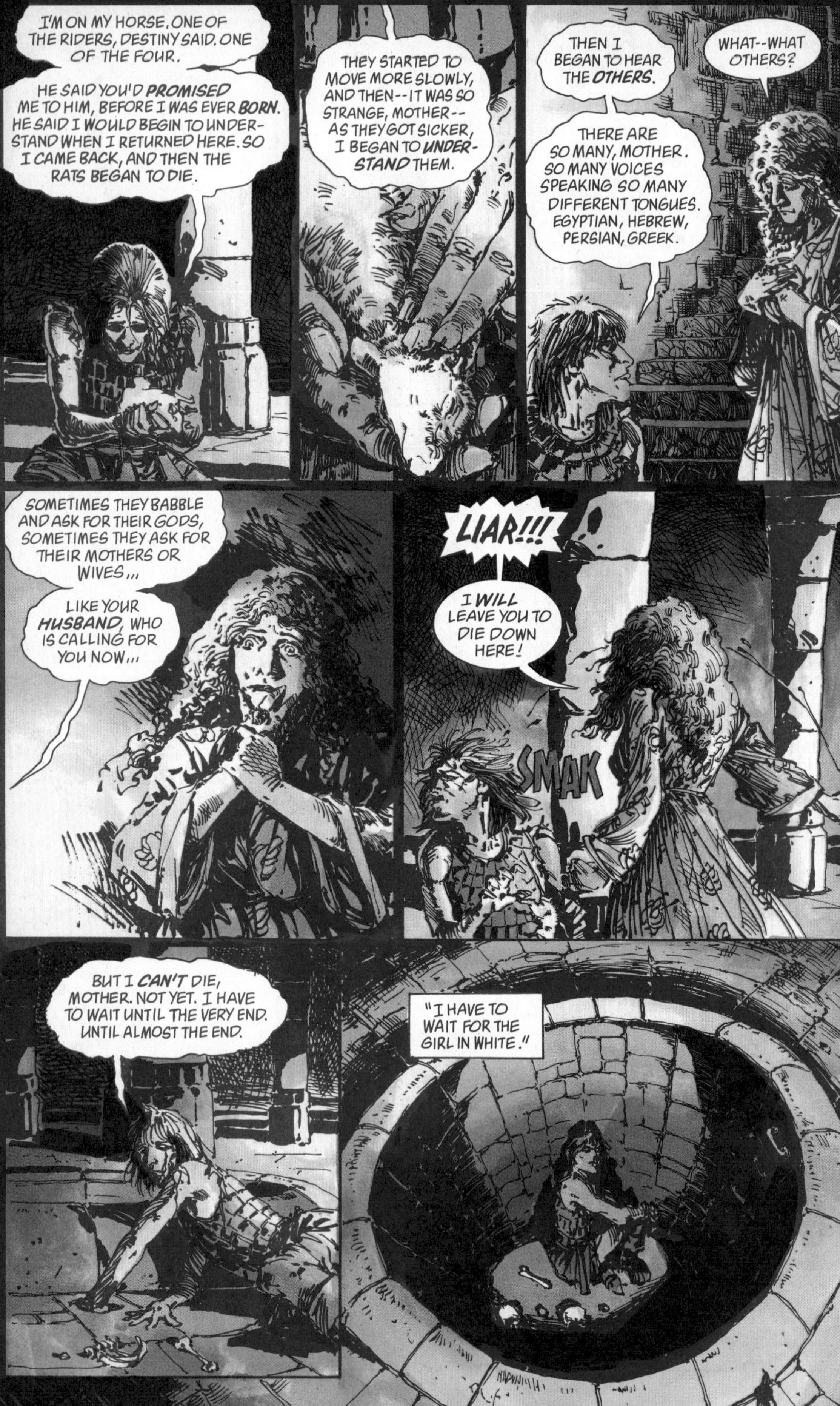
I'M ON MY HORSE, ONE OF THE RIDERS, DESTINY SAID. ONE OF THE FOUR.
HE SAID YOU'D PROMISED ME TO HIM, BEFORE I WAS EVER BORN. HE SAID I WOULD BEGIN TO UNDERSTAND WHEN I RETURNED HERE. SO I CAME BACK, AND THEN THE RATS BEGAN TO DIE.
THEY STARTED TO MOVE MORE SLOWLY, AND THEN--IT WAS SO STRANGE, MOTHER--AS THEY GOT SICKER, I BEGAN TO UNDERSTAND THEM.
THEN I BEGAN TO HEAR THE OTHERS.
WHAT--WHAT OTHERS?
THERE ARE SO MANY, MOTHER. SO MANY VOICES SPEAKING SO MANY DIFFERENT TONGUES. EGYPTIAN, HEBREW, PERSIAN, GREEK.
SOMETIMES THEY BABBLE AND ASK FOR THEIR GODS, SOMETIMES THEY ASK FOR THEIR MOTHERS OR WIVES...
LIKE YOUR HUSBAND, WHO IS CALLING FOR YOU NOW...
LIAR!!!
I WILL LEAVE YOU TO DIE DOWN HERE!
SMAK
BUT I CAN'T DIE, MOTHER. NOT YET. I HAVE TO WAIT UNTIL THE VERY END. UNTIL ALMOST THE END.
"I HAVE TO WAIT FOR THE GIRL IN WHITE."

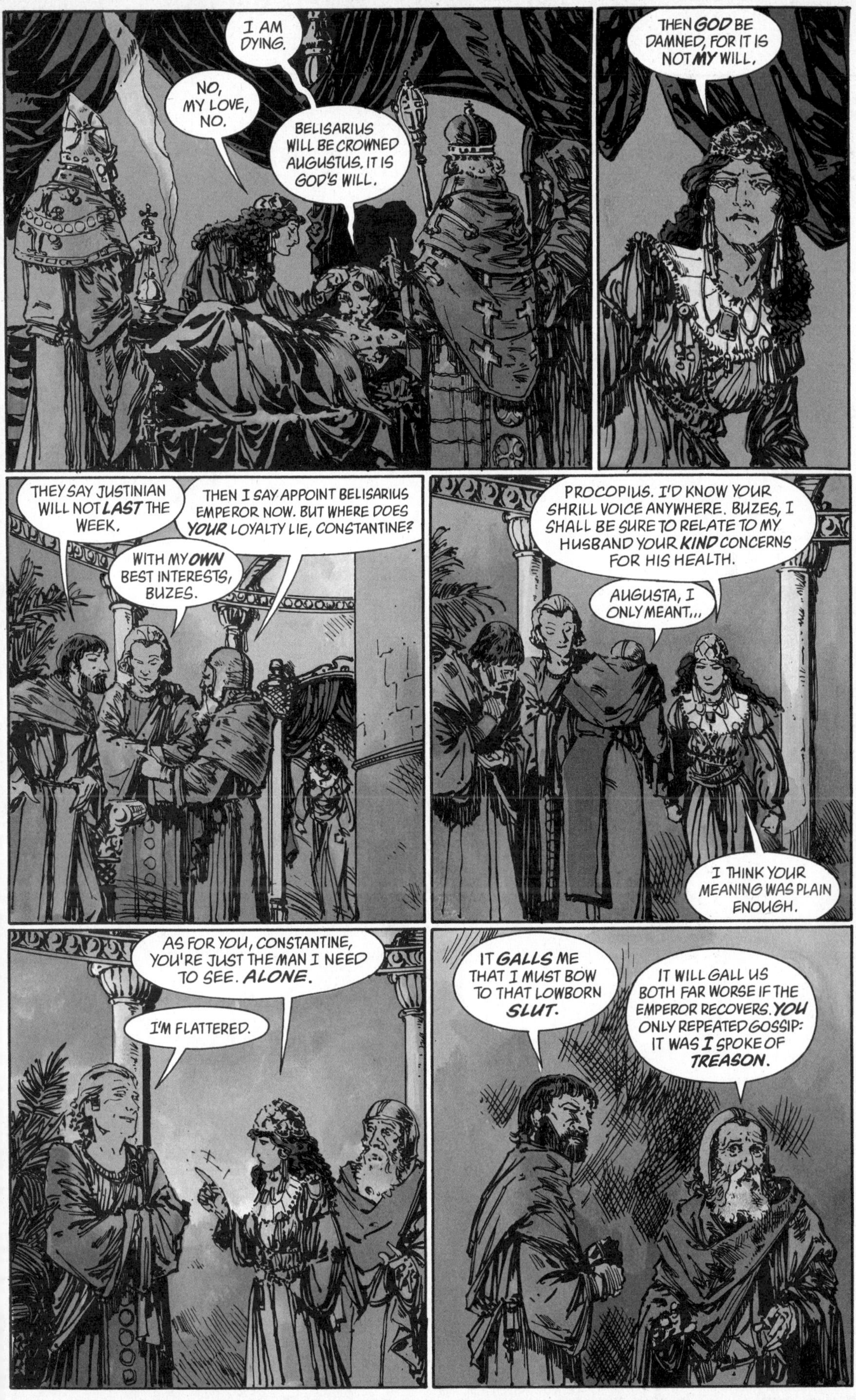
I AM DYING.
NO, MY LOVE, NO.
BELISARIUS WILL BE CROWNED AUGUSTUS. IT IS GOD'S WILL.
THEN GOD BE DAMNED, FOR IT IS NOT MY WILL.
THEY SAY JUSTINIAN WILL NOT LAST THE WEEK.
THEN I SAY APPOINT BELISARIUS EMPEROR NOW. BUT WHERE DOES YOUR LOYALTY LIE, CONSTANTINE?
WITH MY OWN BEST INTERESTS, BUZES.
PROCOPIUS. I'D KNOW YOUR SHRILL VOICE ANYWHERE. BUZES, I SHALL BE SURE TO RELATE TO MY HUSBAND YOUR KIND CONCERNS FOR HIS HEALTH.
AUGUSTA, I ONLY MEANT...
I THINK YOUR MEANING WAS PLAIN ENOUGH.
AS FOR YOU, CONSTANTINE, YOU'RE JUST THE MAN I NEED TO SEE. ALONE.
I'M FLATTERED.
IT GALLS ME THAT I MUST BOW TO THAT LOWBORN SLUT.
IT WILL GALL US BOTH FAR WORSE IF THE EMPEROR RECOVERS. YOU ONLY REPEATED GOSSIP: IT WAS I SPOKE OF TREASON.

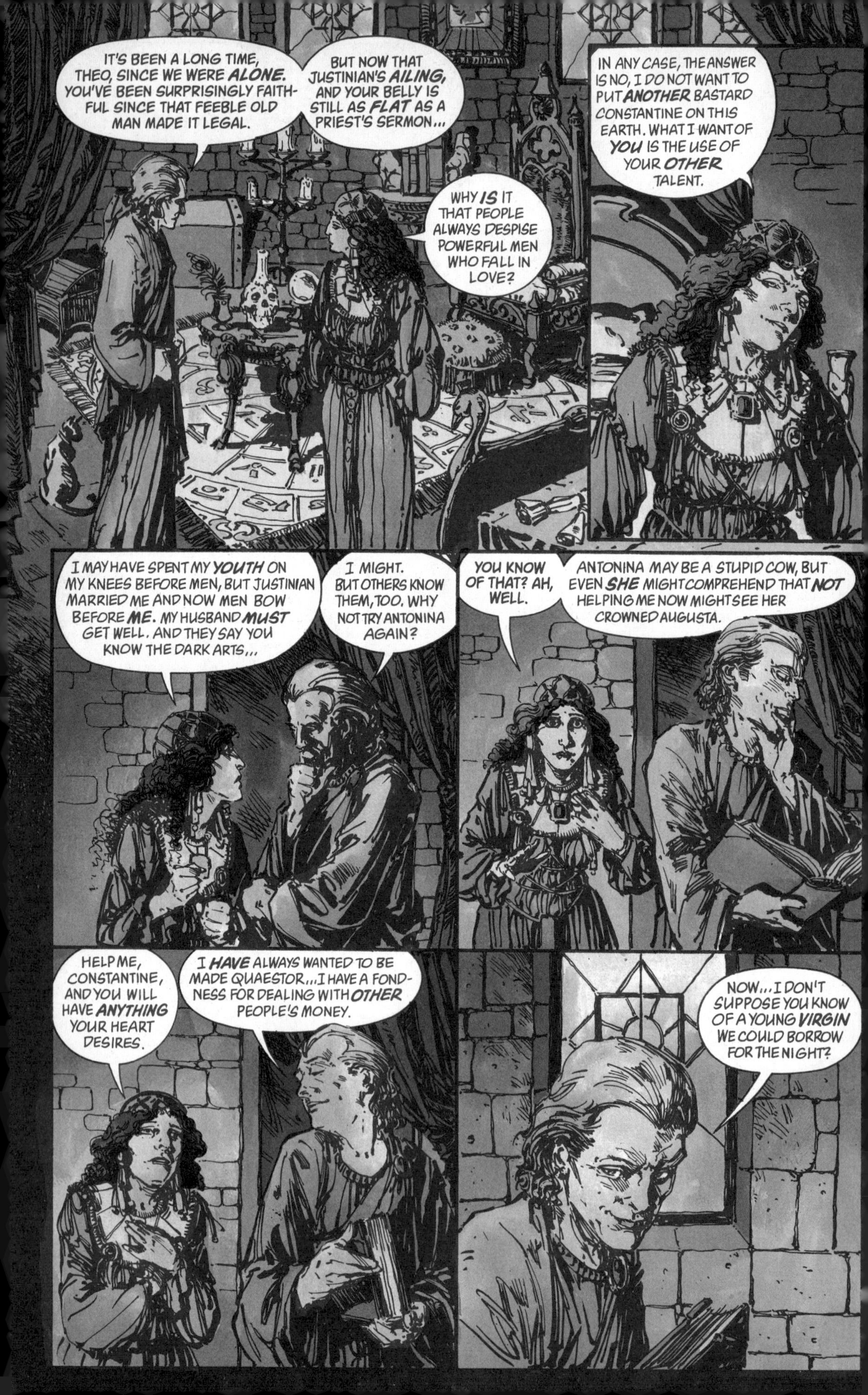
IT'S BEEN A LONG TIME, THEO, SINCE WE WERE ALONE. YOU'VE BEEN SURPRISINGLY FAITHFUL SINCE THAT FEEBLE OLD MAN MADE IT LEGAL.
BUT NOW THAT JUSTINIAN'S AILING, AND YOUR BELLY IS STILL AS FLAT AS A PRIEST'S SERMON...
WHY IS IT THAT PEOPLE ALWAYS DESPISE POWERFUL MEN WHO FALL IN LOVE?
IN ANY CASE, THE ANSWER IS NO, I DO NOT WANT TO PUT ANOTHER BASTARD CONSTANTINE ON THIS EARTH. WHAT I WANT OF YOU IS THE USE OF YOUR OTHER TALENT.
I MAY HAVE SPENT MY YOUTH ON MY KNEES BEFORE MEN, BUT JUSTINIAN MARRIED ME AND NOW MEN BOW BEFORE ME. MY HUSBAND MUST GET WELL. AND THEY SAY YOU KNOW THE DARK ARTS...
I MIGHT. BUT OTHERS KNOW THEM, TOO. WHY NOT TRY ANTONINA AGAIN?
YOU KNOW OF THAT? AH, WELL.
ANTONINA MAY BE A STUPID COW, BUT EVEN SHE MIGHT COMPREHEND THAT NOT HELPING ME NOW MIGHT SEE HER CROWNED AUGUSTA.
HELP ME, CONSTANTINE, AND YOU WILL HAVE ANYTHING YOUR HEART DESIRES.
I HAVE ALWAYS WANTED TO BE MADE QUAESTOR...I HAVE A FONDNESS FOR DEALING WITH OTHER PEOPLE'S MONEY.
NOW...I DON'T SUPPOSE YOU KNOW OF A YOUNG VIRGIN WE COULD BORROW FOR THE NIGHT?

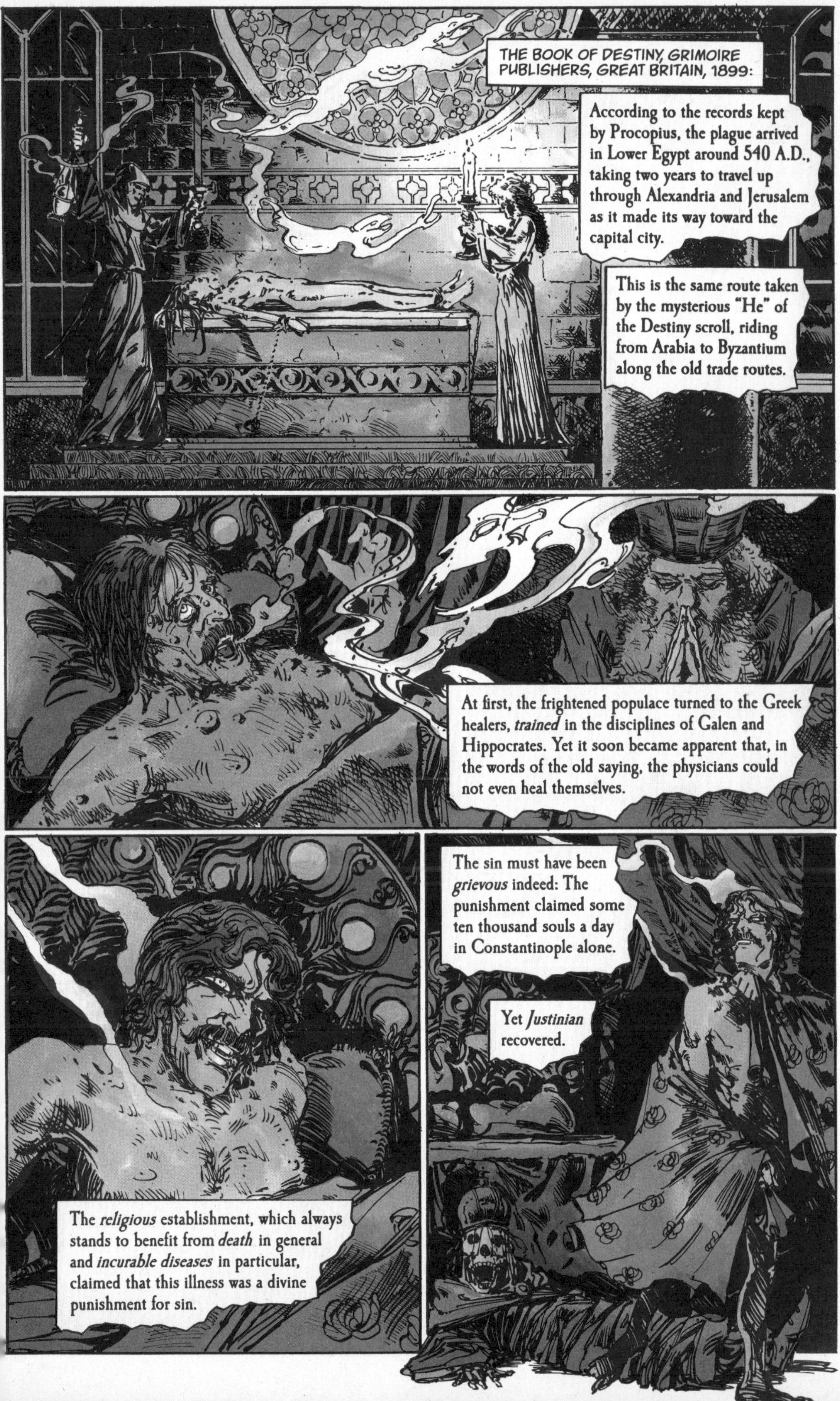
THE BOOK OF DESTINY, GRIMOIRE PUBLISHERS, GREAT BRITAIN, 1899:
According to the records kept by Procopius, the plague arrived in Lower Egypt around 540 A.D., taking two years to travel up through Alexandria and Jerusalem as it made its way toward the capital city.
This is the same route taken by the mysterious "He" of the Destiny scroll, riding from Arabia to Byzantium along the old trade routes.
At first, the frightened populace turned to the Greek healers, *trained* in the disciplines of Galen and Hippocrates. Yet it soon became apparent that, in the words of the old saying, the physicians could not even heal themselves.
The *religious* establishment, which always stands to benefit from *death* in general and *incurable diseases* in particular, claimed that this illness was a divine punishment for sin.
The sin must have been *grievous* indeed: The punishment claimed some ten thousand souls a day in Constantinople alone.
Yet *Justinian* recovered.

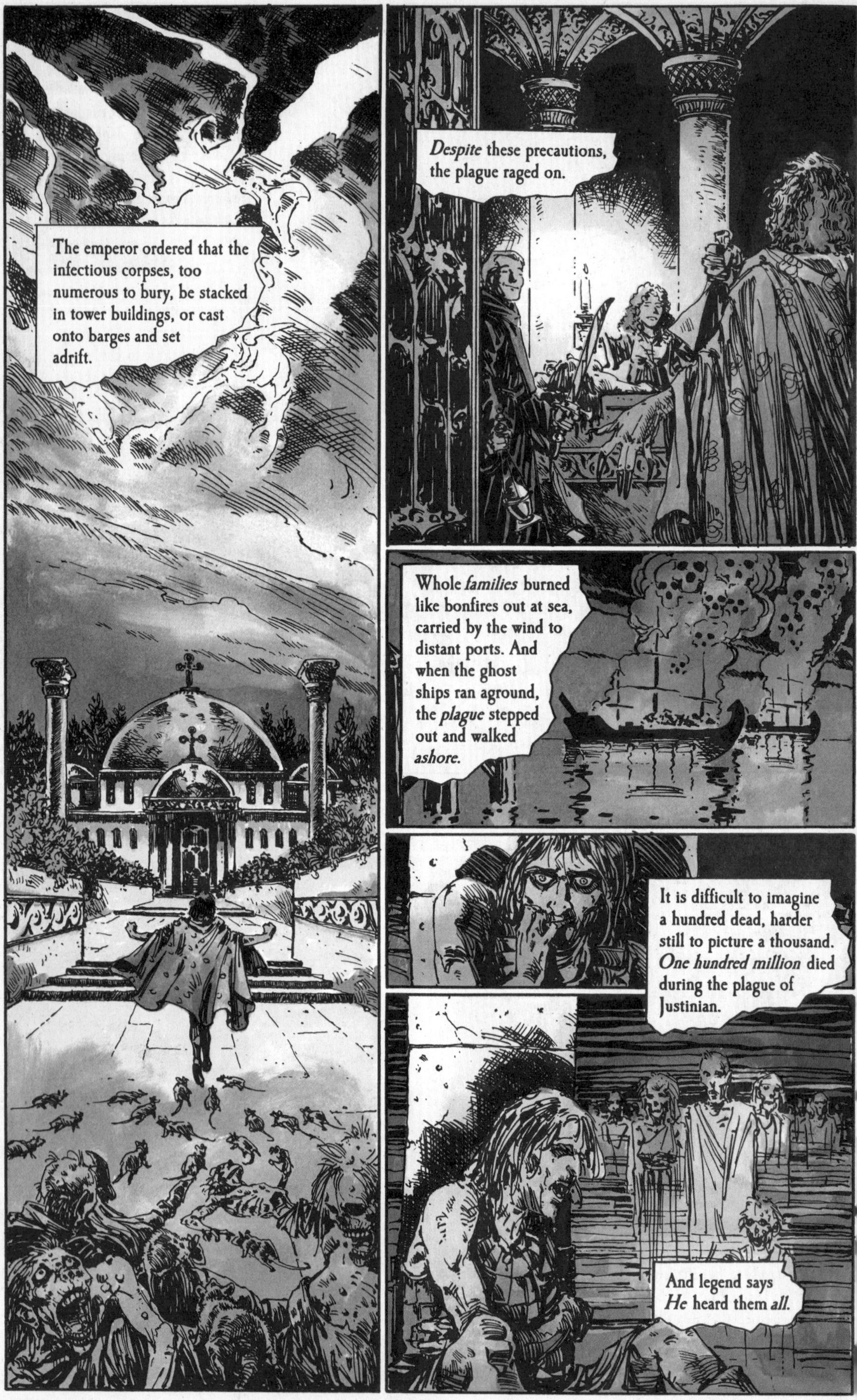
The emperor ordered that the infectious corpses, too numerous to bury, be stacked in tower buildings, or cast onto barges and set adrift.
Despite these precautions, the plague raged on.
Whole *families* burned like bonfires out at sea, carried by the wind to distant ports. And when the ghost ships ran aground, the *plague* stepped out and walked *ashore.*
It is difficult to imagine a hundred dead, harder still to picture a thousand. *One hundred million* died during the plague of Justinian.
And legend says *He* heard them *all.*

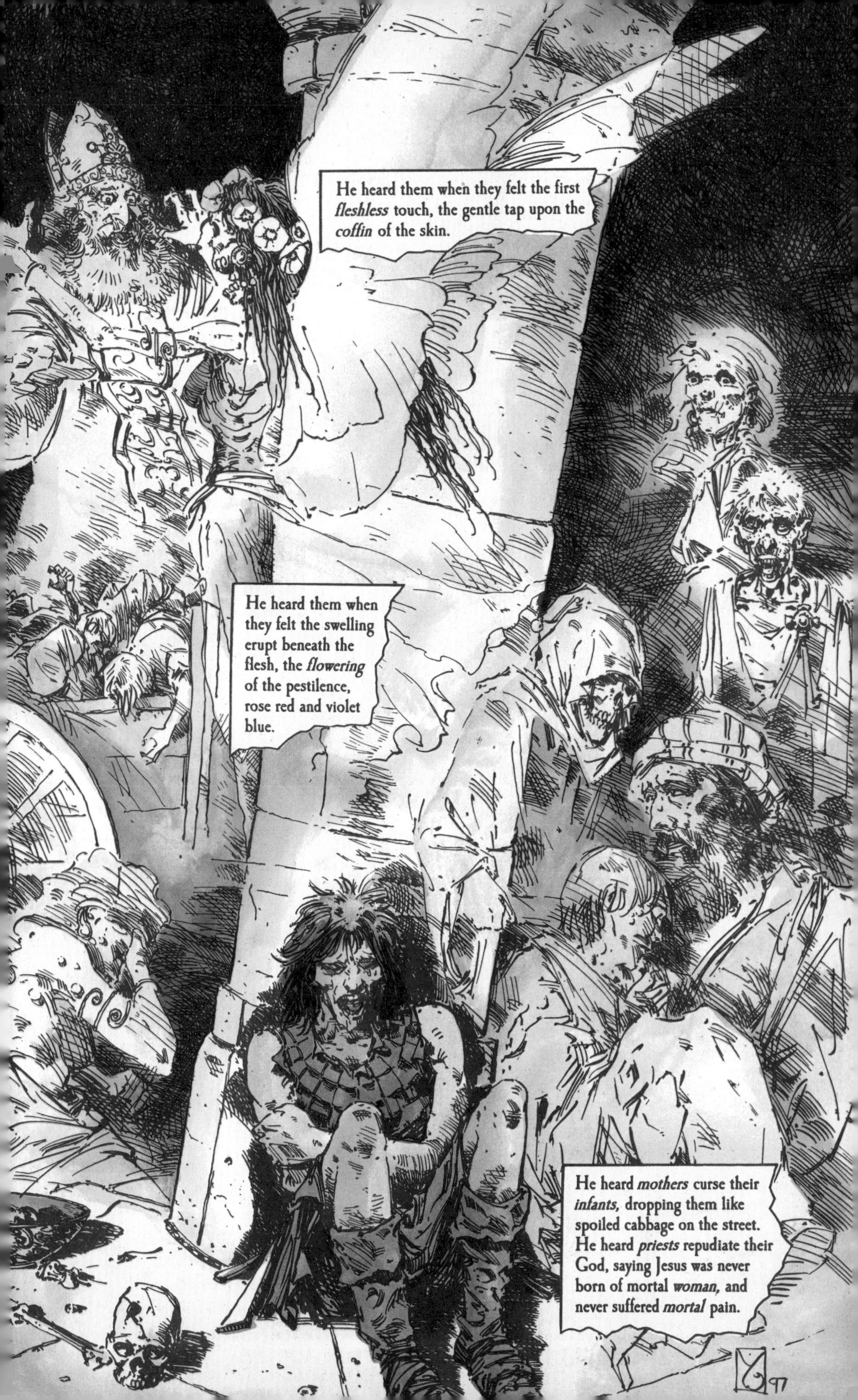
He heard them when they felt the first *fleshless* touch, the gentle tap upon the *coffin* of the skin.
He heard them when they felt the swelling erupt beneath the flesh, the *flowering* of the pestilence, rose red and violet blue.
He heard *mothers* curse their *infants,* dropping them like spoiled cabbage on the street. He heard *priests* repudiate their God, saying Jesus was never born of mortal *woman,* and never suffered *mortal* pain.

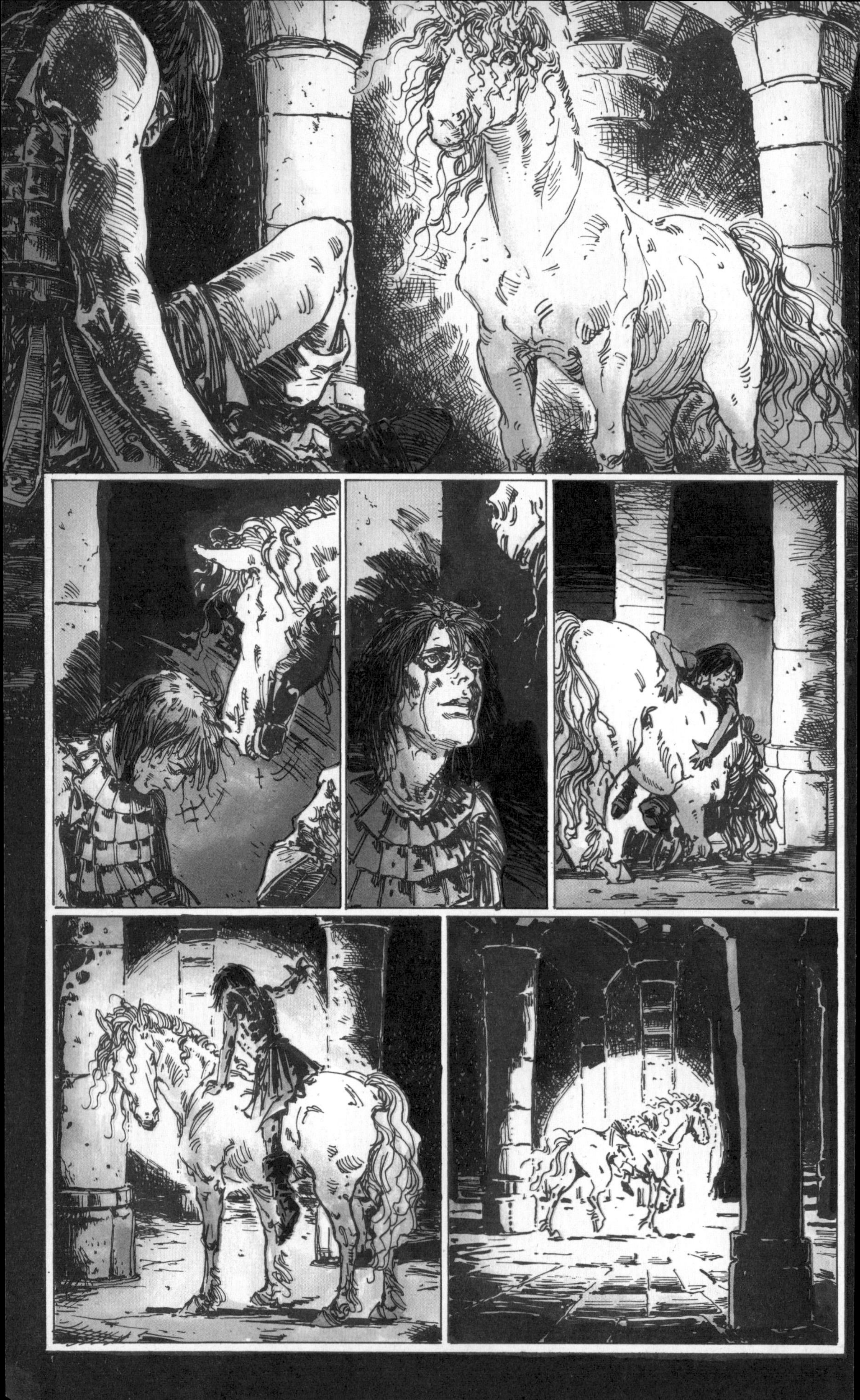

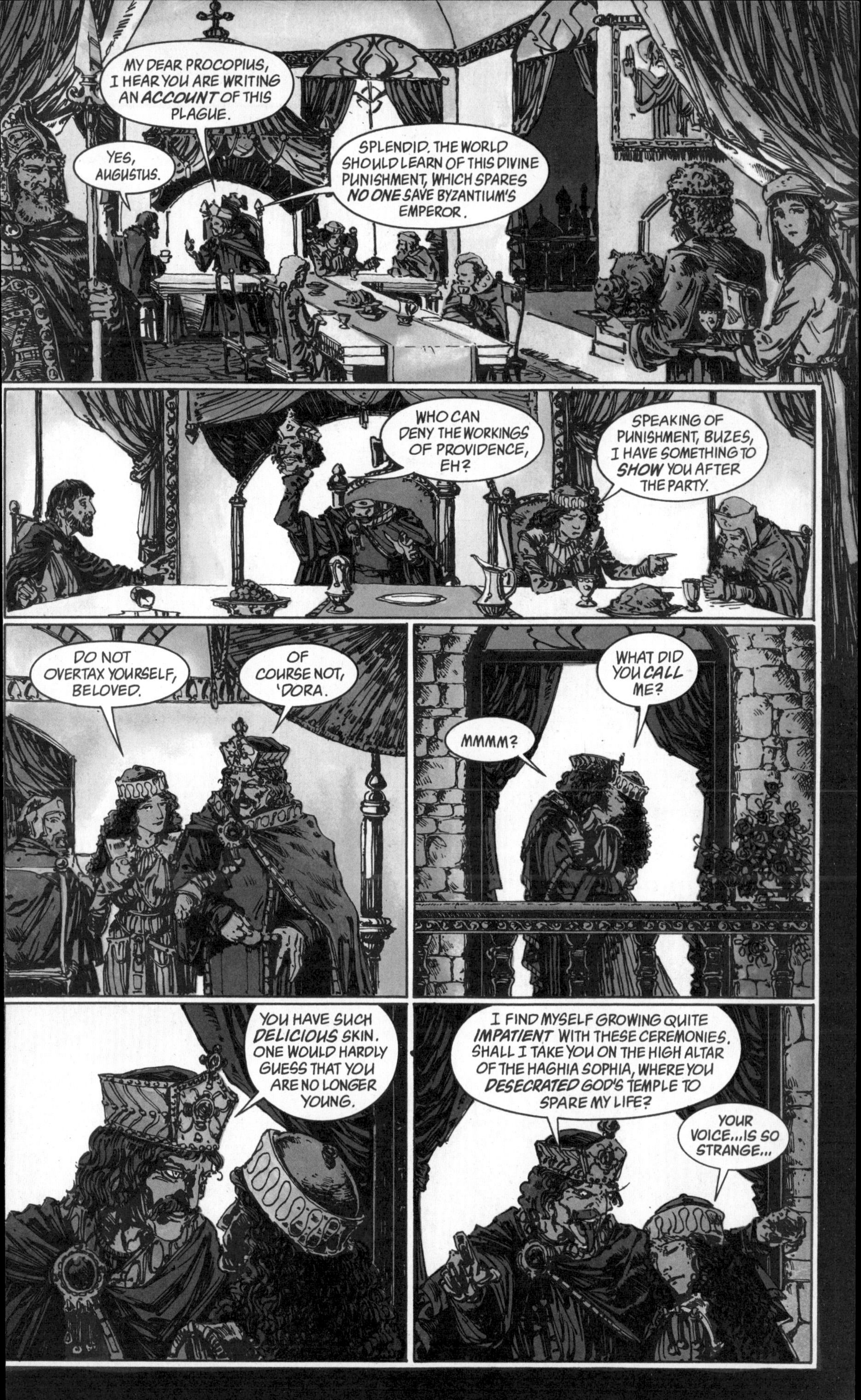
MY DEAR PROCOPIUS, I HEAR YOU ARE WRITING AN ACCOUNT OF THIS PLAGUE.
YES, AUGUSTUS.
SPLENDID. THE WORLD SHOULD LEARN OF THIS DIVINE PUNISHMENT, WHICH SPARES NO ONE SAVE BYZANTIUM'S EMPEROR.
WHO CAN DENY THE WORKINGS OF PROVIDENCE, EH?
SPEAKING OF PUNISHMENT, BUZES, I HAVE SOMETHING TO SHOW YOU AFTER THE PARTY.
DO NOT OVERTAX YOURSELF, BELOVED.
OF COURSE NOT, 'DORA.
WHAT DID YOU CALL ME?
MMMM?
YOU HAVE SUCH DELICIOUS SKIN. ONE WOULD HARDLY GUESS THAT YOU ARE NO LONGER YOUNG.
I FIND MYSELF GROWING QUITE IMPATIENT WITH THESE CEREMONIES. SHALL I TAKE YOU ON THE HIGH ALTAR OF THE HAGHIA SOPHIA, WHERE YOU DESECRATED GOD'S TEMPLE TO SPARE MY LIFE?
YOUR VOICE...IS SO STRANGE...

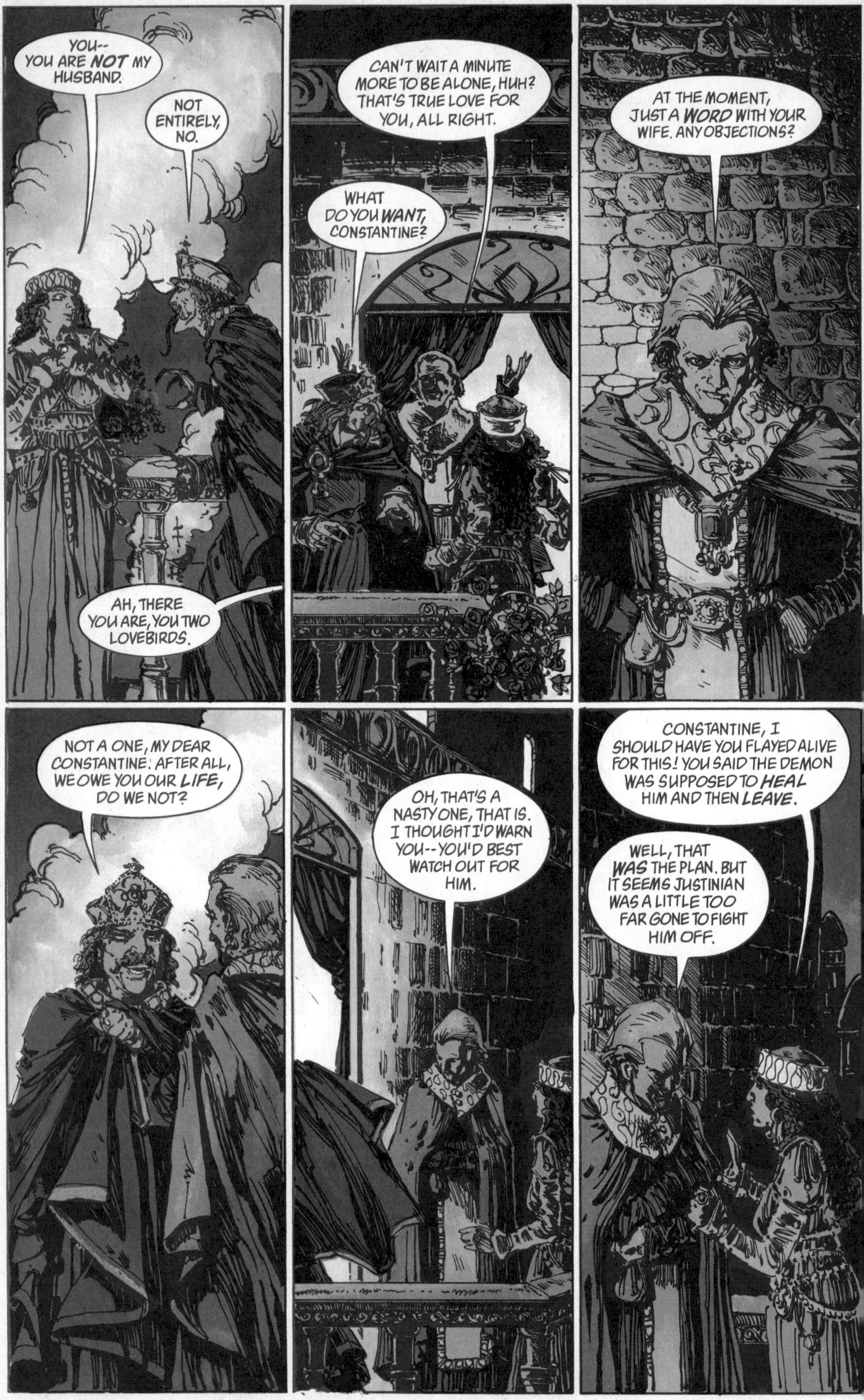
YOU--
YOU ARE NOT MY HUSBAND.
NOT ENTIRELY, NO.
AH, THERE YOU ARE, YOU TWO LOVEBIRDS.
CAN'T WAIT A MINUTE MORE TO BE ALONE, HUH? THAT'S TRUE LOVE FOR YOU, ALL RIGHT.
WHAT DO YOU WANT, CONSTANTINE?
AT THE MOMENT, JUST A WORD WITH YOUR WIFE. ANY OBJECTIONS?
NOT A ONE, MY DEAR CONSTANTINE. AFTER ALL, WE OWE YOU OUR LIFE, DO WE NOT?
OH, THAT'S A NASTY ONE, THAT IS. I THOUGHT I'D WARN YOU--YOU'D BEST WATCH OUT FOR HIM.
CONSTANTINE, I SHOULD HAVE YOU FLAYED ALIVE FOR THIS! YOU SAID THE DEMON WAS SUPPOSED TO HEAL HIM AND THEN LEAVE.
WELL, THAT WAS THE PLAN. BUT IT SEEMS JUSTINIAN WAS A LITTLE TOO FAR GONE TO FIGHT HIM OFF.

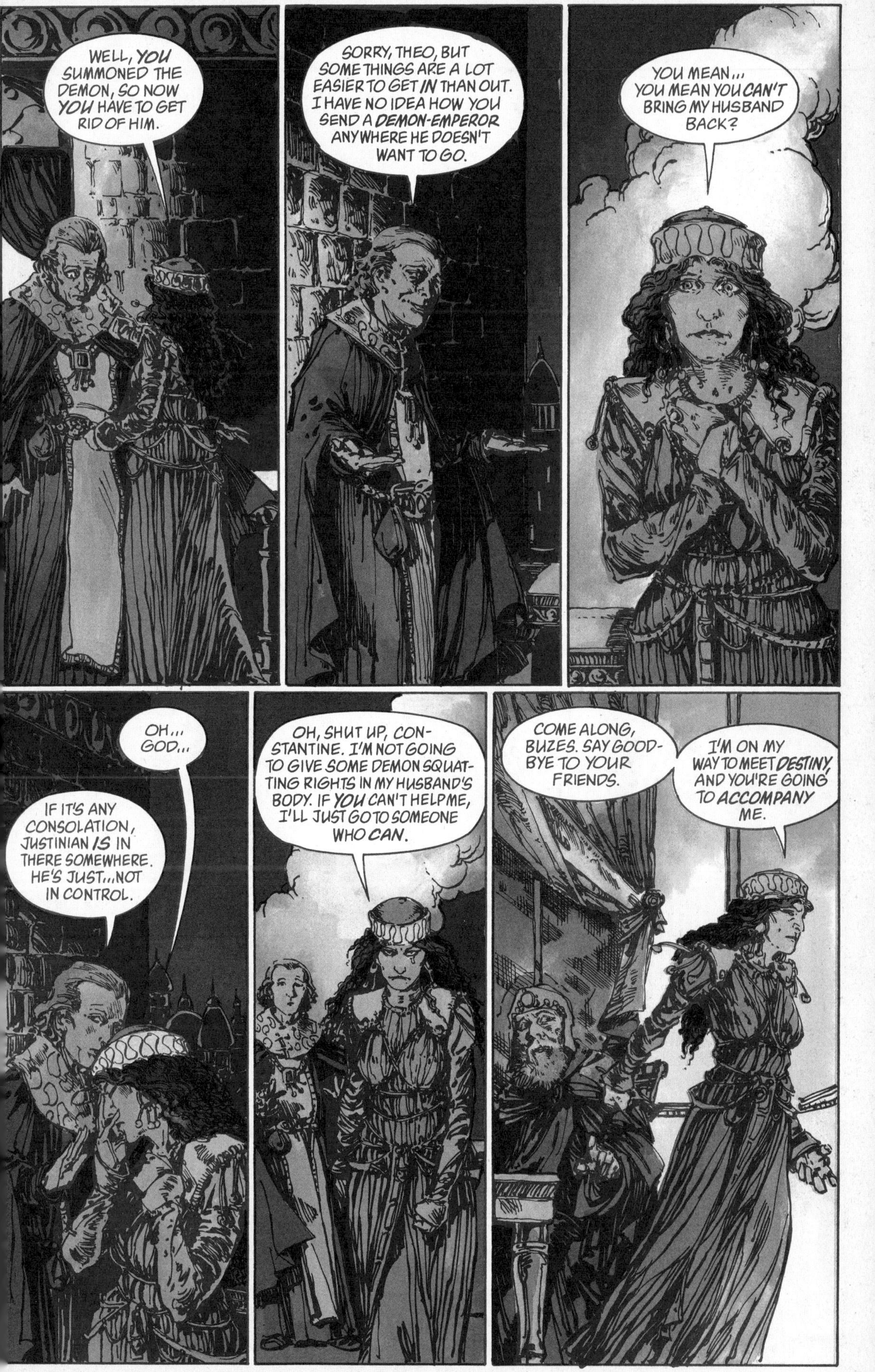
WELL, YOU SUMMONED THE DEMON, SO NOW YOU HAVE TO GET RID OF HIM.
SORRY, THEO, BUT SOME THINGS ARE A LOT EASIER TO GET IN THAN OUT. I HAVE NO IDEA HOW YOU SEND A DEMON-EMPEROR ANYWHERE HE DOESN'T WANT TO GO.
YOU MEAN... YOU MEAN YOU CAN'T BRING MY HUSBAND BACK?
OH... GOD...
IF IT'S ANY CONSOLATION, JUSTINIAN IS IN THERE SOMEWHERE. HE'S JUST...NOT IN CONTROL.
OH, SHUT UP, CON-STANTINE. I'M NOT GOING TO GIVE SOME DEMON SQUAT-TING RIGHTS IN MY HUSBAND'S BODY. IF YOU CAN'T HELP ME, I'LL JUST GO TO SOMEONE WHO CAN.
COME ALONG, BUZES. SAY GOOD-BYE TO YOUR FRIENDS.
I'M ON MY WAY TO MEET DESTINY, AND YOU'RE GOING TO ACCOMPANY ME.

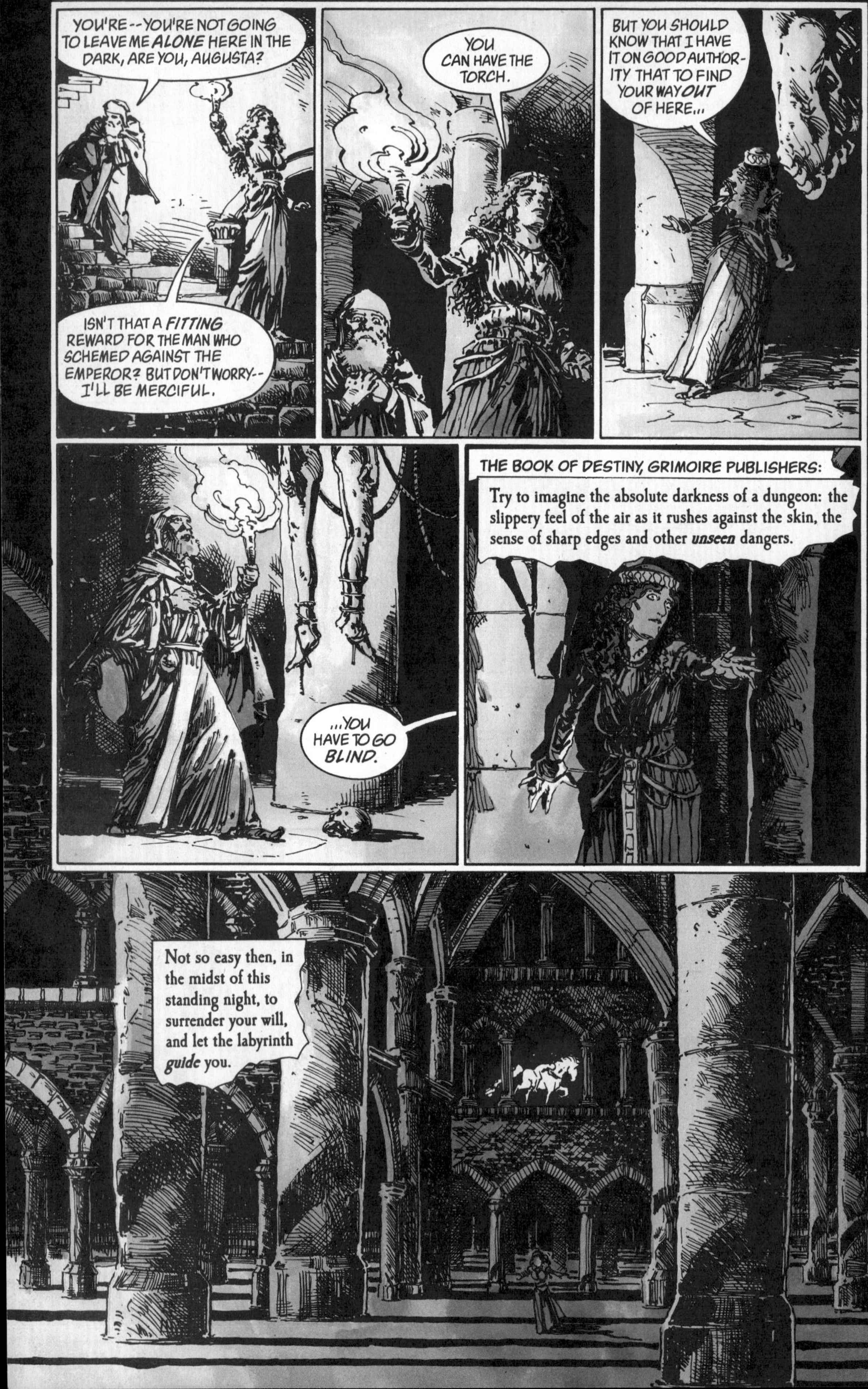
YOU'RE--YOU'RE NOT GOING TO LEAVE ME ALONE HERE IN THE DARK, ARE YOU, AUGUSTA?
ISN'T THAT A FITTING REWARD FOR THE MAN WHO SCHEMED AGAINST THE EMPEROR? BUT DON'T WORRY-- I'LL BE MERCIFUL.
YOU CAN HAVE THE TORCH.
BUT YOU SHOULD KNOW THAT I HAVE IT ON GOOD AUTHOR-ITY THAT TO FIND YOUR WAY OUT OF HERE...
...YOU HAVE TO GO BLIND.
THE BOOK OF DESTINY, GRIMOIRE PUBLISHERS:
Try to imagine the absolute darkness of a dungeon: the slippery feel of the air as it rushes against the skin, the sense of sharp edges and other unseen dangers.
Not so easy then, in the midst of this standing night, to surrender your will, and let the labyrinth guide you.

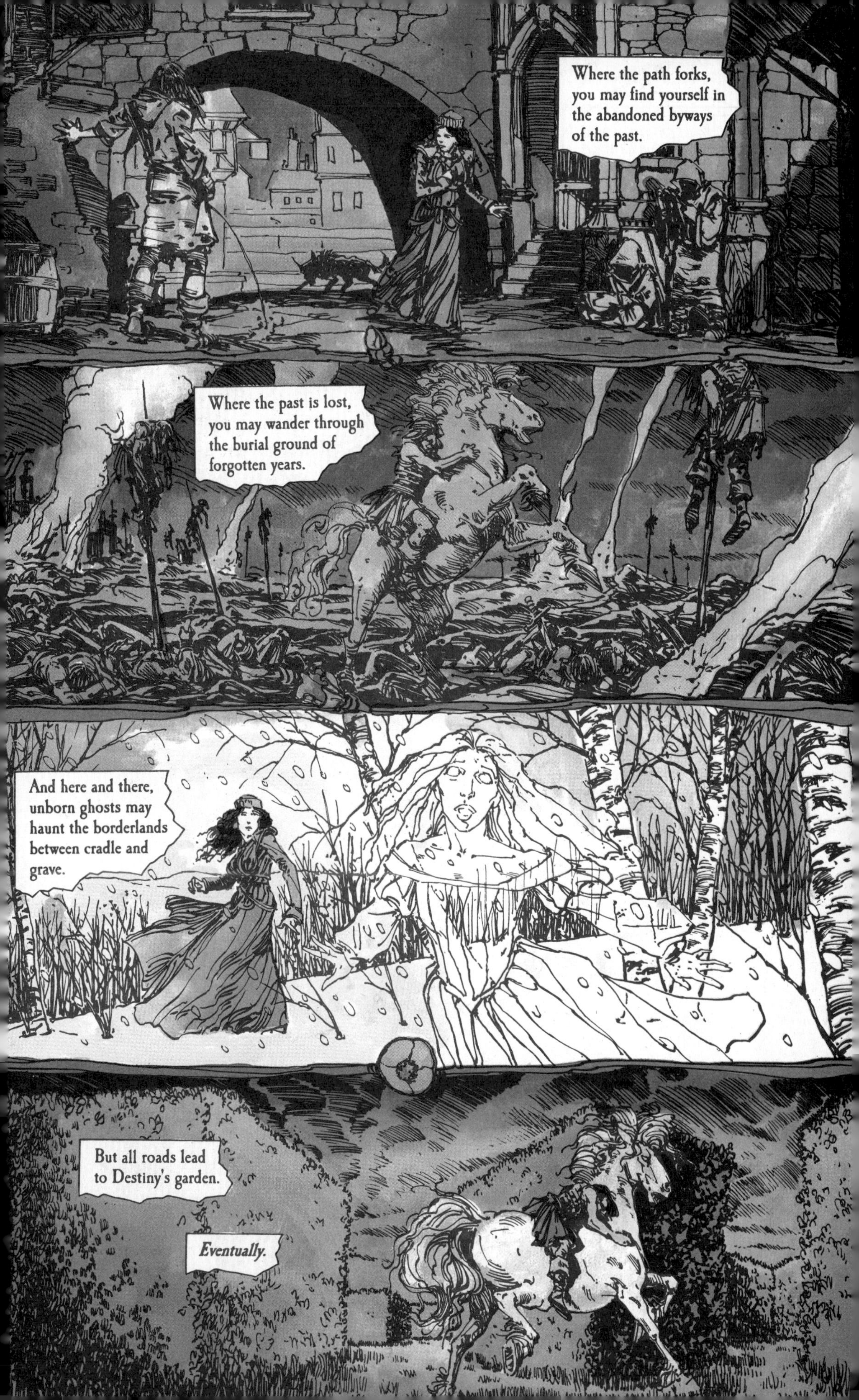
Where the path forks, you may find yourself in the abandoned byways of the past.
Where the past is lost, you may wander through the burial ground of forgotten years.
And here and there, unborn ghosts may haunt the borderlands between cradle and grave.
But all roads lead to Destiny's garden.
Eventually.

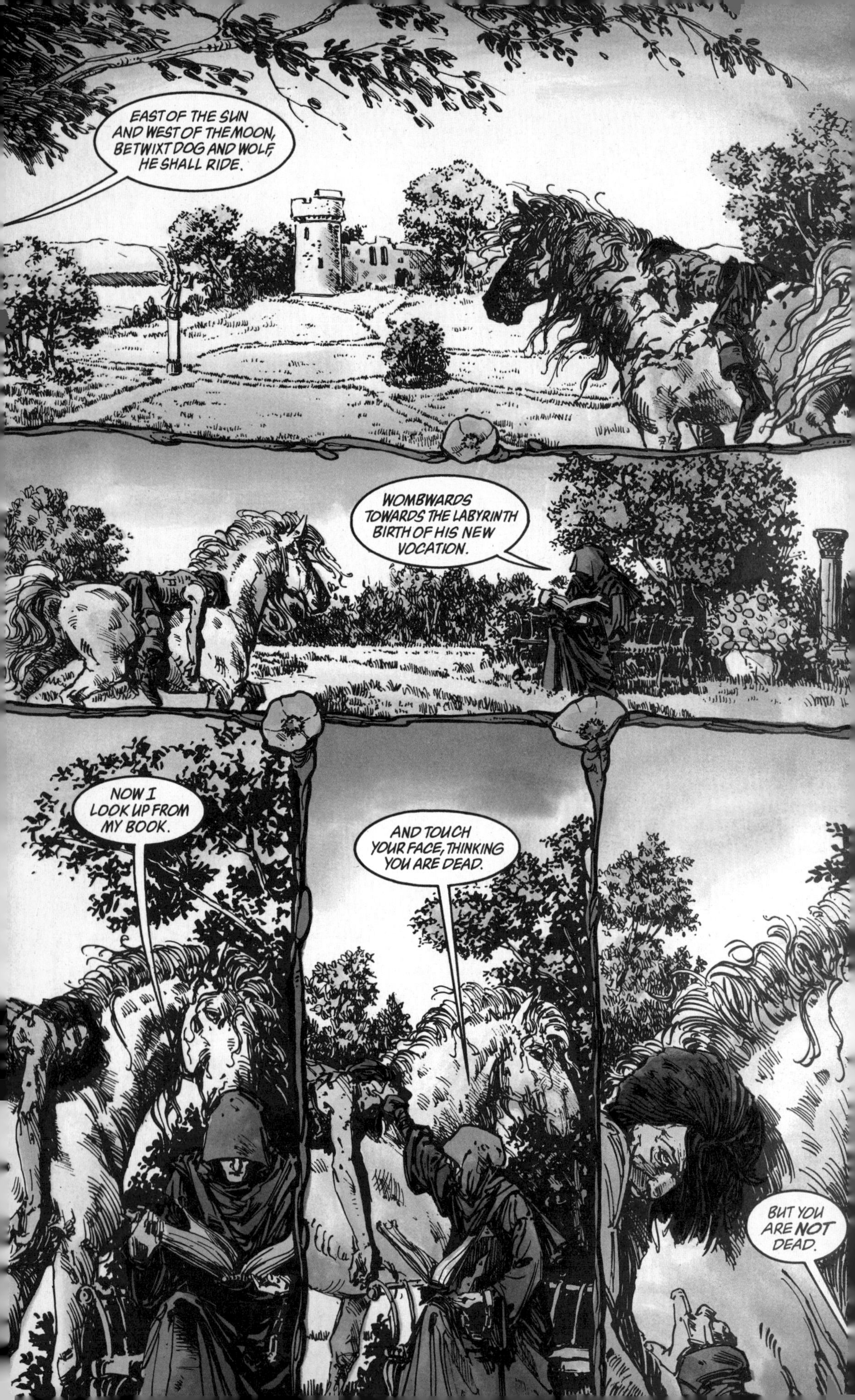
EAST OF THE SUN AND WEST OF THE MOON, BETWIXT DOG AND WOLF, HE SHALL RIDE.
WOMBWARDS TOWARDS THE LABYRINTH BIRTH OF HIS NEW VOCATION.
NOW I LOOK UP FROM MY BOOK.
AND TOUCH YOUR FACE, THINKING YOU ARE DEAD.
BUT YOU ARE NOT DEAD.

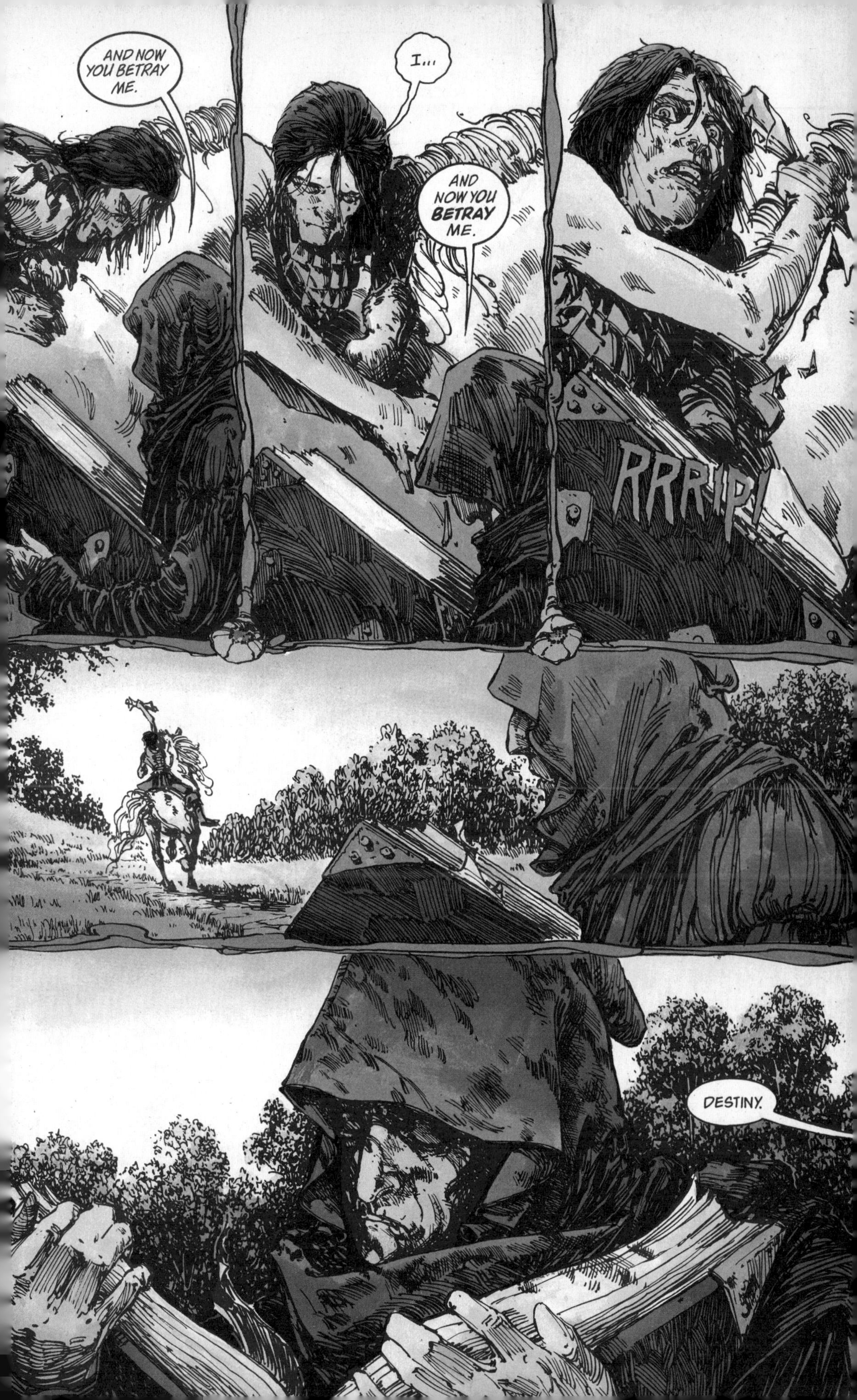
AND NOW YOU BETRAY ME.
I...
AND NOW YOU BETRAY ME.
RRRIP!
DESTINY.

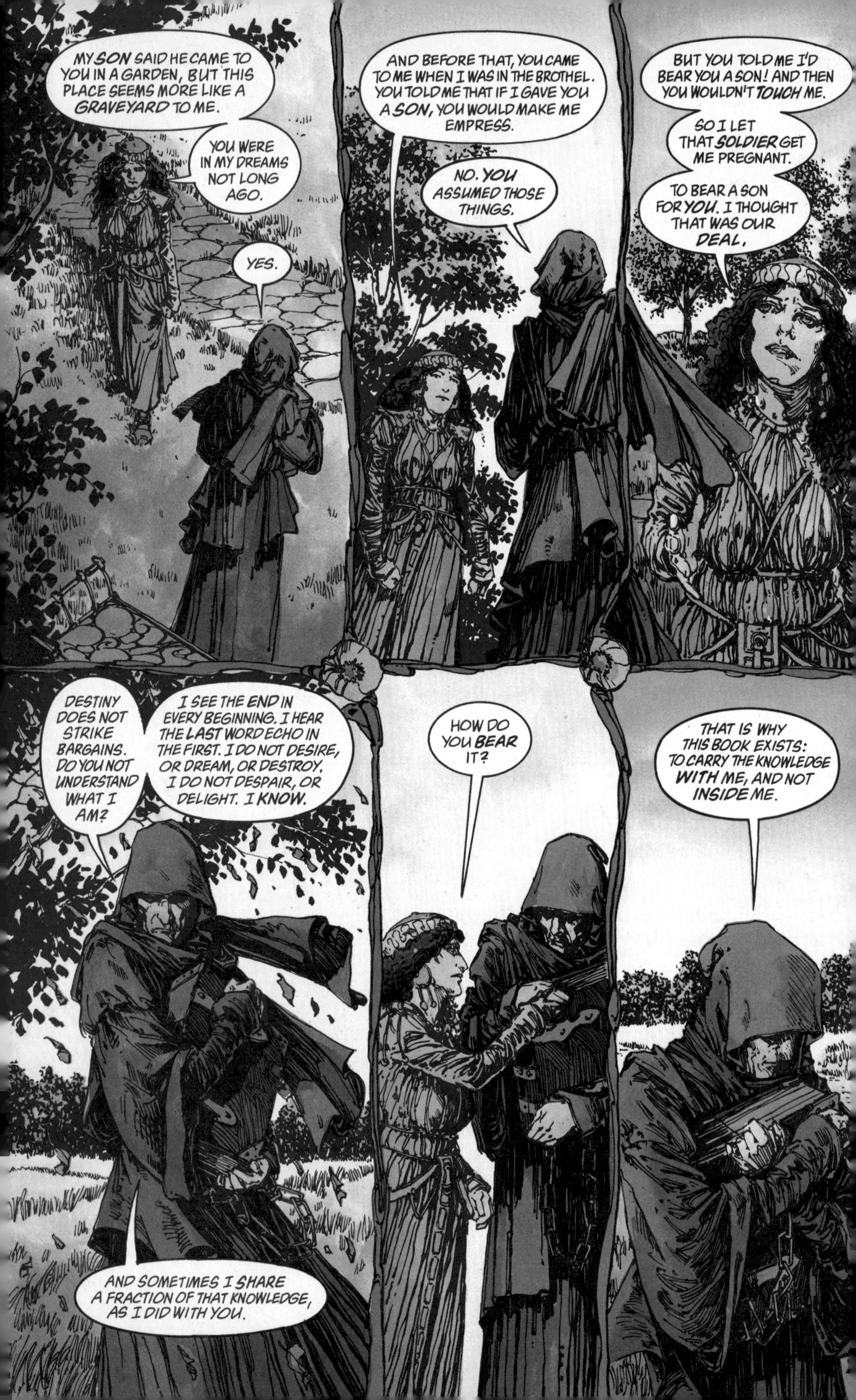
MY SON SAID HE CAME TO YOU IN A GARDEN, BUT THIS PLACE SEEMS MORE LIKE A GRAVEYARD TO ME.
YOU WERE IN MY DREAMS NOT LONG AGO.
YES.
AND BEFORE THAT, YOU CAME TO ME WHEN I WAS IN THE BROTHEL. YOU TOLD ME THAT IF I GAVE YOU A SON, YOU WOULD MAKE ME EMPRESS.
NO. YOU ASSUMED THOSE THINGS.
BUT YOU TOLD ME I'D BEAR YOU A SON! AND THEN YOU WOULDN'T TOUCH ME.
SO I LET THAT SOLDIER GET ME PREGNANT.
TO BEAR A SON FOR YOU. I THOUGHT THAT WAS OUR DEAL.
DESTINY DOES NOT STRIKE BARGAINS. DO YOU NOT UNDERSTAND WHAT I AM?
I SEE THE END IN EVERY BEGINNING. I HEAR THE LAST WORD ECHO IN THE FIRST. I DO NOT DESIRE, OR DREAM, OR DESTROY. I DO NOT DESPAIR, OR DELIGHT. I KNOW.
AND SOMETIMES I SHARE A FRACTION OF THAT KNOWLEDGE, AS I DID WITH YOU.
HOW DO YOU BEAR IT?
THAT IS WHY THIS BOOK EXISTS: TO CARRY THE KNOWLEDGE WITH ME, AND NOT INSIDE ME.

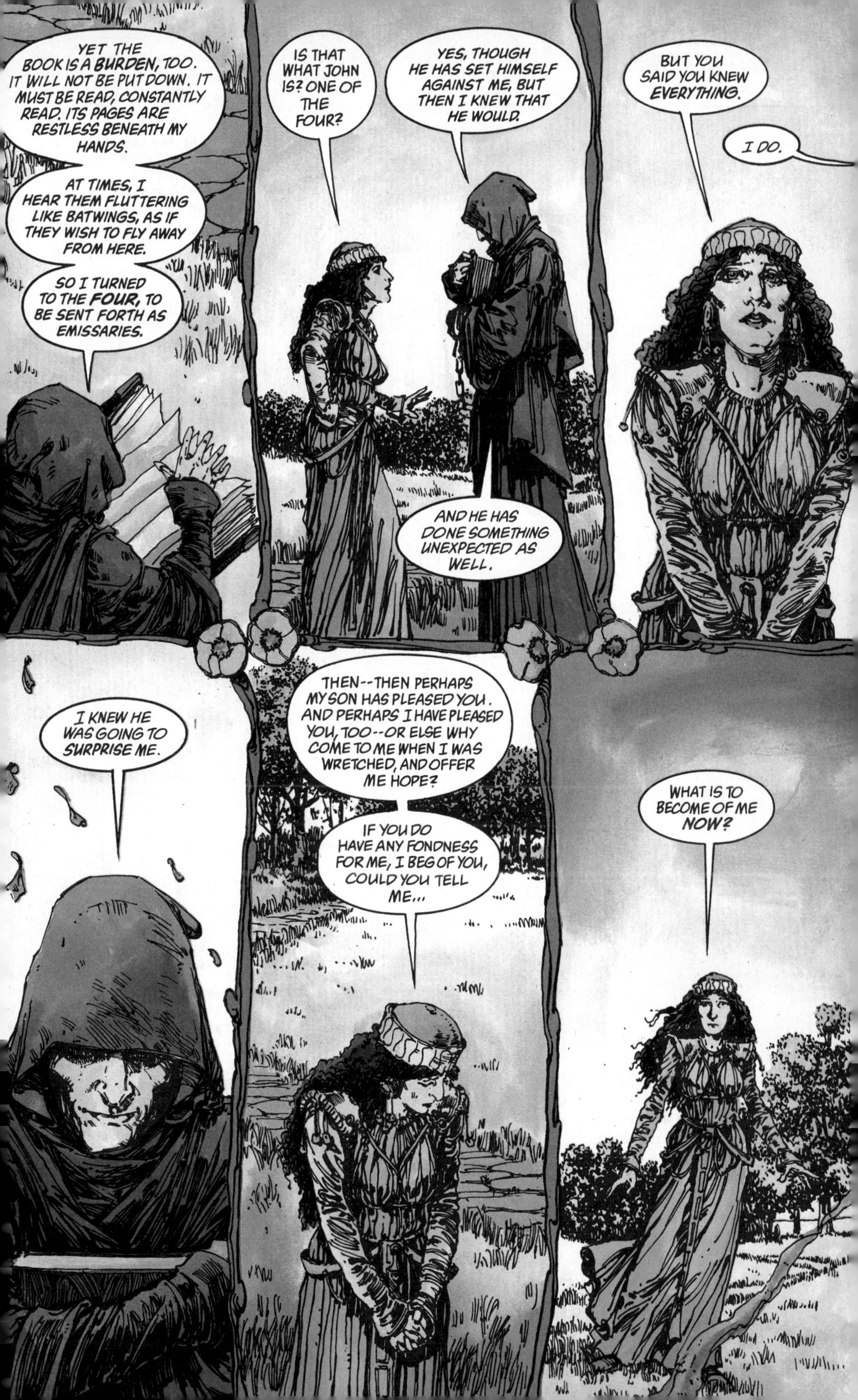
YET THE BOOK IS A BURDEN, TOO. IT WILL NOT BE PUT DOWN. IT MUST BE READ, CONSTANTLY READ. ITS PAGES ARE RESTLESS BENEATH MY HANDS.
AT TIMES, I HEAR THEM FLUTTERING LIKE BATWINGS, AS IF THEY WISH TO FLY AWAY FROM HERE.
SO I TURNED TO THE FOUR, TO BE SENT FORTH AS EMISSARIES.
IS THAT WHAT JOHN IS? ONE OF THE FOUR?
YES, THOUGH HE HAS SET HIMSELF AGAINST ME, BUT THEN I KNEW THAT HE WOULD.
AND HE HAS DONE SOMETHING UNEXPECTED AS WELL.
BUT YOU SAID YOU KNEW EVERYTHING.
I DO.
I KNEW HE WAS GOING TO SURPRISE ME.
THEN--THEN PERHAPS MY SON HAS PLEASED YOU. AND PERHAPS I HAVE PLEASED YOU, TOO--OR ELSE WHY COME TO ME WHEN I WAS WRETCHED, AND OFFER ME HOPE?
IF YOU DO HAVE ANY FONDNESS FOR ME, I BEG OF YOU, COULD YOU TELL ME...
WHAT IS TO BECOME OF ME NOW?

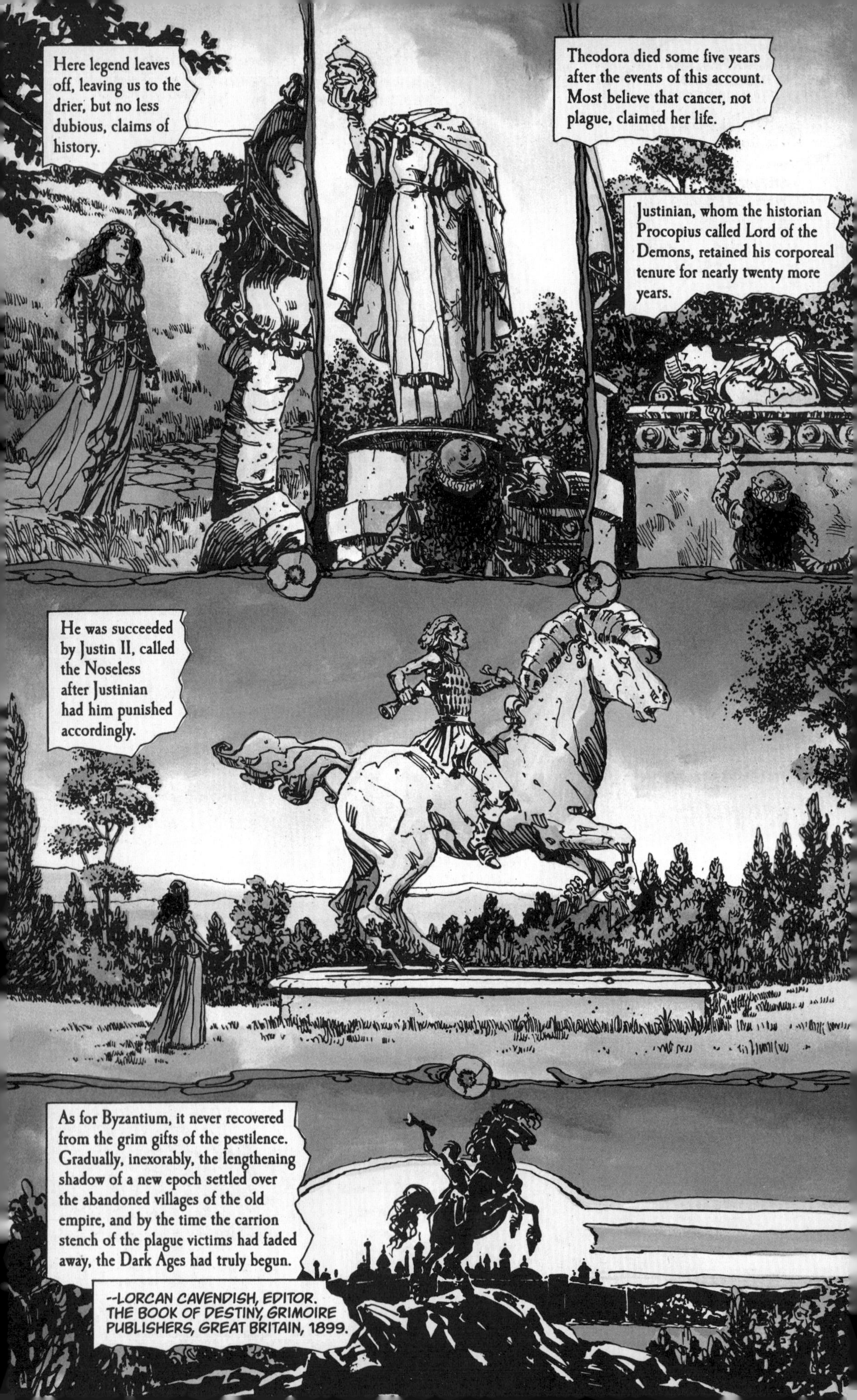

Here legend leaves off, leaving us to the drier, but no less dubious, claims of history.
Theodora died some five years after the events of this account. Most believe that cancer, not plague, claimed her life.
Justinian, whom the historian Procopius called Lord of the Demons, retained his corporeal tenure for nearly twenty more years.
He was succeeded by Justin II, called the Noseless after Justinian had him punished accordingly.
As for Byzantium, it never recovered from the grim gifts of the pestilence. Gradually, inexorably, the lengthening shadow of a new epoch settled over the abandoned villages of the old empire, and by the time the carrion stench of the plague victims had faded away, the Dark Ages had truly begun.
--LORCAN CAVENDISH, EDITOR. THE BOOK OF DESTINY, GRIMOIRE PUBLISHERS, GREAT BRITAIN, 1899.

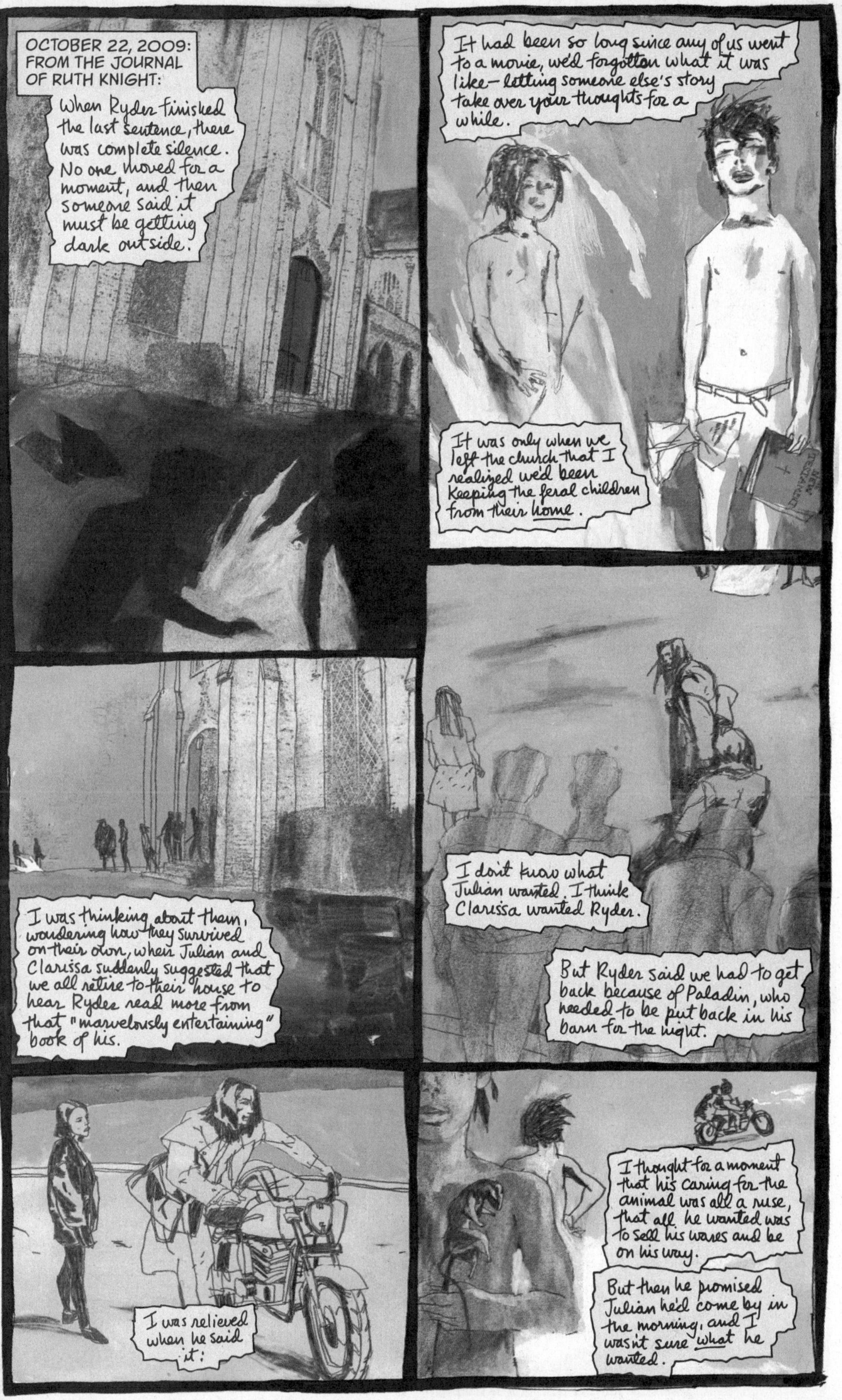

OCTOBER 22, 2009: FROM THE JOURNAL OF RUTH KNIGHT:
When Ryder finished the last sentence, there was complete silence. No one moved for a moment, and then someone said it must be getting dark outside.
It had been so long since any of us went to a movie, we'd forgotten what it was like—letting someone else's story take over your thoughts for a while.
It was only when we left the church that I realized we'd been keeping the feral children from their home.
I was thinking about them, wondering how they survived on their own, when Julian and Clarissa suddenly suggested that we all retire to their house to hear Ryder read more from that "marvelously entertaining" book of his.
I don't know what Julian wanted. I think Clarissa wanted Ryder.
But Ryder said we had to get back because of Paladin, who needed to be put back in his barn for the night.
I was relieved when he said it:
I thought for a moment that his caring for the animal was all a ruse, that all he wanted was to sell his wares and be on his way.
But then he promised Julian he'd come by in the morning, and I wasn't sure what he wanted.

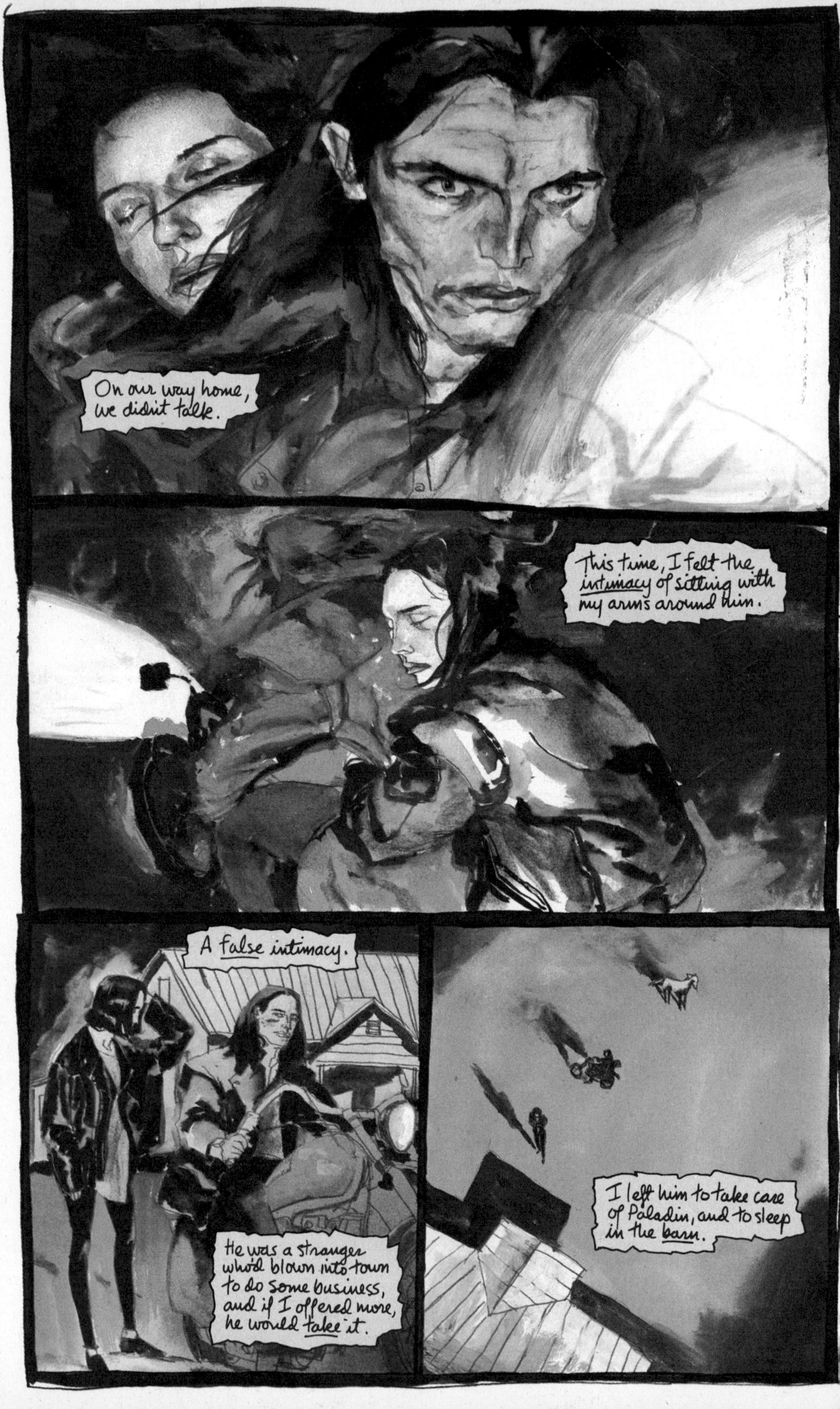
On our way home, we didn't talk.
This time, I felt the intimacy of sitting with my arms around him.
A false intimacy.
He was a stranger who'd blown into town to do some business, and if I offered more, he would take it.
I left him to take care of Paladin, and to sleep in the barn.

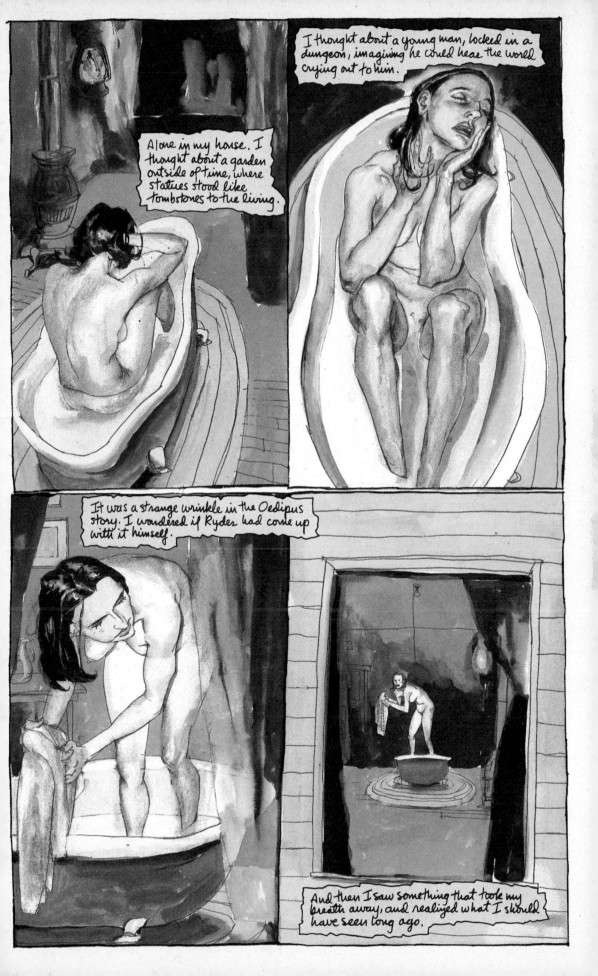

Alone in my house, I thought about a garden outside of time, where statues stood like tombstones to the living.

I thought about a young man, locked in a dungeon, imagining he could hear the world crying out to him.

It was a strange wrinkle in the Oedipus story. I wondered if Ryder had come up with it himself.

And then I saw something that took my breath away, and realized what I should have seen long ago.

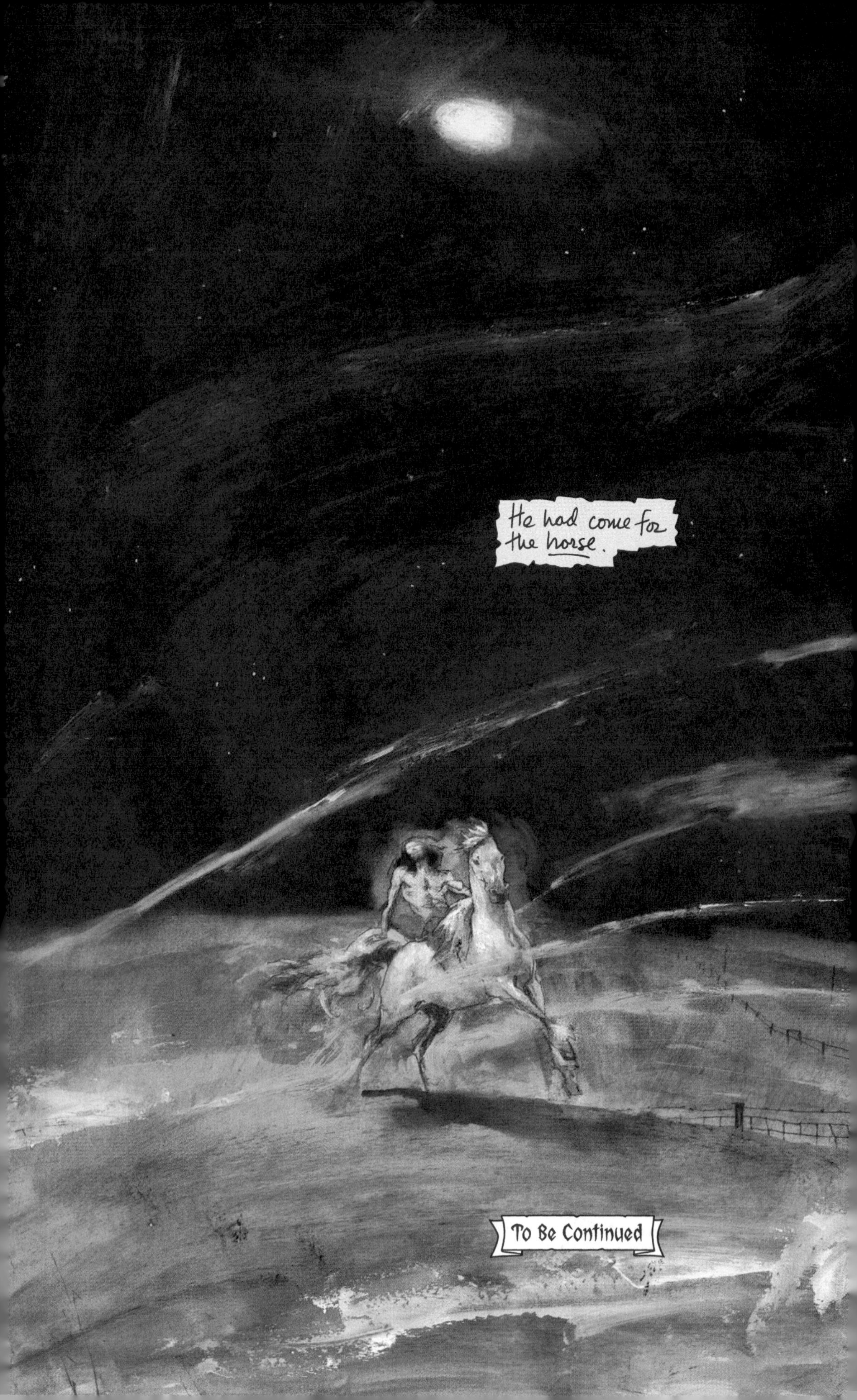
He had come for the horse.
To Be Continued

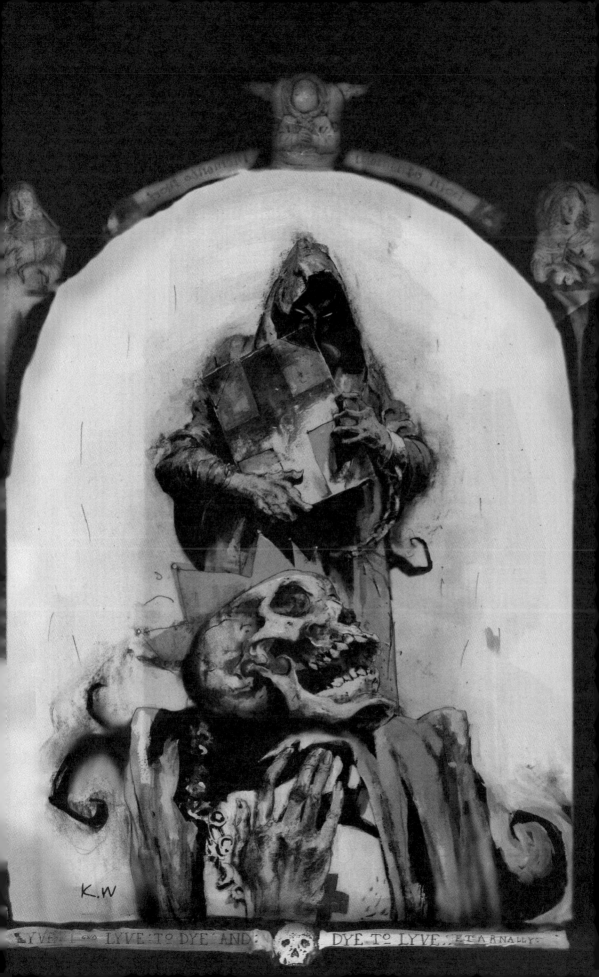

LYVE TO DYE AND DYE TO LYVE ETARNALLY

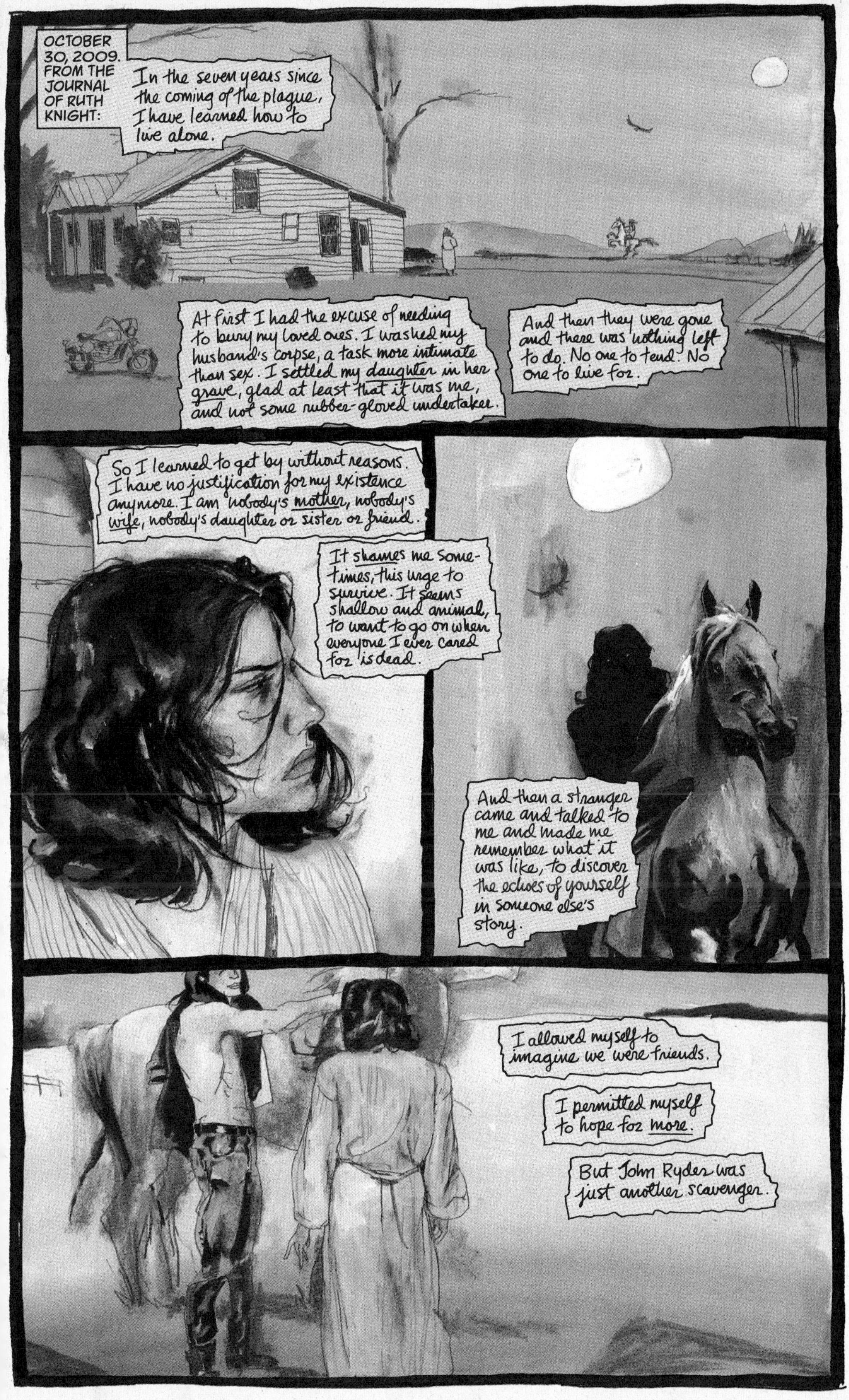
OCTOBER 30, 2009. FROM THE JOURNAL OF RUTH KNIGHT:
In the seven years since the coming of the plague, I have learned how to live alone.
At first I had the excuse of needing to bury my loved ones. I washed my husband's corpse, a task more intimate than sex. I settled my daughter in her grave, glad at least that it was me, and not some rubber-gloved undertaker.
And then they were gone and there was nothing left to do. No one to tend. No one to live for.
So I learned to get by without reasons. I have no justification for my existence anymore. I am nobody's mother, nobody's wife, nobody's daughter or sister or friend.
It shames me sometimes, this urge to survive. It seems shallow and animal, to want to go on when everyone I ever cared for is dead.
And then a stranger came and talked to me and made me remember what it was like, to discover the echoes of yourself in someone else's story.
I allowed myself to imagine we were friends.
I permitted myself to hope for more.
But John Ryder was just another scavenger.

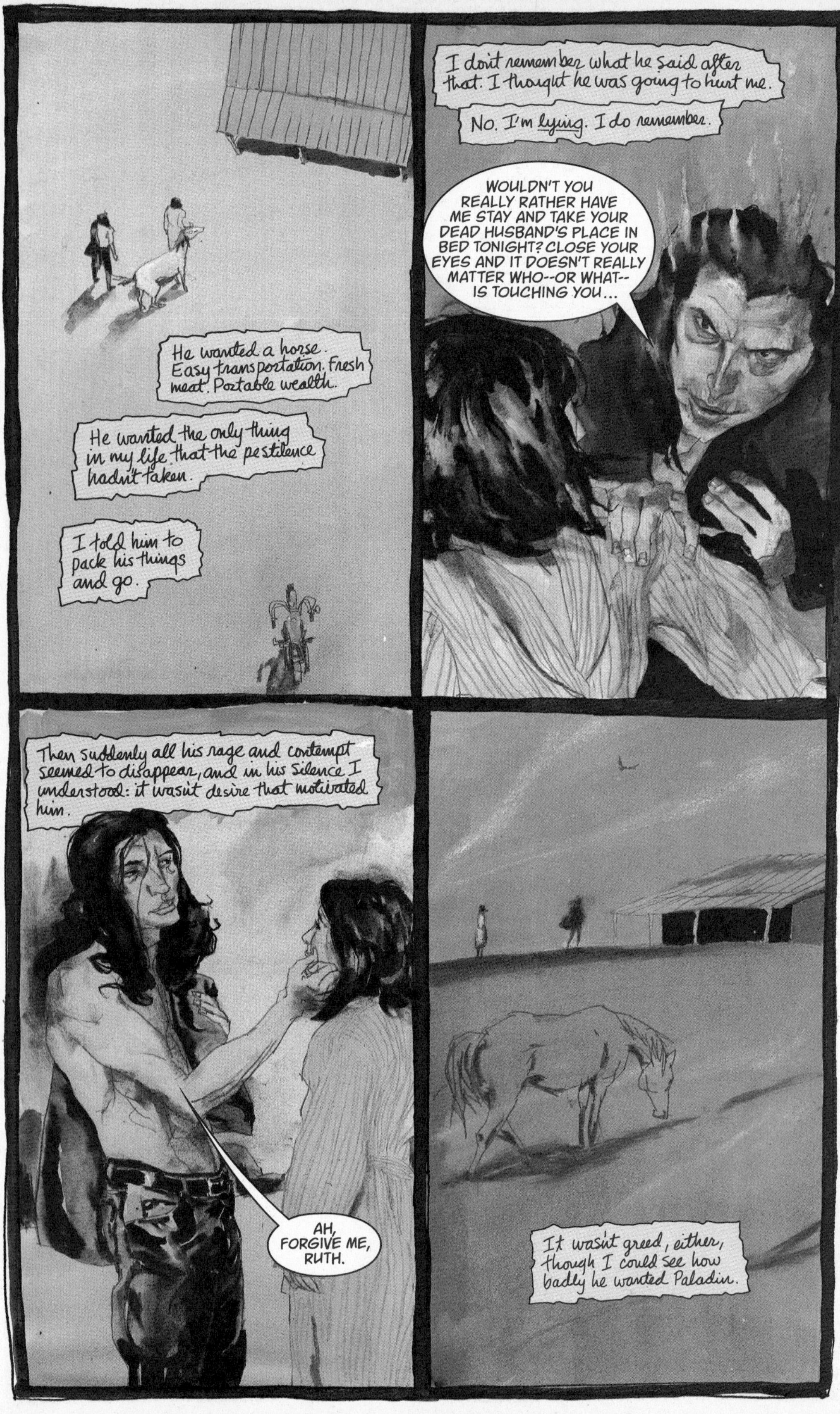
He wanted a horse. Easy transportation. Fresh meat. Portable wealth.
He wanted the only thing in my life that the pestilence hadn't taken.
I told him to pack his things and go.
I don't remember what he said after that. I thought he was going to hurt me.
No. I'm lying. I do remember.
WOULDN'T YOU REALLY RATHER HAVE ME STAY AND TAKE YOUR DEAD HUSBAND'S PLACE IN BED TONIGHT? CLOSE YOUR EYES AND IT DOESN'T REALLY MATTER WHO--OR WHAT--IS TOUCHING YOU...
Then suddenly all his rage and contempt seemed to disappear, and in his silence I understood: it wasn't desire that motivated him.
AH, FORGIVE ME, RUTH.
It wasn't greed, either, though I could see how badly he wanted Paladin.

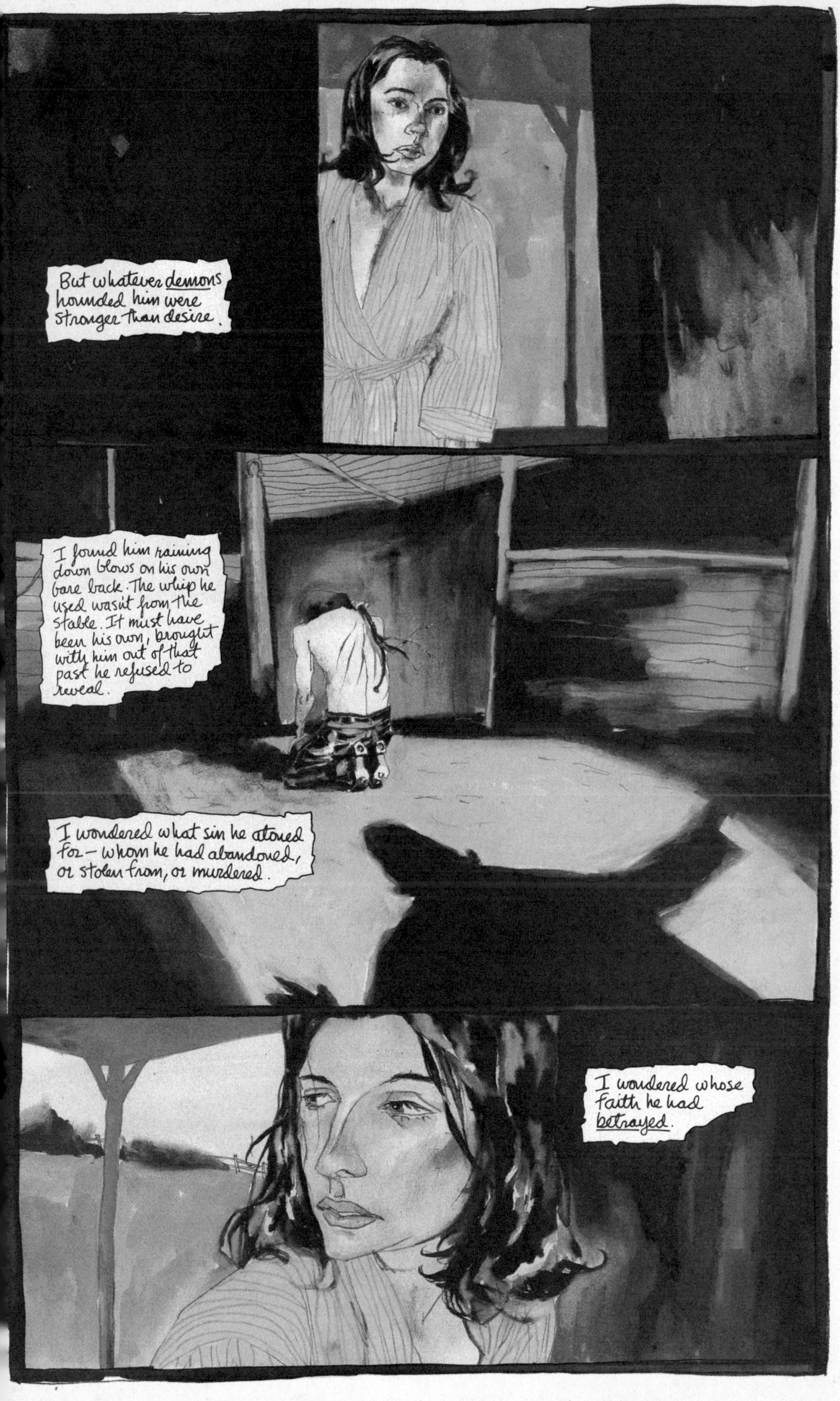
But whatever demons hounded him were stronger than desire.
I found him raining down blows on his own bare back. The whip he used wasn't from the stable. It must have been his own, brought with him out of that past he refused to reveal.
I wondered what sin he atoned for — whom he had abandoned, or stolen from, or murdered.
I wondered whose faith he had betrayed.

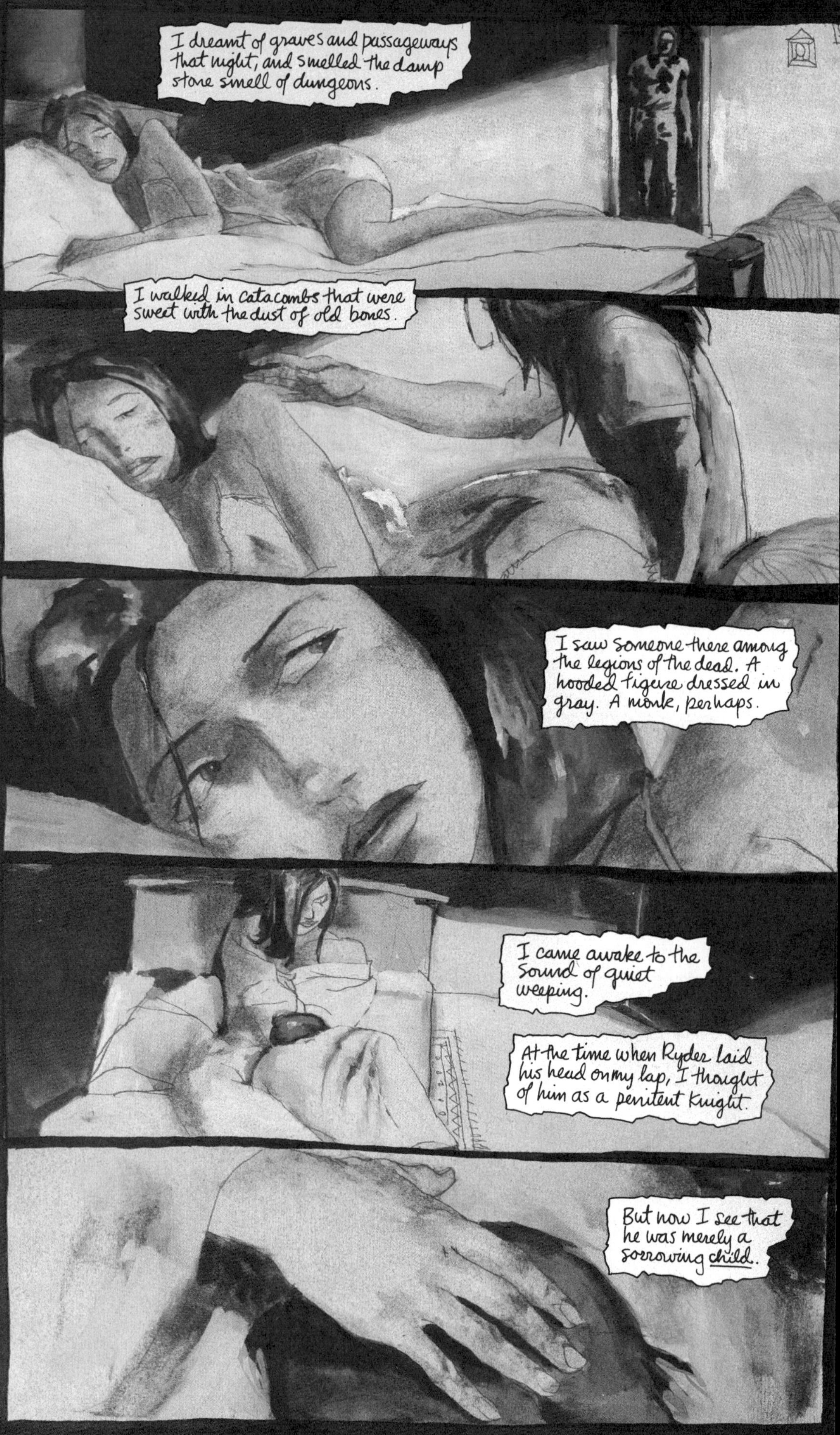
I dreamt of graves and passageways that night, and smelled the damp stone smell of dungeons.
I walked in catacombs that were sweet with the dust of old bones.
I saw someone there among the legions of the dead. A hooded figure dressed in gray. A monk, perhaps.
I came awake to the sound of quiet weeping.
At the time when Ryder laid his head on my lap, I thought of him as a penitent knight.
But now I see that he was merely a sorrowing child.

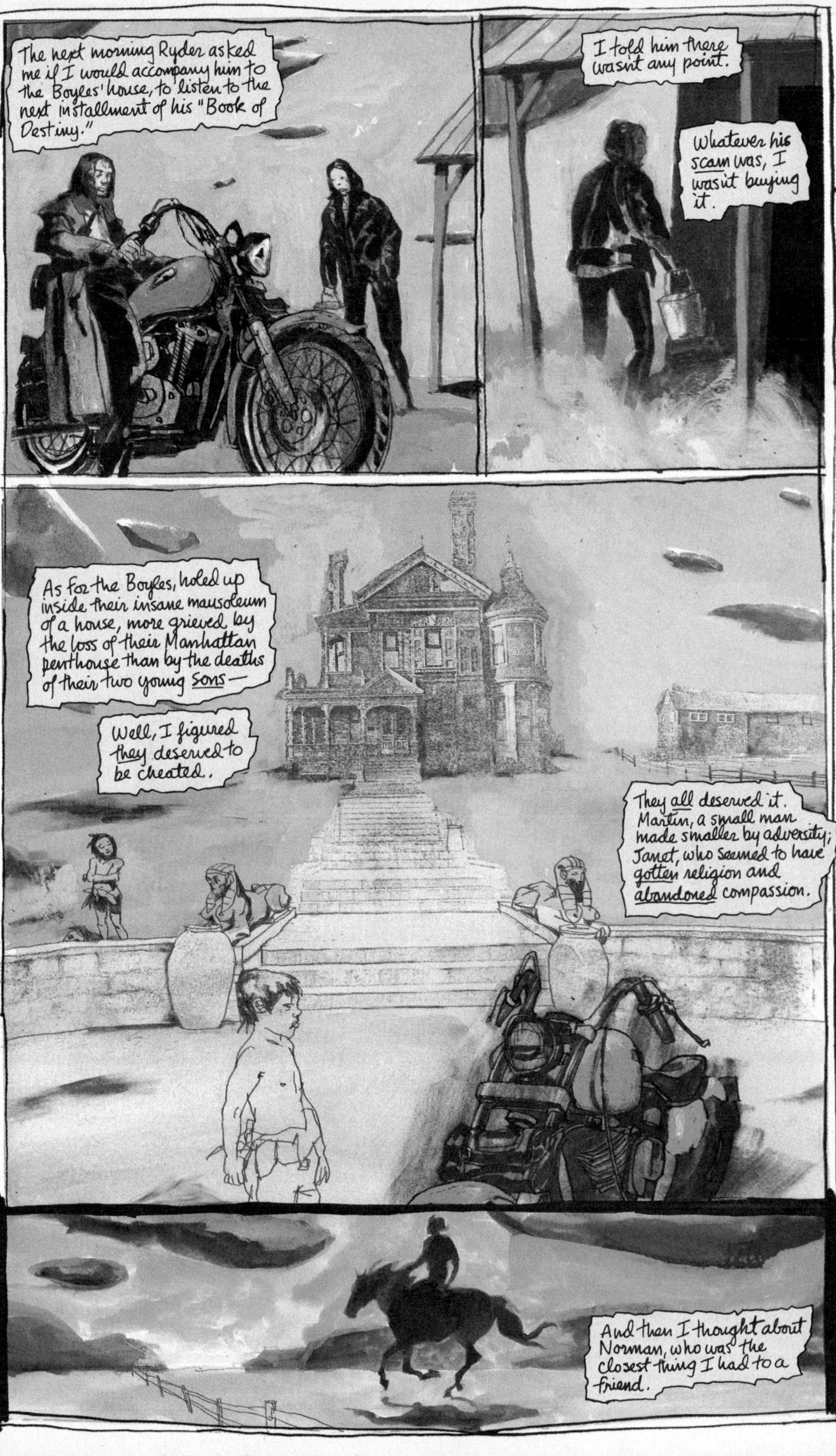
The next morning Ryder asked me if I would accompany him to the Boyles' house, to listen to the next installment of his "Book of Destiny."
I told him there wasn't any point.
Whatever his scam was, I wasn't buying it.
As for the Boyles, holed up inside their insane mausoleum of a house, more grieved by the loss of their Manhattan penthouse than by the deaths of their two young sons—
Well, I figured they deserved to be cheated.
They all deserved it. Martin, a small man made smaller by adversity; Janet, who seemed to have gotten religion and abandoned compassion.
And then I thought about Norman, who was the closest thing I had to a friend.

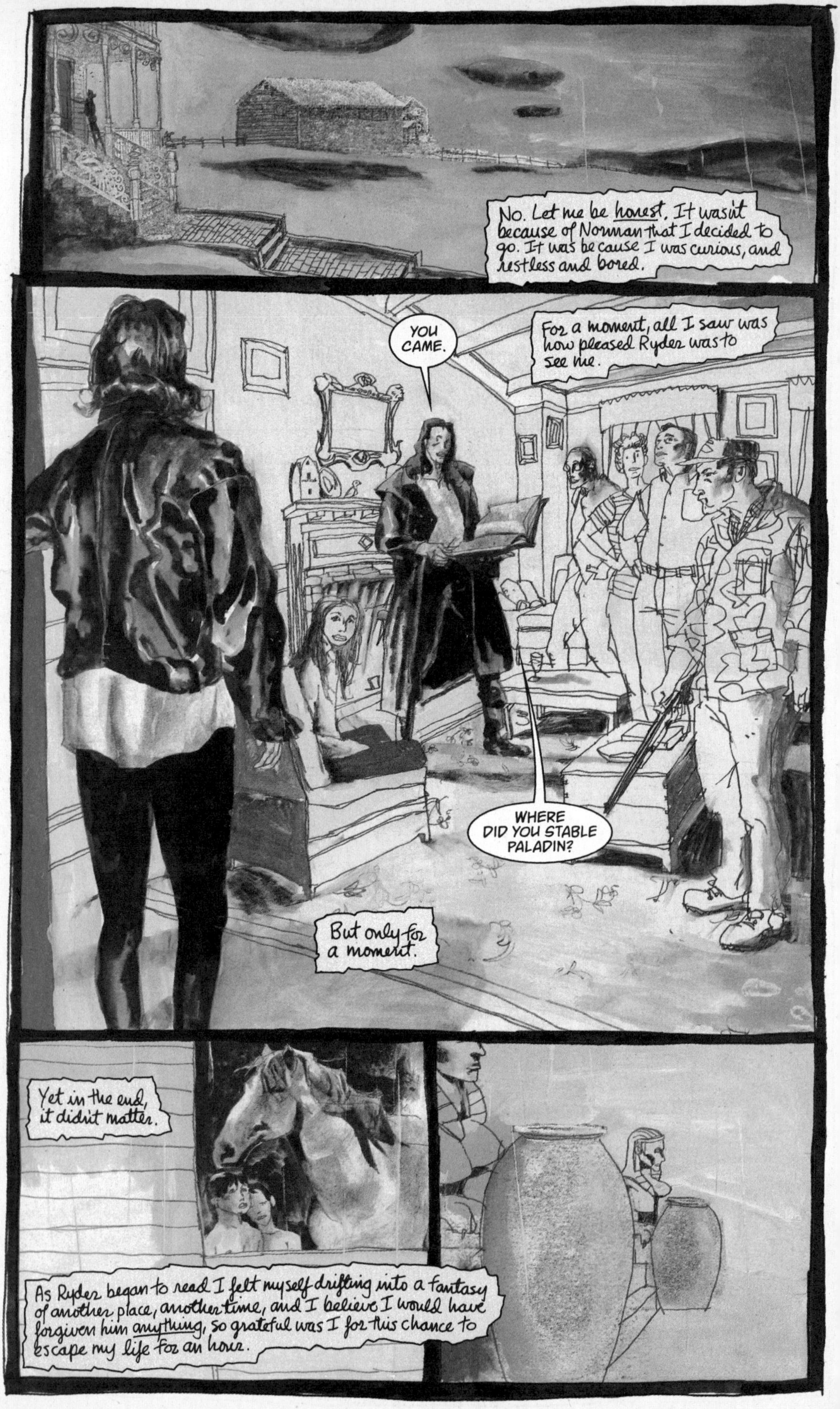
No. Let me be honest. It wasn't because of Norman that I decided to go. It was be cause I was curious, and restless and bored.
YOU CAME.
For a moment, all I saw was how pleased Ryder was to see me.
WHERE DID YOU STABLE PALADIN?
But only for a moment.
Yet in the end, it didn't matter.
As Ryder began to read I felt myself drifting into a fantasy of another place, another time, and I believe I would have forgiven him anything, so grateful was I for this chance to escape my life for an hour.

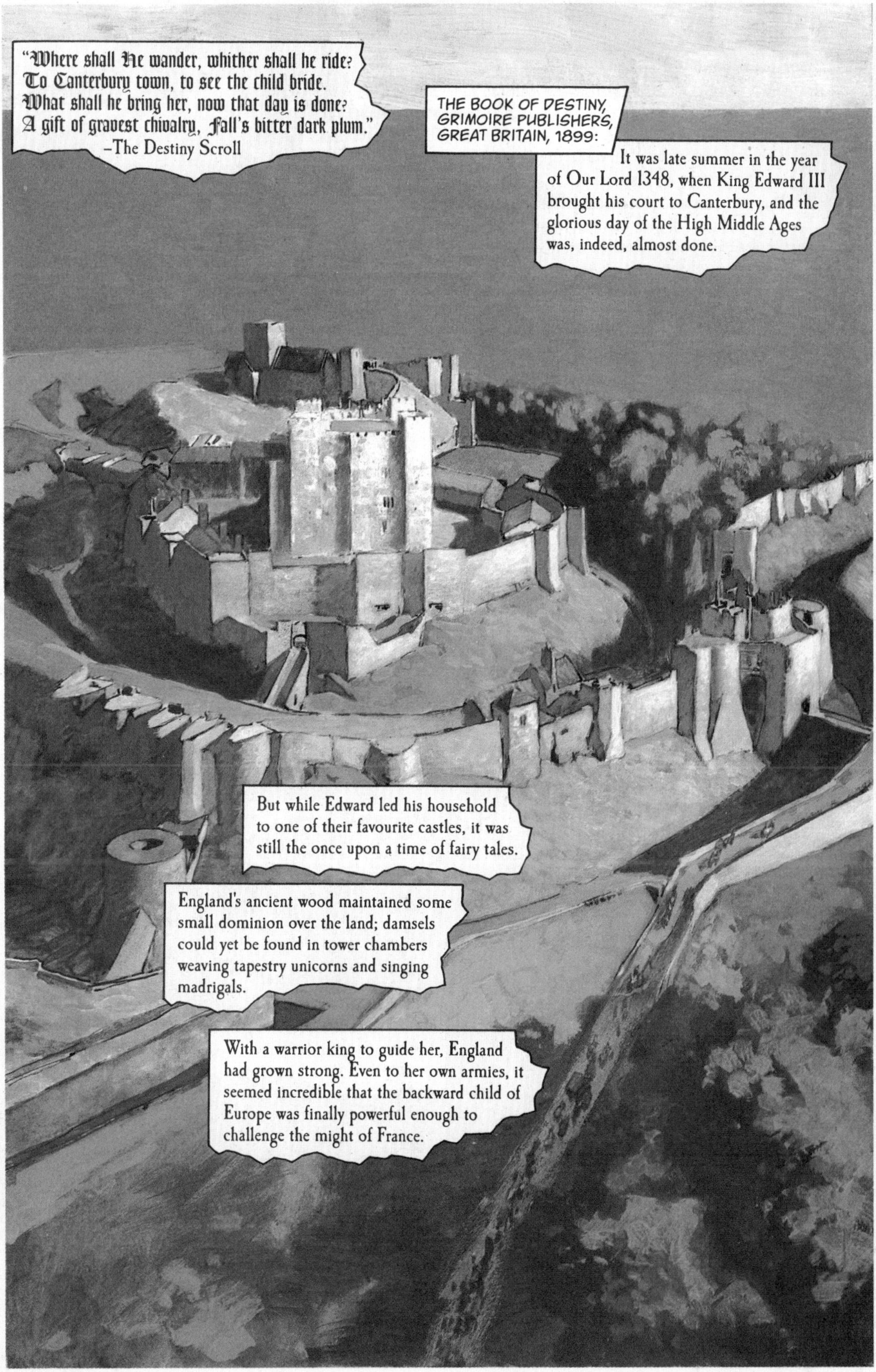
"Where shall He wander, whither shall he ride?
To Canterbury town, to see the child bride.
What shall he bring her, now that day is done?
A gift of gravest chivalry, Fall's bitter dark plum."
–The Destiny Scroll
THE BOOK OF DESTINY, GRIMOIRE PUBLISHERS, GREAT BRITAIN, 1899:
It was late summer in the year of Our Lord 1348, when King Edward III brought his court to Canterbury, and the glorious day of the High Middle Ages was, indeed, almost done.
But while Edward led his household to one of their favourite castles, it was still the once upon a time of fairy tales.
England's ancient wood maintained some small dominion over the land; damsels could yet be found in tower chambers weaving tapestry unicorns and singing madrigals.
With a warrior king to guide her, England had grown strong. Even to her own armies, it seemed incredible that the backward child of Europe was finally powerful enough to challenge the might of France.

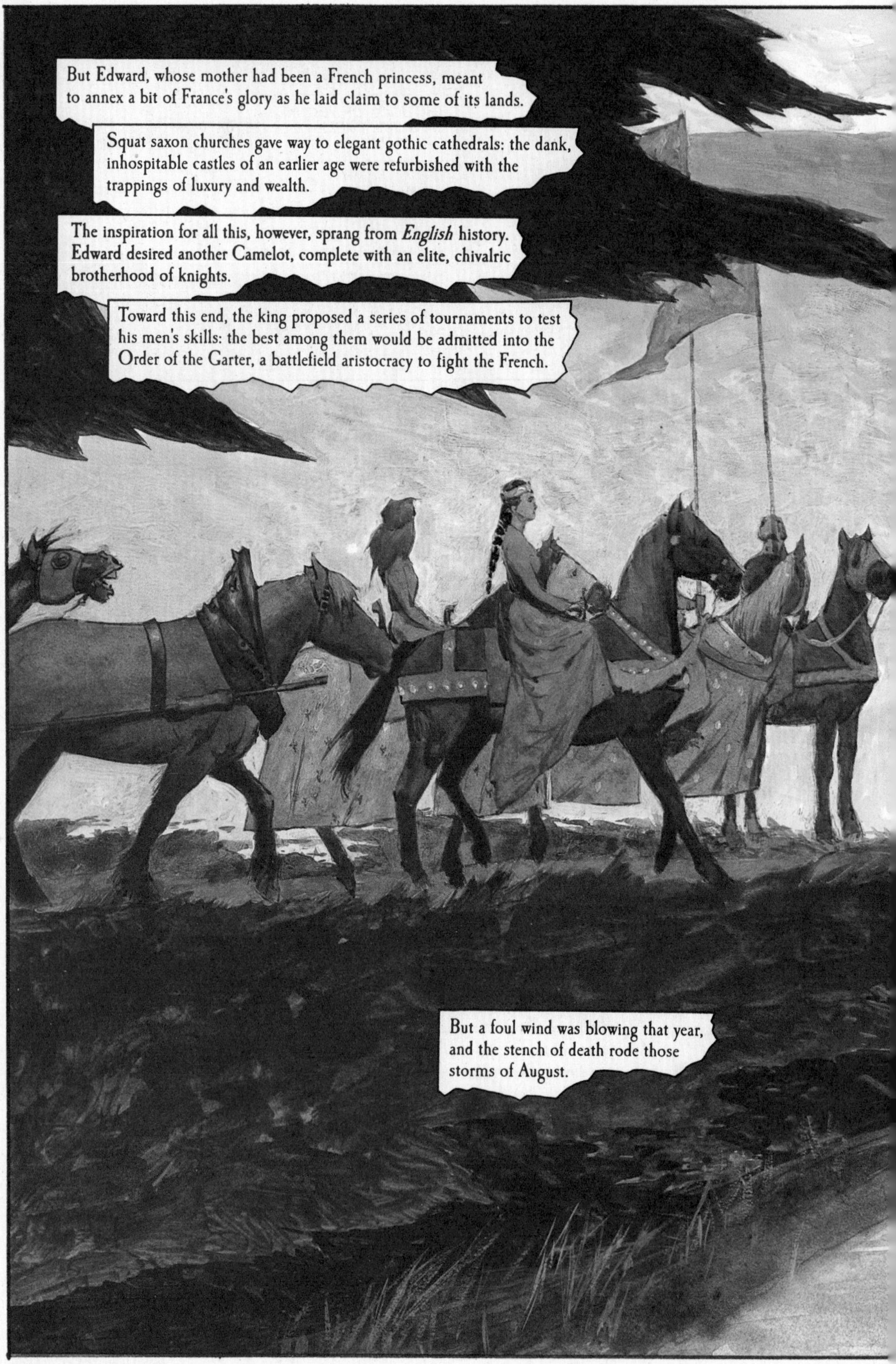
But Edward, whose mother had been a French princess, meant to annex a bit of France's glory as he laid claim to some of its lands.
Squat saxon churches gave way to elegant gothic cathedrals: the dank, inhospitable castles of an earlier age were refurbished with the trappings of luxury and wealth.
The inspiration for all this, however, sprang from *English* history. Edward desired another Camelot, complete with an elite, chivalric brotherhood of knights.
Toward this end, the king proposed a series of tournaments to test his men's skills: the best among them would be admitted into the Order of the Garter, a battlefield aristocracy to fight the French.
But a foul wind was blowing that year, and the stench of death rode those storms of August.

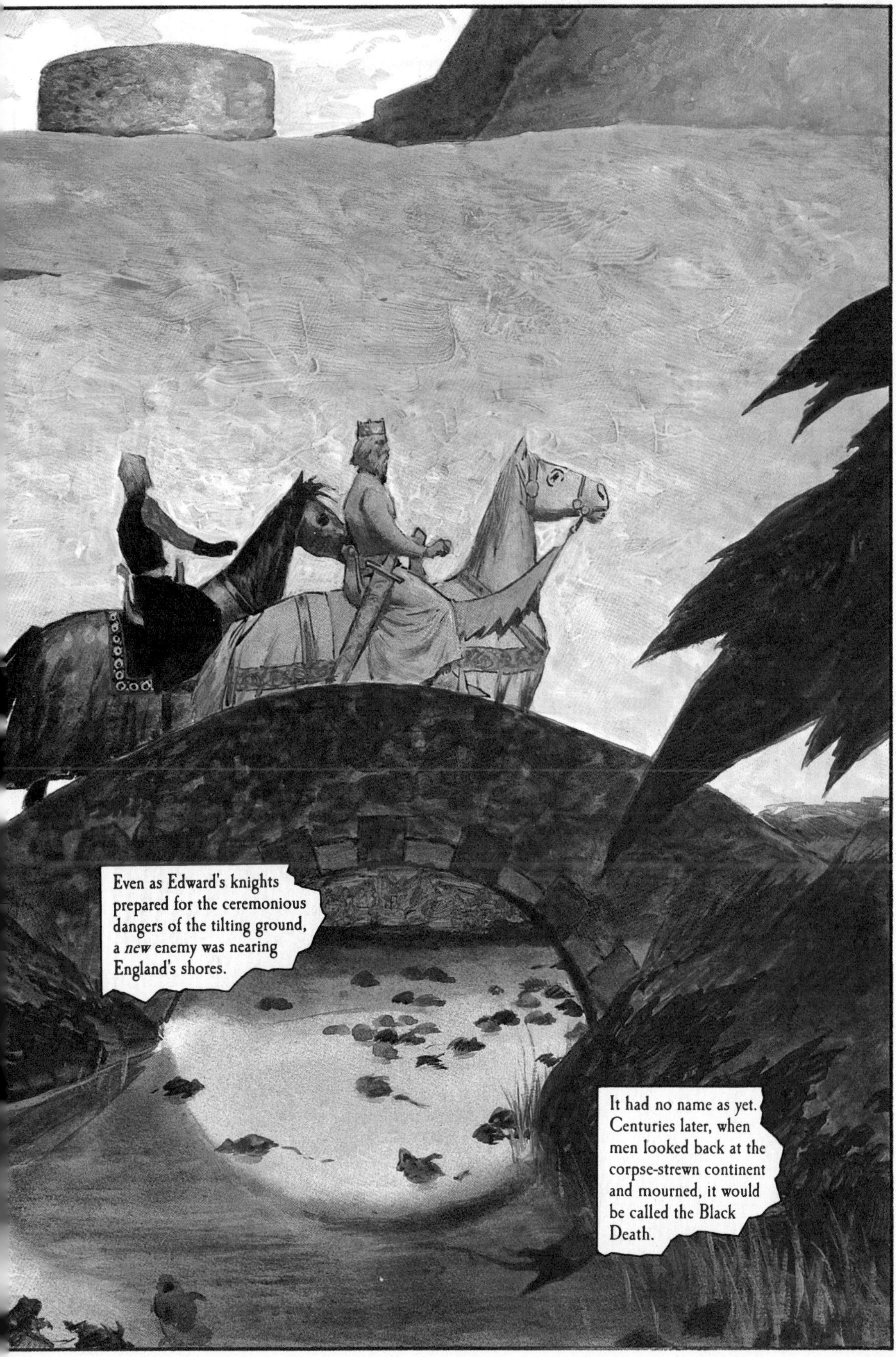
Even as Edward's knights prepared for the ceremonious dangers of the tilting ground, a *new* enemy was nearing England's shores.
It had no name as yet. Centuries later, when men looked back at the corpse-strewn continent and mourned, it would be called the Black Death.

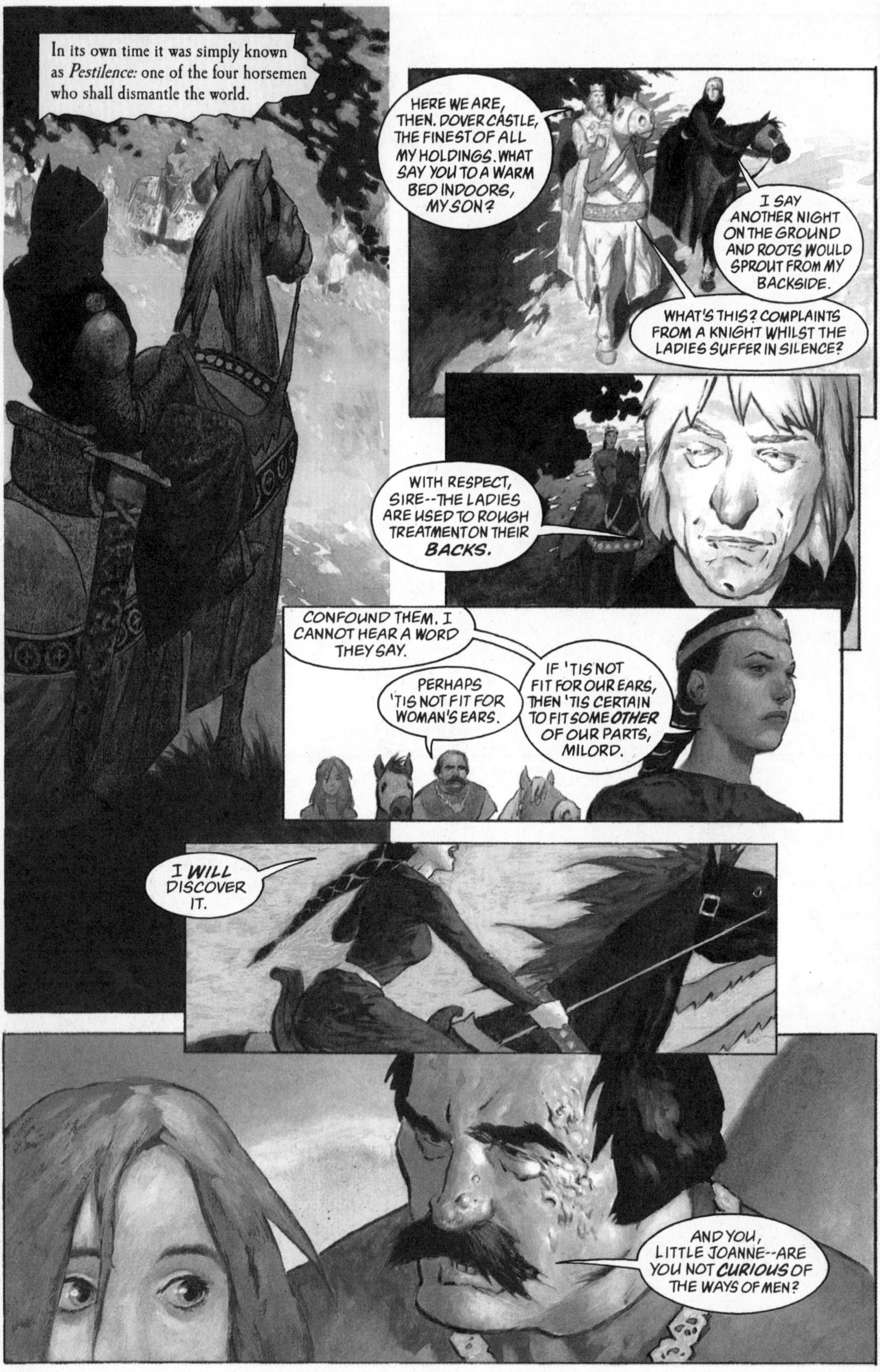

In its own time it was simply known as *Pestilence:* one of the four horsemen who shall dismantle the world.
HERE WE ARE, THEN. DOVER CASTLE, THE FINEST OF ALL MY HOLDINGS. WHAT SAY YOU TO A WARM BED INDOORS, MY SON?
I SAY ANOTHER NIGHT ON THE GROUND AND ROOTS WOULD SPROUT FROM MY BACKSIDE.
WHAT'S THIS? COMPLAINTS FROM A KNIGHT WHILST THE LADIES SUFFER IN SILENCE?
WITH RESPECT, SIRE--THE LADIES ARE USED TO ROUGH TREATMENT ON THEIR **BACKS.**
CONFOUND THEM. I CANNOT HEAR A WORD THEY SAY.
PERHAPS 'TIS NOT FIT FOR WOMAN'S EARS.
IF 'TIS NOT FIT FOR OUR EARS, THEN 'TIS CERTAIN TO FIT SOME ***OTHER*** OF OUR PARTS, MILORD.
I ***WILL*** DISCOVER IT.
AND YOU, LITTLE JOANNE--ARE YOU NOT ***CURIOUS*** OF THE WAYS OF MEN?

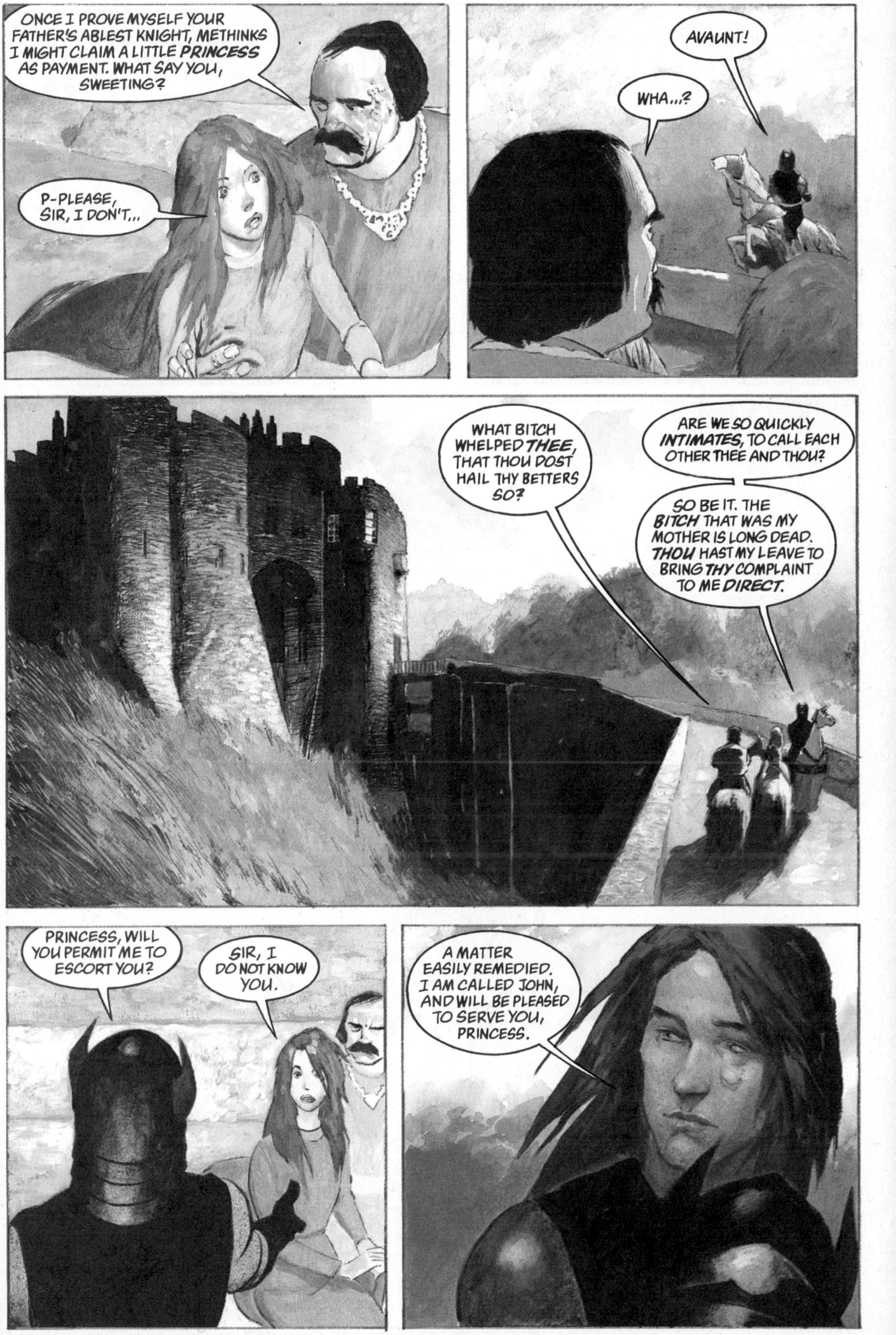
ONCE I PROVE MYSELF YOUR FATHER'S ABLEST KNIGHT, METHINKS I MIGHT CLAIM A LITTLE PRINCESS AS PAYMENT. WHAT SAY YOU, SWEETING?
P-PLEASE, SIR, I DON'T...
AVAUNT!
WHA...?
WHAT BITCH WHELPED THEE, THAT THOU DOST HAIL THY BETTERS SO?
ARE WE SO QUICKLY INTIMATES, TO CALL EACH OTHER THEE AND THOU?
SO BE IT. THE BITCH THAT WAS MY MOTHER IS LONG DEAD. THOU HAST MY LEAVE TO BRING THY COMPLAINT TO ME DIRECT.
PRINCESS, WILL YOU PERMIT ME TO ESCORT YOU?
SIR, I DO NOT KNOW YOU.
A MATTER EASILY REMEDIED. I AM CALLED JOHN, AND WILL BE PLEASED TO SERVE YOU, PRINCESS.

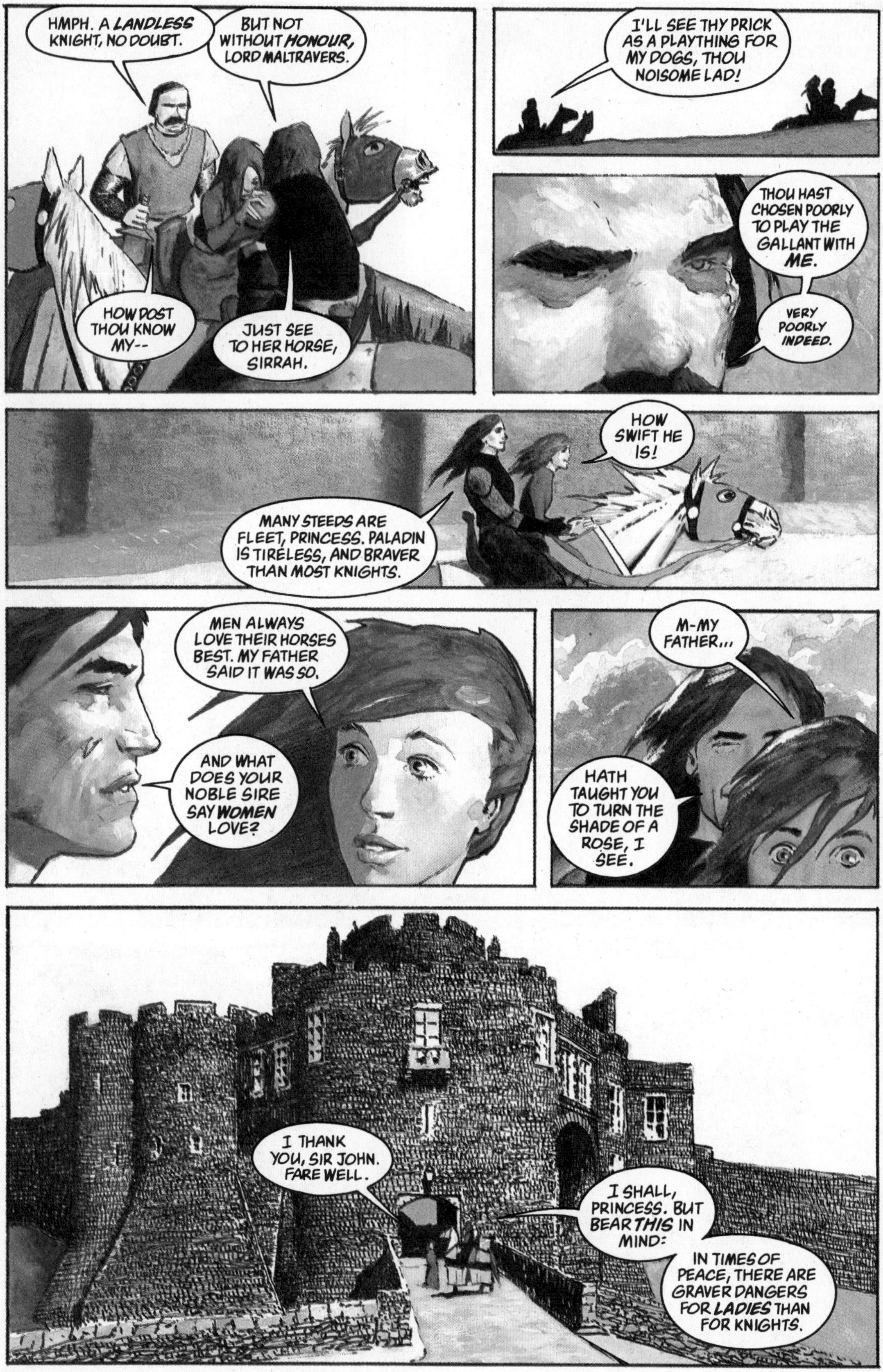
HMPH. A LANDLESS KNIGHT, NO DOUBT.
BUT NOT WITHOUT HONOUR, LORD MALTRAVERS.
HOW DOST THOU KNOW MY--
JUST SEE TO HER HORSE, SIRRAH.
I'LL SEE THY PRICK AS A PLAYTHING FOR MY DOGS, THOU NOISOME LAD!
THOU HAST CHOSEN POORLY TO PLAY THE GALLANT WITH ME.
VERY POORLY INDEED.
HOW SWIFT HE IS!
MANY STEEDS ARE FLEET, PRINCESS. PALADIN IS TIRELESS, AND BRAVER THAN MOST KNIGHTS.
MEN ALWAYS LOVE THEIR HORSES BEST. MY FATHER SAID IT WAS SO.
AND WHAT DOES YOUR NOBLE SIRE SAY WOMEN LOVE?
M-MY FATHER...
HATH TAUGHT YOU TO TURN THE SHADE OF A ROSE, I SEE.
I THANK YOU, SIR JOHN. FARE WELL.
I SHALL, PRINCESS. BUT BEAR THIS IN MIND:
IN TIMES OF PEACE, THERE ARE GRAVER DANGERS FOR LADIES THAN FOR KNIGHTS.

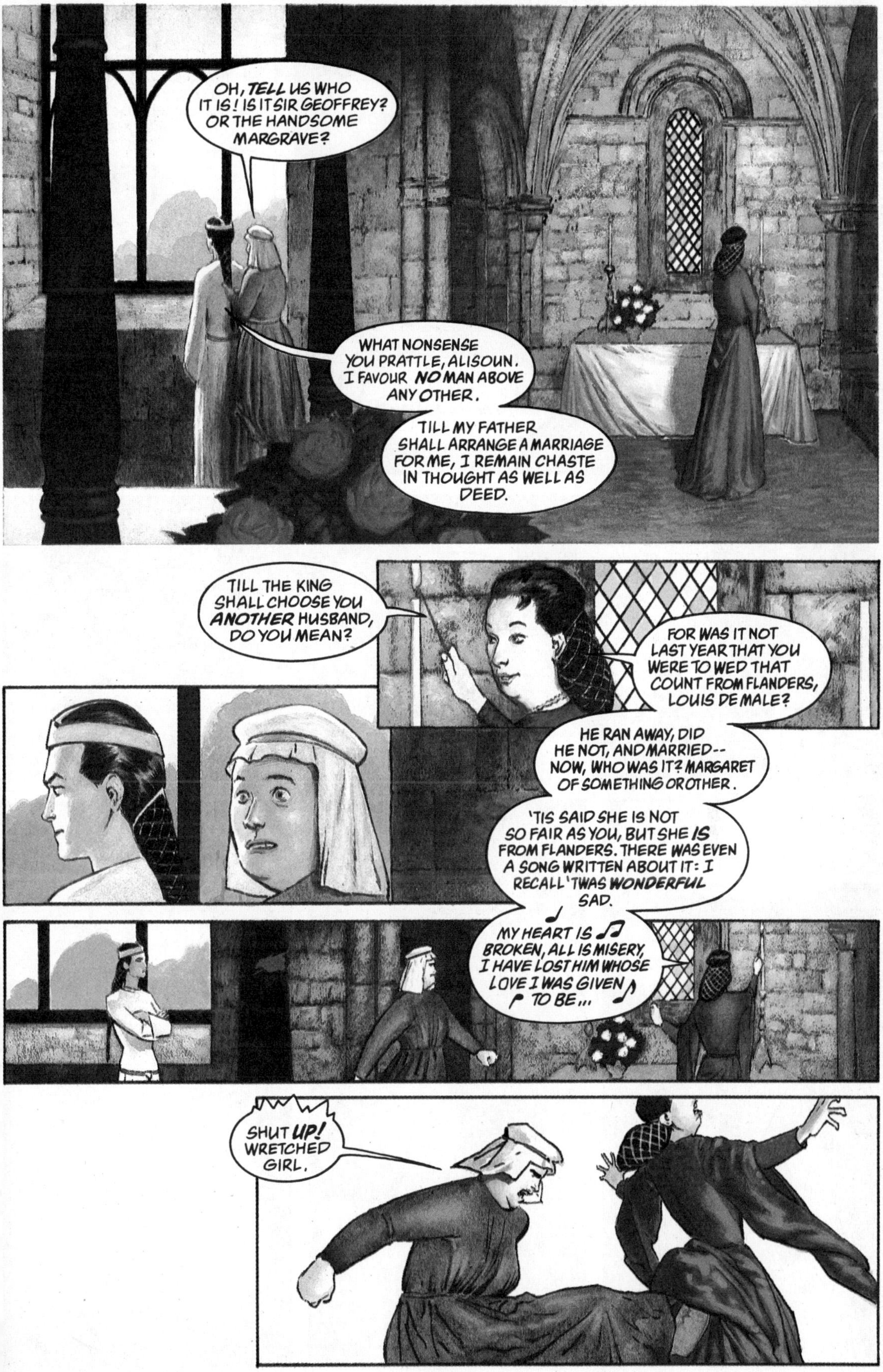
OH, TELL US WHO IT IS! IS IT SIR GEOFFREY? OR THE HANDSOME MARGRAVE?
WHAT NONSENSE YOU PRATTLE, ALISOUN. I FAVOUR NO MAN ABOVE ANY OTHER.
TILL MY FATHER SHALL ARRANGE A MARRIAGE FOR ME, I REMAIN CHASTE IN THOUGHT AS WELL AS DEED.
TILL THE KING SHALL CHOOSE YOU ANOTHER HUSBAND, DO YOU MEAN?
FOR WAS IT NOT LAST YEAR THAT YOU WERE TO WED THAT COUNT FROM FLANDERS, LOUIS DE MALE?
HE RAN AWAY, DID HE NOT, AND MARRIED-- NOW, WHO WAS IT? MARGARET OF SOMETHING OR OTHER.
'TIS SAID SHE IS NOT SO FAIR AS YOU, BUT SHE IS FROM FLANDERS. THERE WAS EVEN A SONG WRITTEN ABOUT IT: I RECALL 'TWAS WONDERFUL SAD.
MY HEART IS BROKEN, ALL IS MISERY, I HAVE LOST HIM WHOSE LOVE I WAS GIVEN TO BE...
SHUT UP! WRETCHED GIRL.

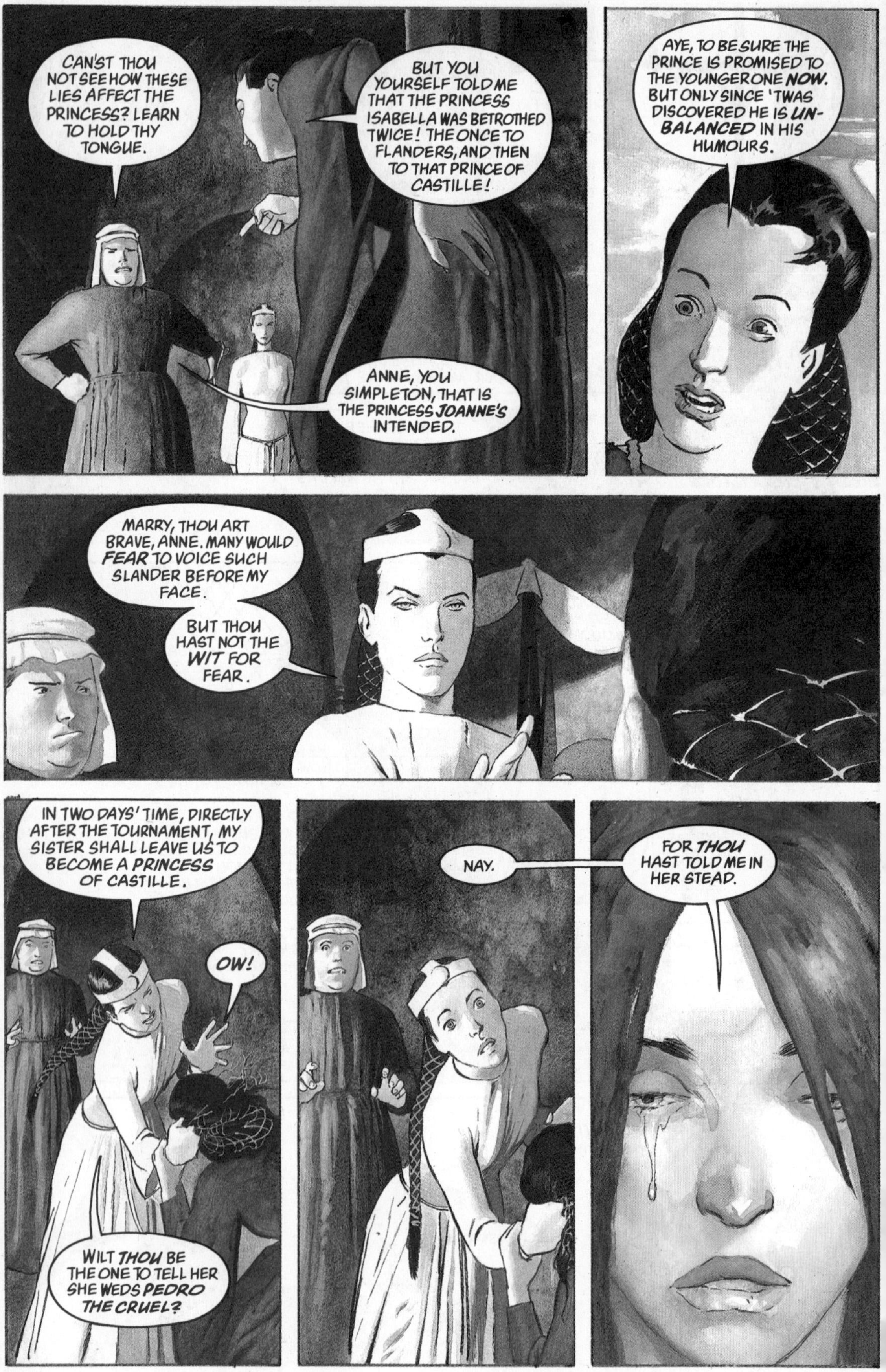
CAN'ST THOU NOT SEE HOW THESE LIES AFFECT THE PRINCESS? LEARN TO HOLD THY TONGUE.
BUT YOU YOURSELF TOLD ME THAT THE PRINCESS ISABELLA WAS BETROTHED TWICE! THE ONCE TO FLANDERS, AND THEN TO THAT PRINCE OF CASTILLE!
ANNE, YOU SIMPLETON, THAT IS THE PRINCESS JOANNE'S INTENDED.
AYE, TO BE SURE THE PRINCE IS PROMISED TO THE YOUNGER ONE NOW. BUT ONLY SINCE 'TWAS DISCOVERED HE IS UNBALANCED IN HIS HUMOURS.
MARRY, THOU ART BRAVE, ANNE. MANY WOULD FEAR TO VOICE SUCH SLANDER BEFORE MY FACE.
BUT THOU HAST NOT THE WIT FOR FEAR.
IN TWO DAYS' TIME, DIRECTLY AFTER THE TOURNAMENT, MY SISTER SHALL LEAVE US TO BECOME A PRINCESS OF CASTILLE.
OW!
WILT THOU BE THE ONE TO TELL HER SHE WEDS PEDRO THE CRUEL?
NAY.
FOR THOU HAST TOLD ME IN HER STEAD.

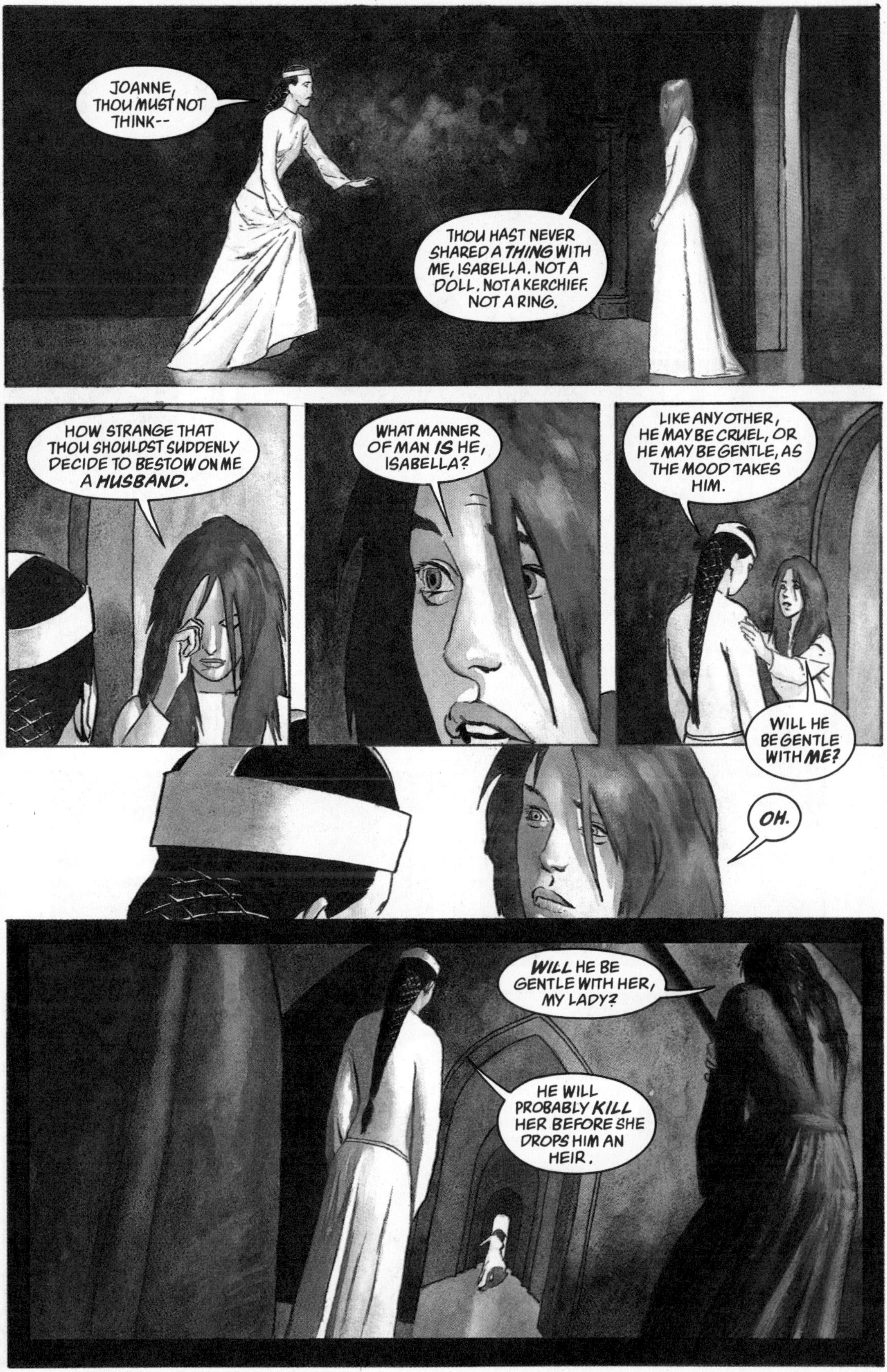
JOANNE, THOU MUST NOT THINK--
THOU HAST NEVER SHARED A THING WITH ME, ISABELLA. NOT A DOLL. NOT A KERCHIEF. NOT A RING.
HOW STRANGE THAT THOU SHOULDST SUDDENLY DECIDE TO BESTOW ON ME A HUSBAND.
WHAT MANNER OF MAN IS HE, ISABELLA?
LIKE ANY OTHER, HE MAY BE CRUEL, OR HE MAY BE GENTLE, AS THE MOOD TAKES HIM.
WILL HE BE GENTLE WITH ME?
OH.
WILL HE BE GENTLE WITH HER, MY LADY?
HE WILL PROBABLY KILL HER BEFORE SHE DROPS HIM AN HEIR.

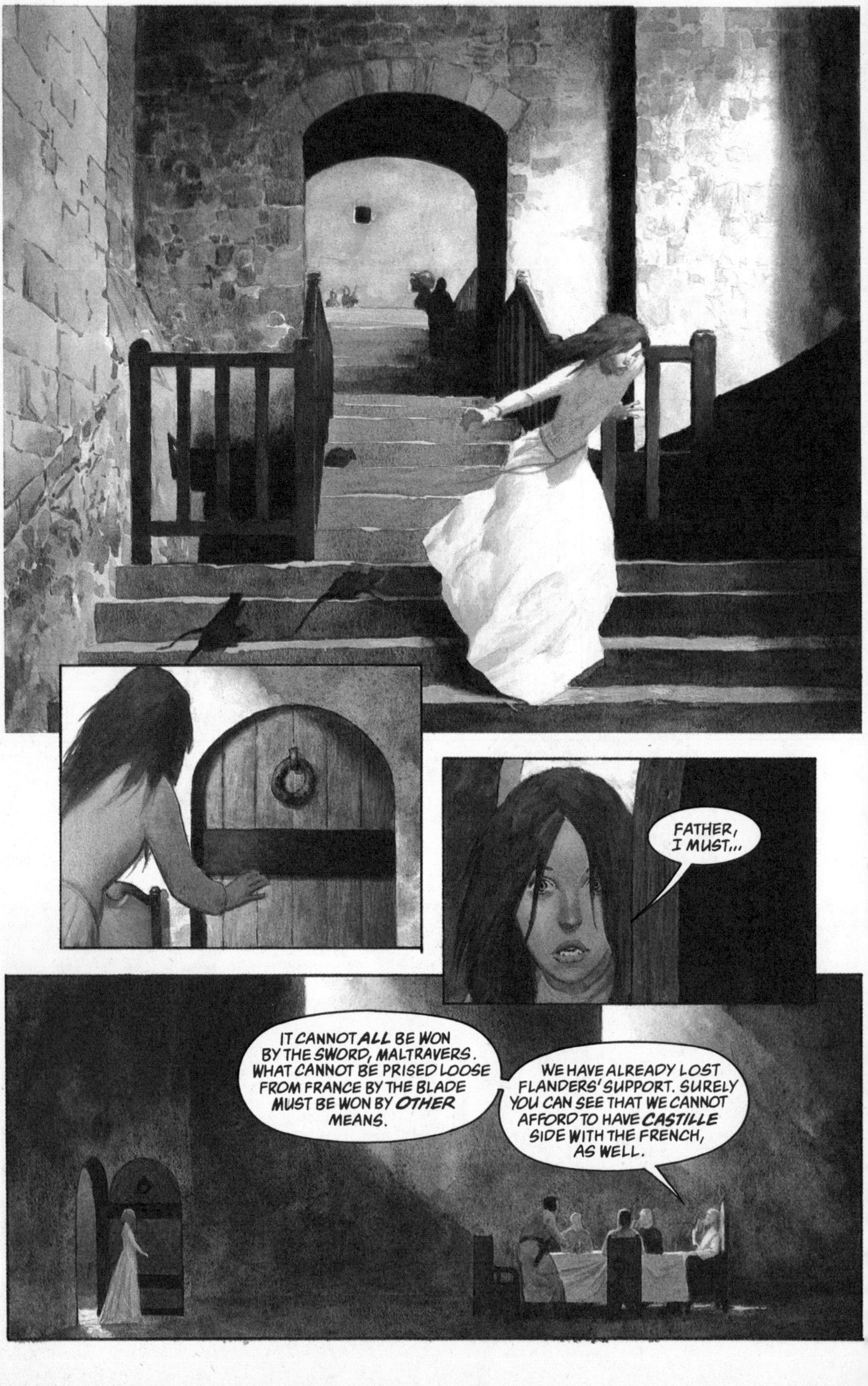
FATHER, I MUST...
IT CANNOT ALL BE WON BY THE SWORD, MALTRAVERS. WHAT CANNOT BE PRISED LOOSE FROM FRANCE BY THE BLADE MUST BE WON BY OTHER MEANS.
WE HAVE ALREADY LOST FLANDERS' SUPPORT. SURELY YOU CAN SEE THAT WE CANNOT AFFORD TO HAVE CASTILLE SIDE WITH THE FRENCH, AS WELL.

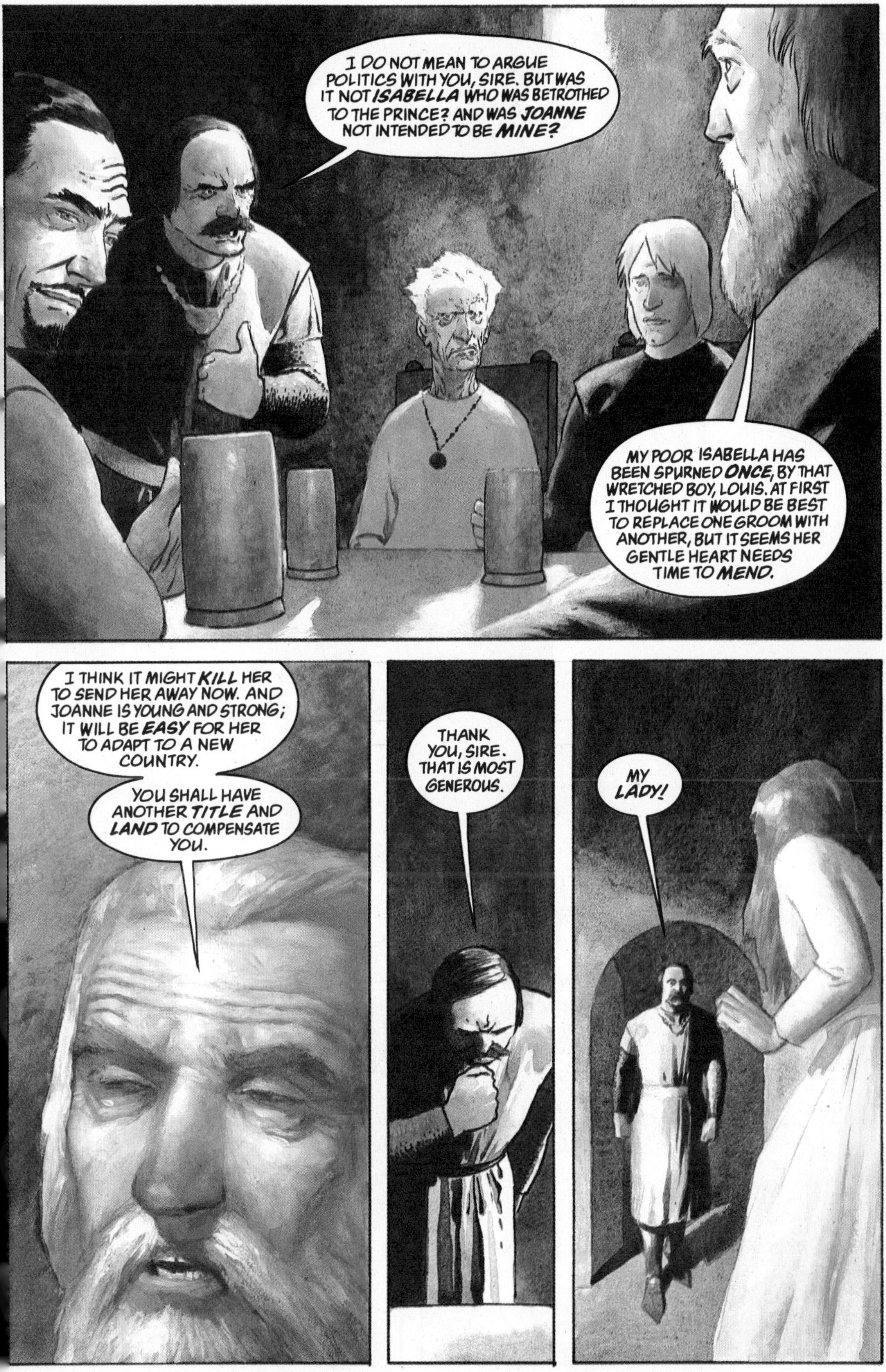
I DO NOT MEAN TO ARGUE POLITICS WITH YOU, SIRE. BUT WAS IT NOT ISABELLA WHO WAS BETROTHED TO THE PRINCE? AND WAS JOANNE NOT INTENDED TO BE MINE?
MY POOR ISABELLA HAS BEEN SPURNED ONCE, BY THAT WRETCHED BOY, LOUIS. AT FIRST I THOUGHT IT WOULD BE BEST TO REPLACE ONE GROOM WITH ANOTHER, BUT IT SEEMS HER GENTLE HEART NEEDS TIME TO MEND.
I THINK IT MIGHT KILL HER TO SEND HER AWAY NOW. AND JOANNE IS YOUNG AND STRONG; IT WILL BE EASY FOR HER TO ADAPT TO A NEW COUNTRY.
YOU SHALL HAVE ANOTHER TITLE AND LAND TO COMPENSATE YOU.
THANK YOU, SIRE. THAT IS MOST GENEROUS.
MY LADY!

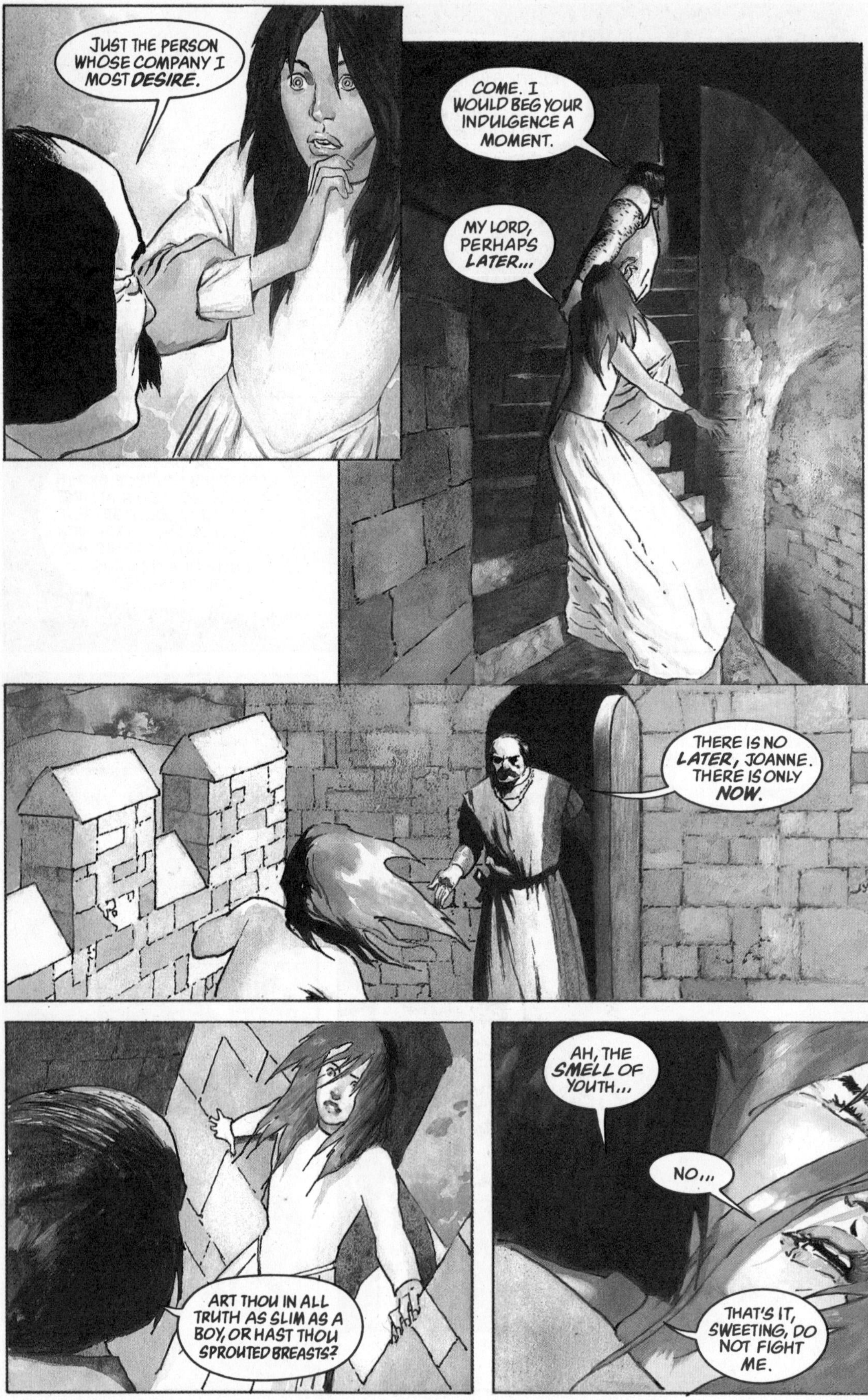
JUST THE PERSON WHOSE COMPANY I MOST DESIRE.
COME. I WOULD BEG YOUR INDULGENCE A MOMENT.
MY LORD, PERHAPS LATER...
THERE IS NO LATER, JOANNE. THERE IS ONLY NOW.
ART THOU IN ALL TRUTH AS SLIM AS A BOY, OR HAST THOU SPROUTED BREASTS?
AH, THE SMELL OF YOUTH...
NO...
THAT'S IT, SWEETING, DO NOT FIGHT ME.

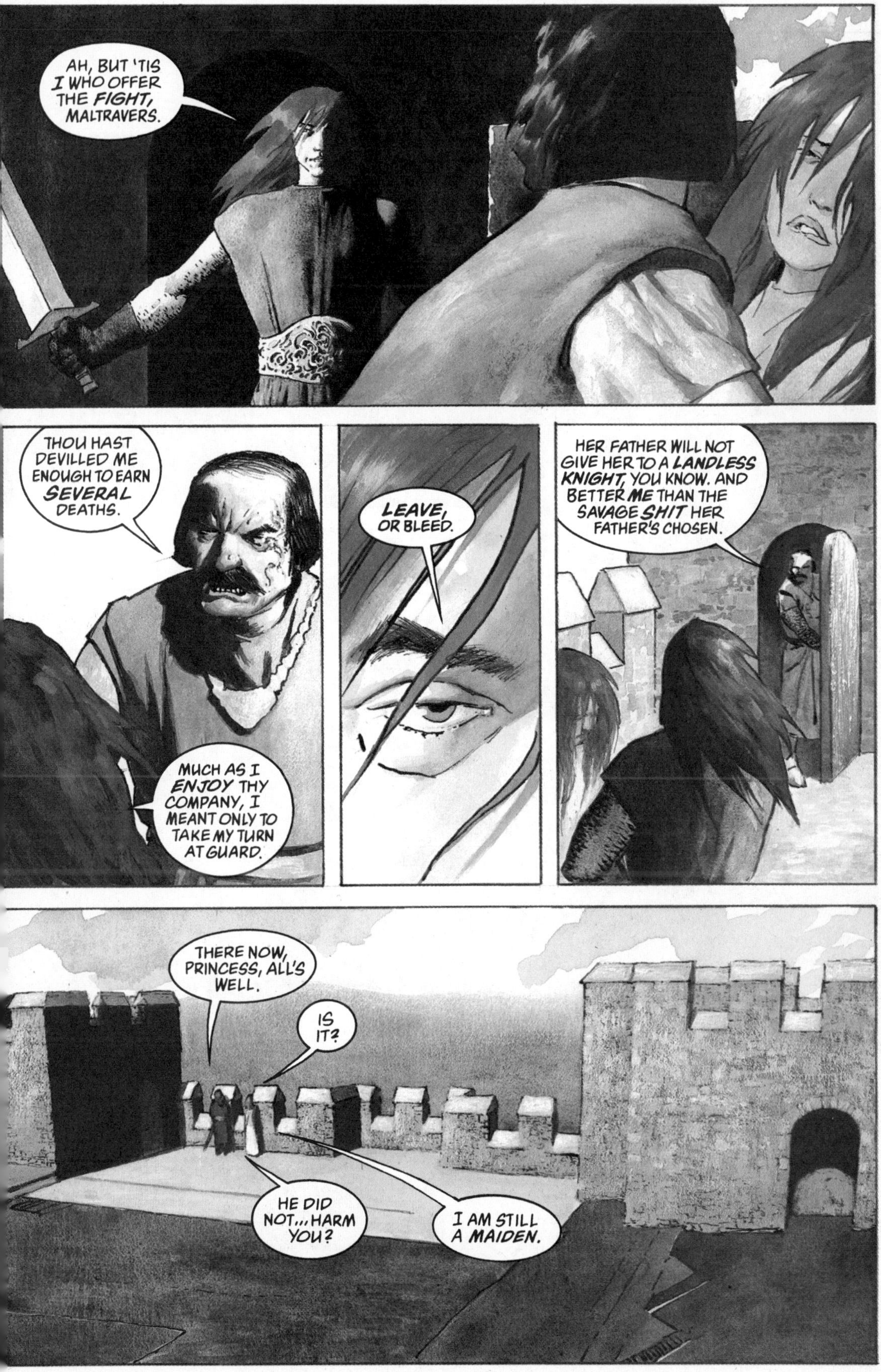
AH, BUT 'TIS I WHO OFFER THE FIGHT, MALTRAVERS.
THOU HAST DEVILLED ME ENOUGH TO EARN SEVERAL DEATHS.
MUCH AS I ENJOY THY COMPANY, I MEANT ONLY TO TAKE MY TURN AT GUARD.
LEAVE, OR BLEED.
HER FATHER WILL NOT GIVE HER TO A LANDLESS KNIGHT, YOU KNOW. AND BETTER ME THAN THE SAVAGE SHIT HER FATHER'S CHOSEN.
THERE NOW, PRINCESS, ALL'S WELL.
IS IT?
HE DID NOT... HARM YOU?
I AM STILL A MAIDEN.

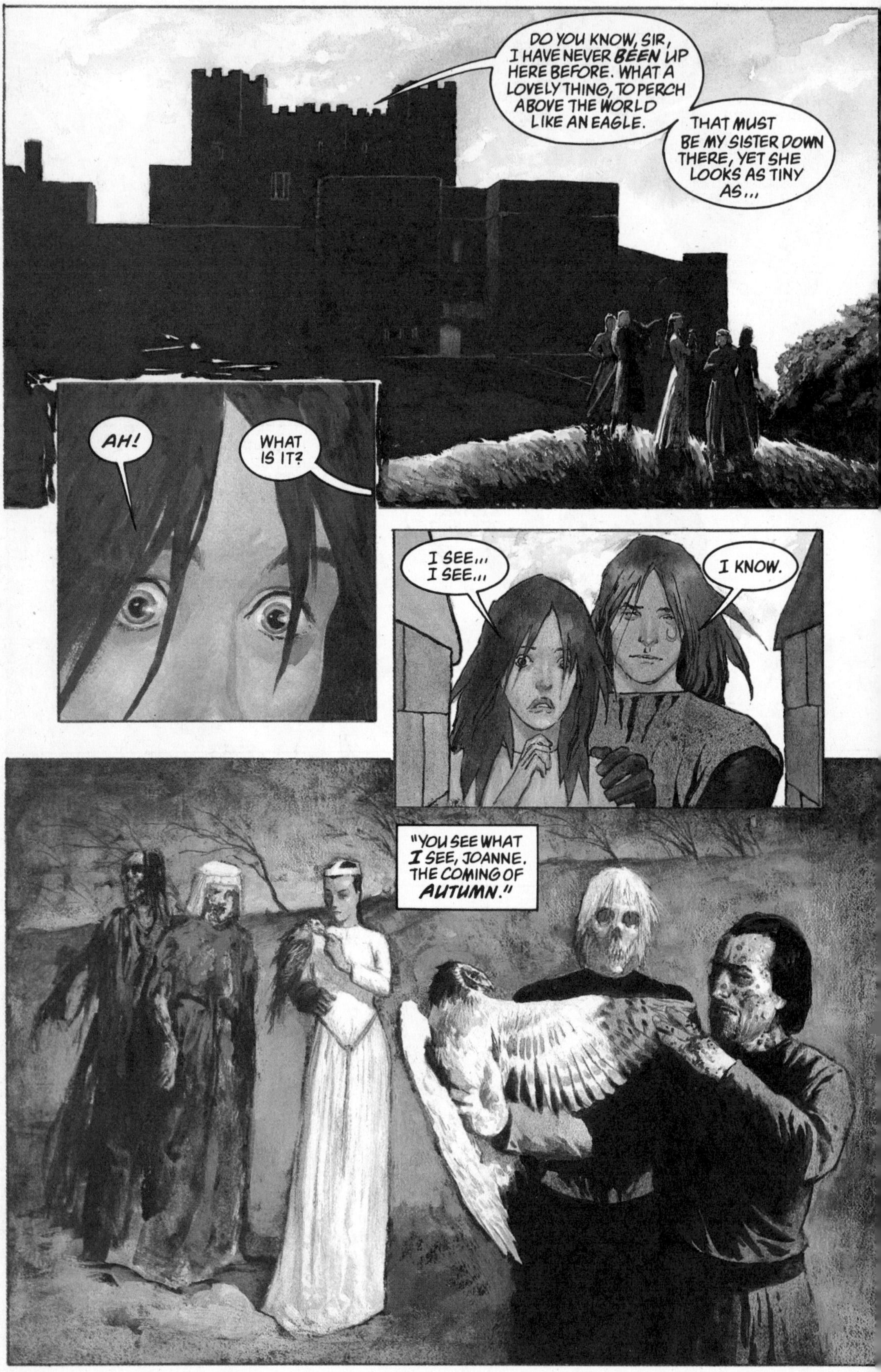
DO YOU KNOW, SIR, I HAVE NEVER BEEN UP HERE BEFORE. WHAT A LOVELY THING, TO PERCH ABOVE THE WORLD LIKE AN EAGLE.
THAT MUST BE MY SISTER DOWN THERE, YET SHE LOOKS AS TINY AS...
AH!
WHAT IS IT?
I SEE... I SEE...
I KNOW.
"YOU SEE WHAT I SEE, JOANNE. THE COMING OF AUTUMN."

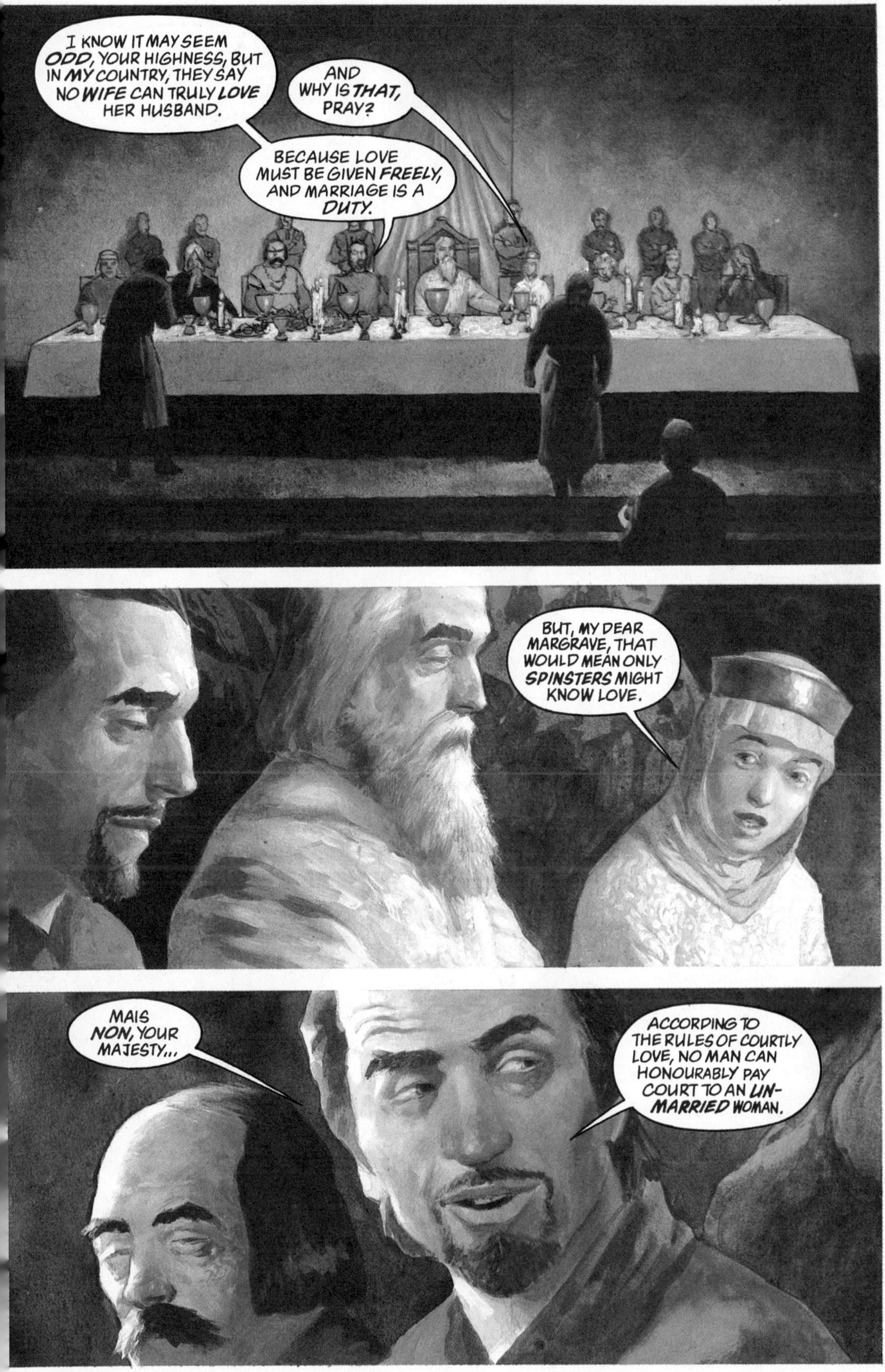
I KNOW IT MAY SEEM ODD, YOUR HIGHNESS, BUT IN MY COUNTRY, THEY SAY NO WIFE CAN TRULY LOVE HER HUSBAND.
AND WHY IS THAT, PRAY?
BECAUSE LOVE MUST BE GIVEN FREELY, AND MARRIAGE IS A DUTY.
BUT, MY DEAR MARGRAVE, THAT WOULD MEAN ONLY SPINSTERS MIGHT KNOW LOVE.
MAIS NON, YOUR MAJESTY...
ACCORDING TO THE RULES OF COURTLY LOVE, NO MAN CAN HONOURABLY PAY COURT TO AN UN-MARRIED WOMAN.

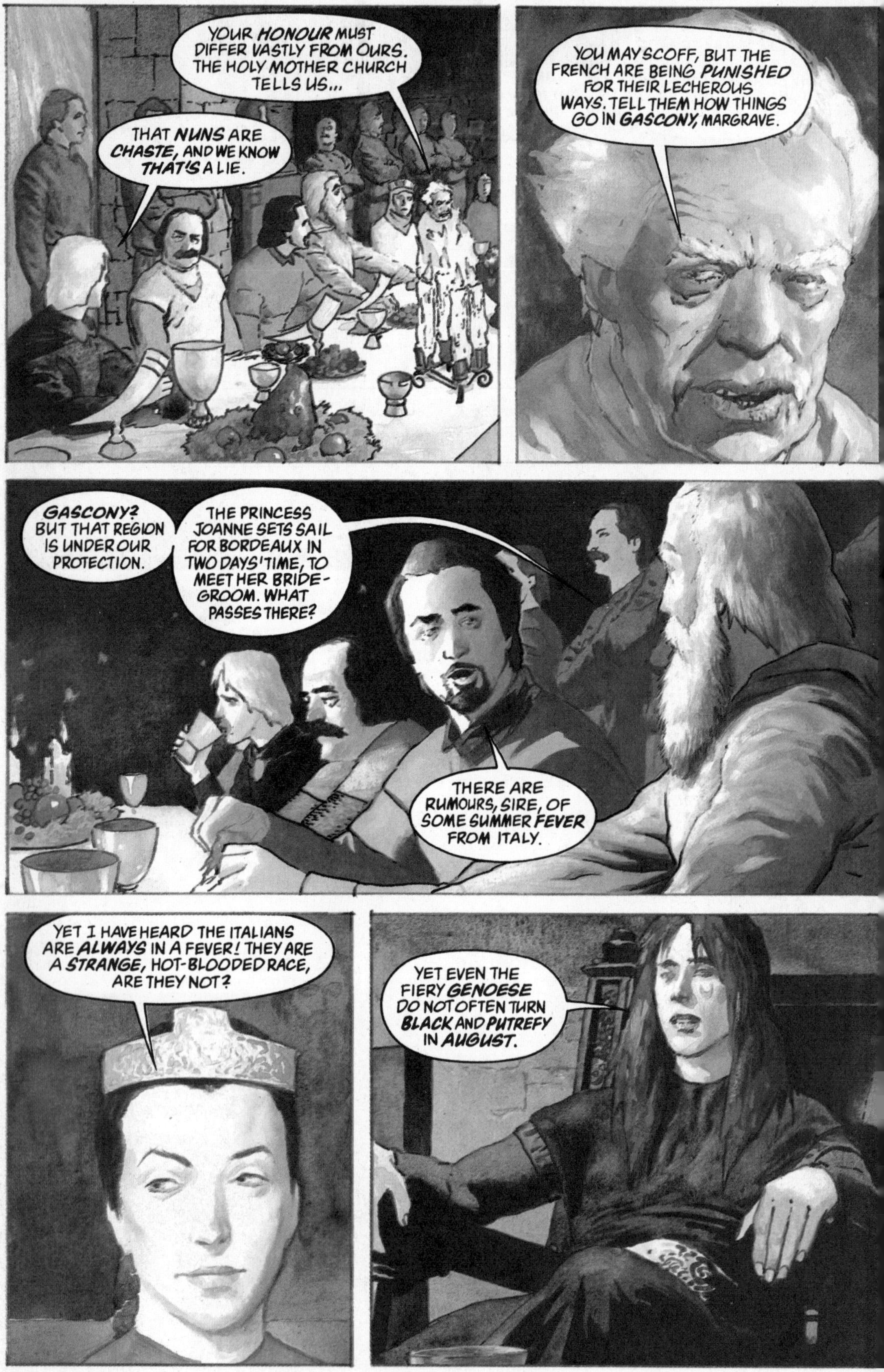

YOUR HONOUR MUST DIFFER VASTLY FROM OURS. THE HOLY MOTHER CHURCH TELLS US...
THAT NUNS ARE CHASTE, AND WE KNOW THAT'S A LIE.
YOU MAY SCOFF, BUT THE FRENCH ARE BEING PUNISHED FOR THEIR LECHEROUS WAYS. TELL THEM HOW THINGS GO IN GASCONY, MARGRAVE.
GASCONY? BUT THAT REGION IS UNDER OUR PROTECTION.
THE PRINCESS JOANNE SETS SAIL FOR BORDEAUX IN TWO DAYS' TIME, TO MEET HER BRIDE-GROOM. WHAT PASSES THERE?
THERE ARE RUMOURS, SIRE, OF SOME SUMMER FEVER FROM ITALY.
YET I HAVE HEARD THE ITALIANS ARE ALWAYS IN A FEVER! THEY ARE A STRANGE, HOT-BLOODED RACE, ARE THEY NOT?
YET EVEN THE FIERY GENOESE DO NOT OFTEN TURN BLACK AND PUTREFY IN AUGUST.

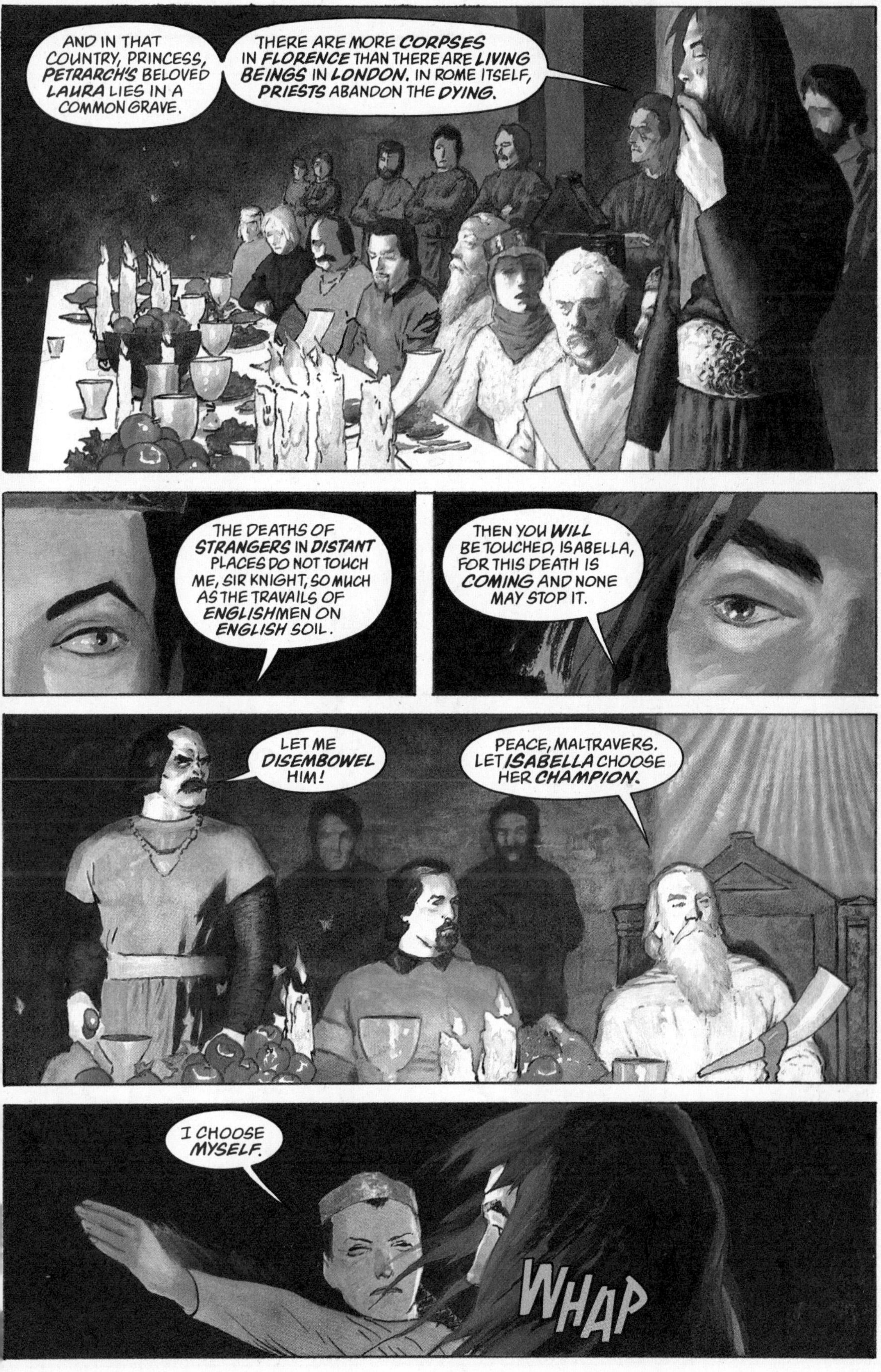
AND IN THAT COUNTRY, PRINCESS, PETRARCH'S BELOVED LAURA LIES IN A COMMON GRAVE.
THERE ARE MORE CORPSES IN FLORENCE THAN THERE ARE LIVING BEINGS IN LONDON. IN ROME ITSELF, PRIESTS ABANDON THE DYING.
THE DEATHS OF STRANGERS IN DISTANT PLACES DO NOT TOUCH ME, SIR KNIGHT, SO MUCH AS THE TRAVAILS OF ENGLISHMEN ON ENGLISH SOIL.
THEN YOU WILL BE TOUCHED, ISABELLA, FOR THIS DEATH IS COMING AND NONE MAY STOP IT.
LET ME DISEMBOWEL HIM!
PEACE, MALTRAVERS. LET ISABELLA CHOOSE HER CHAMPION.
I CHOOSE MYSELF.
WHAP

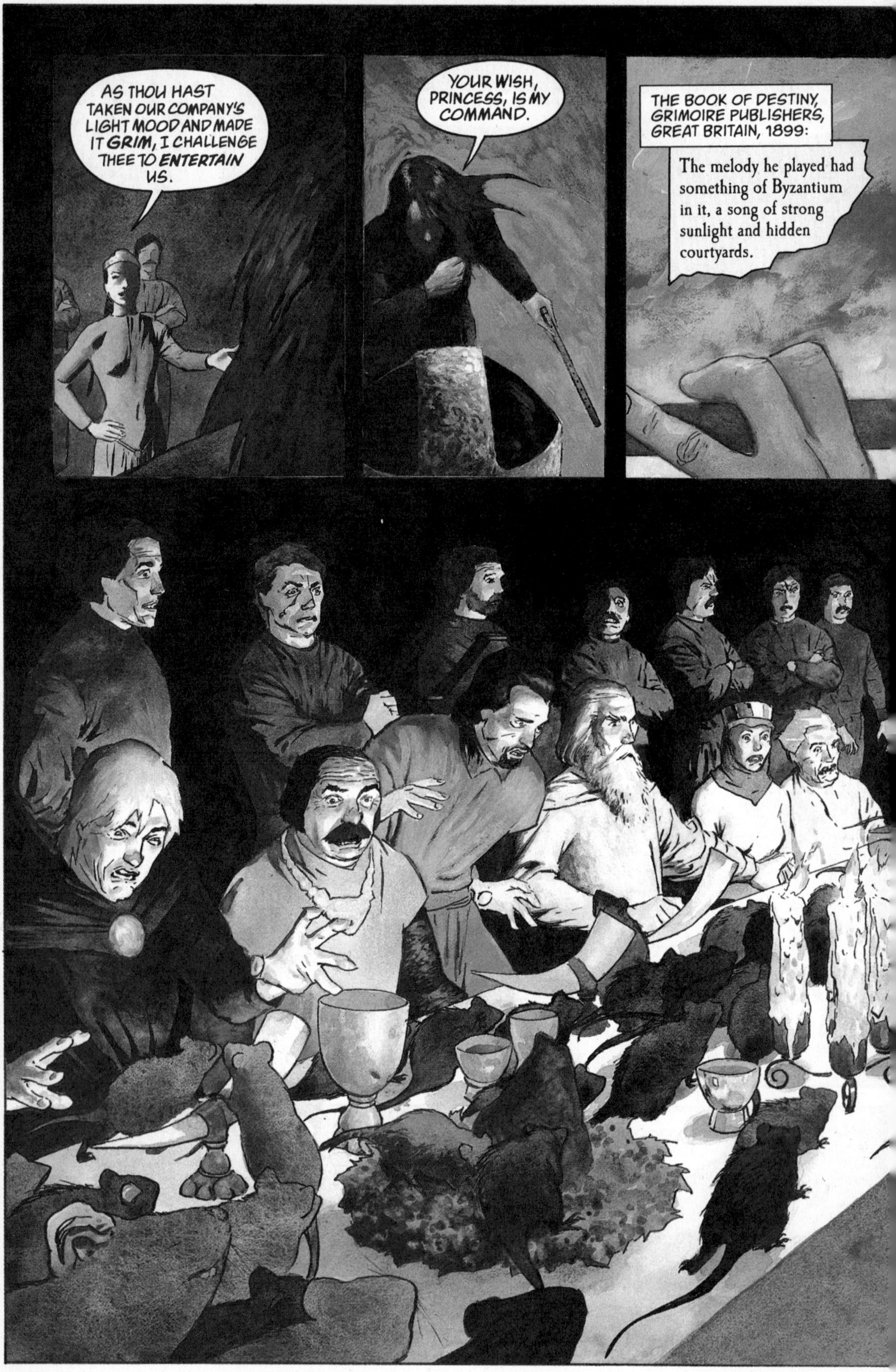
AS THOU HAST TAKEN OUR COMPANY'S LIGHT MOOD AND MADE IT GRIM, I CHALLENGE THEE TO ENTERTAIN US.
YOUR WISH, PRINCESS, IS MY COMMAND.
THE BOOK OF DESTINY, GRIMOIRE PUBLISHERS, GREAT BRITAIN, 1899:
The melody he played had something of Byzantium in it, a song of strong sunlight and hidden courtyards.

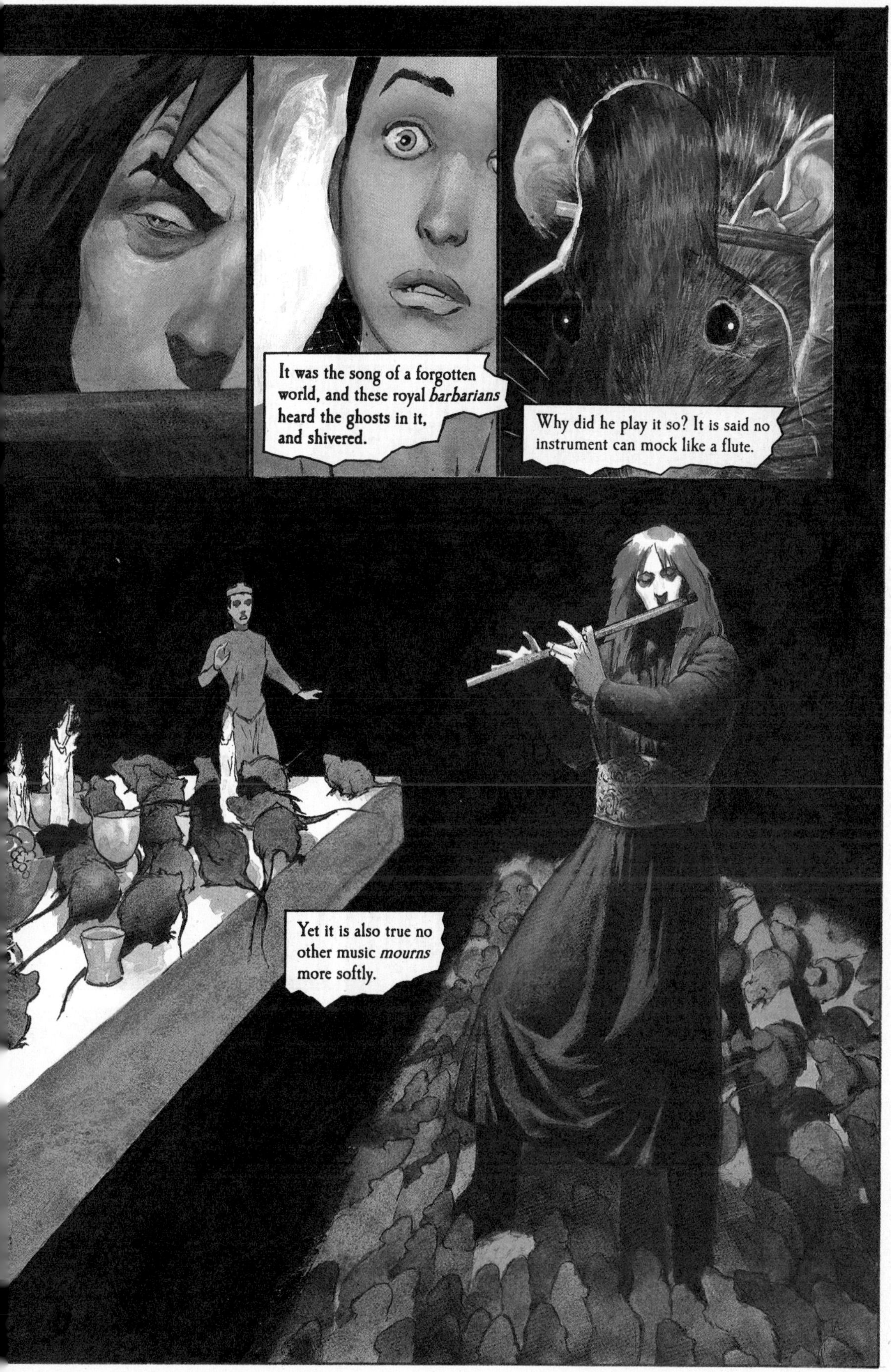
It was the song of a forgotten world, and these royal *barbarians* heard the ghosts in it, and shivered.
Why did he play it so? It is said no instrument can mock like a flute.
Yet it is also true no other music *mourns* more softly.

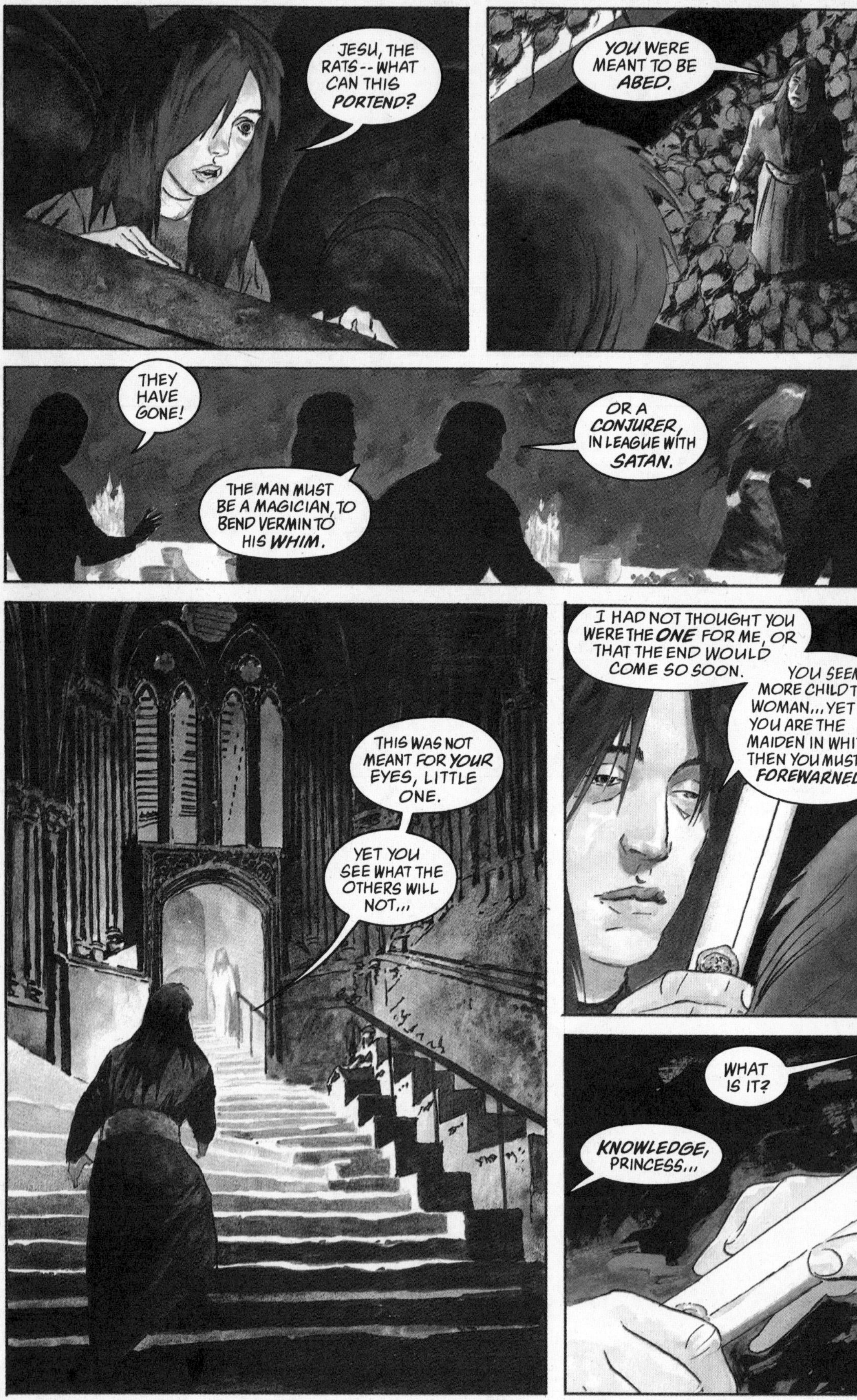
JESU, THE RATS--WHAT CAN THIS PORTEND?
YOU WERE MEANT TO BE ABED.
THEY HAVE GONE!
THE MAN MUST BE A MAGICIAN, TO BEND VERMIN TO HIS WHIM.
OR A CONJURER, IN LEAGUE WITH SATAN.
THIS WAS NOT MEANT FOR YOUR EYES, LITTLE ONE.
YET YOU SEE WHAT THE OTHERS WILL NOT...
I HAD NOT THOUGHT YOU WERE THE ONE FOR ME, OR THAT THE END WOULD COME SO SOON.
YOU SEEM MORE CHILD THAN WOMAN... YET IF YOU ARE THE MAIDEN IN WHITE, THEN YOU MUST BE FOREWARNED.
WHAT IS IT?
KNOWLEDGE, PRINCESS...

"OF THE KIND *EVE* PLUCKED AND OFFERED *ADAM*."

OH, GET YOU *GONE*, JOANNE.

BUT OUR LADY MOTHER SAID I WAS NOT TO LEAVE YOU ALONE WITH...

YOU CALL THIS *ALONE*? 'TIS HARVEST FAIR!

AND IN ALL TRUTH, THE *JEWEL* YOU WERE TOLD TO PROTECT WAS LONG SINCE *LOST* BY ME.

IF YE'LL FORGIVE ME, MILADY, YE LOOKS LIKE ONE THAT NEEDS A FORTUNE TOLD.

METHINKS *THIS* MIGHT BE A FORTUNE OF A KIND, YET MUCH OF THE SENSE ESCAPES ME. 'TIS LATIN, I SUPPOSE, BUT A STRANGE SORT.

I READ PALMS, MILADY, NOT LETTERS.

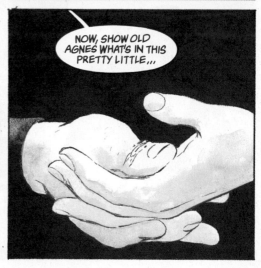

NOW, SHOW OLD AGNES WHAT'S IN THIS PRETTY LITTLE...

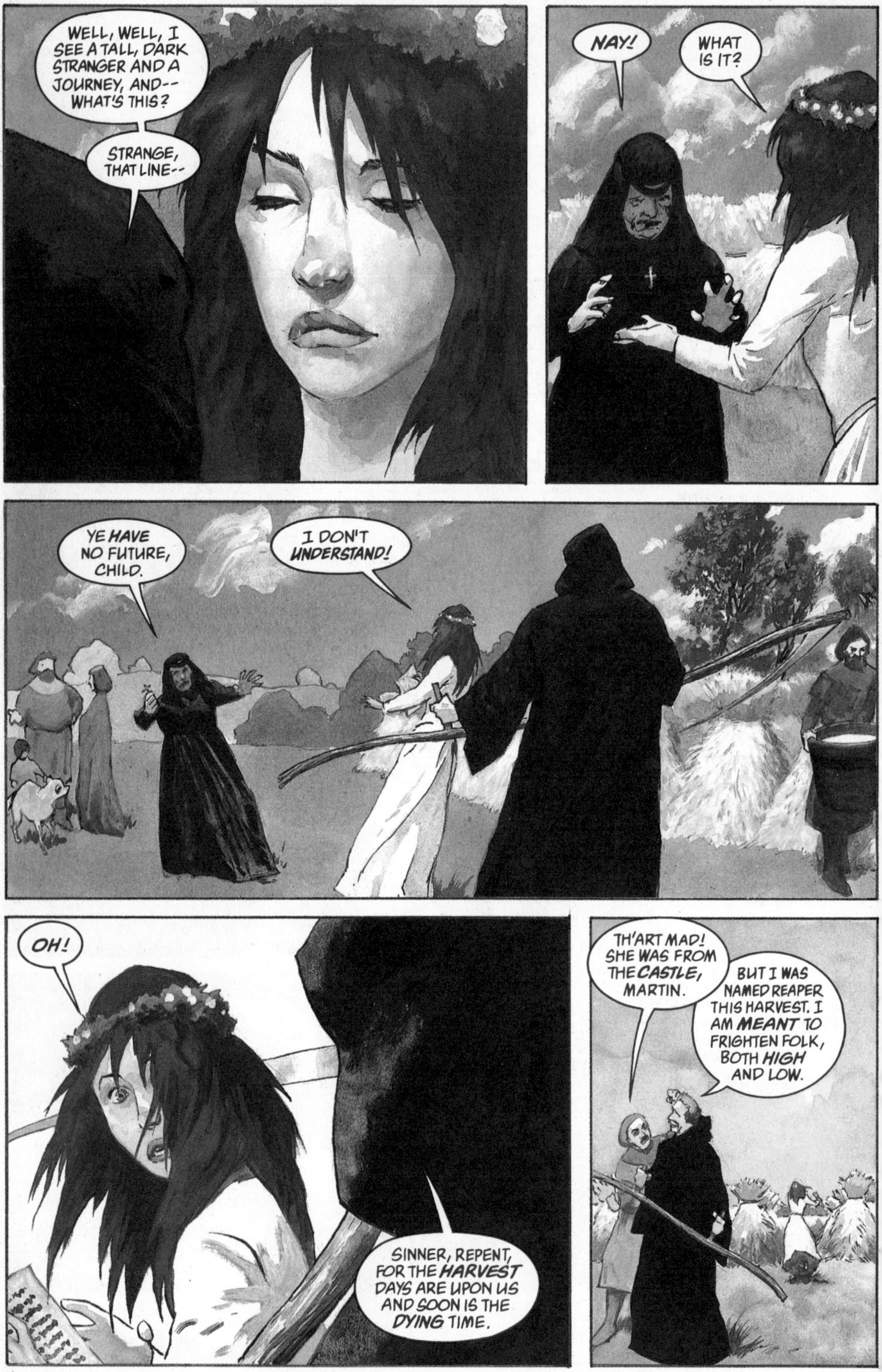
WELL, WELL, I SEE A TALL, DARK STRANGER AND A JOURNEY, AND-- WHAT'S THIS?
STRANGE, THAT LINE--
NAY!
WHAT IS IT?
YE HAVE NO FUTURE, CHILD.
I DON'T UNDERSTAND!
OH!
SINNER, REPENT, FOR THE HARVEST DAYS ARE UPON US AND SOON IS THE DYING TIME.
TH'ART MAD! SHE WAS FROM THE CASTLE, MARTIN.
BUT I WAS NAMED REAPER THIS HARVEST. I AM MEANT TO FRIGHTEN FOLK, BOTH HIGH AND LOW.

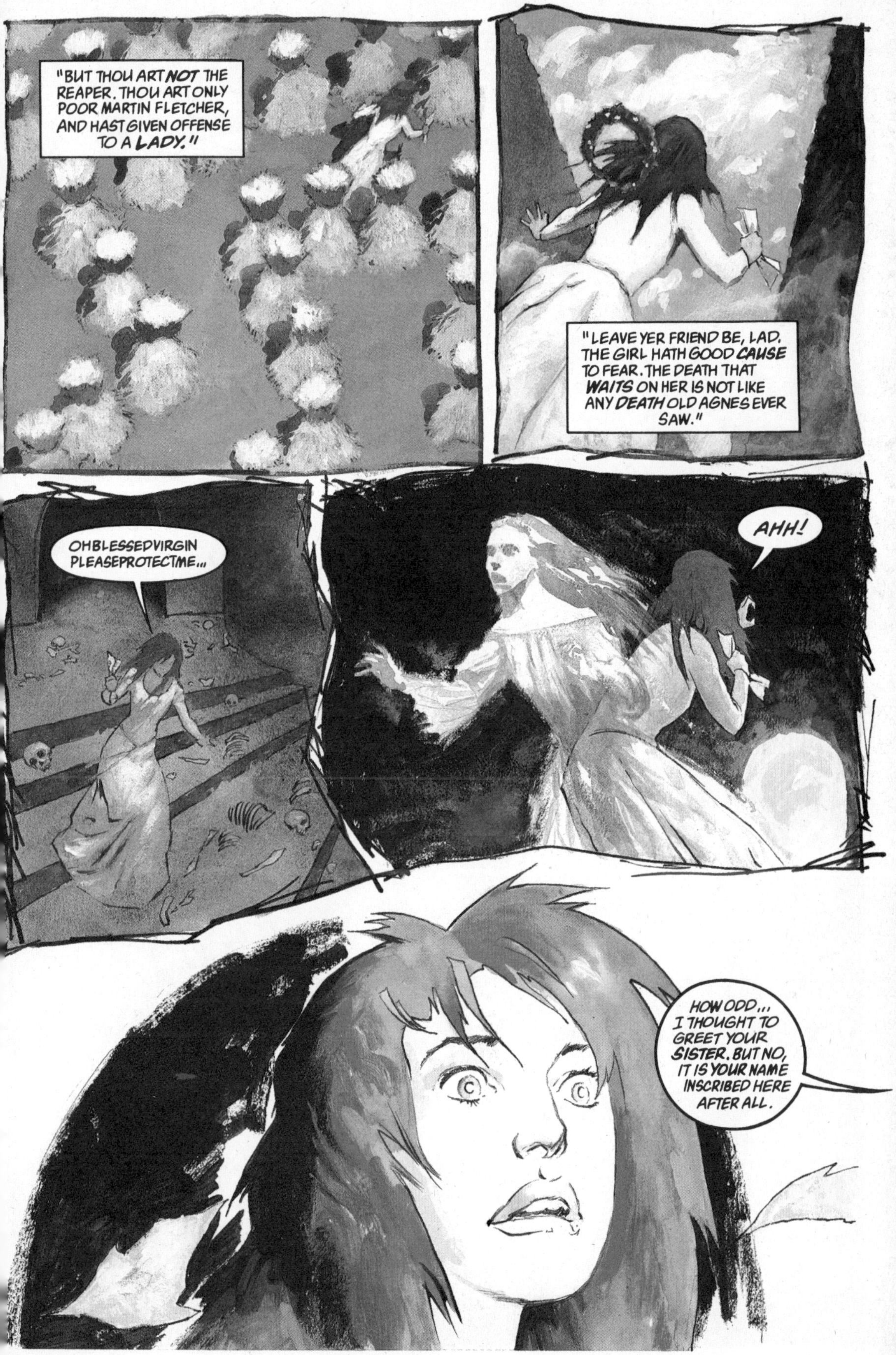
"BUT THOU ART NOT THE REAPER. THOU ART ONLY POOR MARTIN FLETCHER, AND HAST GIVEN OFFENSE TO A LADY."
"LEAVE YER FRIEND BE, LAD. THE GIRL HATH GOOD CAUSE TO FEAR. THE DEATH THAT WAITS ON HER IS NOT LIKE ANY DEATH OLD AGNES EVER SAW."
OHBLESSEDVIRGIN PLEASEPROTECTME...
AHH!
HOW ODD... I THOUGHT TO GREET YOUR SISTER. BUT NO, IT IS YOUR NAME INSCRIBED HERE AFTER ALL.

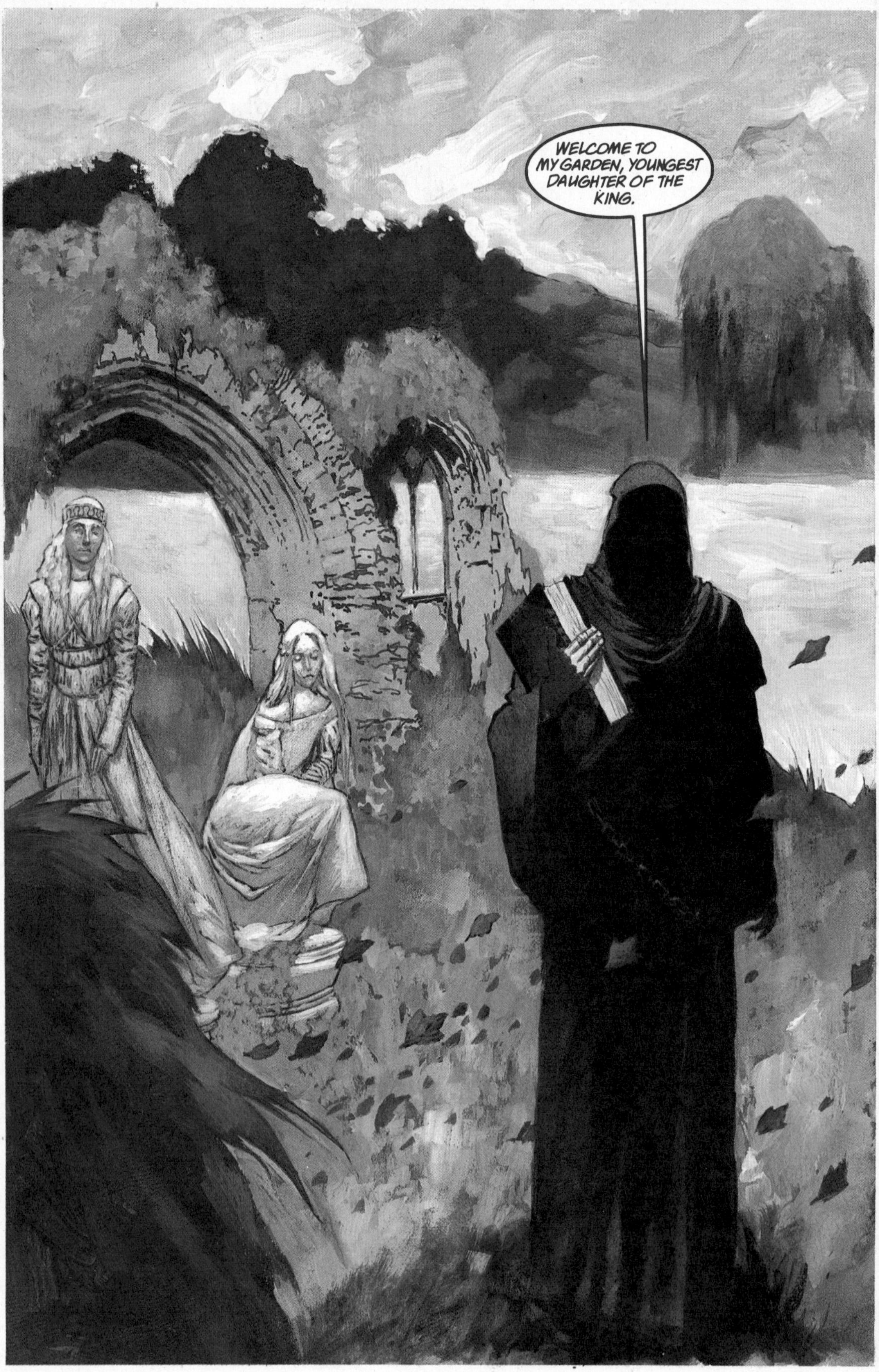
WELCOME TO MY GARDEN, YOUNGEST DAUGHTER OF THE KING.

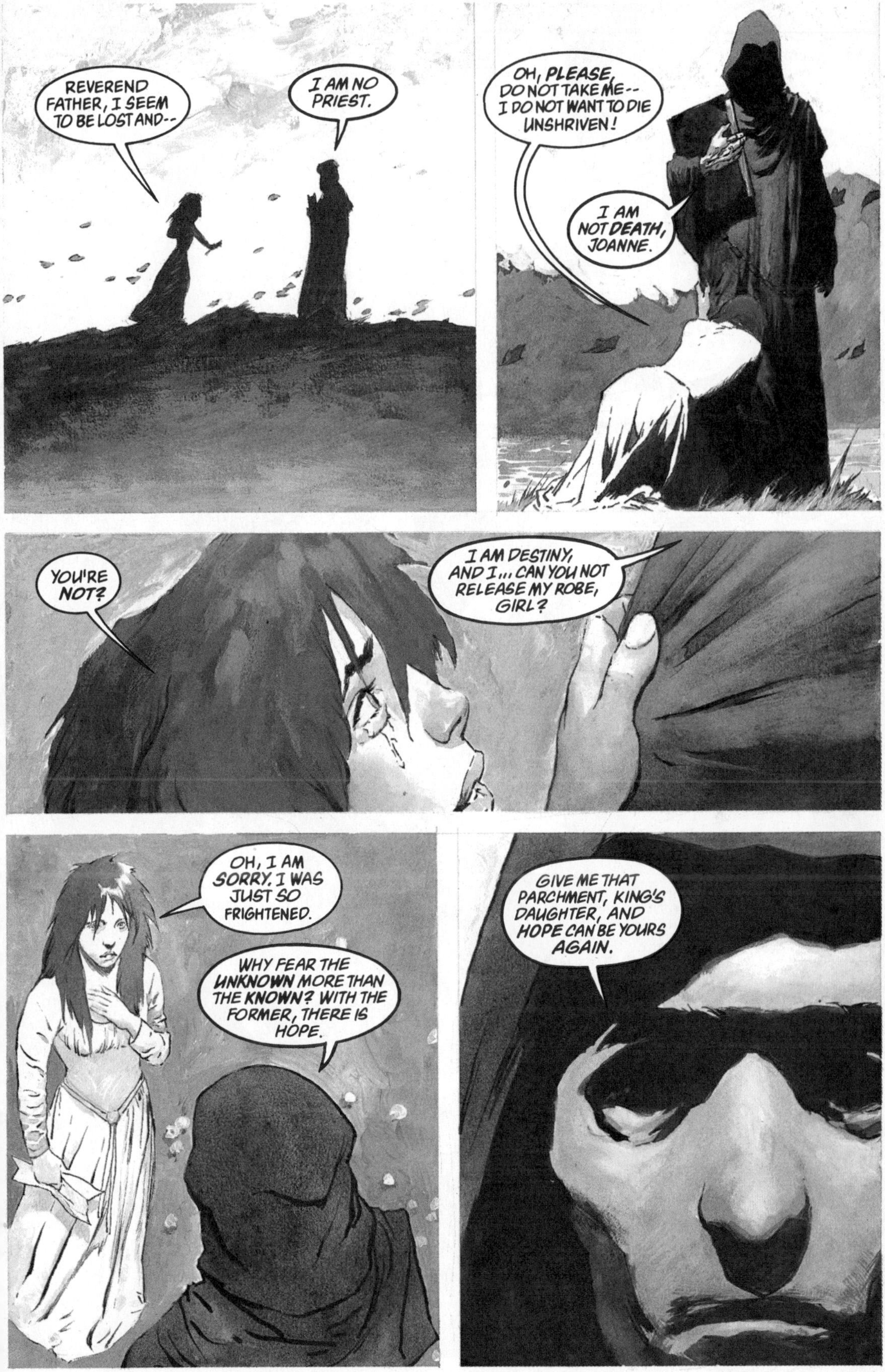
REVEREND FATHER, I SEEM TO BE LOST AND--
I AM NO PRIEST.
OH, PLEASE, DO NOT TAKE ME-- I DO NOT WANT TO DIE UNSHRIVEN!
I AM NOT DEATH, JOANNE.
YOU'RE NOT?
I AM DESTINY, AND I... CAN YOU NOT RELEASE MY ROBE, GIRL?
OH, I AM SORRY. I WAS JUST SO FRIGHTENED.
WHY FEAR THE UNKNOWN MORE THAN THE KNOWN? WITH THE FORMER, THERE IS HOPE.
GIVE ME THAT PARCHMENT, KING'S DAUGHTER, AND HOPE CAN BE YOURS AGAIN.

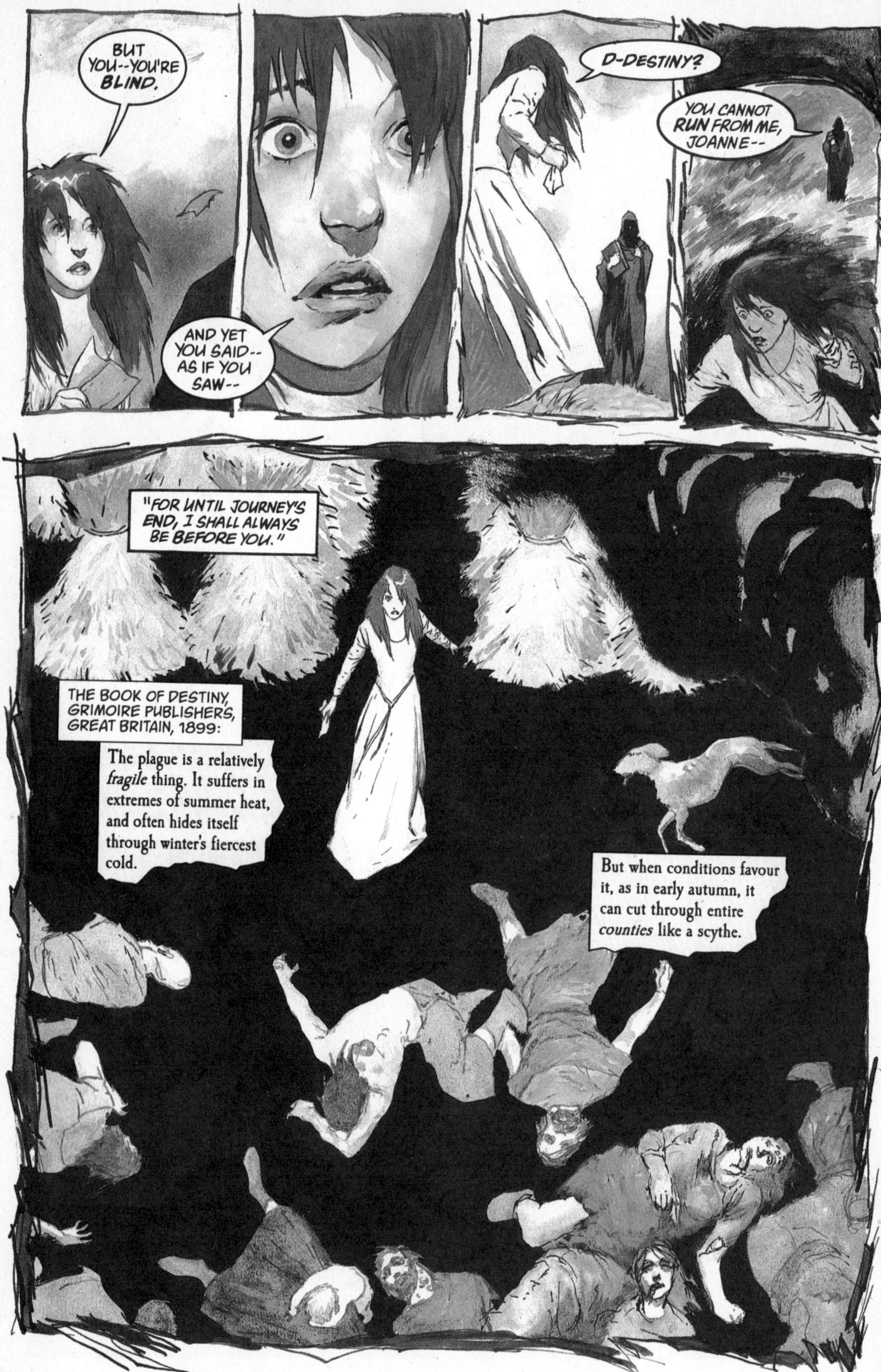
BUT YOU--YOU'RE BLIND.
AND YET YOU SAID-- AS IF YOU SAW--
D-DESTINY?
YOU CANNOT RUN FROM ME, JOANNE--
"FOR UNTIL JOURNEY'S END, I SHALL ALWAYS BE BEFORE YOU."
THE BOOK OF DESTINY, GRIMOIRE PUBLISHERS, GREAT BRITAIN, 1899:
The plague is a relatively fragile thing. It suffers in extremes of summer heat, and often hides itself through winter's fiercest cold.
But when conditions favour it, as in early autumn, it can cut through entire counties like a scythe.

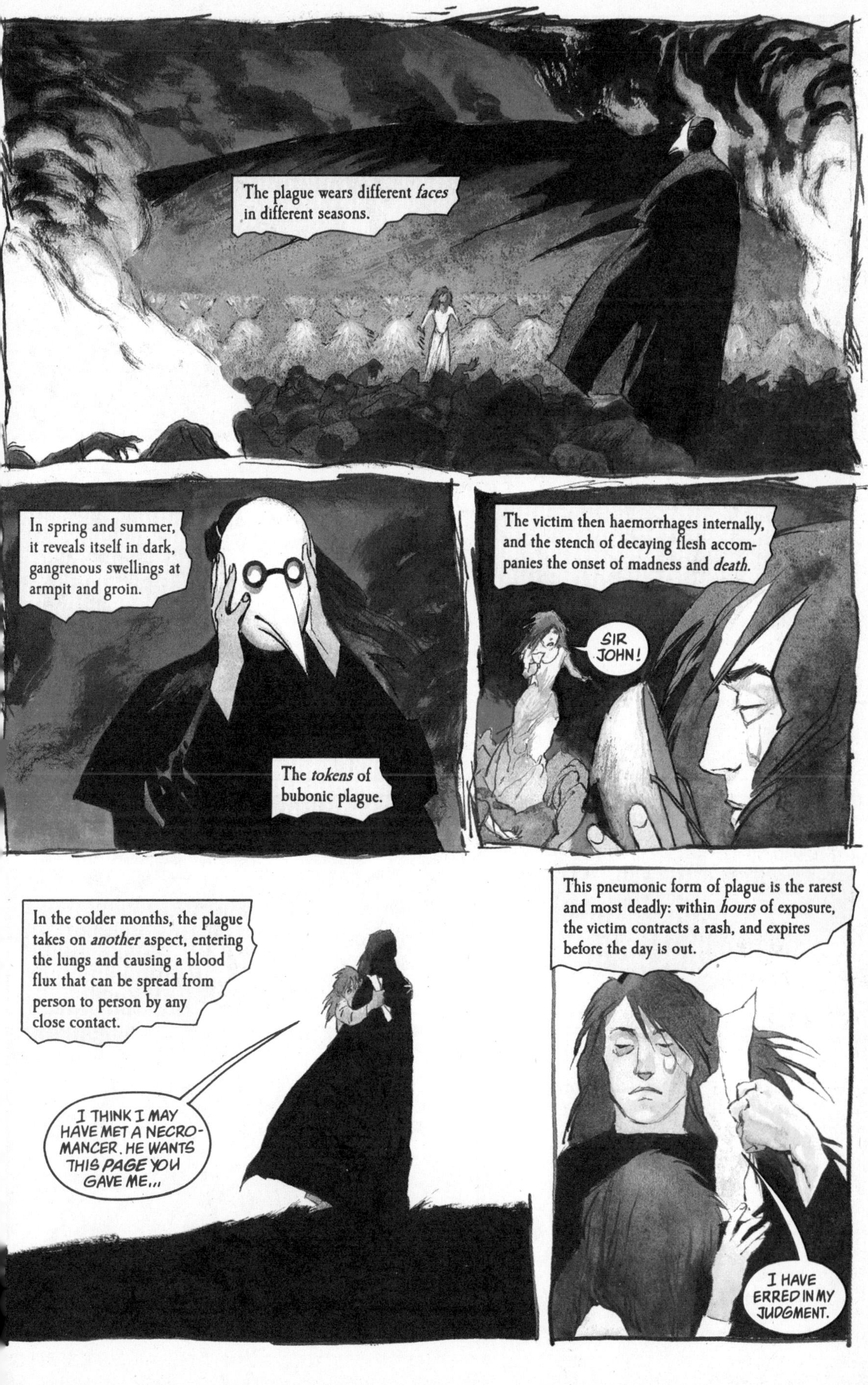
The plague wears different *faces* in different seasons.
In spring and summer, it reveals itself in dark, gangrenous swellings at armpit and groin.
The *tokens* of bubonic plague.
The victim then haemorrhages internally, and the stench of decaying flesh accompanies the onset of madness and *death*.
SIR JOHN!
In the colder months, the plague takes on *another* aspect, entering the lungs and causing a blood flux that can be spread from person to person by any close contact.
I THINK I MAY HAVE MET A NECROMANCER. HE WANTS THIS *PAGE* YOU GAVE ME...
This pneumonic form of plague is the rarest and most deadly: within *hours* of exposure, the victim contracts a rash, and expires before the day is out.
I HAVE ERRED IN MY JUDGMENT.

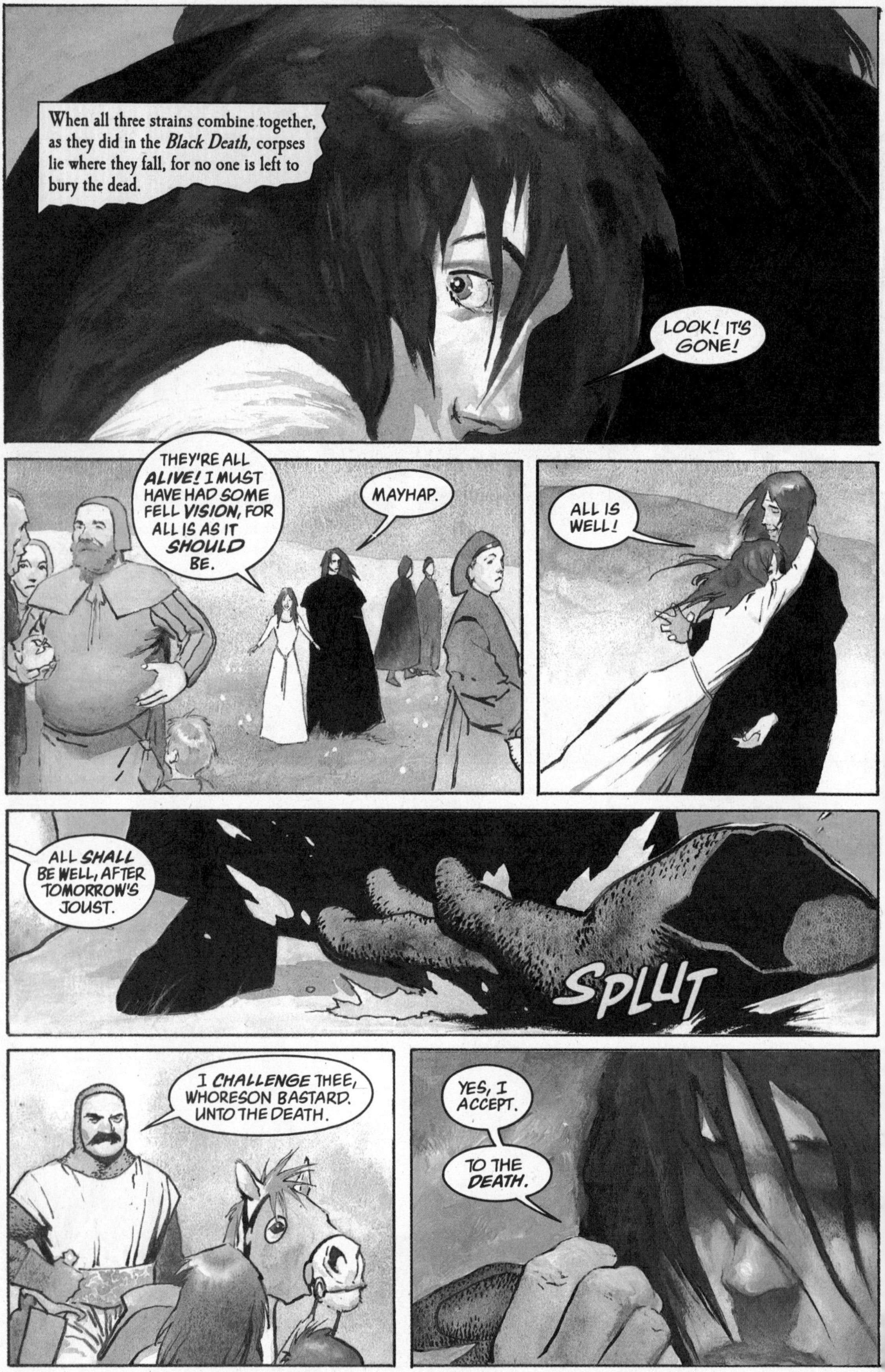
When all three strains combine together, as they did in the *Black Death*, corpses lie where they fall, for no one is left to bury the dead.
LOOK! IT'S GONE!
THEY'RE ALL ALIVE! I MUST HAVE HAD SOME FELL VISION, FOR ALL IS AS IT SHOULD BE.
MAYHAP.
ALL IS WELL!
ALL SHALL BE WELL, AFTER TOMORROW'S JOUST.
SPLUT
I CHALLENGE THEE, WHORESON BASTARD. UNTO THE DEATH.
YES, I ACCEPT.
TO THE DEATH.

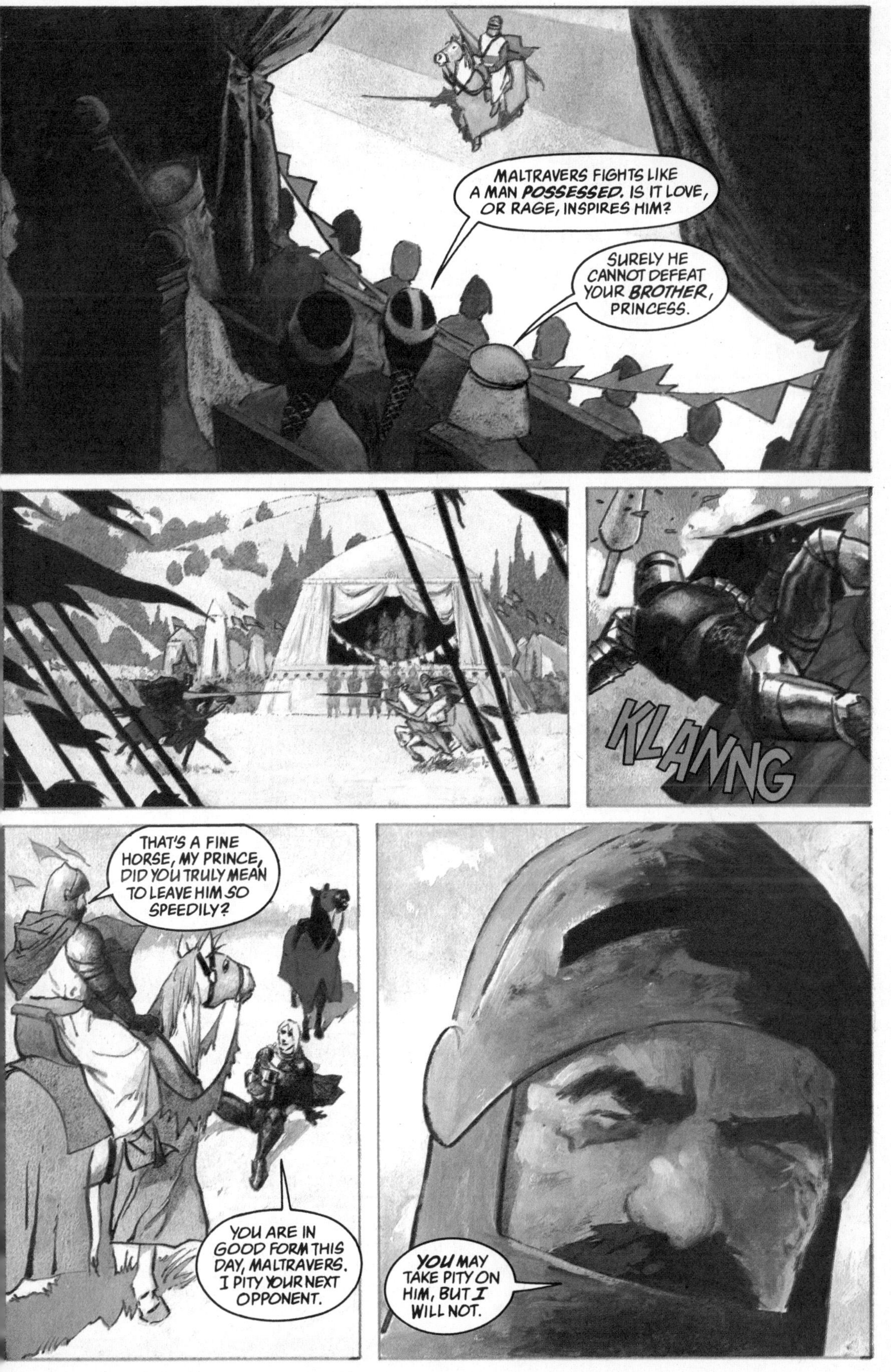
MALTRAVERS FIGHTS LIKE A MAN POSSESSED. IS IT LOVE, OR RAGE, INSPIRES HIM?
SURELY HE CANNOT DEFEAT YOUR BROTHER, PRINCESS.
KLANNG
THAT'S A FINE HORSE, MY PRINCE, DID YOU TRULY MEAN TO LEAVE HIM SO SPEEDILY?
YOU ARE IN GOOD FORM THIS DAY, MALTRAVERS. I PITY YOUR NEXT OPPONENT.
YOU MAY TAKE PITY ON HIM, BUT I WILL NOT.

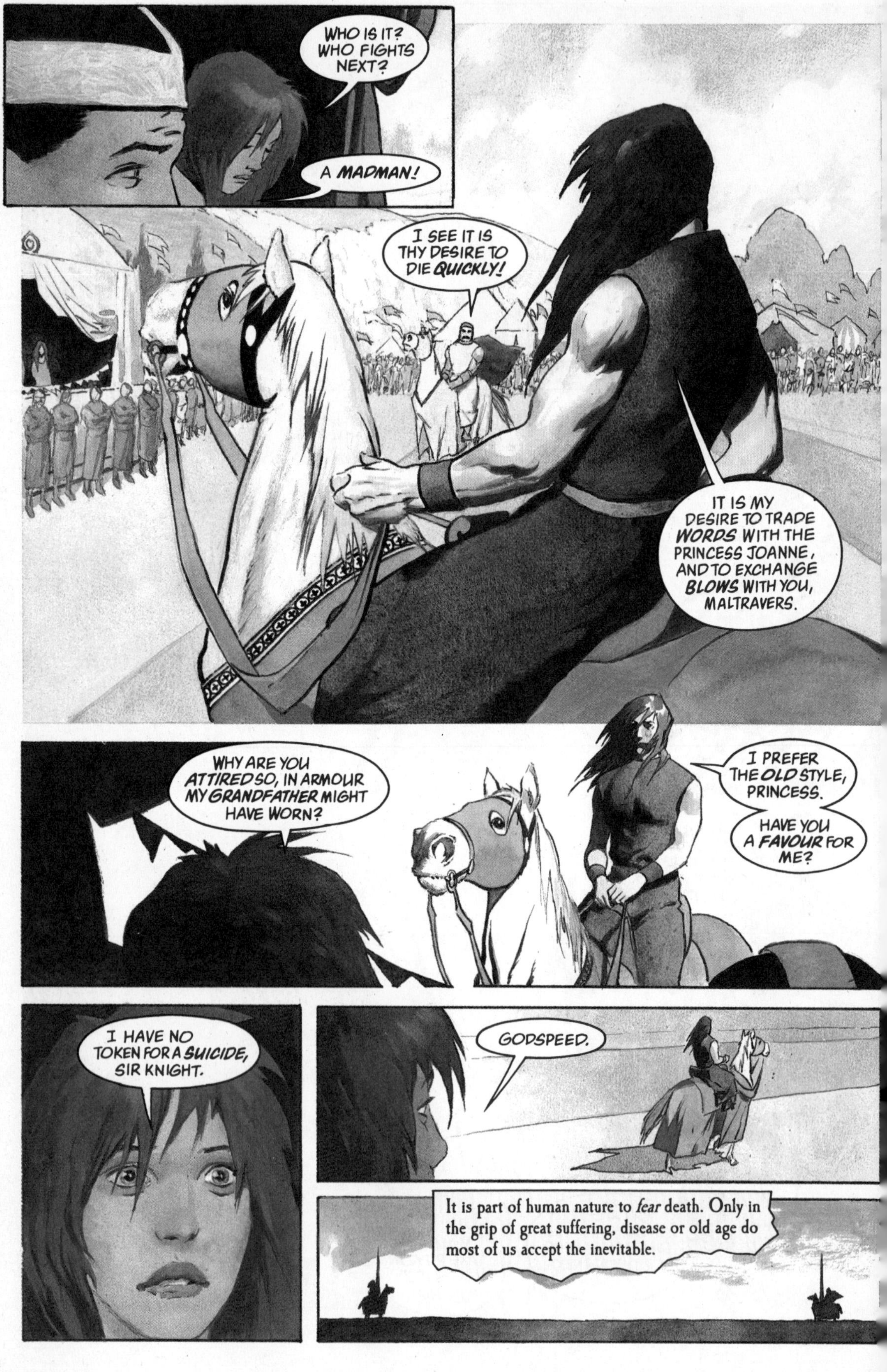
WHO IS IT? WHO FIGHTS NEXT?
A MADMAN!
I SEE IT IS THY DESIRE TO DIE QUICKLY!
IT IS MY DESIRE TO TRADE WORDS WITH THE PRINCESS JOANNE, AND TO EXCHANGE BLOWS WITH YOU, MALTRAVERS.
WHY ARE YOU ATTIRED SO, IN ARMOUR MY GRANDFATHER MIGHT HAVE WORN?
I PREFER THE OLD STYLE, PRINCESS.
HAVE YOU A FAVOUR FOR ME?
I HAVE NO TOKEN FOR A SUICIDE, SIR KNIGHT.
GODSPEED.
It is part of human nature to fear death. Only in the grip of great suffering, disease or old age do most of us accept the inevitable.

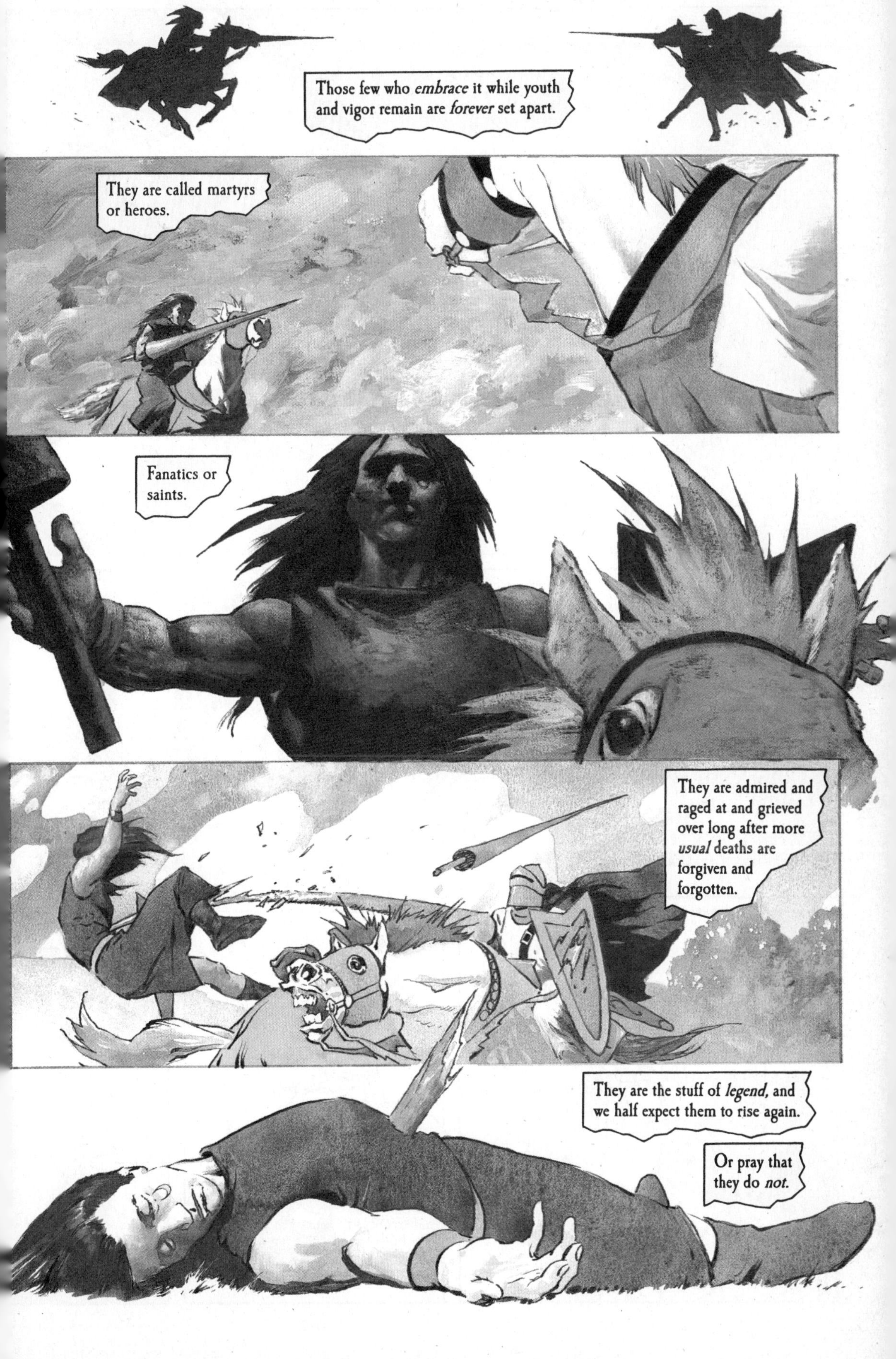
Those few who *embrace* it while youth and vigor remain are *forever* set apart.
They are called martyrs or heroes.
Fanatics or saints.
They are admired and raged at and grieved over long after more *usual* deaths are forgiven and forgotten.
They are the stuff of *legend,* and we half expect them to rise again.
Or pray that they do *not.*

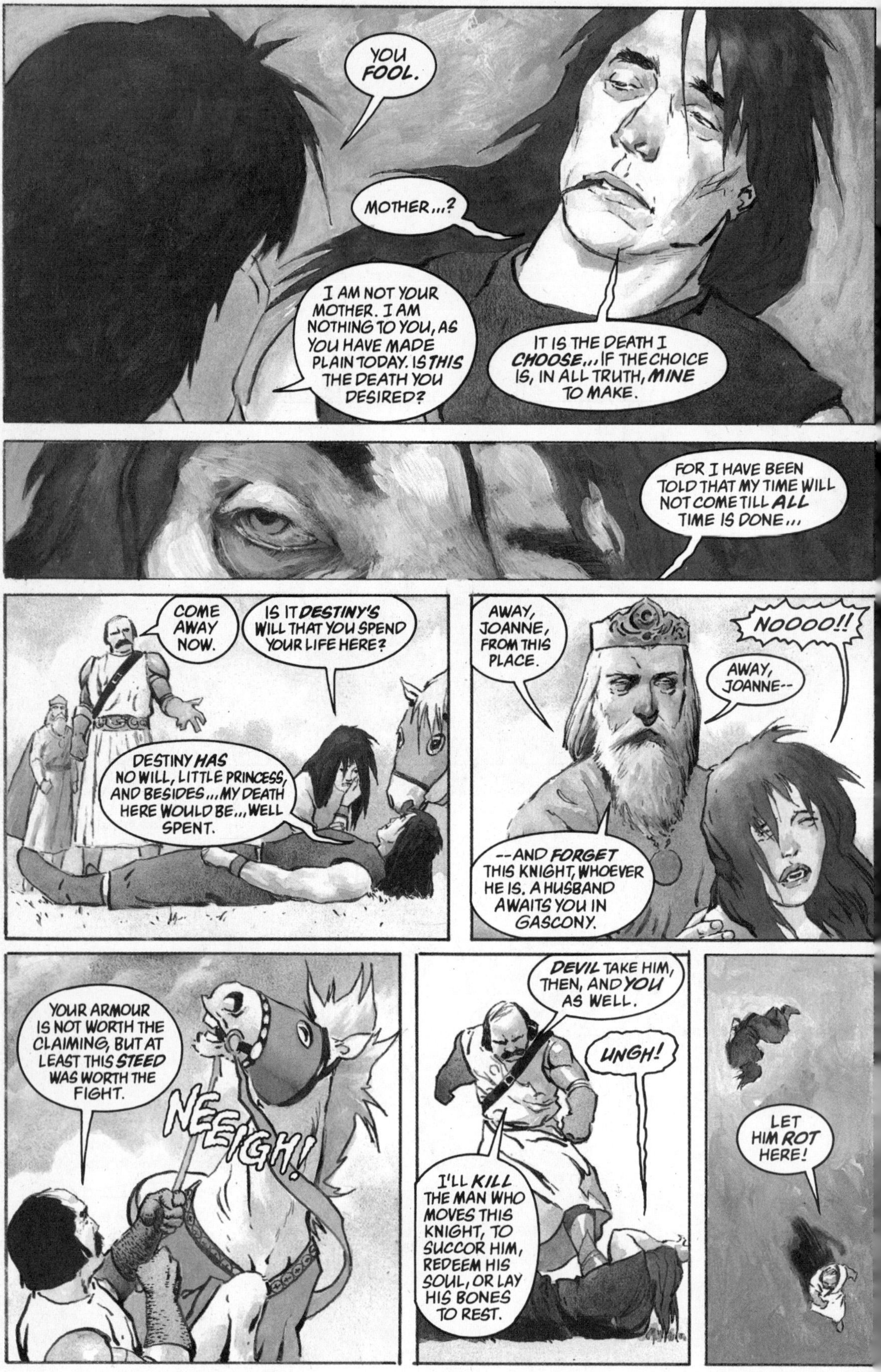
YOU FOOL.
MOTHER...?
I AM NOT YOUR MOTHER. I AM NOTHING TO YOU, AS YOU HAVE MADE PLAIN TODAY. IS THIS THE DEATH YOU DESIRED?
IT IS THE DEATH I CHOOSE... IF THE CHOICE IS, IN ALL TRUTH, MINE TO MAKE.
FOR I HAVE BEEN TOLD THAT MY TIME WILL NOT COME TILL ALL TIME IS DONE...
COME AWAY NOW.
IS IT DESTINY'S WILL THAT YOU SPEND YOUR LIFE HERE?
DESTINY HAS NO WILL, LITTLE PRINCESS, AND BESIDES... MY DEATH HERE WOULD BE... WELL SPENT.
AWAY, JOANNE, FROM THIS PLACE.
NOOOO!!
AWAY, JOANNE--
--AND FORGET THIS KNIGHT, WHOEVER HE IS. A HUSBAND AWAITS YOU IN GASCONY.
YOUR ARMOUR IS NOT WORTH THE CLAIMING, BUT AT LEAST THIS STEED WAS WORTH THE FIGHT.
NEEIGH!
DEVIL TAKE HIM, THEN, AND YOU AS WELL.
UNGH!
I'LL KILL THE MAN WHO MOVES THIS KNIGHT, TO SUCCOR HIM, REDEEM HIS SOUL, OR LAY HIS BONES TO REST.
LET HIM ROT HERE!

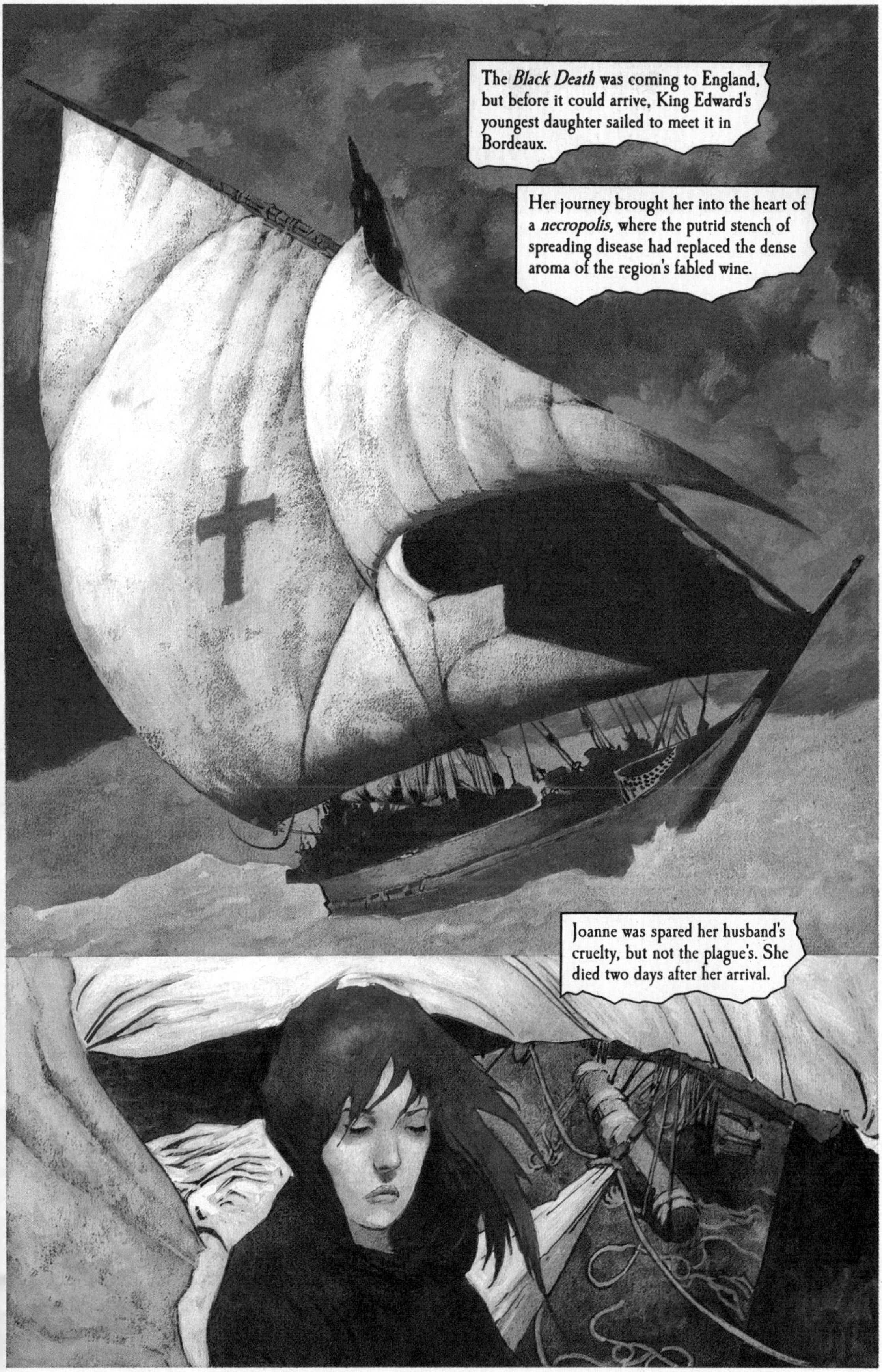
The *Black Death* was coming to England, but before it could arrive, King Edward's youngest daughter sailed to meet it in Bordeaux.
Her journey brought her into the heart of a *necropolis,* where the putrid stench of spreading disease had replaced the dense aroma of the region's fabled wine.
Joanne was spared her husband's cruelty, but not the plague's. She died two days after her arrival.

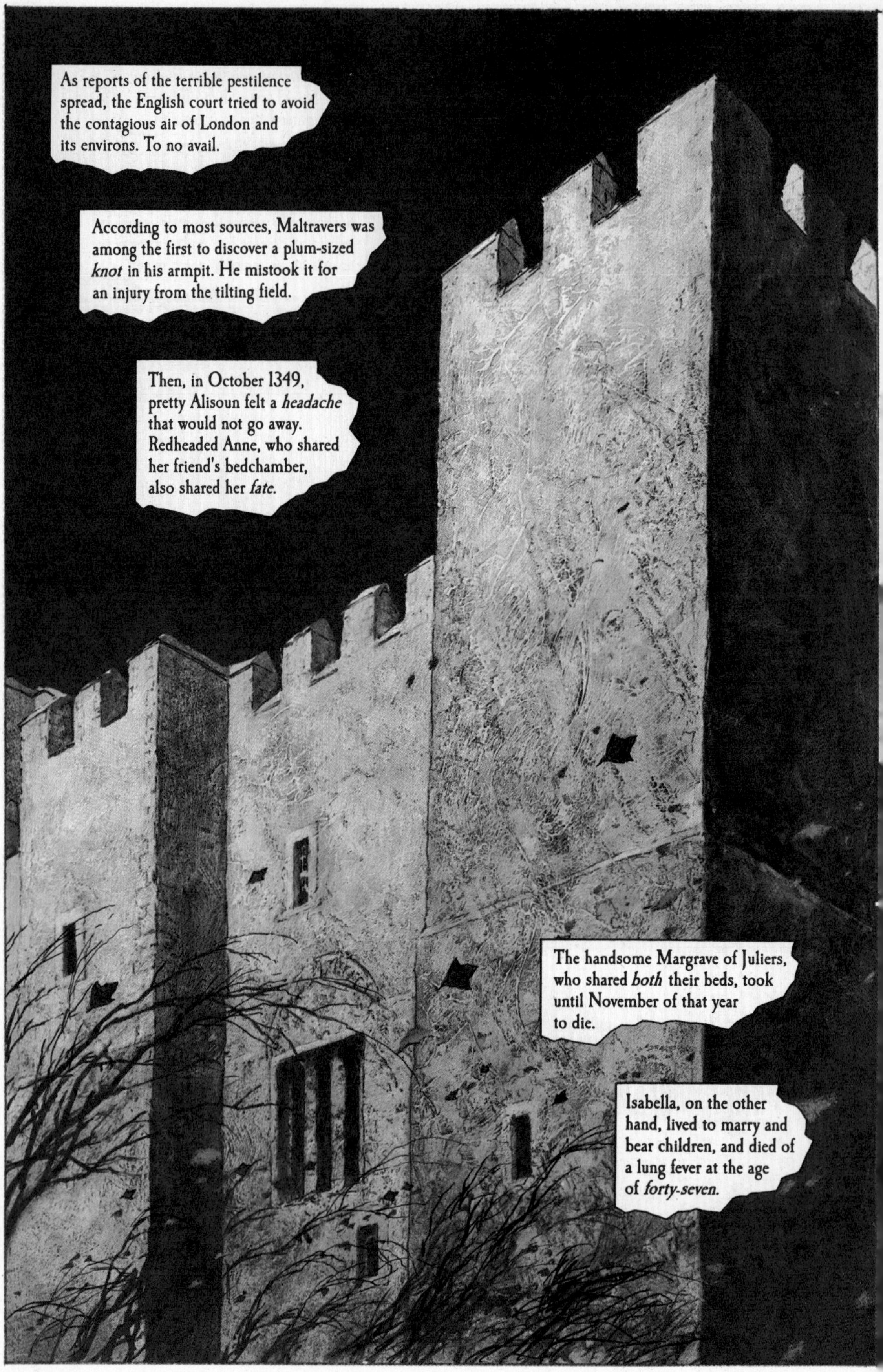
As reports of the terrible pestilence spread, the English court tried to avoid the contagious air of London and its environs. To no avail.
According to most sources, Maltravers was among the first to discover a plum-sized *knot* in his armpit. He mistook it for an injury from the tilting field.
Then, in October 1349, pretty Alisoun felt a *headache* that would not go away. Redheaded Anne, who shared her friend's bedchamber, also shared her *fate*.
The handsome Margrave of Juliers, who shared *both* their beds, took until November of that year to die.
Isabella, on the other hand, lived to marry and bear children, and died of a lung fever at the age of *forty-seven*.

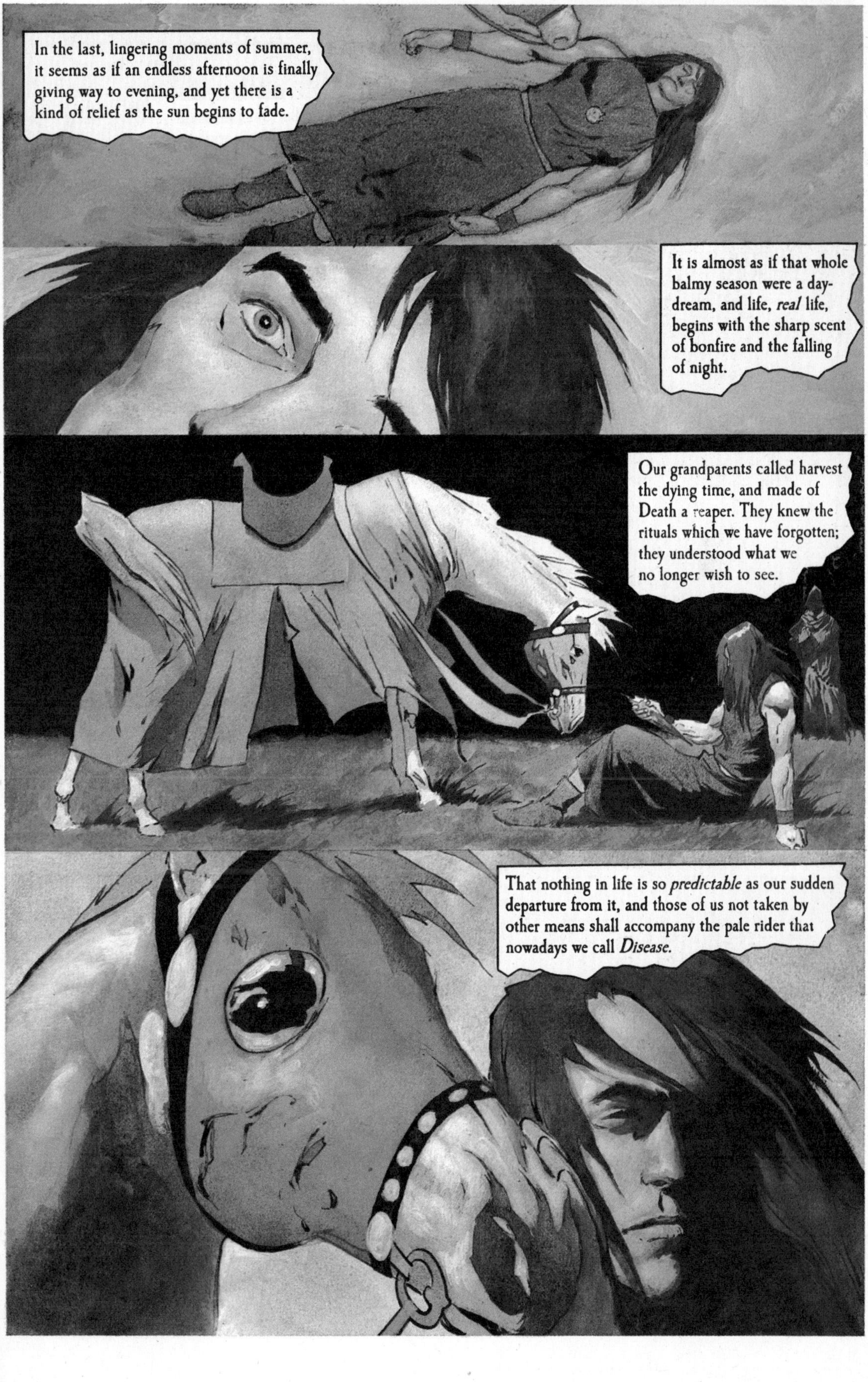
In the last, lingering moments of summer, it seems as if an endless afternoon is finally giving way to evening, and yet there is a kind of relief as the sun begins to fade.
It is almost as if that whole balmy season were a day-dream, and life, *real* life, begins with the sharp scent of bonfire and the falling of night.
Our grandparents called harvest the dying time, and made of Death a reaper. They knew the rituals which we have forgotten; they understood what we no longer wish to see.
That nothing in life is so *predictable* as our sudden departure from it, and those of us not taken by other means shall accompany the pale rider that nowadays we call *Disease.*

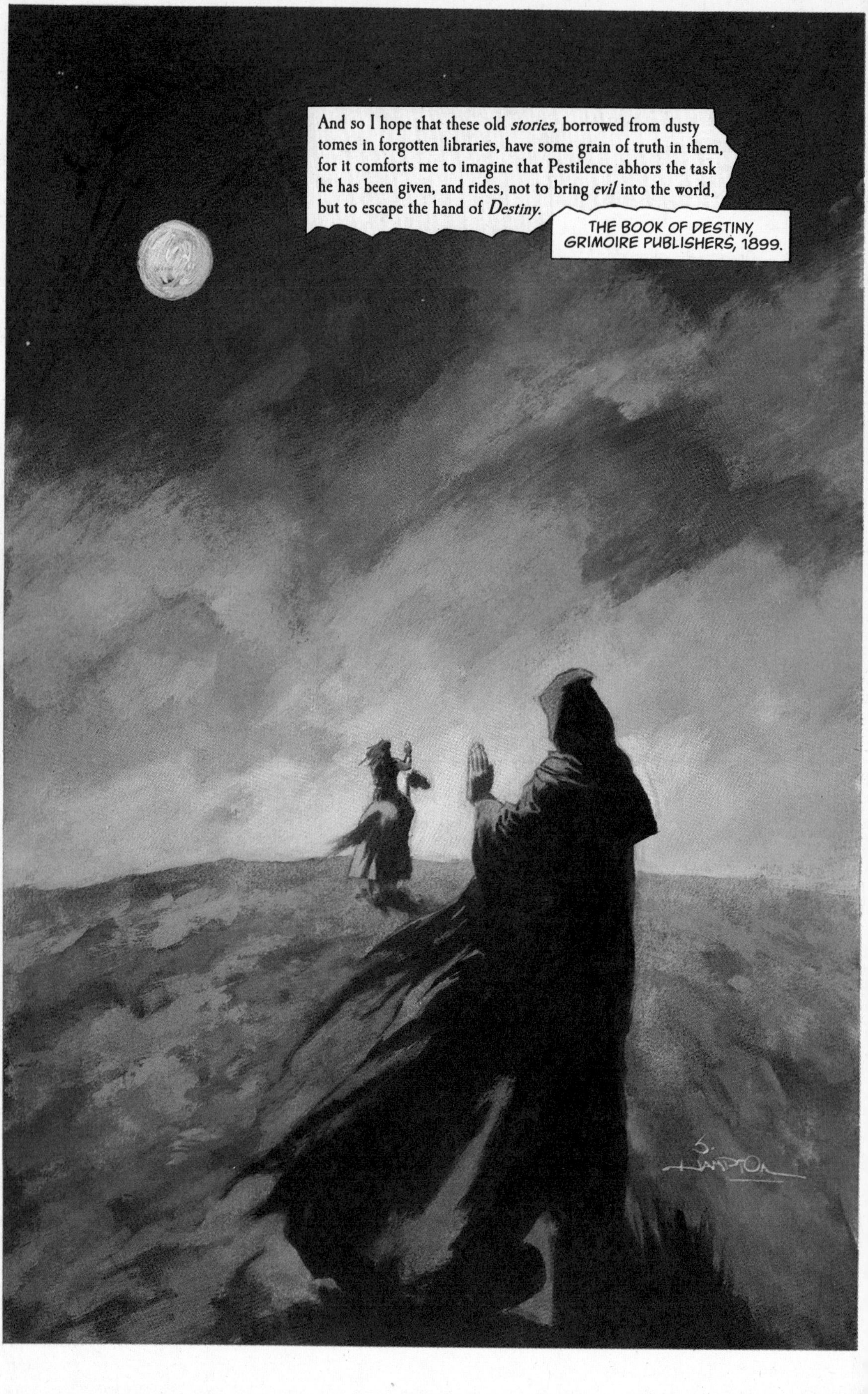
And so I hope that these old *stories*, borrowed from dusty tomes in forgotten libraries, have some grain of truth in them, for it comforts me to imagine that Pestilence abhors the task he has been given, and rides, not to bring *evil* into the world, but to escape the hand of *Destiny*.
THE BOOK OF DESTINY, GRIMOIRE PUBLISHERS, 1899.

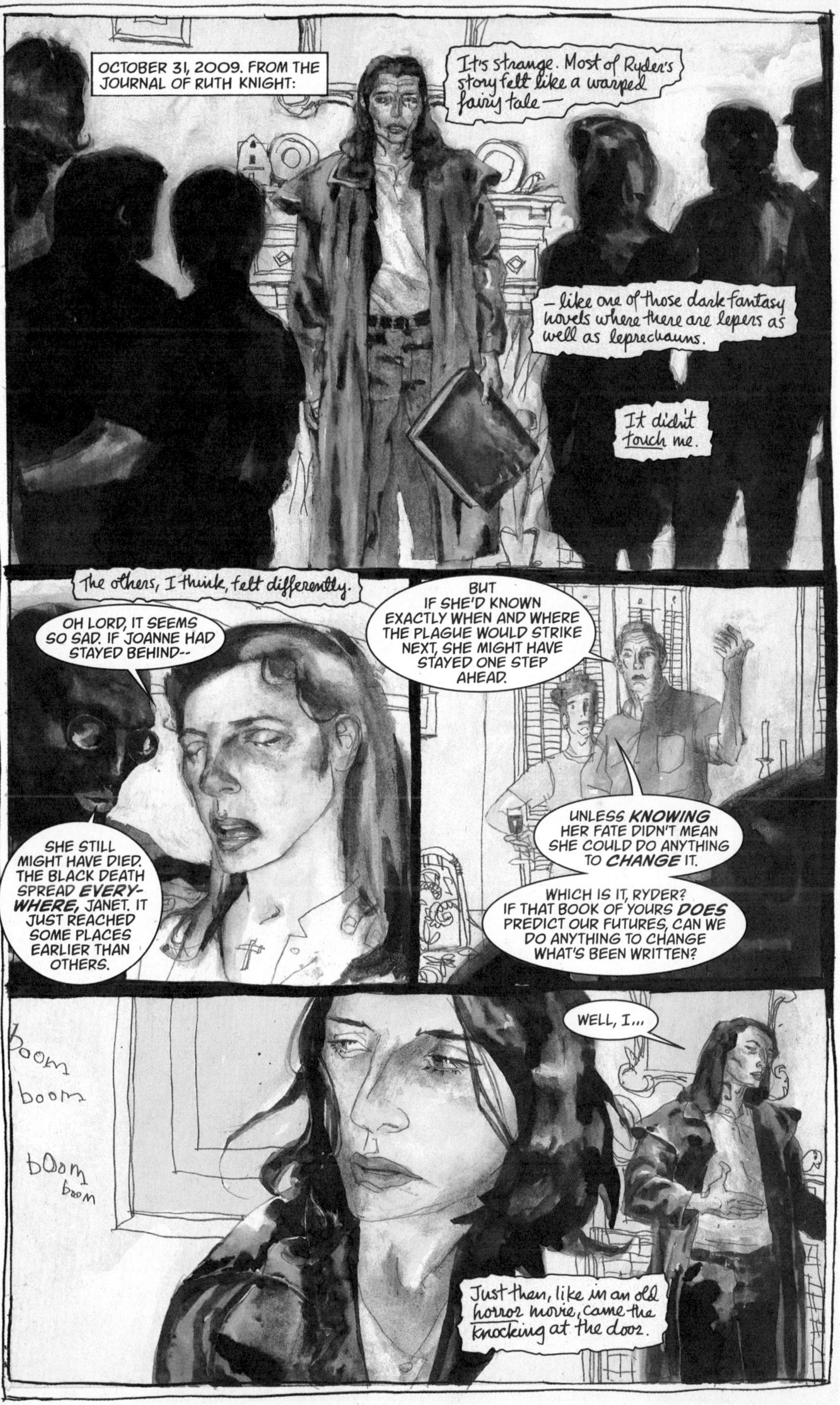
OCTOBER 31, 2009. FROM THE JOURNAL OF RUTH KNIGHT:
It's strange. Most of Ryder's story felt like a warped fairy tale—
—like one of those dark fantasy novels where there are lepers as well as leprechauns.
It didn't touch me.
The others, I think, felt differently.
OH LORD, IT SEEMS SO SAD. IF JOANNE HAD STAYED BEHIND--
SHE STILL MIGHT HAVE DIED. THE BLACK DEATH SPREAD EVERY-WHERE, JANET. IT JUST REACHED SOME PLACES EARLIER THAN OTHERS.
BUT IF SHE'D KNOWN EXACTLY WHEN AND WHERE THE PLAGUE WOULD STRIKE NEXT, SHE MIGHT HAVE STAYED ONE STEP AHEAD.
UNLESS KNOWING HER FATE DIDN'T MEAN SHE COULD DO ANYTHING TO CHANGE IT.
WHICH IS IT, RYDER? IF THAT BOOK OF YOURS DOES PREDICT OUR FUTURES, CAN WE DO ANYTHING TO CHANGE WHAT'S BEEN WRITTEN?
boom boom boom boom
WELL, I...
Just then, like in an old horror movie, came the knocking at the door.

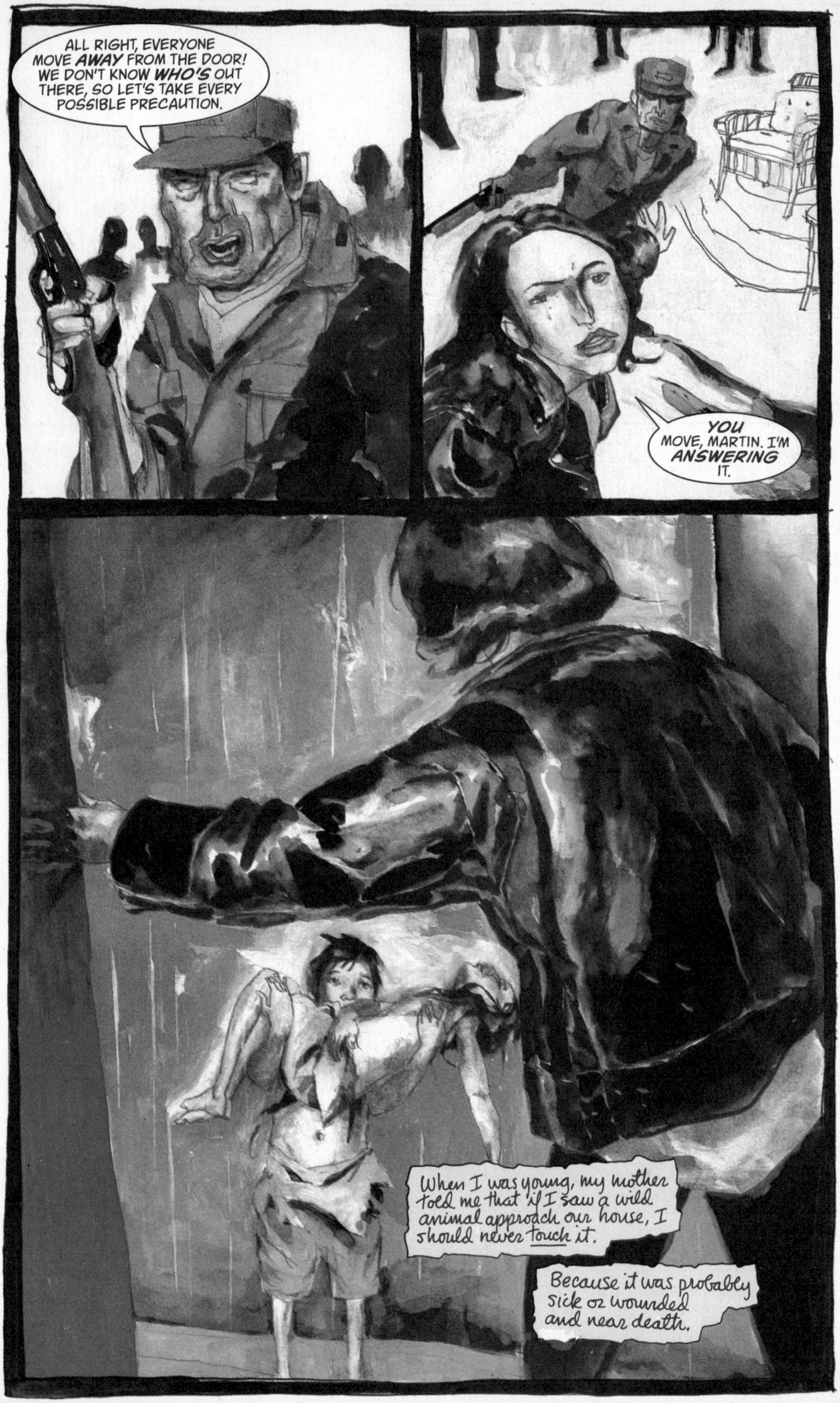
ALL RIGHT, EVERYONE MOVE AWAY FROM THE DOOR! WE DON'T KNOW WHO'S OUT THERE, SO LET'S TAKE EVERY POSSIBLE PRECAUTION.
YOU MOVE, MARTIN. I'M ANSWERING IT.
When I was young, my mother told me that if I saw a wild animal approach our house, I should never touch it.
Because it was probably sick or wounded and near death.

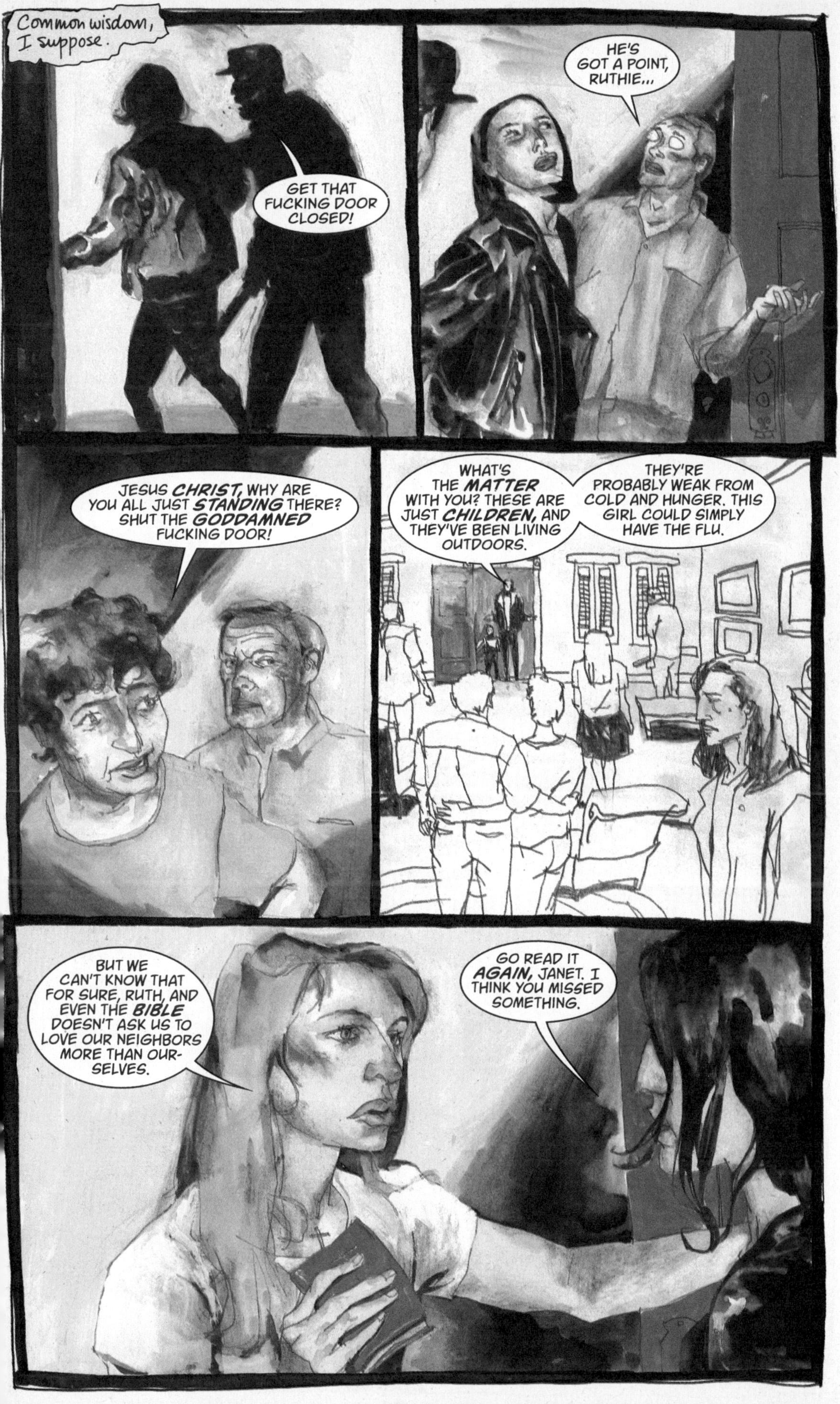
Common wisdom, I suppose.
GET THAT FUCKING DOOR CLOSED!
HE'S GOT A POINT, RUTHIE...
JESUS CHRIST, WHY ARE YOU ALL JUST STANDING THERE? SHUT THE GODDAMNED FUCKING DOOR!
WHAT'S THE MATTER WITH YOU? THESE ARE JUST CHILDREN, AND THEY'VE BEEN LIVING OUTDOORS.
THEY'RE PROBABLY WEAK FROM COLD AND HUNGER. THIS GIRL COULD SIMPLY HAVE THE FLU.
BUT WE CAN'T KNOW THAT FOR SURE, RUTH, AND EVEN THE BIBLE DOESN'T ASK US TO LOVE OUR NEIGHBORS MORE THAN OUR-SELVES.
GO READ IT AGAIN, JANET. I THINK YOU MISSED SOMETHING.

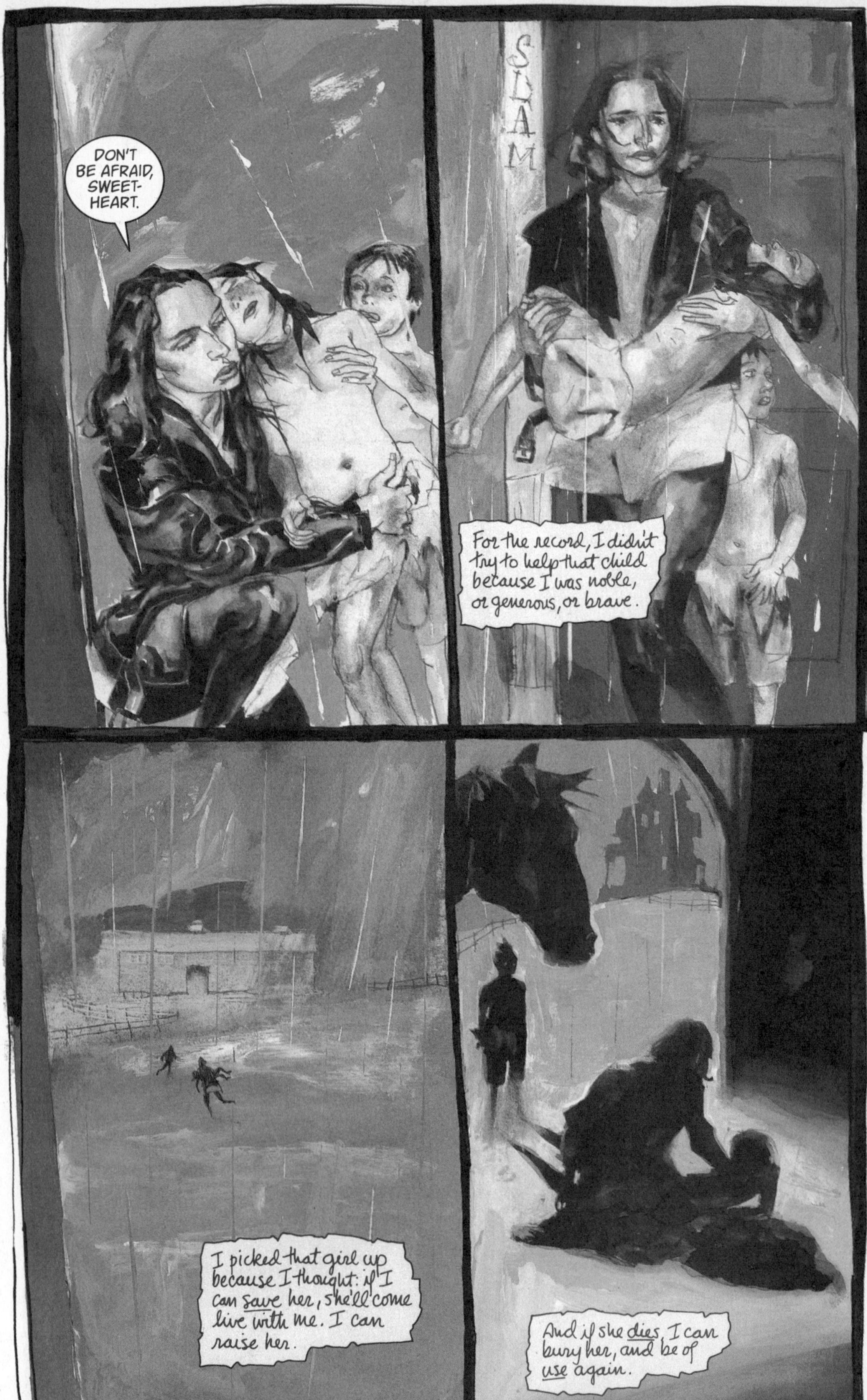
DON'T BE AFRAID, SWEET-HEART.
SLAM
For the record, I didn't try to help that child because I was noble, or generous, or brave.
I picked that girl up because I thought: if I can save her, she'll come live with me. I can raise her.
And if she dies, I can bury her, and be of use again.

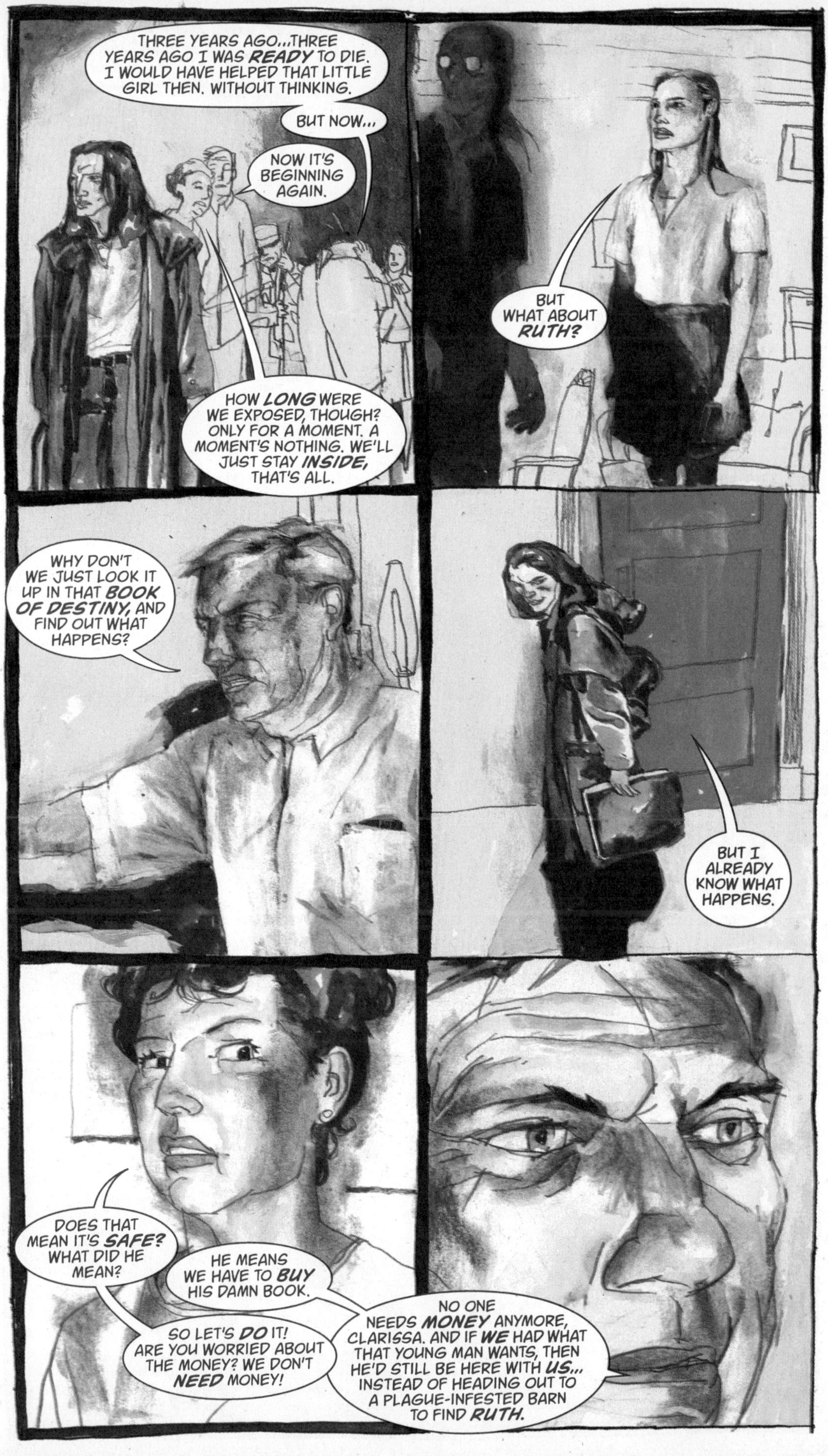
THREE YEARS AGO...THREE YEARS AGO I WAS READY TO DIE. I WOULD HAVE HELPED THAT LITTLE GIRL THEN. WITHOUT THINKING.
BUT NOW...
NOW IT'S BEGINNING AGAIN.
HOW LONG WERE WE EXPOSED, THOUGH? ONLY FOR A MOMENT. A MOMENT'S NOTHING. WE'LL JUST STAY INSIDE, THAT'S ALL.
BUT WHAT ABOUT RUTH?
WHY DON'T WE JUST LOOK IT UP IN THAT BOOK OF DESTINY, AND FIND OUT WHAT HAPPENS?
BUT I ALREADY KNOW WHAT HAPPENS.
DOES THAT MEAN IT'S SAFE? WHAT DID HE MEAN?
HE MEANS WE HAVE TO BUY HIS DAMN BOOK.
SO LET'S DO IT! ARE YOU WORRIED ABOUT THE MONEY? WE DON'T NEED MONEY!
NO ONE NEEDS MONEY ANYMORE, CLARISSA. AND IF WE HAD WHAT THAT YOUNG MAN WANTS, THEN HE'D STILL BE HERE WITH US... INSTEAD OF HEADING OUT TO A PLAGUE-INFESTED BARN TO FIND RUTH.

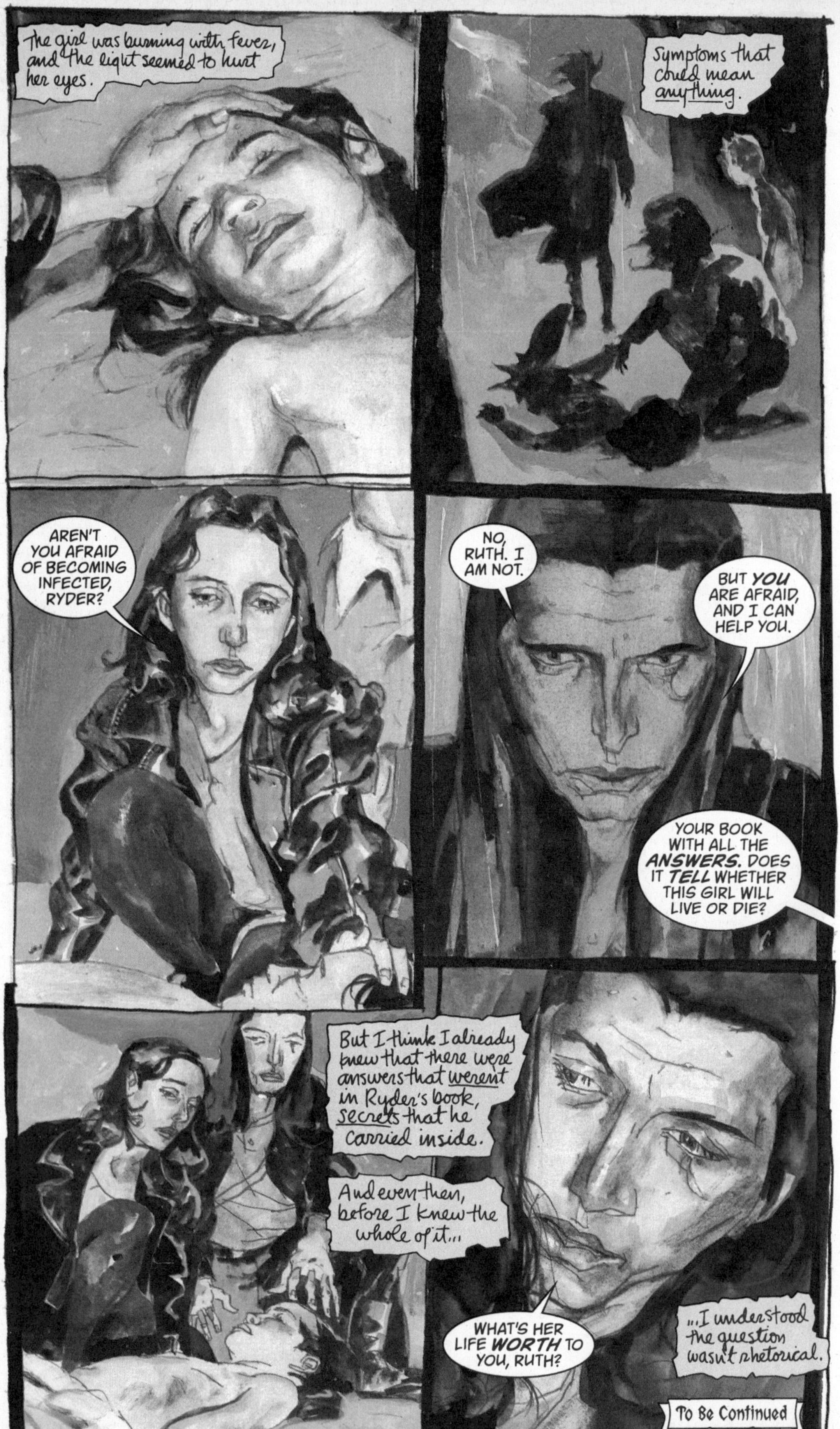
The girl was burning with fever, and the light seemed to hurt her eyes.
Symptoms that could mean anything.
AREN'T YOU AFRAID OF BECOMING INFECTED, RYDER?
NO, RUTH. I AM NOT.
BUT YOU ARE AFRAID, AND I CAN HELP YOU.
YOUR BOOK WITH ALL THE ANSWERS. DOES IT TELL WHETHER THIS GIRL WILL LIVE OR DIE?
But I think I already knew that there were answers that weren't in Ryder's book, secrets that he carried inside.
And even then, before I knew the whole of it...
WHAT'S HER LIFE WORTH TO YOU, RUTH?
...I understood the question wasn't rhetorical.
To Be Continued

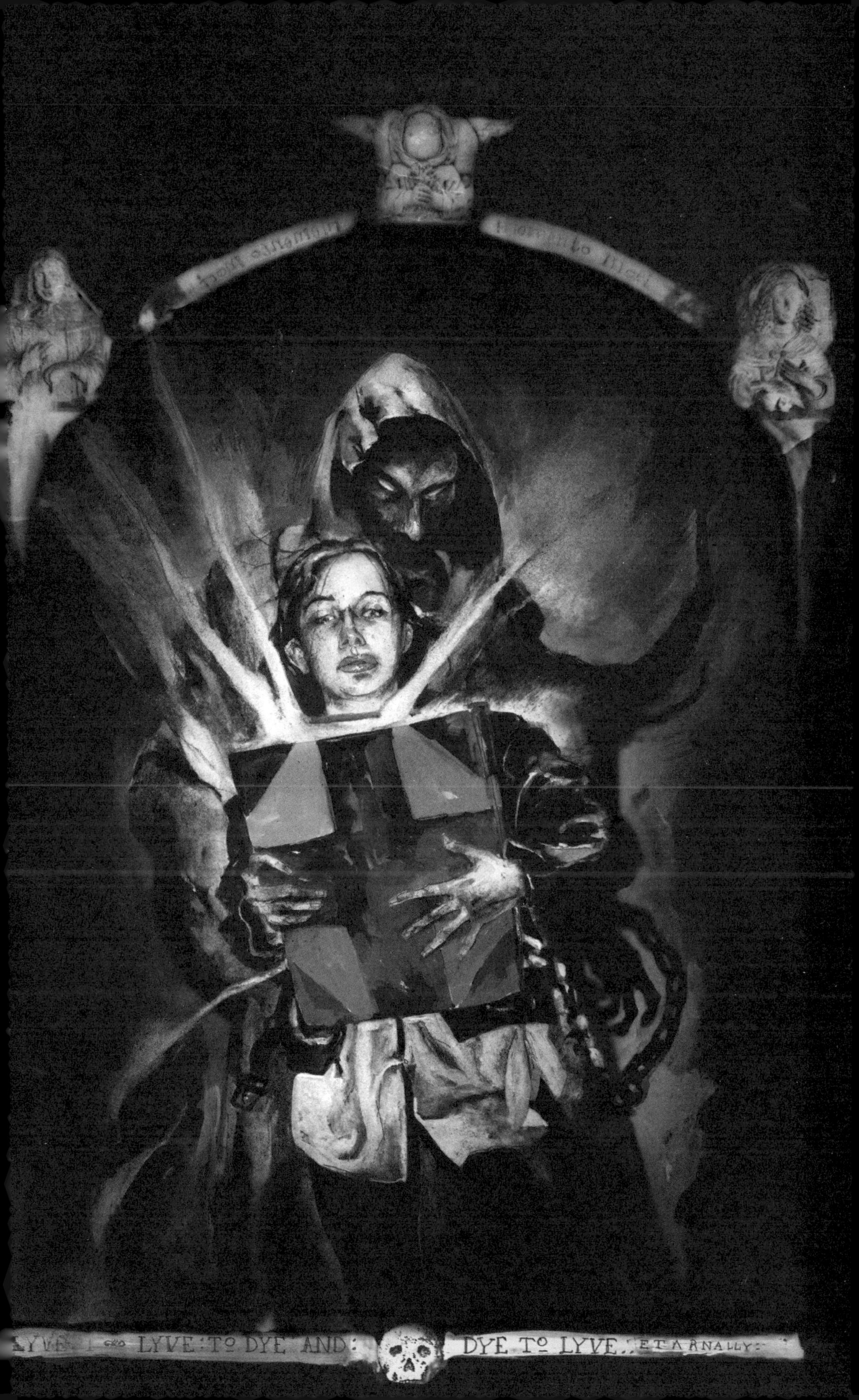
LYVE TO DYE AND:
DYE TO LYVE.: ETARNALLY:

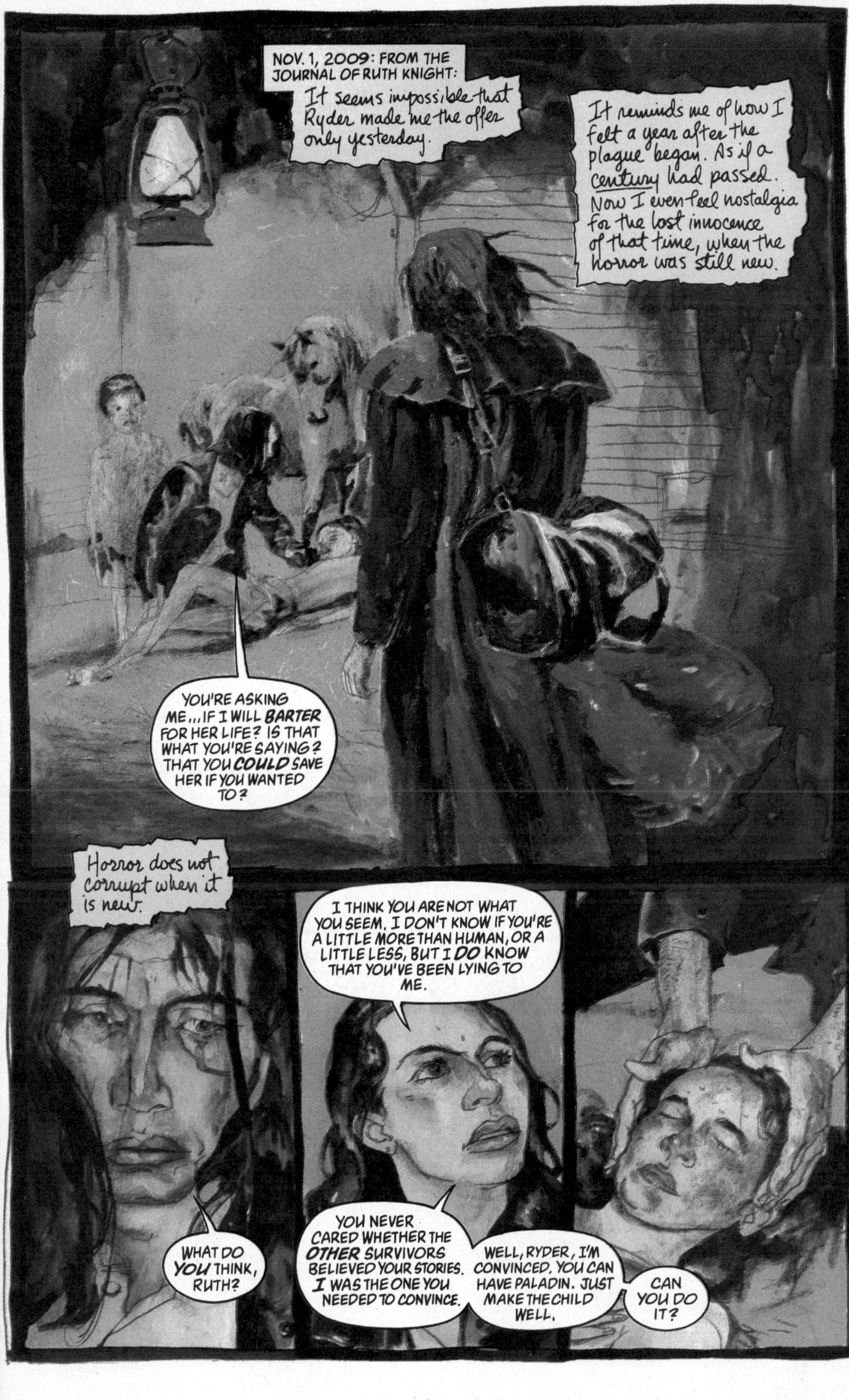
NOV. 1, 2009: FROM THE JOURNAL OF RUTH KNIGHT:
It seems impossible that Ryder made me the offer only yesterday.
It reminds me of how I felt a year after the plague began. As if a century had passed. Now I even feel nostalgia for the lost innocence of that time, when the horror was still new.
YOU'RE ASKING ME... IF I WILL BARTER FOR HER LIFE? IS THAT WHAT YOU'RE SAYING? THAT YOU COULD SAVE HER IF YOU WANTED TO?
Horror does not corrupt when it is new.
WHAT DO YOU THINK, RUTH?
I THINK YOU ARE NOT WHAT YOU SEEM. I DON'T KNOW IF YOU'RE A LITTLE MORE THAN HUMAN, OR A LITTLE LESS, BUT I DO KNOW THAT YOU'VE BEEN LYING TO ME.
YOU NEVER CARED WHETHER THE OTHER SURVIVORS BELIEVED YOUR STORIES. I WAS THE ONE YOU NEEDED TO CONVINCE.
WELL, RYDER, I'M CONVINCED. YOU CAN HAVE PALADIN. JUST MAKE THE CHILD WELL.
CAN YOU DO IT?

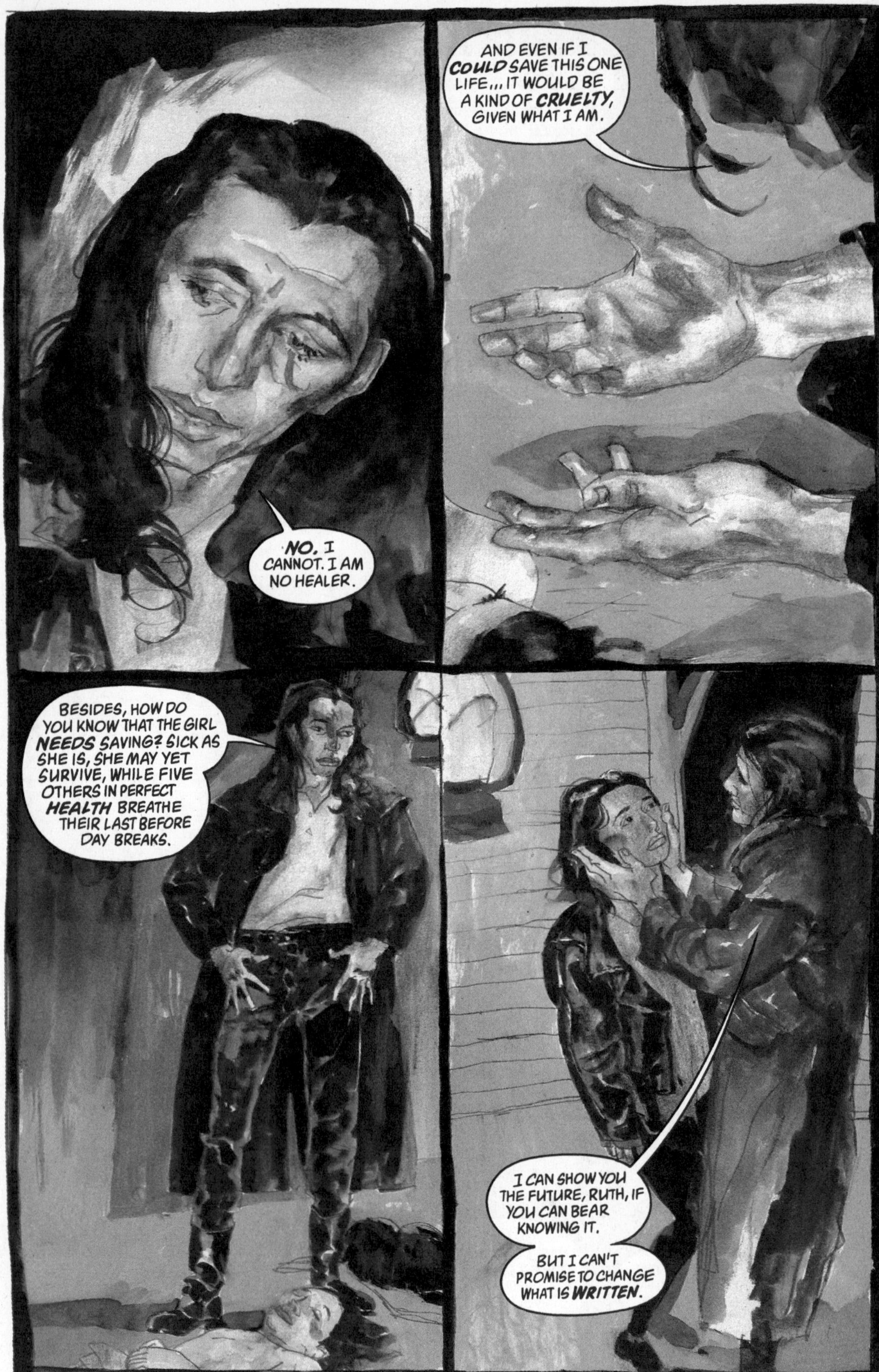
NO. I CANNOT. I AM NO HEALER.
AND EVEN IF I COULD SAVE THIS ONE LIFE... IT WOULD BE A KIND OF CRUELTY, GIVEN WHAT I AM.
BESIDES, HOW DO YOU KNOW THAT THE GIRL NEEDS SAVING? SICK AS SHE IS, SHE MAY YET SURVIVE, WHILE FIVE OTHERS IN PERFECT HEALTH BREATHE THEIR LAST BEFORE DAY BREAKS.
I CAN SHOW YOU THE FUTURE, RUTH, IF YOU CAN BEAR KNOWING IT.
BUT I CAN'T PROMISE TO CHANGE WHAT IS WRITTEN.

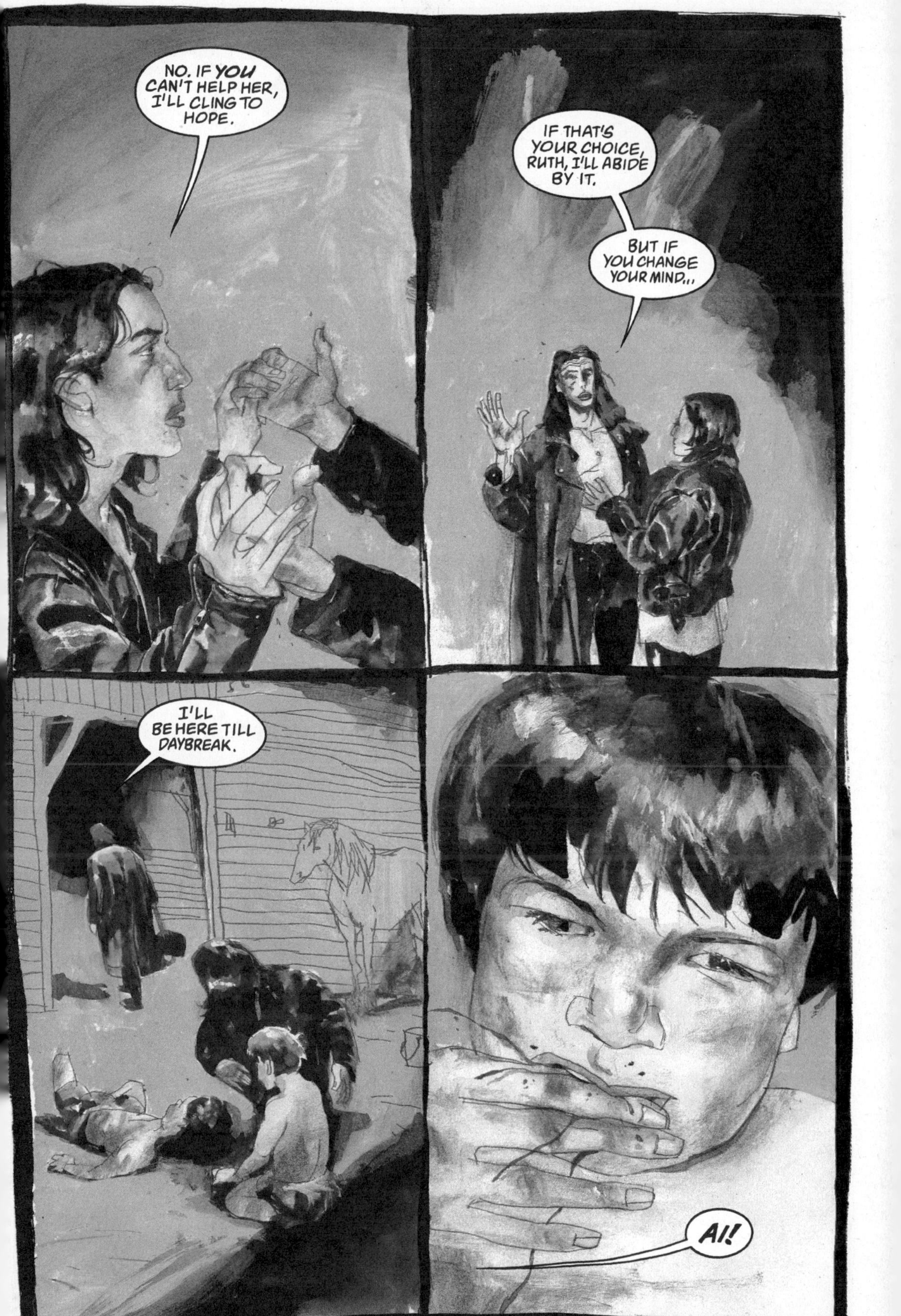
NO. IF YOU CAN'T HELP HER, I'LL CLING TO HOPE.
IF THAT'S YOUR CHOICE, RUTH, I'LL ABIDE BY IT.
BUT IF YOU CHANGE YOUR MIND...
I'LL BE HERE TILL DAYBREAK.
AI!

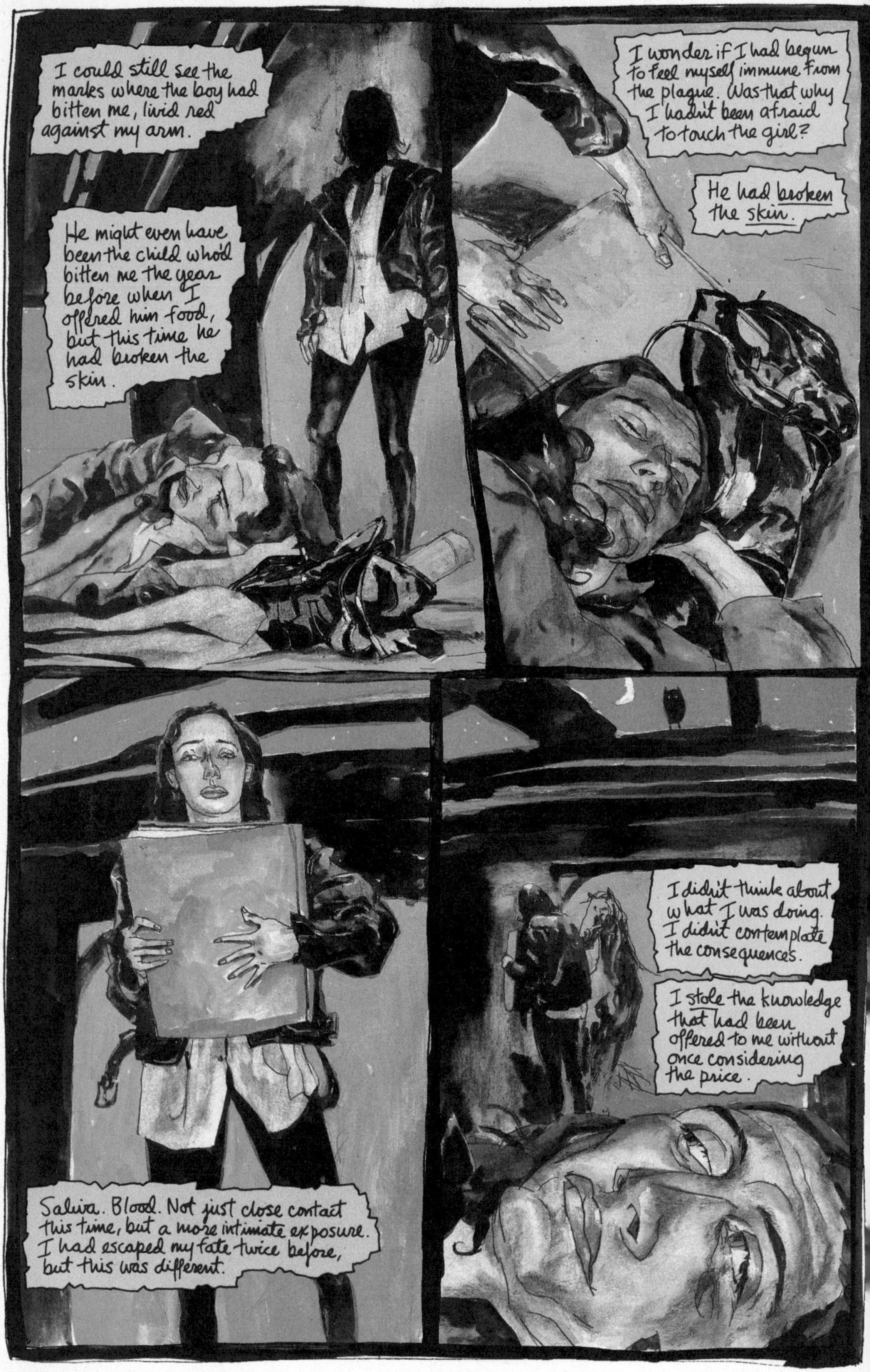
I could still see the marks where the boy had bitten me, livid red against my arm.
He might even have been the child who'd bitten me the year before when I offered him food, but this time he had broken the skin.
I wonder if I had begun to feel myself immune from the plague. Was that why I hadn't been afraid to touch the girl?
He had broken the skin.
Saliva. Blood. Not just close contact this time, but a more intimate exposure. I had escaped my fate twice before, but this was different.
I didn't think about what I was doing. I didn't contemplate the consequences.
I stole the knowledge that had been offered to me without once considering the price.

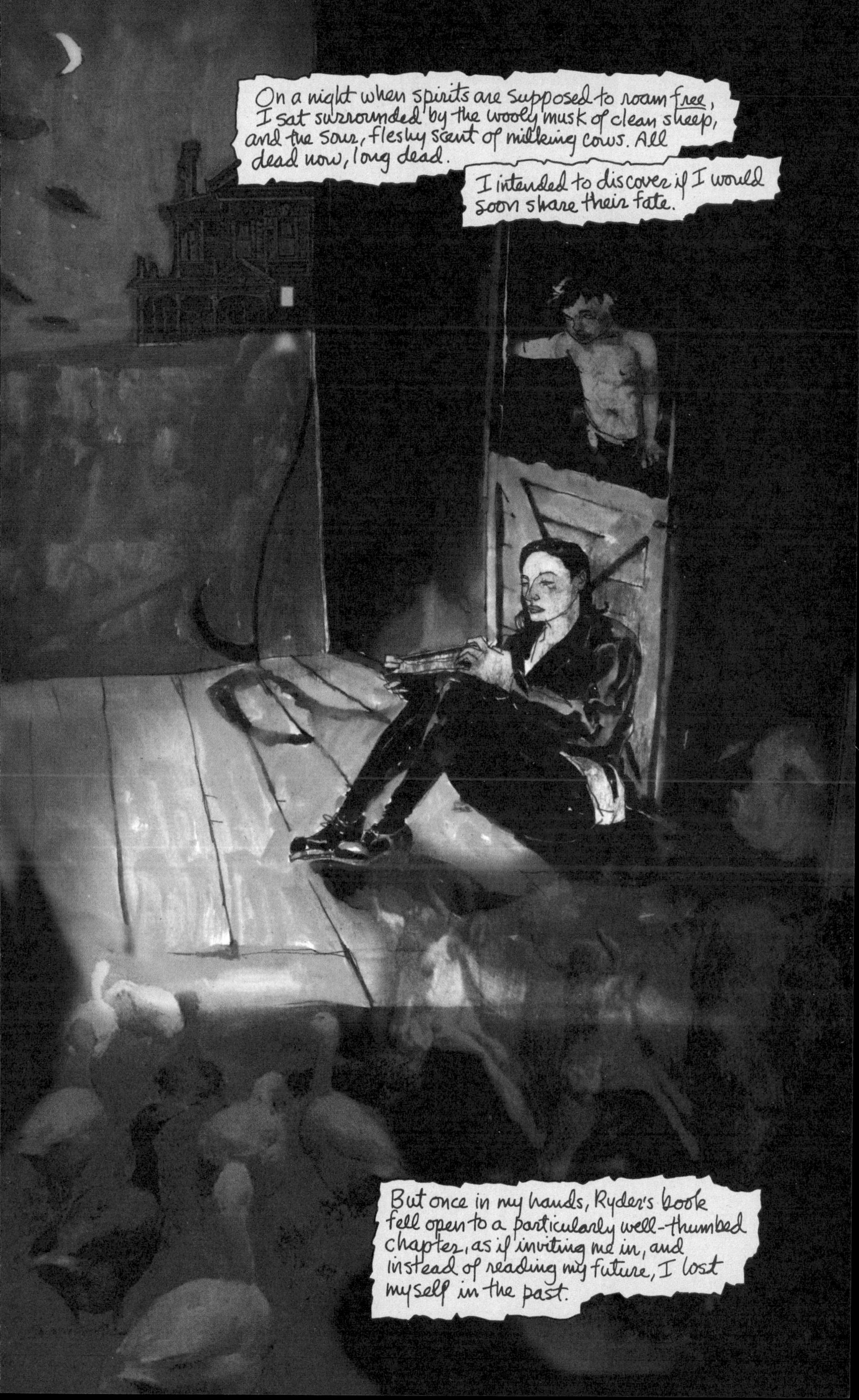
On a night when spirits are supposed to roam free, I sat surrounded by the wooly musk of clean sheep, and the sour, fleshy scent of milking cows. All dead now, long dead.
I intended to discover if I would soon share their fate.
But once in my hands, Ryder's book fell open to a particularly well-thumbed chapter, as if inviting me in, and instead of reading my future, I lost myself in the past.

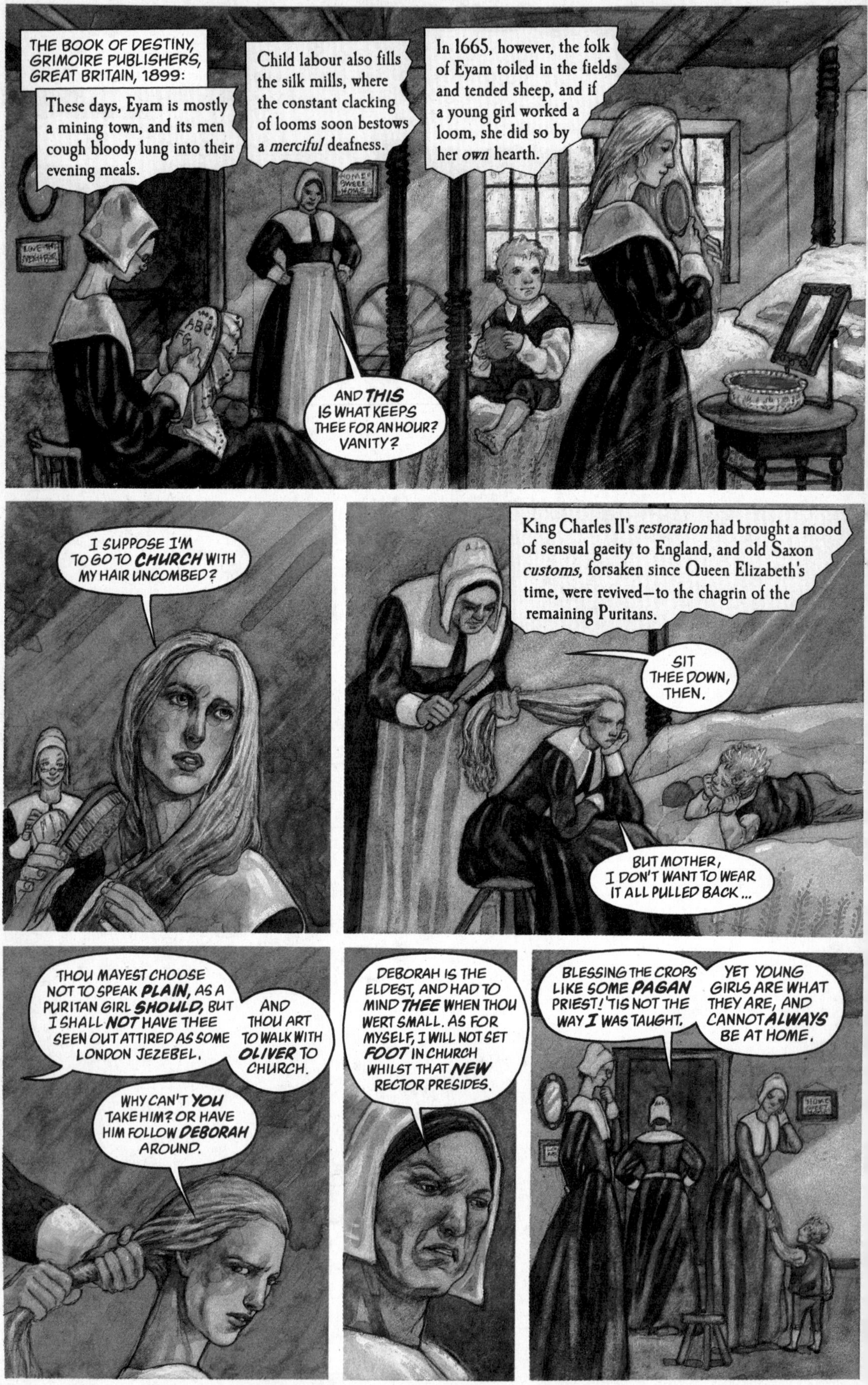
THE BOOK OF DESTINY, GRIMOIRE PUBLISHERS, GREAT BRITAIN, 1899:
These days, Eyam is mostly a mining town, and its men cough bloody lung into their evening meals.
Child labour also fills the silk mills, where the constant clacking of looms soon bestows a *merciful* deafness.
In 1665, however, the folk of Eyam toiled in the fields and tended sheep, and if a young girl worked a loom, she did so by her *own* hearth.
AND **THIS** IS WHAT KEEPS THEE FOR AN HOUR? VANITY?
I SUPPOSE I'M TO GO TO **CHURCH** WITH MY HAIR UNCOMBED?
King Charles II's *restoration* had brought a mood of sensual gaeity to England, and old Saxon *customs,* forsaken since Queen Elizabeth's time, were revived—to the chagrin of the remaining Puritans.
SIT THEE DOWN, THEN.
BUT MOTHER, I DON'T WANT TO WEAR IT ALL PULLED BACK...
THOU MAYEST CHOOSE NOT TO SPEAK **PLAIN,** AS A PURITAN GIRL **SHOULD,** BUT I SHALL **NOT** HAVE THEE SEEN OUT ATTIRED AS SOME LONDON JEZEBEL.
AND THOU ART TO WALK WITH **OLIVER** TO CHURCH.
WHY CAN'T **YOU** TAKE HIM? OR HAVE HIM FOLLOW **DEBORAH** AROUND.
DEBORAH IS THE ELDEST, AND HAD TO MIND **THEE** WHEN THOU WERT SMALL. AS FOR MYSELF, I WILL NOT SET **FOOT** IN CHURCH WHILST THAT **NEW** RECTOR PRESIDES.
BLESSING THE CROPS LIKE SOME **PAGAN** PRIEST! 'TIS NOT THE WAY **I** WAS TAUGHT.
YET YOUNG GIRLS ARE WHAT THEY ARE, AND CANNOT **ALWAYS** BE AT HOME.

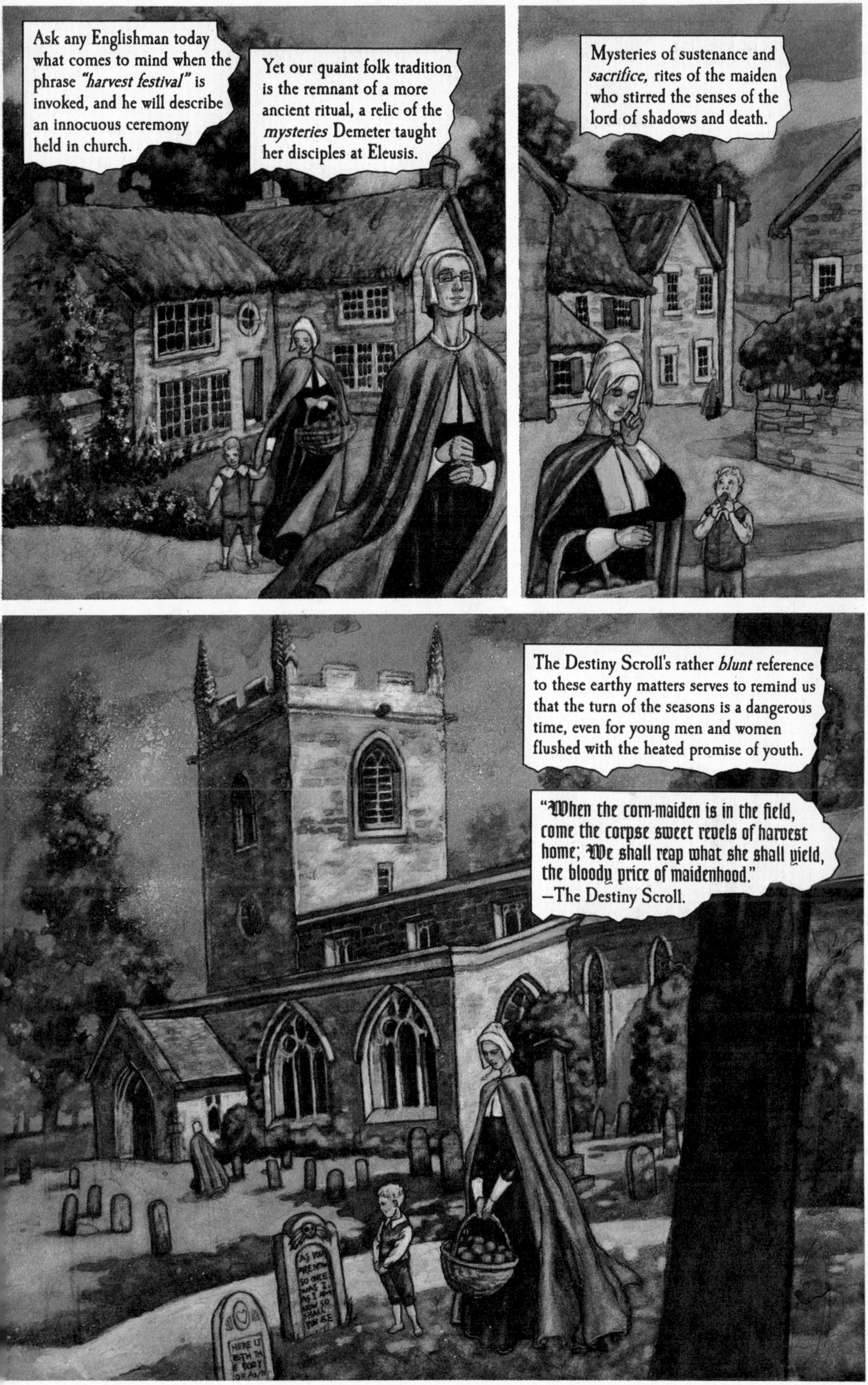

Ask any Englishman today what comes to mind when the phrase *"harvest festival"* is invoked, and he will describe an innocuous ceremony held in church.
Yet our quaint folk tradition is the remnant of a more ancient ritual, a relic of the *mysteries* Demeter taught her disciples at Eleusis.
Mysteries of sustenance and *sacrifice,* rites of the maiden who stirred the senses of the lord of shadows and death.
The Destiny Scroll's rather *blunt* reference to these earthy matters serves to remind us that the turn of the seasons is a dangerous time, even for young men and women flushed with the heated promise of youth.
"When the corn-maiden is in the field, come the corpse sweet revels of harvest home; We shall reap what she shall yield, the bloody price of maidenhood."
—The Destiny Scroll.

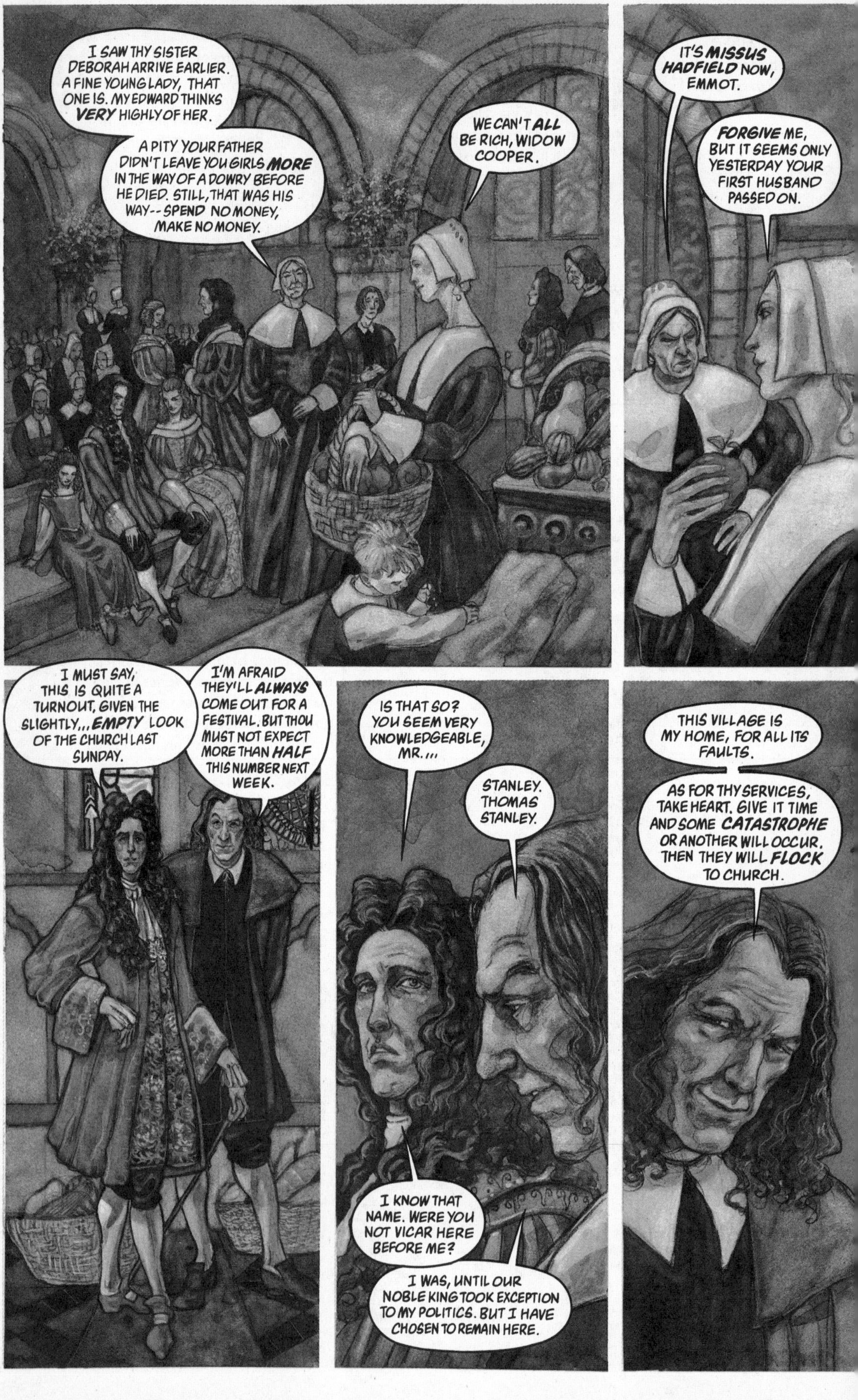
I SAW THY SISTER DEBORAH ARRIVE EARLIER. A FINE YOUNG LADY, THAT ONE IS. MY EDWARD THINKS VERY HIGHLY OF HER.
A PITY YOUR FATHER DIDN'T LEAVE YOU GIRLS MORE IN THE WAY OF A DOWRY BEFORE HE DIED. STILL, THAT WAS HIS WAY-- SPEND NO MONEY, MAKE NO MONEY.
WE CAN'T ALL BE RICH, WIDOW COOPER.
IT'S MISSUS HADFIELD NOW, EMMOT.
FORGIVE ME, BUT IT SEEMS ONLY YESTERDAY YOUR FIRST HUSBAND PASSED ON.
I MUST SAY, THIS IS QUITE A TURNOUT, GIVEN THE SLIGHTLY... EMPTY LOOK OF THE CHURCH LAST SUNDAY.
I'M AFRAID THEY'LL ALWAYS COME OUT FOR A FESTIVAL. BUT THOU MUST NOT EXPECT MORE THAN HALF THIS NUMBER NEXT WEEK.
IS THAT SO? YOU SEEM VERY KNOWLEDGEABLE, MR....
STANLEY. THOMAS STANLEY.
I KNOW THAT NAME. WERE YOU NOT VICAR HERE BEFORE ME?
I WAS, UNTIL OUR NOBLE KING TOOK EXCEPTION TO MY POLITICS. BUT I HAVE CHOSEN TO REMAIN HERE.
THIS VILLAGE IS MY HOME, FOR ALL ITS FAULTS.
AS FOR THY SERVICES, TAKE HEART. GIVE IT TIME AND SOME CATASTROPHE OR ANOTHER WILL OCCUR. THEN THEY WILL FLOCK TO CHURCH.

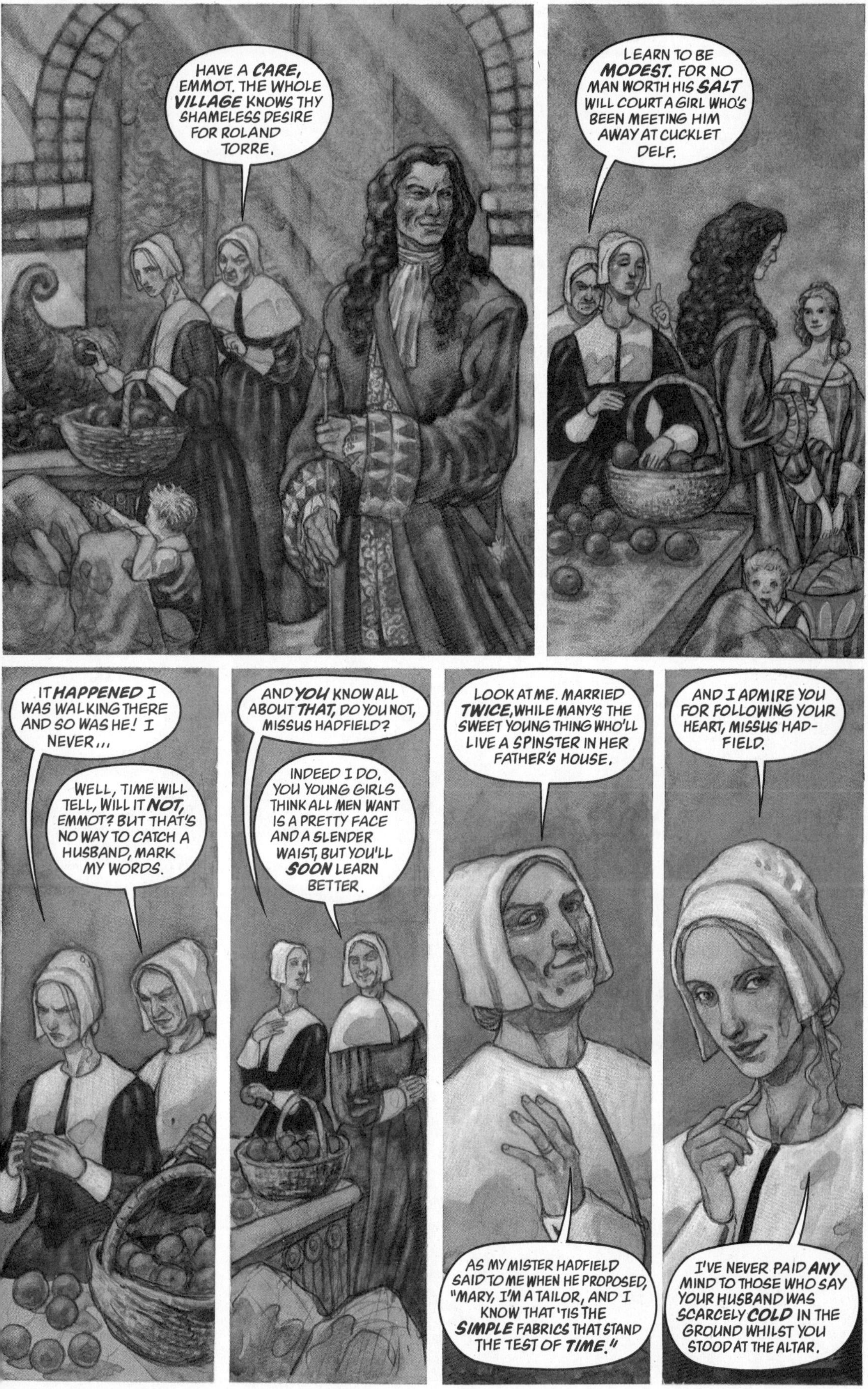
HAVE A CARE, EMMOT. THE WHOLE VILLAGE KNOWS THY SHAMELESS DESIRE FOR ROLAND TORRE.
LEARN TO BE MODEST. FOR NO MAN WORTH HIS SALT WILL COURT A GIRL WHO'S BEEN MEETING HIM AWAY AT CUCKLET DELF.
IT HAPPENED I WAS WALKING THERE AND SO WAS HE! I NEVER...
WELL, TIME WILL TELL, WILL IT NOT, EMMOT? BUT THAT'S NO WAY TO CATCH A HUSBAND, MARK MY WORDS.
AND YOU KNOW ALL ABOUT THAT, DO YOU NOT, MISSUS HADFIELD?
INDEED I DO. YOU YOUNG GIRLS THINK ALL MEN WANT IS A PRETTY FACE AND A SLENDER WAIST, BUT YOU'LL SOON LEARN BETTER.
LOOK AT ME. MARRIED TWICE, WHILE MANY'S THE SWEET YOUNG THING WHO'LL LIVE A SPINSTER IN HER FATHER'S HOUSE.
AS MY MISTER HADFIELD SAID TO ME WHEN HE PROPOSED, "MARY, I'M A TAILOR, AND I KNOW THAT 'TIS THE SIMPLE FABRICS THAT STAND THE TEST OF TIME."
AND I ADMIRE YOU FOR FOLLOWING YOUR HEART, MISSUS HADFIELD.
I'VE NEVER PAID ANY MIND TO THOSE WHO SAY YOUR HUSBAND WAS SCARCELY COLD IN THE GROUND WHILST YOU STOOD AT THE ALTAR.

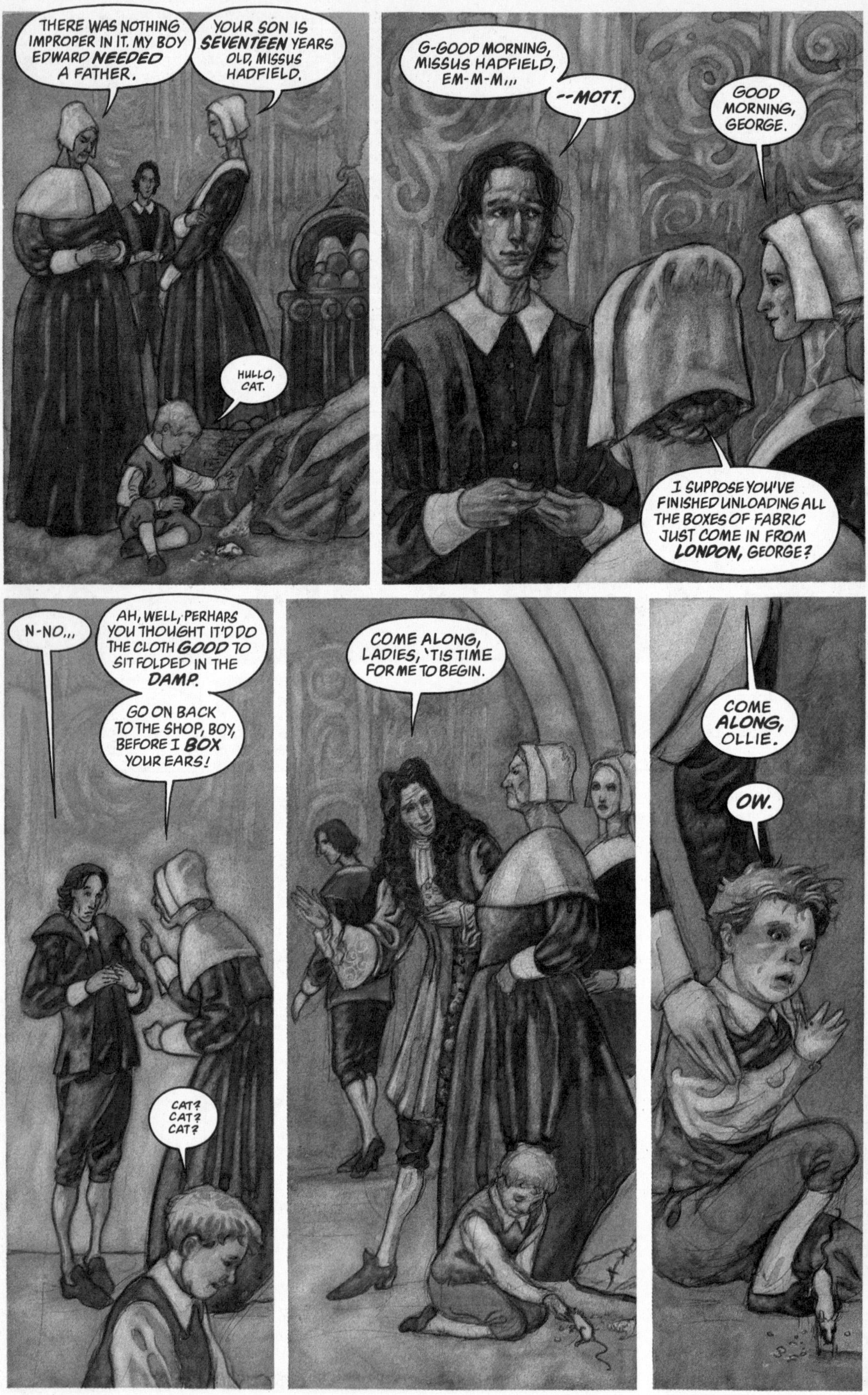
THERE WAS NOTHING IMPROPER IN IT. MY BOY EDWARD **NEEDED** A FATHER.
YOUR SON IS **SEVENTEEN** YEARS OLD, MISSUS HADFIELD.
HULLO, CAT.
G-GOOD MORNING, MISSUS HADFIELD, EM-M-M...
--MOTT.
GOOD MORNING, GEORGE.
I SUPPOSE YOU'VE FINISHED UNLOADING ALL THE BOXES OF FABRIC JUST COME IN FROM **LONDON**, GEORGE?
N-NO...
AH, WELL, PERHAPS YOU THOUGHT IT'D DO THE CLOTH **GOOD** TO SIT FOLDED IN THE **DAMP**.
GO ON BACK TO THE SHOP, BOY, BEFORE I **BOX** YOUR EARS!
CAT? CAT? CAT?
COME ALONG, LADIES, 'TIS TIME FOR ME TO BEGIN.
COME **ALONG**, OLLIE.
OW.

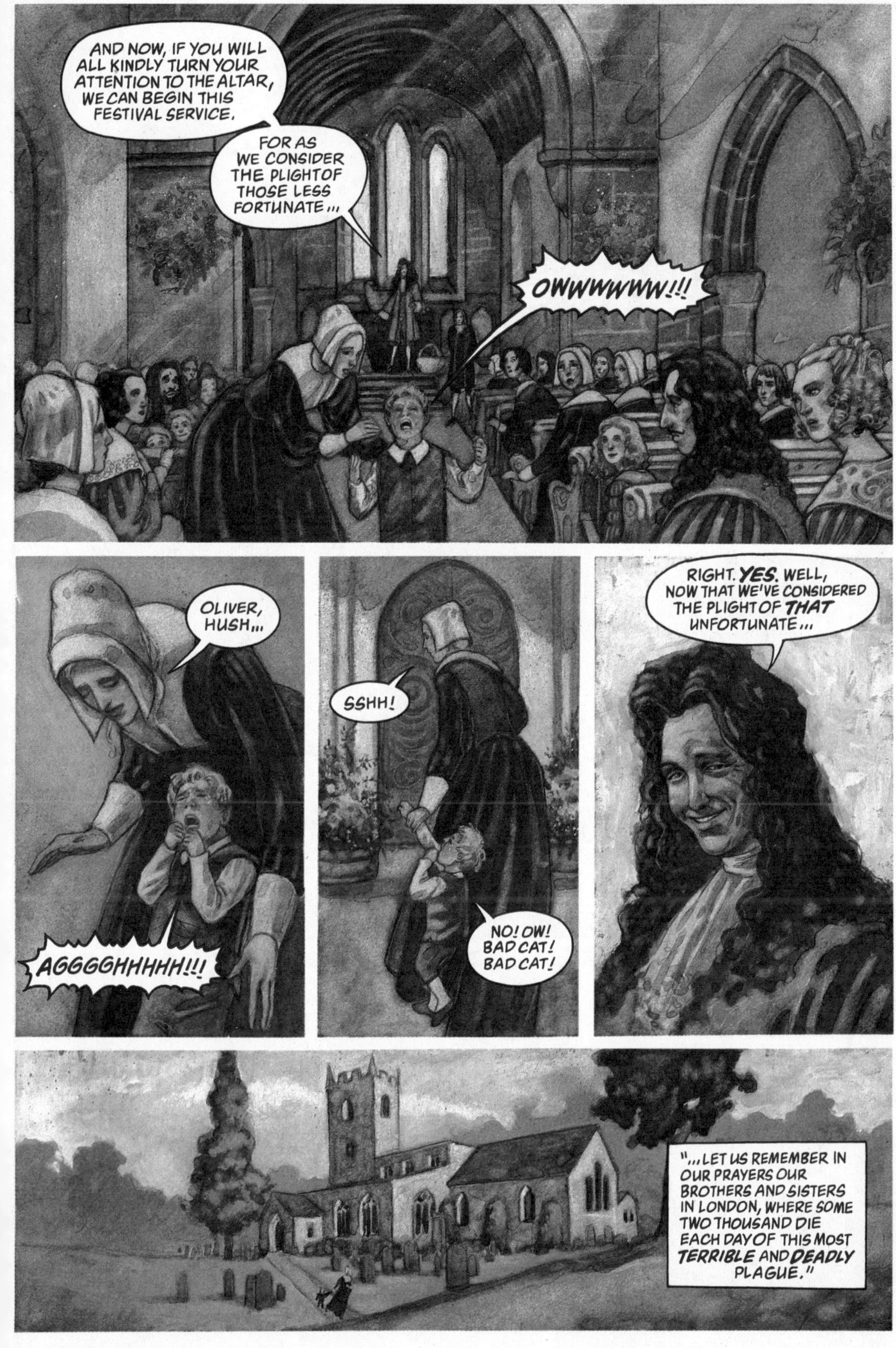
AND NOW, IF YOU WILL ALL KINDLY TURN YOUR ATTENTION TO THE ALTAR, WE CAN BEGIN THIS FESTIVAL SERVICE.
FOR AS WE CONSIDER THE PLIGHT OF THOSE LESS FORTUNATE...
OWWWWWW!!!
OLIVER, HUSH...
AGGGGHHHHH!!!
SSHH!
NO! OW! BAD CAT! BAD CAT!
RIGHT. **YES.** WELL, NOW THAT WE'VE CONSIDERED THE PLIGHT OF **THAT** UNFORTUNATE...
"...LET US REMEMBER IN OUR PRAYERS OUR BROTHERS AND SISTERS IN LONDON, WHERE SOME TWO THOUSAND DIE EACH DAY OF THIS MOST **TERRIBLE** AND **DEADLY** PLAGUE."

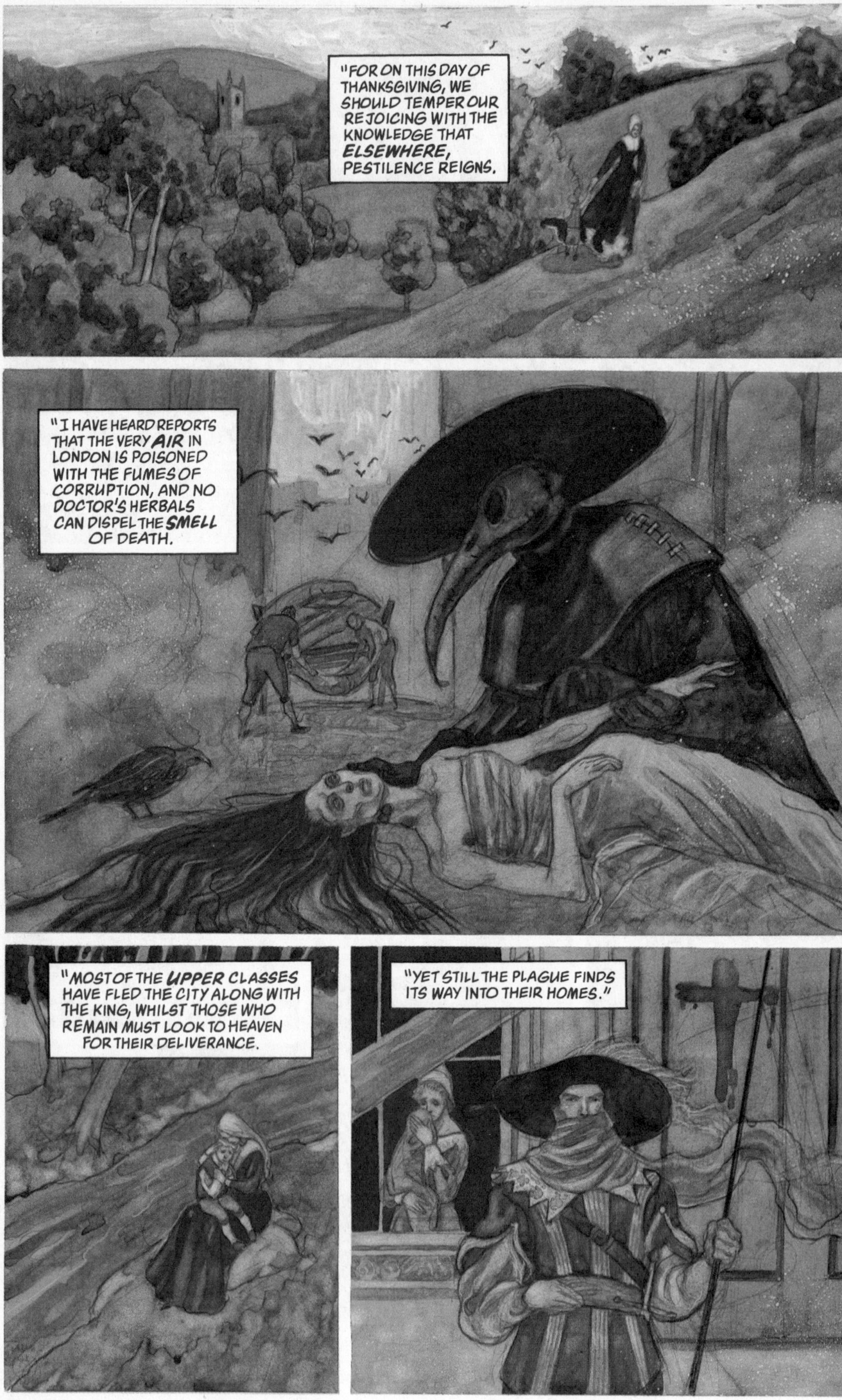
"FOR ON THIS DAY OF THANKSGIVING, WE SHOULD TEMPER OUR REJOICING WITH THE KNOWLEDGE THAT ELSEWHERE, PESTILENCE REIGNS.
"I HAVE HEARD REPORTS THAT THE VERY AIR IN LONDON IS POISONED WITH THE FUMES OF CORRUPTION, AND NO DOCTOR'S HERBALS CAN DISPEL THE SMELL OF DEATH.
"MOST OF THE UPPER CLASSES HAVE FLED THE CITY ALONG WITH THE KING, WHILST THOSE WHO REMAIN MUST LOOK TO HEAVEN FOR THEIR DELIVERANCE.
"YET STILL THE PLAGUE FINDS ITS WAY INTO THEIR HOMES."

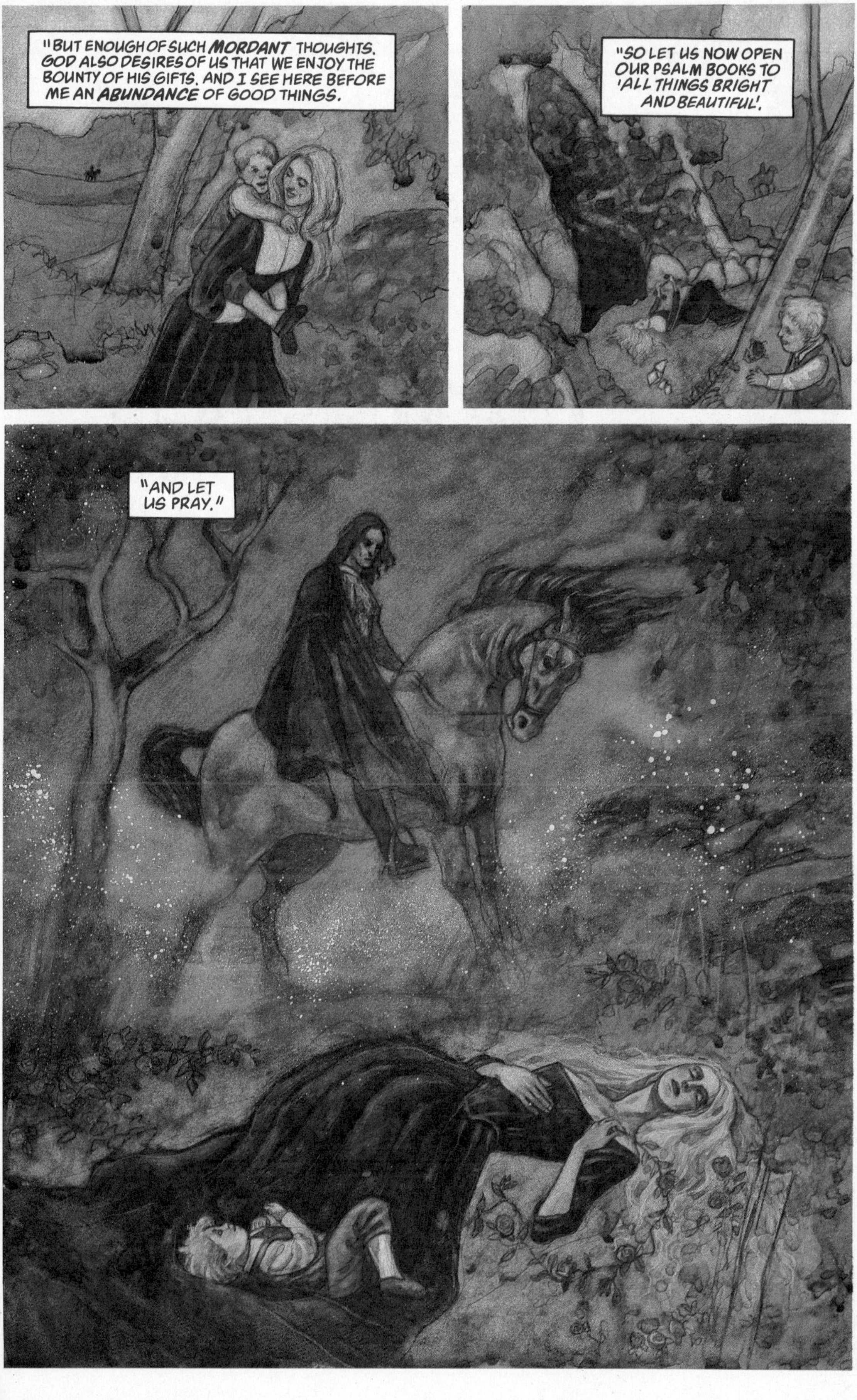
"BUT ENOUGH OF SUCH MORDANT THOUGHTS. GOD ALSO DESIRES OF US THAT WE ENJOY THE BOUNTY OF HIS GIFTS. AND I SEE HERE BEFORE ME AN ABUNDANCE OF GOOD THINGS.
"SO LET US NOW OPEN OUR PSALM BOOKS TO 'ALL THINGS BRIGHT AND BEAUTIFUL'.
"AND LET US PRAY."

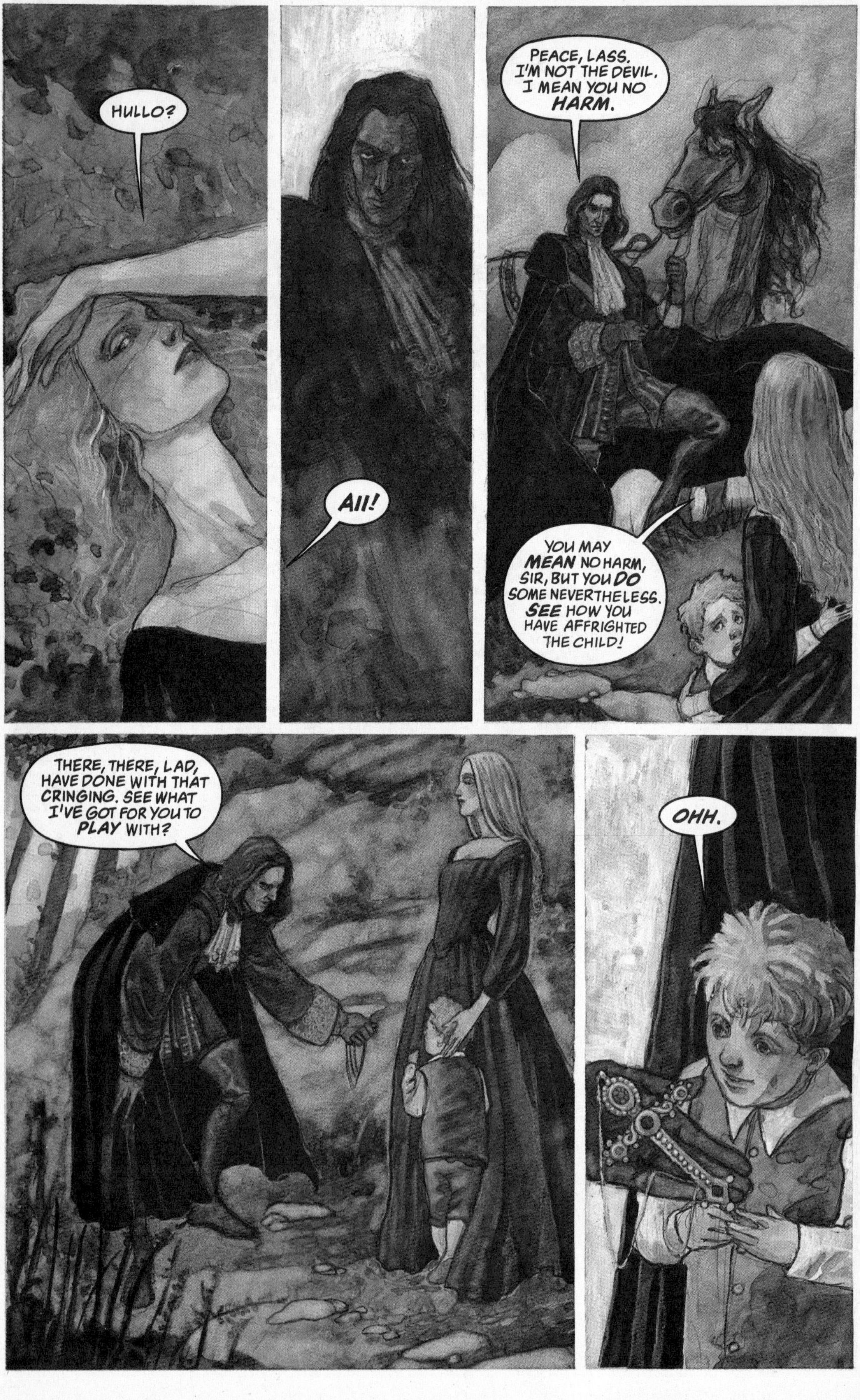
HULLO?
AII!
PEACE, LASS. I'M NOT THE DEVIL. I MEAN YOU NO HARM.
YOU MAY MEAN NO HARM, SIR, BUT YOU DO SOME NEVERTHELESS. SEE HOW YOU HAVE AFFRIGHTED THE CHILD!
THERE, THERE, LAD, HAVE DONE WITH THAT CRINGING. SEE WHAT I'VE GOT FOR YOU TO PLAY WITH?
OHH.

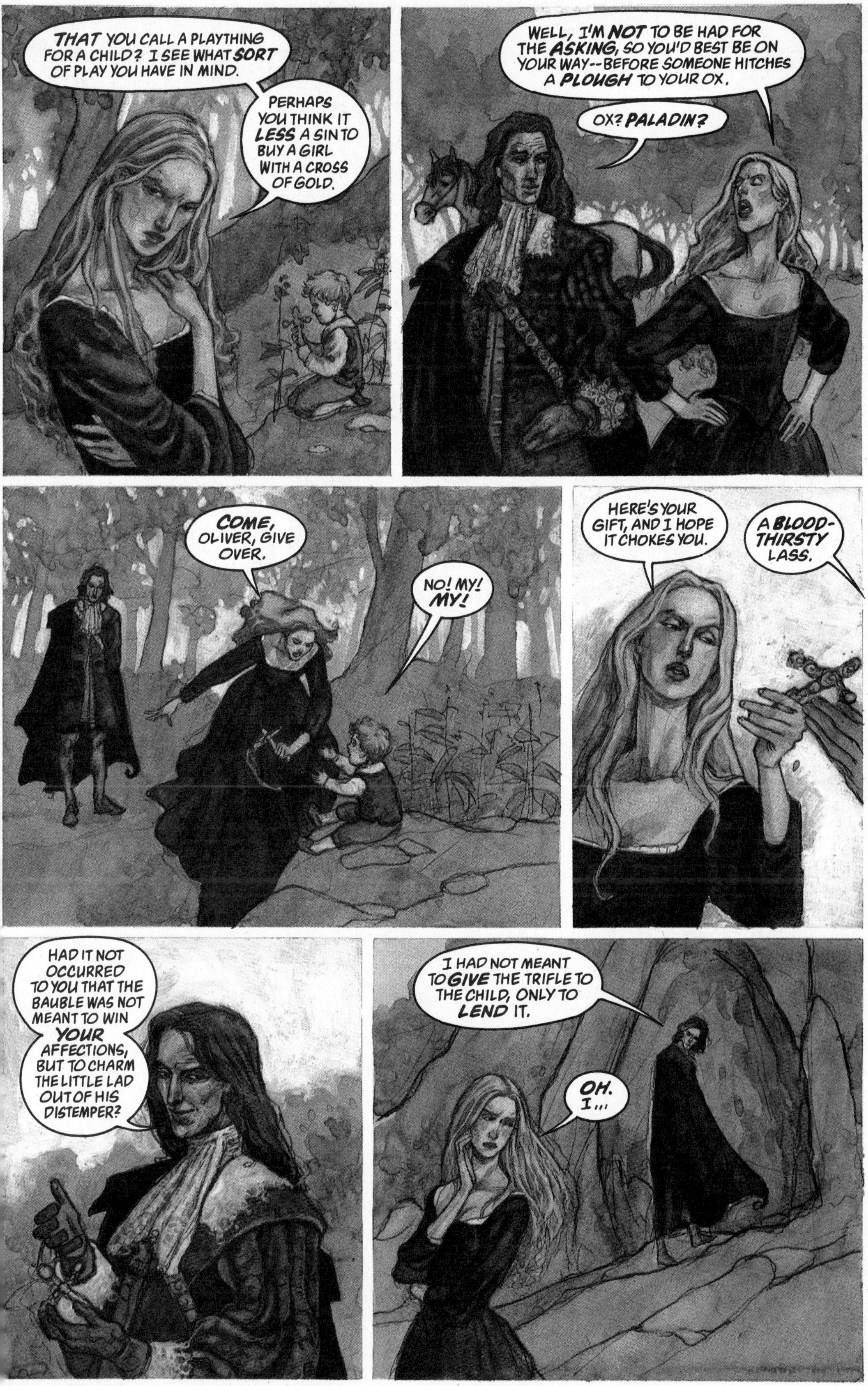
THAT YOU CALL A PLAYTHING FOR A CHILD? I SEE WHAT SORT OF PLAY YOU HAVE IN MIND.
PERHAPS YOU THINK IT LESS A SIN TO BUY A GIRL WITH A CROSS OF GOLD.
WELL, I'M NOT TO BE HAD FOR THE ASKING, SO YOU'D BEST BE ON YOUR WAY--BEFORE SOMEONE HITCHES A PLOUGH TO YOUR OX.
OX? PALADIN?
COME, OLIVER, GIVE OVER.
NO! MY! MY!
HERE'S YOUR GIFT, AND I HOPE IT CHOKES YOU.
A BLOOD-THIRSTY LASS.
HAD IT NOT OCCURRED TO YOU THAT THE BAUBLE WAS NOT MEANT TO WIN YOUR AFFECTIONS, BUT TO CHARM THE LITTLE LAD OUT OF HIS DISTEMPER?
I HAD NOT MEANT TO GIVE THE TRIFLE TO THE CHILD, ONLY TO LEND IT.
OH. I...

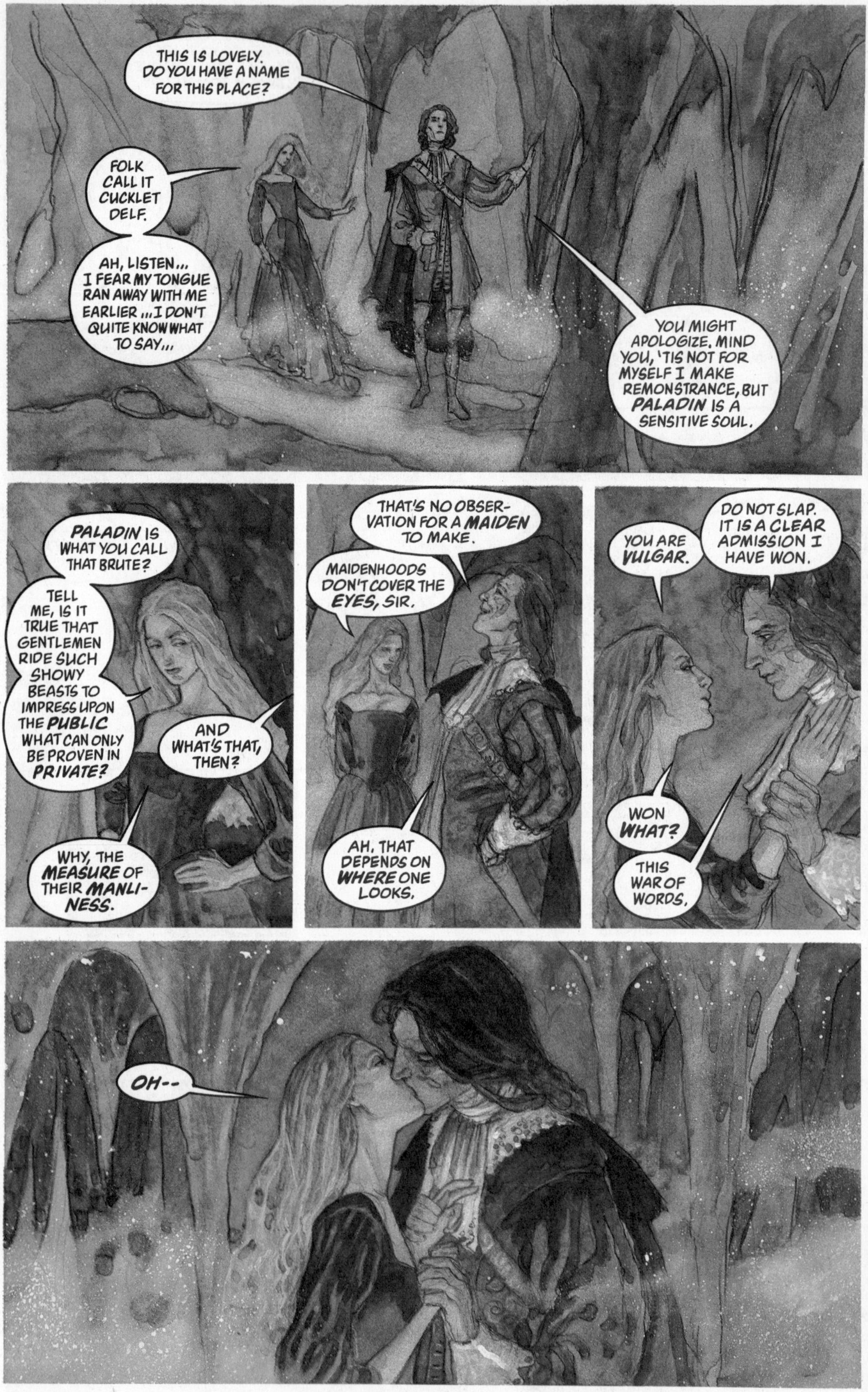
THIS IS LOVELY. DO YOU HAVE A NAME FOR THIS PLACE?
FOLK CALL IT CUCKLET DELF.
AH, LISTEN... I FEAR MY TONGUE RAN AWAY WITH ME EARLIER ...I DON'T QUITE KNOW WHAT TO SAY...
YOU MIGHT APOLOGIZE. MIND YOU, 'TIS NOT FOR MYSELF I MAKE REMONSTRANCE, BUT PALADIN IS A SENSITIVE SOUL.
PALADIN IS WHAT YOU CALL THAT BRUTE?
TELL ME, IS IT TRUE THAT GENTLEMEN RIDE SUCH SHOWY BEASTS TO IMPRESS UPON THE PUBLIC WHAT CAN ONLY BE PROVEN IN PRIVATE?
AND WHAT'S THAT, THEN?
WHY, THE MEASURE OF THEIR MANLINESS.
THAT'S NO OBSERVATION FOR A MAIDEN TO MAKE.
MAIDENHOODS DON'T COVER THE EYES, SIR.
AH, THAT DEPENDS ON WHERE ONE LOOKS.
YOU ARE VULGAR.
DO NOT SLAP. IT IS A CLEAR ADMISSION I HAVE WON.
WON WHAT?
THIS WAR OF WORDS.
OH--

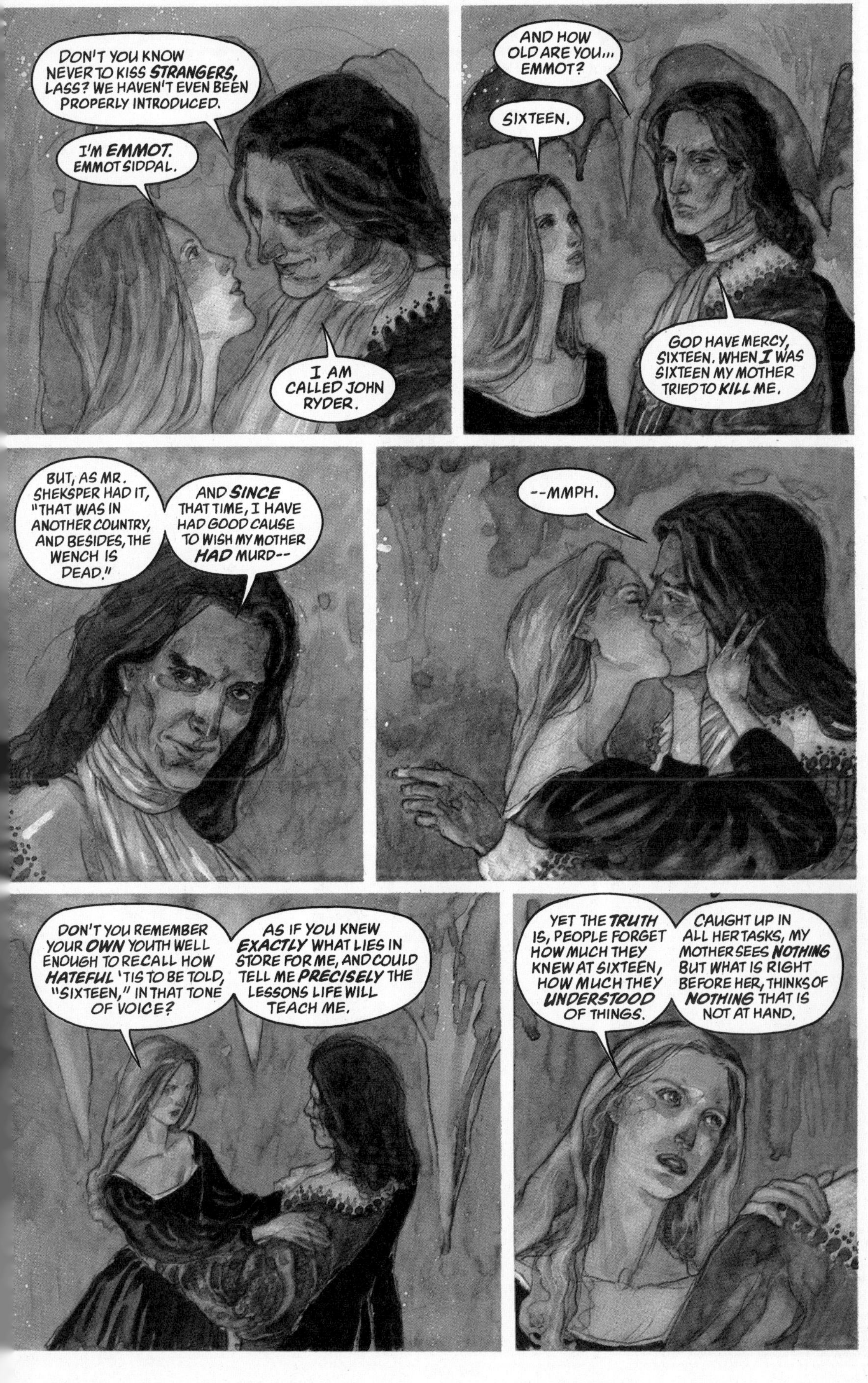
DON'T YOU KNOW NEVER TO KISS STRANGERS, LASS? WE HAVEN'T EVEN BEEN PROPERLY INTRODUCED.
I'M EMMOT. EMMOT SIDDAL.
I AM CALLED JOHN RYDER.
AND HOW OLD ARE YOU... EMMOT?
SIXTEEN.
GOD HAVE MERCY, SIXTEEN. WHEN I WAS SIXTEEN MY MOTHER TRIED TO KILL ME.
BUT, AS MR. SHEKSPER HAD IT, "THAT WAS IN ANOTHER COUNTRY, AND BESIDES, THE WENCH IS DEAD."
AND SINCE THAT TIME, I HAVE HAD GOOD CAUSE TO WISH MY MOTHER HAD MURD--
--MMPH.
DON'T YOU REMEMBER YOUR OWN YOUTH WELL ENOUGH TO RECALL HOW HATEFUL 'TIS TO BE TOLD, "SIXTEEN," IN THAT TONE OF VOICE?
AS IF YOU KNEW EXACTLY WHAT LIES IN STORE FOR ME, AND COULD TELL ME PRECISELY THE LESSONS LIFE WILL TEACH ME.
YET THE TRUTH IS, PEOPLE FORGET HOW MUCH THEY KNEW AT SIXTEEN, HOW MUCH THEY UNDERSTOOD OF THINGS.
CAUGHT UP IN ALL HER TASKS, MY MOTHER SEES NOTHING BUT WHAT IS RIGHT BEFORE HER, THINKS OF NOTHING THAT IS NOT AT HAND.

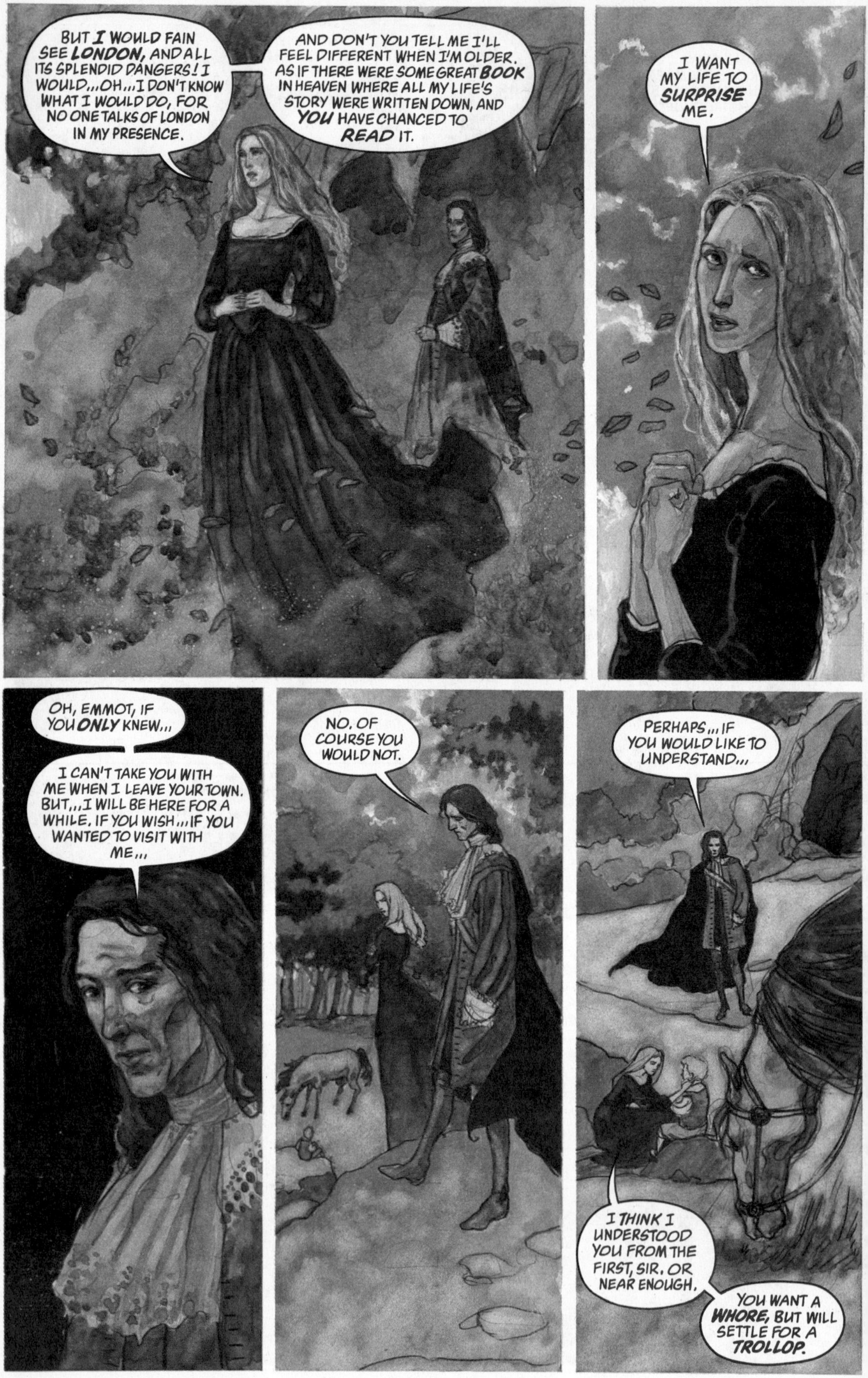
BUT I WOULD FAIN SEE LONDON, AND ALL ITS SPLENDID DANGERS! I WOULD...OH...I DON'T KNOW WHAT I WOULD DO, FOR NO ONE TALKS OF LONDON IN MY PRESENCE.
AND DON'T YOU TELL ME I'LL FEEL DIFFERENT WHEN I'M OLDER. AS IF THERE WERE SOME GREAT BOOK IN HEAVEN WHERE ALL MY LIFE'S STORY WERE WRITTEN DOWN, AND YOU HAVE CHANCED TO READ IT.
I WANT MY LIFE TO SURPRISE ME.
OH, EMMOT, IF YOU ONLY KNEW...
I CAN'T TAKE YOU WITH ME WHEN I LEAVE YOUR TOWN. BUT...I WILL BE HERE FOR A WHILE. IF YOU WISH...IF YOU WANTED TO VISIT WITH ME...
NO. OF COURSE YOU WOULD NOT.
PERHAPS...IF YOU WOULD LIKE TO UNDERSTAND...
I THINK I UNDERSTOOD YOU FROM THE FIRST, SIR. OR NEAR ENOUGH.
YOU WANT A WHORE, BUT WILL SETTLE FOR A TROLLOP.

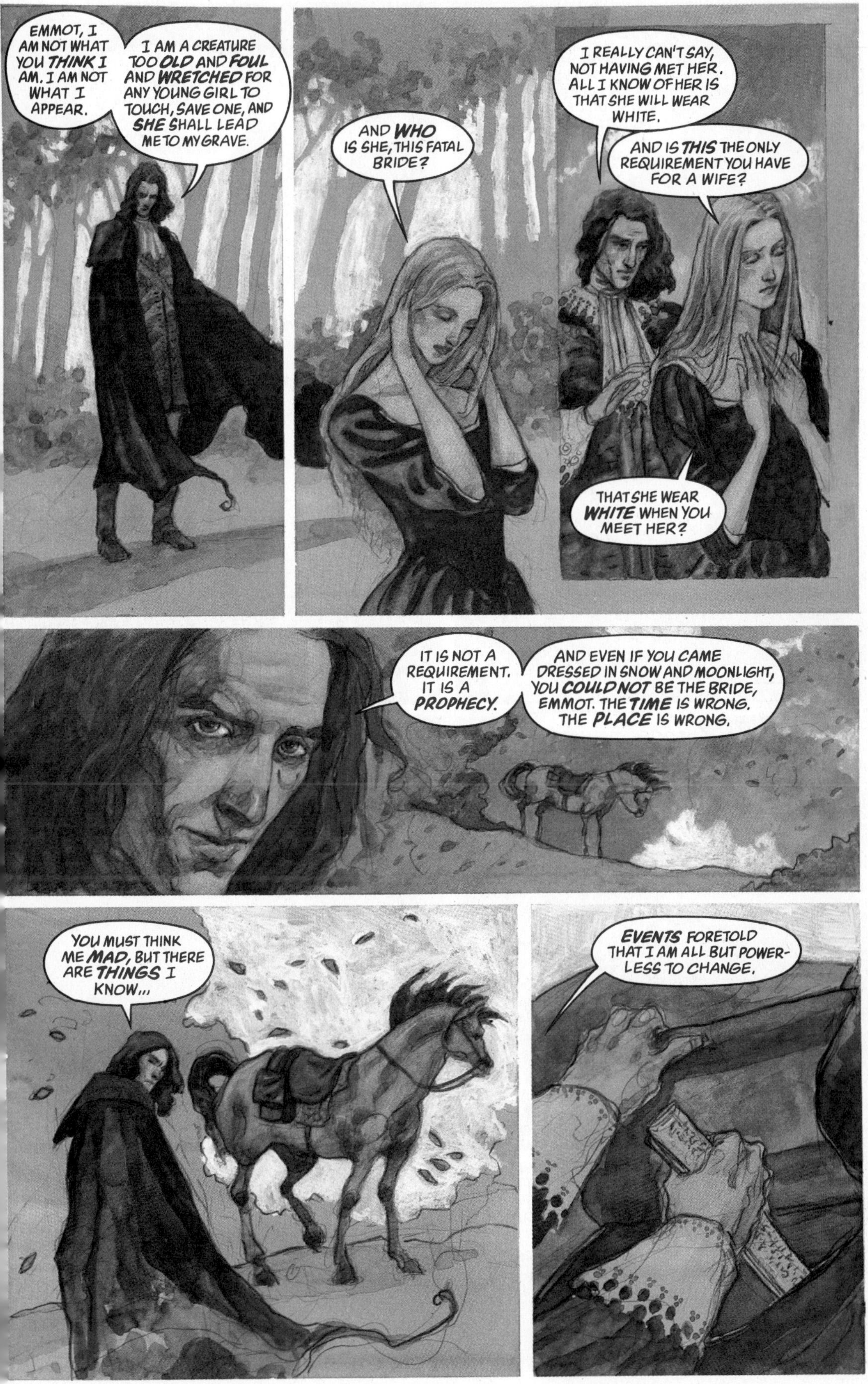
EMMOT, I AM NOT WHAT YOU THINK I AM. I AM NOT WHAT I APPEAR.
I AM A CREATURE TOO OLD AND FOUL AND WRETCHED FOR ANY YOUNG GIRL TO TOUCH, SAVE ONE, AND SHE SHALL LEAD ME TO MY GRAVE.
AND WHO IS SHE, THIS FATAL BRIDE?
I REALLY CAN'T SAY, NOT HAVING MET HER. ALL I KNOW OF HER IS THAT SHE WILL WEAR WHITE.
AND IS THIS THE ONLY REQUIREMENT YOU HAVE FOR A WIFE?
THAT SHE WEAR WHITE WHEN YOU MEET HER?
IT IS NOT A REQUIREMENT. IT IS A PROPHECY.
AND EVEN IF YOU CAME DRESSED IN SNOW AND MOONLIGHT, YOU COULD NOT BE THE BRIDE, EMMOT. THE TIME IS WRONG. THE PLACE IS WRONG.
YOU MUST THINK ME MAD, BUT THERE ARE THINGS I KNOW...
EVENTS FORETOLD THAT I AM ALL BUT POWER-LESS TO CHANGE.

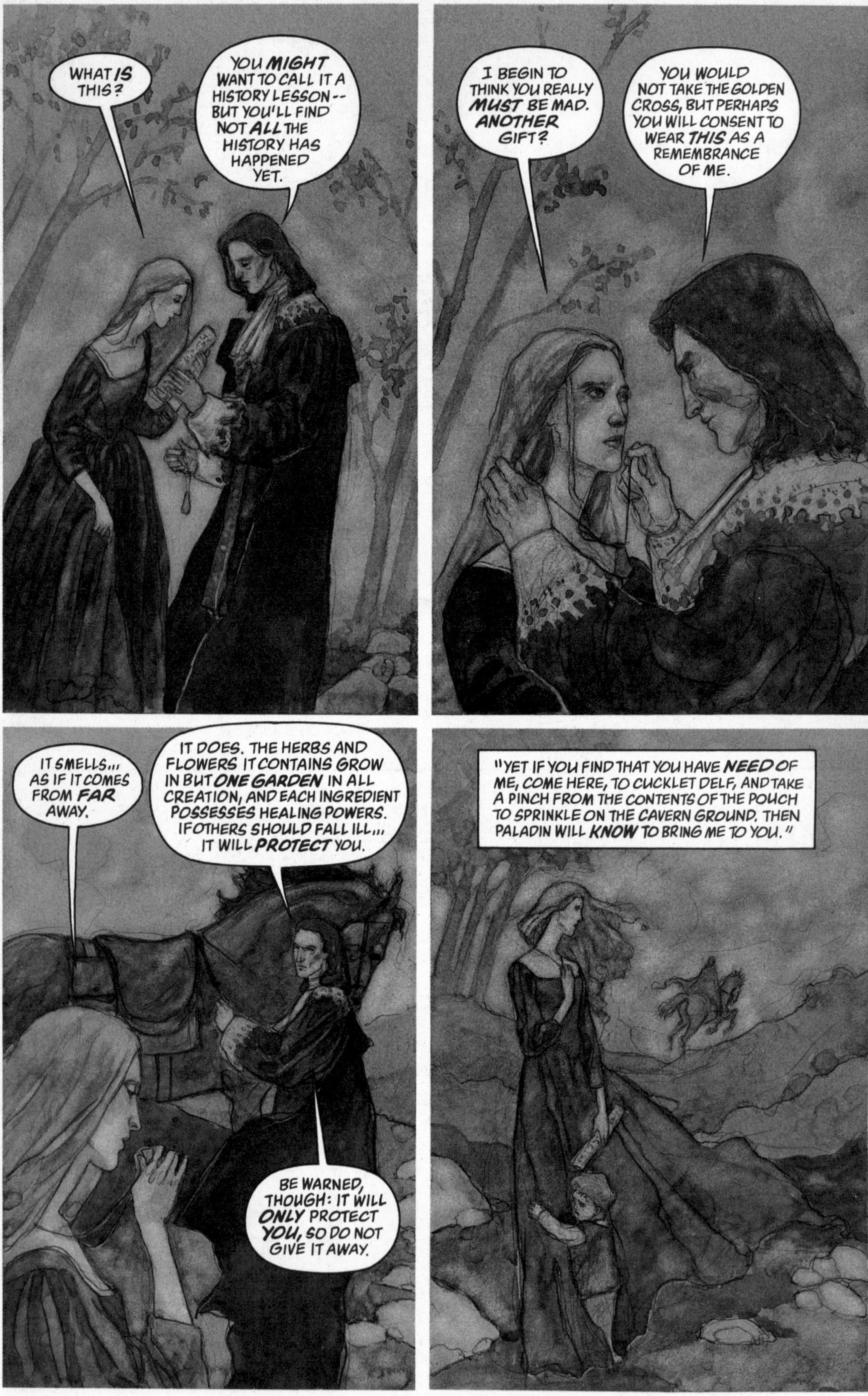
WHAT IS THIS?
YOU MIGHT WANT TO CALL IT A HISTORY LESSON-- BUT YOU'LL FIND NOT ALL THE HISTORY HAS HAPPENED YET.
I BEGIN TO THINK YOU REALLY MUST BE MAD. ANOTHER GIFT?
YOU WOULD NOT TAKE THE GOLDEN CROSS, BUT PERHAPS YOU WILL CONSENT TO WEAR THIS AS A REMEMBRANCE OF ME.
IT SMELLS... AS IF IT COMES FROM FAR AWAY.
IT DOES. THE HERBS AND FLOWERS IT CONTAINS GROW IN BUT ONE GARDEN IN ALL CREATION, AND EACH INGREDIENT POSSESSES HEALING POWERS. IF OTHERS SHOULD FALL ILL... IT WILL PROTECT YOU.
BE WARNED, THOUGH: IT WILL ONLY PROTECT YOU, SO DO NOT GIVE IT AWAY.
"YET IF YOU FIND THAT YOU HAVE NEED OF ME, COME HERE, TO CUCKLET DELF, AND TAKE A PINCH FROM THE CONTENTS OF THE POUCH TO SPRINKLE ON THE CAVERN GROUND. THEN PALADIN WILL KNOW TO BRING ME TO YOU."

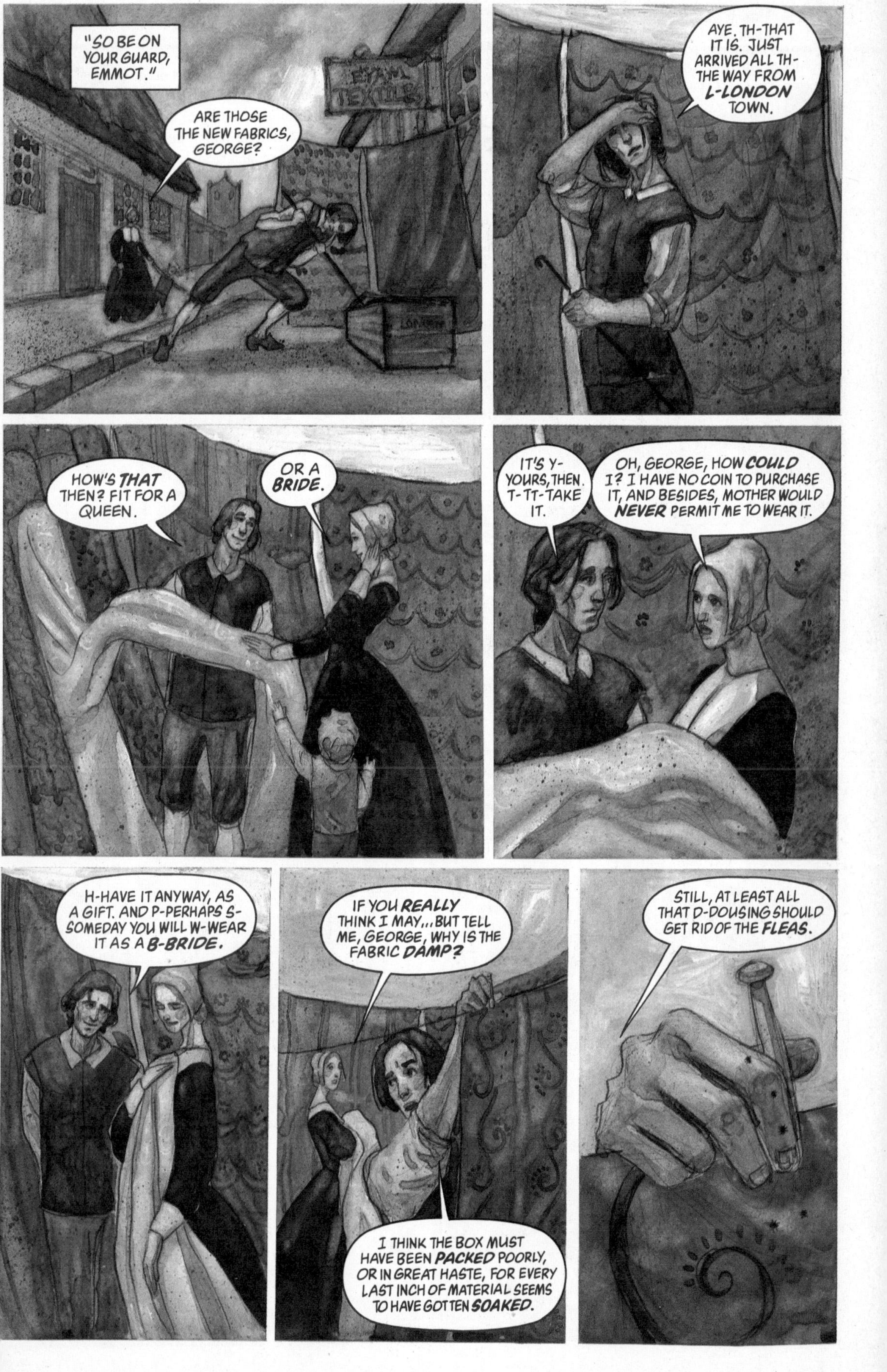
"SO BE ON YOUR GUARD, EMMOT."
ARE THOSE THE NEW FABRICS, GEORGE?
AYE. TH-THAT IT IS. JUST ARRIVED ALL TH-THE WAY FROM L-LONDON TOWN.
HOW'S THAT THEN? FIT FOR A QUEEN.
OR A BRIDE.
IT'S Y-YOURS, THEN. T-TT-TAKE IT.
OH, GEORGE, HOW COULD I? I HAVE NO COIN TO PURCHASE IT, AND BESIDES, MOTHER WOULD NEVER PERMIT ME TO WEAR IT.
H-HAVE IT ANYWAY, AS A GIFT. AND P-PERHAPS S-SOMEDAY YOU WILL W-WEAR IT AS A B-BRIDE.
IF YOU REALLY THINK I MAY... BUT TELL ME, GEORGE, WHY IS THE FABRIC DAMP?
I THINK THE BOX MUST HAVE BEEN PACKED POORLY, OR IN GREAT HASTE, FOR EVERY LAST INCH OF MATERIAL SEEMS TO HAVE GOTTEN SOAKED.
STILL, AT LEAST ALL THAT D-DOUSING SHOULD GET RID OF THE FLEAS.

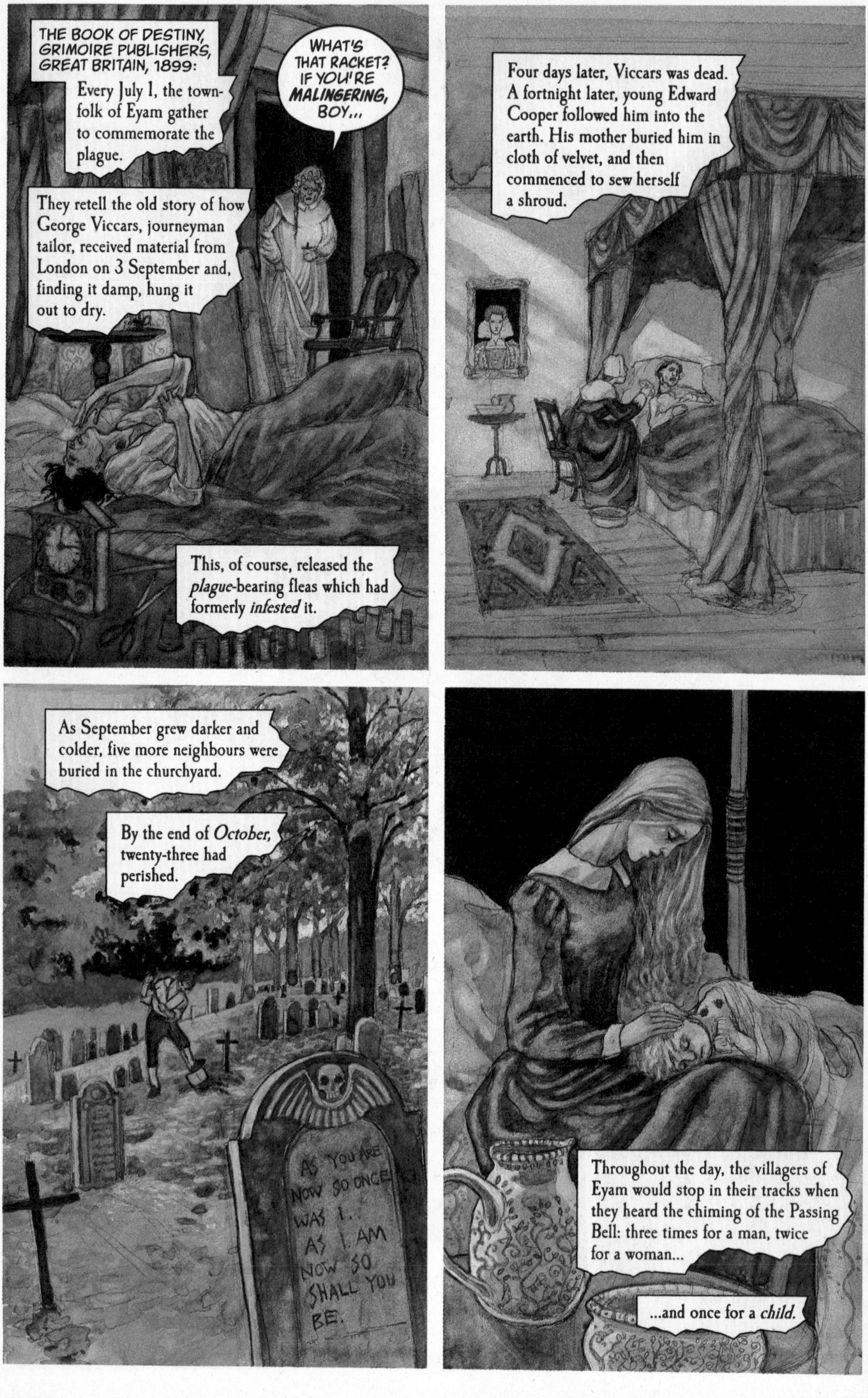
THE BOOK OF DESTINY, GRIMOIRE PUBLISHERS, GREAT BRITAIN, 1899:
Every July 1, the townfolk of Eyam gather to commemorate the plague.
WHAT'S THAT RACKET? IF YOU'RE MALINGERING, BOY...
They retell the old story of how George Viccars, journeyman tailor, received material from London on 3 September and, finding it damp, hung it out to dry.
This, of course, released the *plague*-bearing fleas which had formerly *infested* it.
Four days later, Viccars was dead. A fortnight later, young Edward Cooper followed him into the earth. His mother buried him in cloth of velvet, and then commenced to sew herself a shroud.
As September grew darker and colder, five more neighbours were buried in the churchyard.
By the end of *October,* twenty-three had perished.
AS YOU ARE NOW SO ONCE WAS I. AS I AM NOW SO SHALL YOU BE.
Throughout the day, the villagers of Eyam would stop in their tracks when they heard the chiming of the Passing Bell: three times for a man, twice for a woman...
...and once for a *child.*

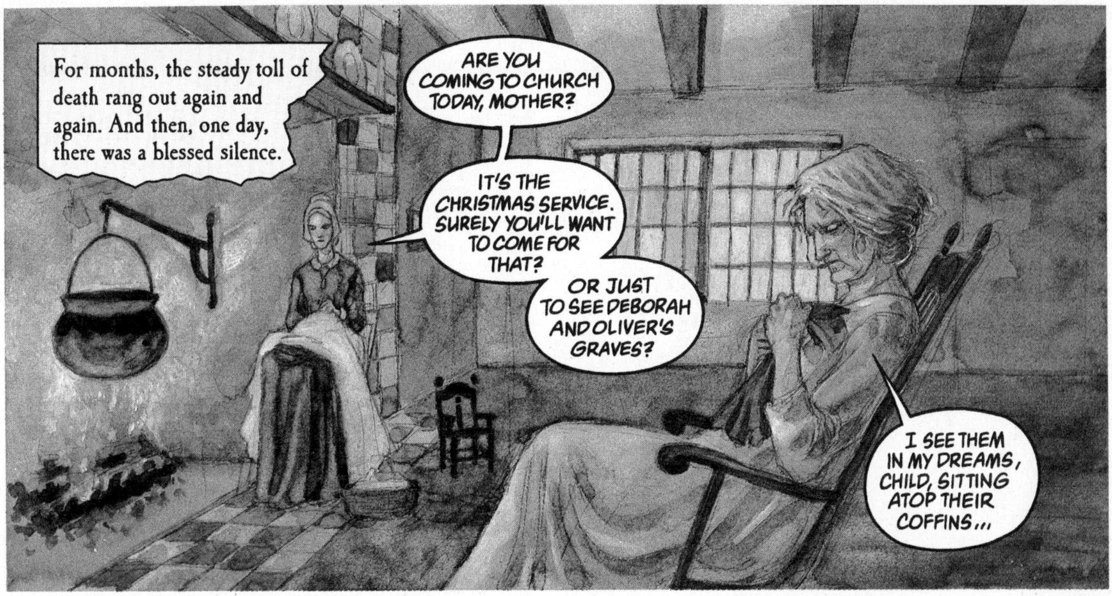
For months, the steady toll of death rang out again and again. And then, one day, there was a blessed silence.
ARE YOU COMING TO CHURCH TODAY, MOTHER?
IT'S THE CHRISTMAS SERVICE. SURELY YOU'LL WANT TO COME FOR THAT?
OR JUST TO SEE DEBORAH AND OLIVER'S GRAVES?
I SEE THEM IN MY DREAMS, CHILD, SITTING ATOP THEIR COFFINS...

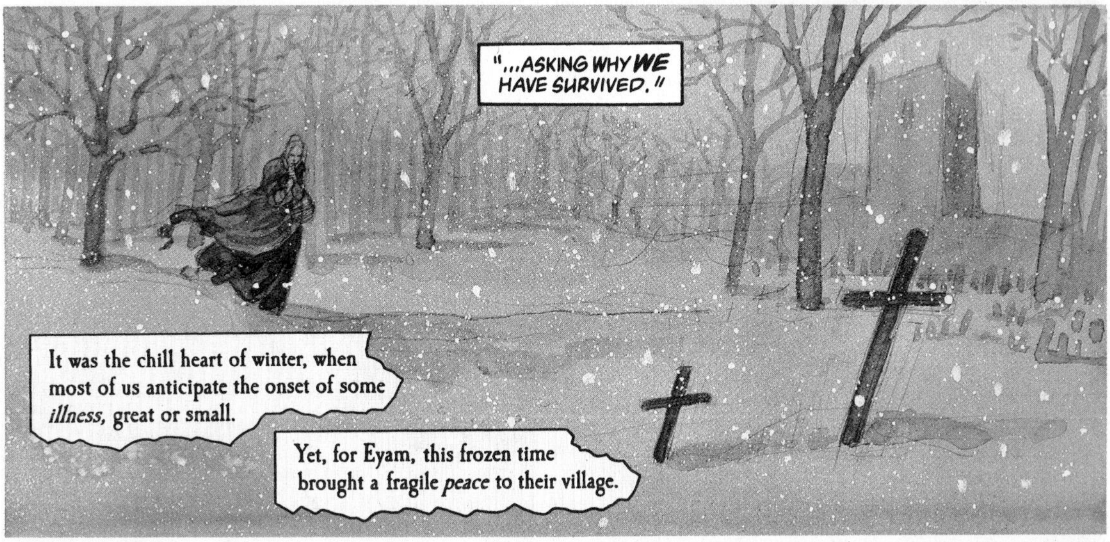
"...ASKING WHY *WE* HAVE SURVIVED."
It was the chill heart of winter, when most of us anticipate the onset of some *illness,* great or small.
Yet, for Eyam, this frozen time brought a fragile *peace* to their village.

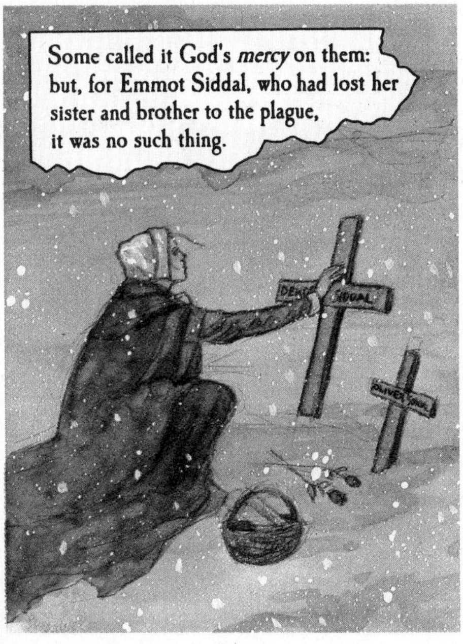
Some called it God's *mercy* on them: but, for Emmot Siddal, who had lost her sister and brother to the plague, it was no such thing.

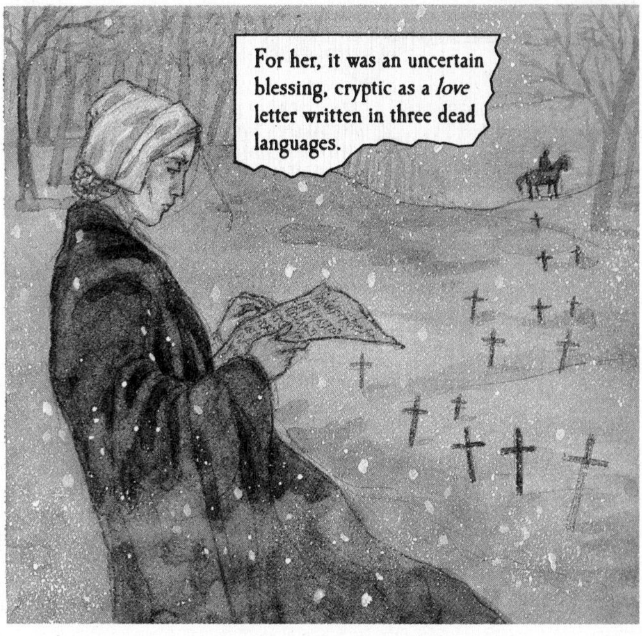
For her, it was an uncertain blessing, cryptic as a *love* letter written in three dead languages.

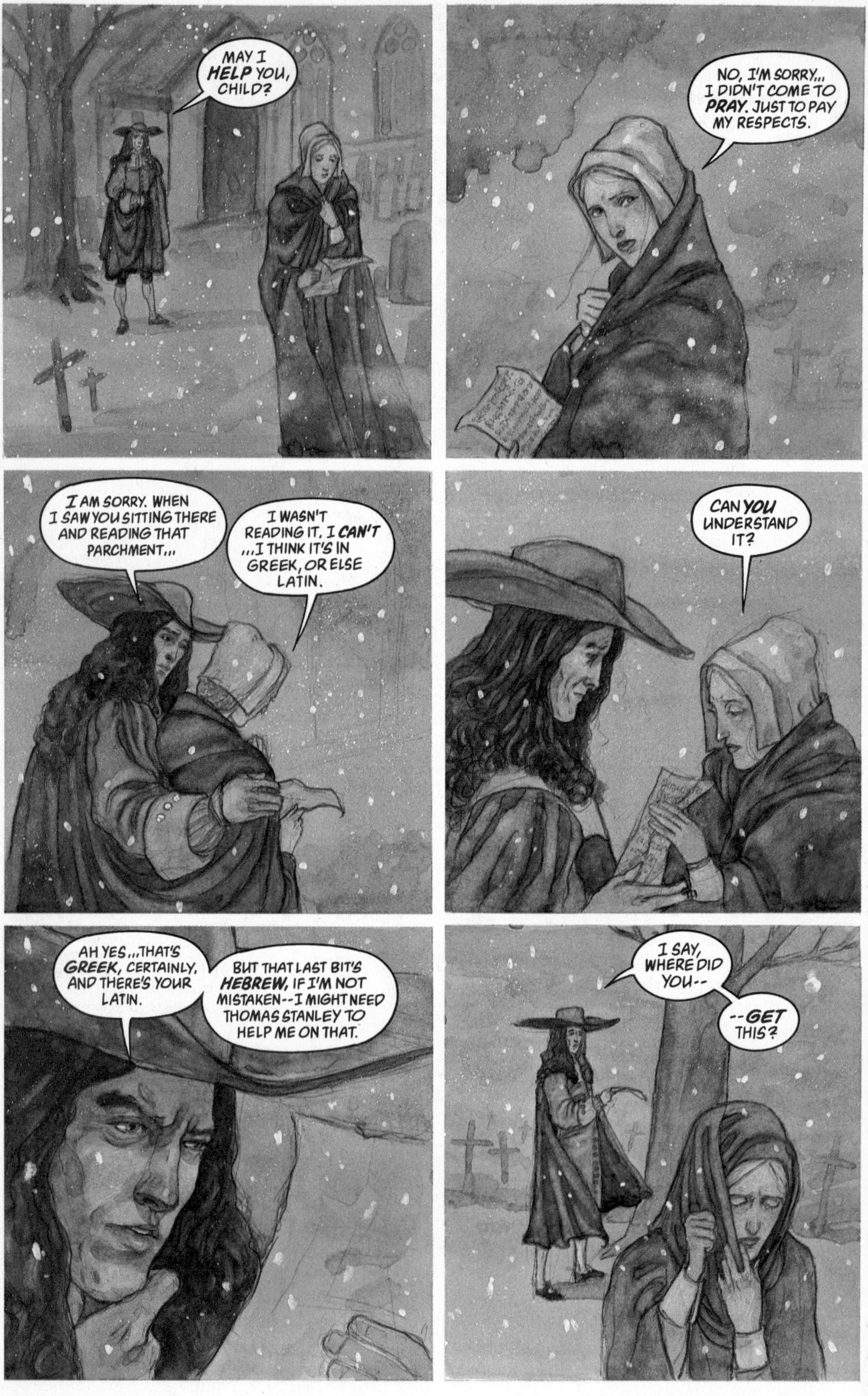
MAY I HELP YOU, CHILD?
NO, I'M SORRY... I DIDN'T COME TO PRAY. JUST TO PAY MY RESPECTS.
I AM SORRY. WHEN I SAW YOU SITTING THERE AND READING THAT PARCHMENT...
I WASN'T READING IT. I CAN'T ...I THINK IT'S IN GREEK, OR ELSE LATIN.
CAN YOU UNDERSTAND IT?
AH YES...THAT'S GREEK, CERTAINLY. AND THERE'S YOUR LATIN.
BUT THAT LAST BIT'S HEBREW, IF I'M NOT MISTAKEN--I MIGHT NEED THOMAS STANLEY TO HELP ME ON THAT.
I SAY, WHERE DID YOU--
--GET THIS?

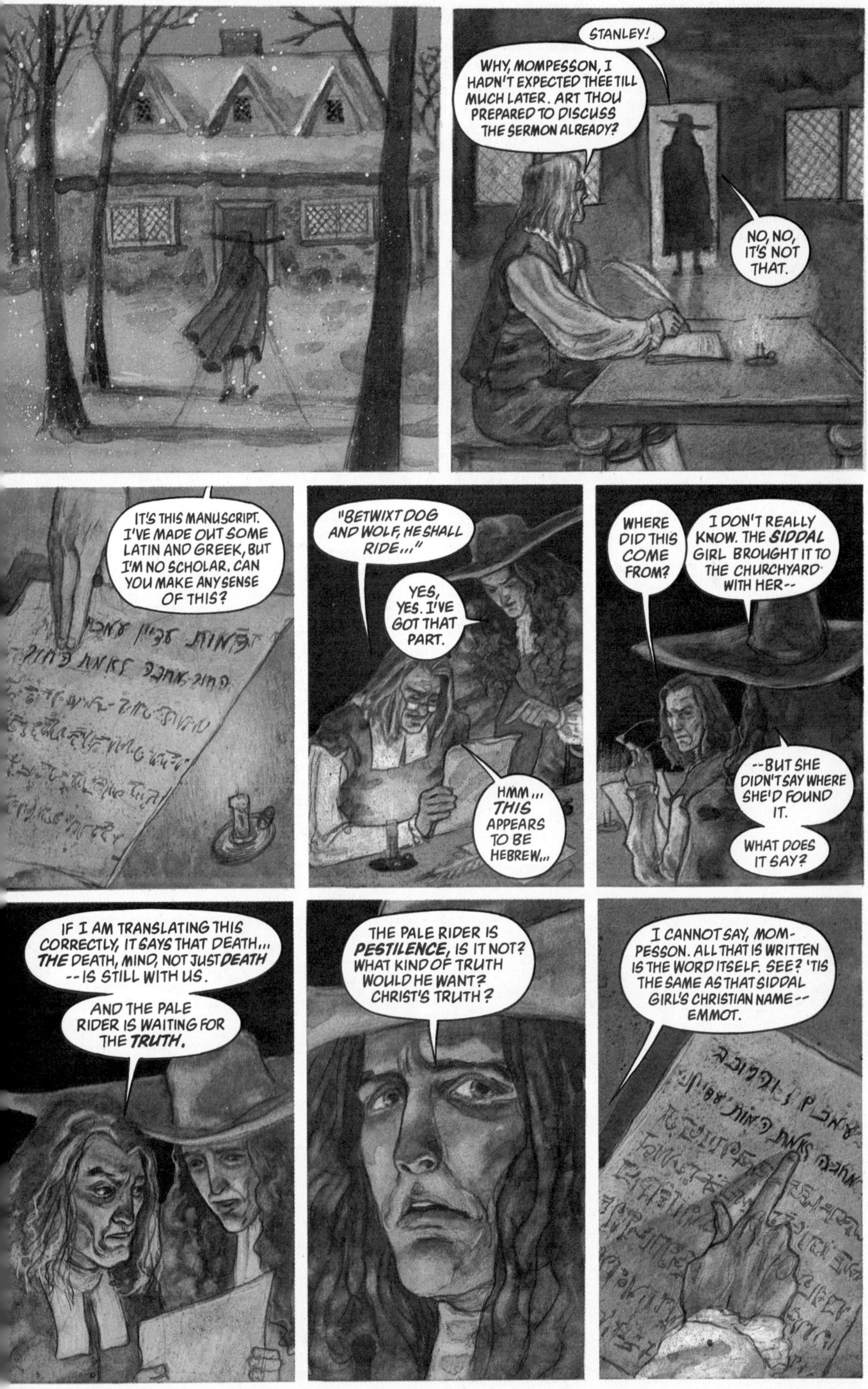
STANLEY!
WHY, MOMPESSON, I HADN'T EXPECTED THEE TILL MUCH LATER. ART THOU PREPARED TO DISCUSS THE SERMON ALREADY?
NO, NO, IT'S NOT THAT.
IT'S THIS MANUSCRIPT. I'VE MADE OUT SOME LATIN AND GREEK, BUT I'M NO SCHOLAR. CAN YOU MAKE ANY SENSE OF THIS?
"BETWIXT DOG AND WOLF, HE SHALL RIDE..."
YES, YES. I'VE GOT THAT PART.
HMM... THIS APPEARS TO BE HEBREW...
WHERE DID THIS COME FROM?
I DON'T REALLY KNOW. THE SIDDAL GIRL BROUGHT IT TO THE CHURCHYARD WITH HER--
--BUT SHE DIDN'T SAY WHERE SHE'D FOUND IT.
WHAT DOES IT SAY?
IF I AM TRANSLATING THIS CORRECTLY, IT SAYS THAT DEATH... THE DEATH, MIND, NOT JUST DEATH --IS STILL WITH US.
AND THE PALE RIDER IS WAITING FOR THE TRUTH.
THE PALE RIDER IS PESTILENCE, IS IT NOT? WHAT KIND OF TRUTH WOULD HE WANT? CHRIST'S TRUTH?
I CANNOT SAY, MOMPESSON. ALL THAT IS WRITTEN IS THE WORD ITSELF. SEE? 'TIS THE SAME AS THAT SIDDAL GIRL'S CHRISTIAN NAME-- EMMOT.

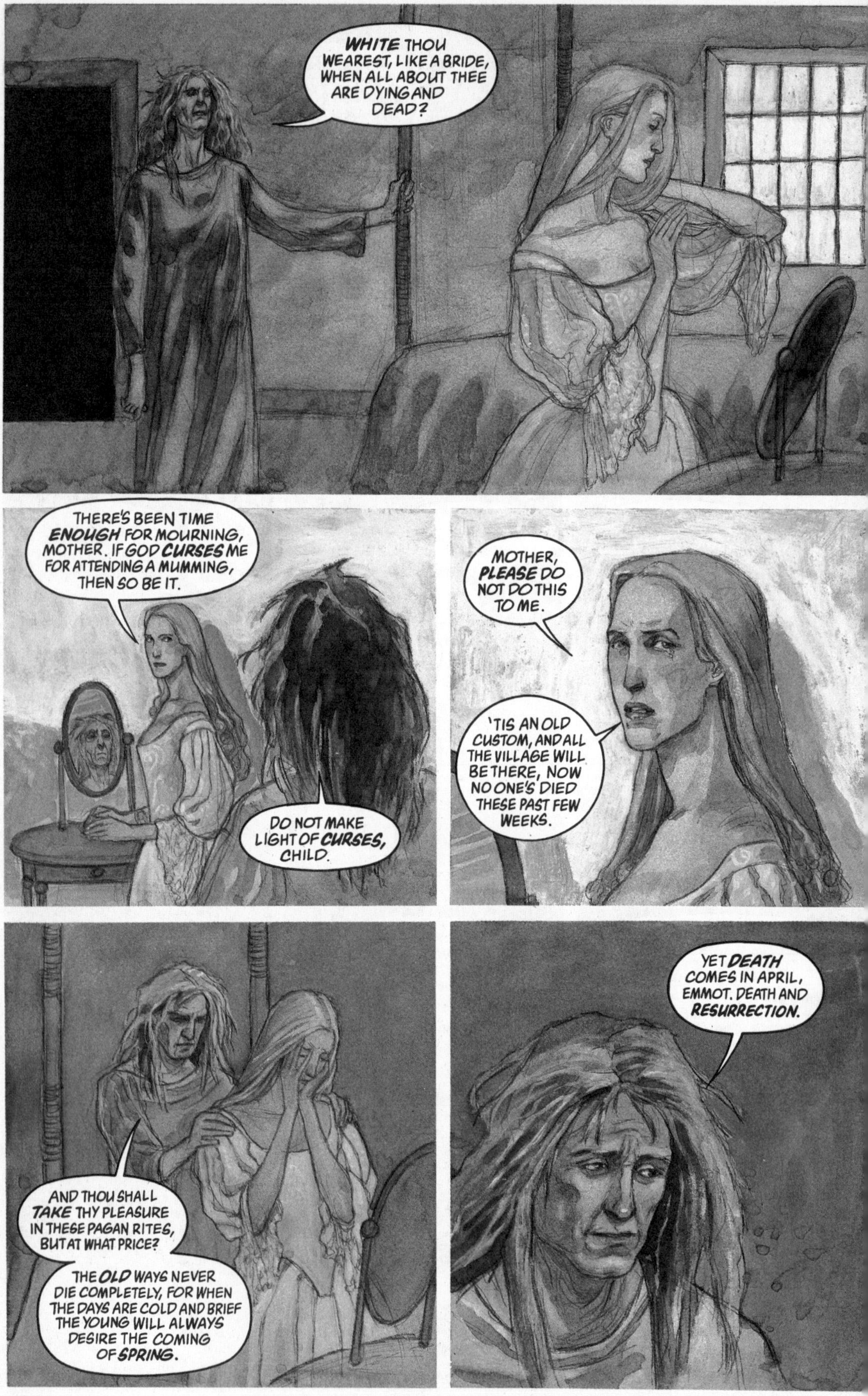
WHITE THOU WEAREST, LIKE A BRIDE, WHEN ALL ABOUT THEE ARE DYING AND DEAD?
THERE'S BEEN TIME ENOUGH FOR MOURNING, MOTHER. IF GOD CURSES ME FOR ATTENDING A MUMMING, THEN SO BE IT.
DO NOT MAKE LIGHT OF CURSES, CHILD.
MOTHER, PLEASE DO NOT DO THIS TO ME.
'TIS AN OLD CUSTOM, AND ALL THE VILLAGE WILL BE THERE, NOW NO ONE'S DIED THESE PAST FEW WEEKS.
AND THOU SHALL TAKE THY PLEASURE IN THESE PAGAN RITES, BUT AT WHAT PRICE?
THE OLD WAYS NEVER DIE COMPLETELY, FOR WHEN THE DAYS ARE COLD AND BRIEF THE YOUNG WILL ALWAYS DESIRE THE COMING OF SPRING.
YET DEATH COMES IN APRIL, EMMOT. DEATH AND RESURRECTION.

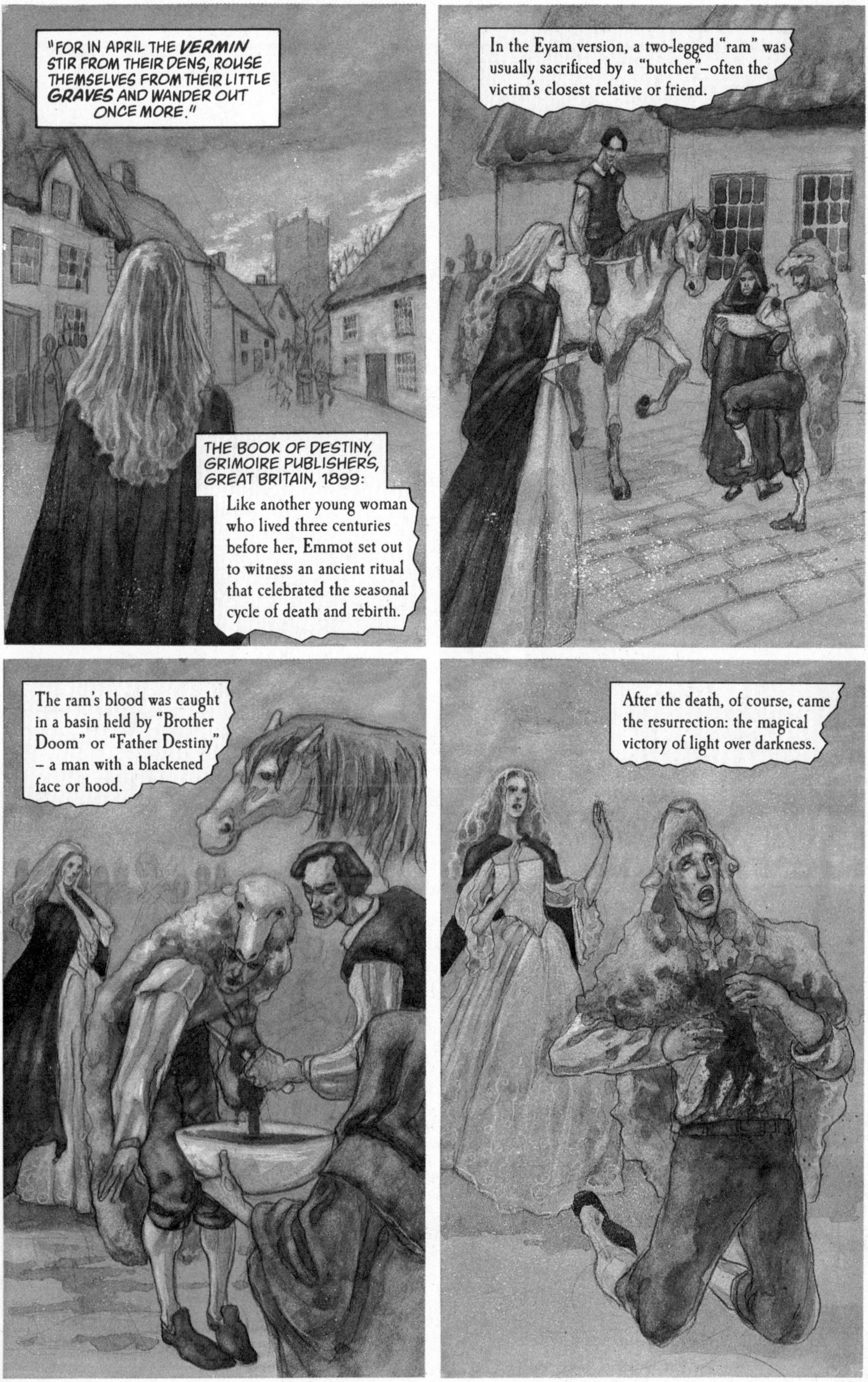
"FOR IN APRIL THE VERMIN STIR FROM THEIR DENS, ROUSE THEMSELVES FROM THEIR LITTLE GRAVES AND WANDER OUT ONCE MORE."
THE BOOK OF DESTINY, GRIMOIRE PUBLISHERS, GREAT BRITAIN, 1899:
Like another young woman who lived three centuries before her, Emmot set out to witness an ancient ritual that celebrated the seasonal cycle of death and rebirth.
In the Eyam version, a two-legged "ram" was usually sacrificed by a "butcher"–often the victim's closest relative or friend.
The ram's blood was caught in a basin held by "Brother Doom" or "Father Destiny" – a man with a blackened face or hood.
After the death, of course, came the resurrection: the magical victory of light over darkness.

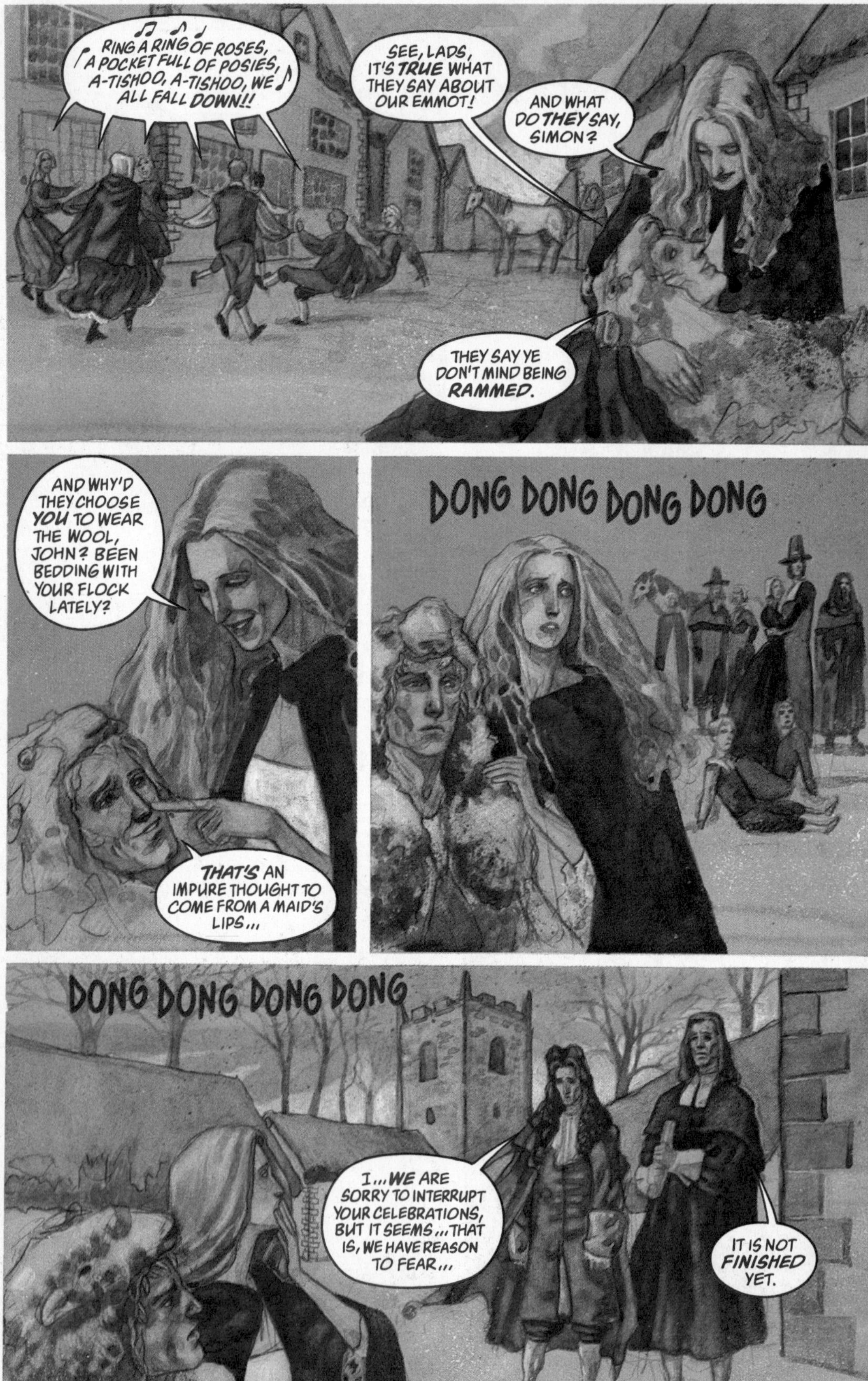
RING A RING OF ROSES, A POCKET FULL OF POSIES, A-TISHOO, A-TISHOO, WE ALL FALL DOWN!!
SEE, LADS, IT'S TRUE WHAT THEY SAY ABOUT OUR EMMOT!
AND WHAT DO THEY SAY, SIMON?
THEY SAY YE DON'T MIND BEING RAMMED.
AND WHY'D THEY CHOOSE YOU TO WEAR THE WOOL, JOHN? BEEN BEDDING WITH YOUR FLOCK LATELY?
THAT'S AN IMPURE THOUGHT TO COME FROM A MAID'S LIPS...
DONG DONG DONG DONG
DONG DONG DONG DONG
I... WE ARE SORRY TO INTERRUPT YOUR CELEBRATIONS, BUT IT SEEMS... THAT IS, WE HAVE REASON TO FEAR...
IT IS NOT FINISHED YET.

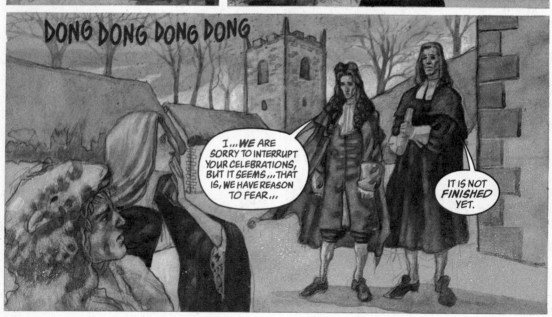

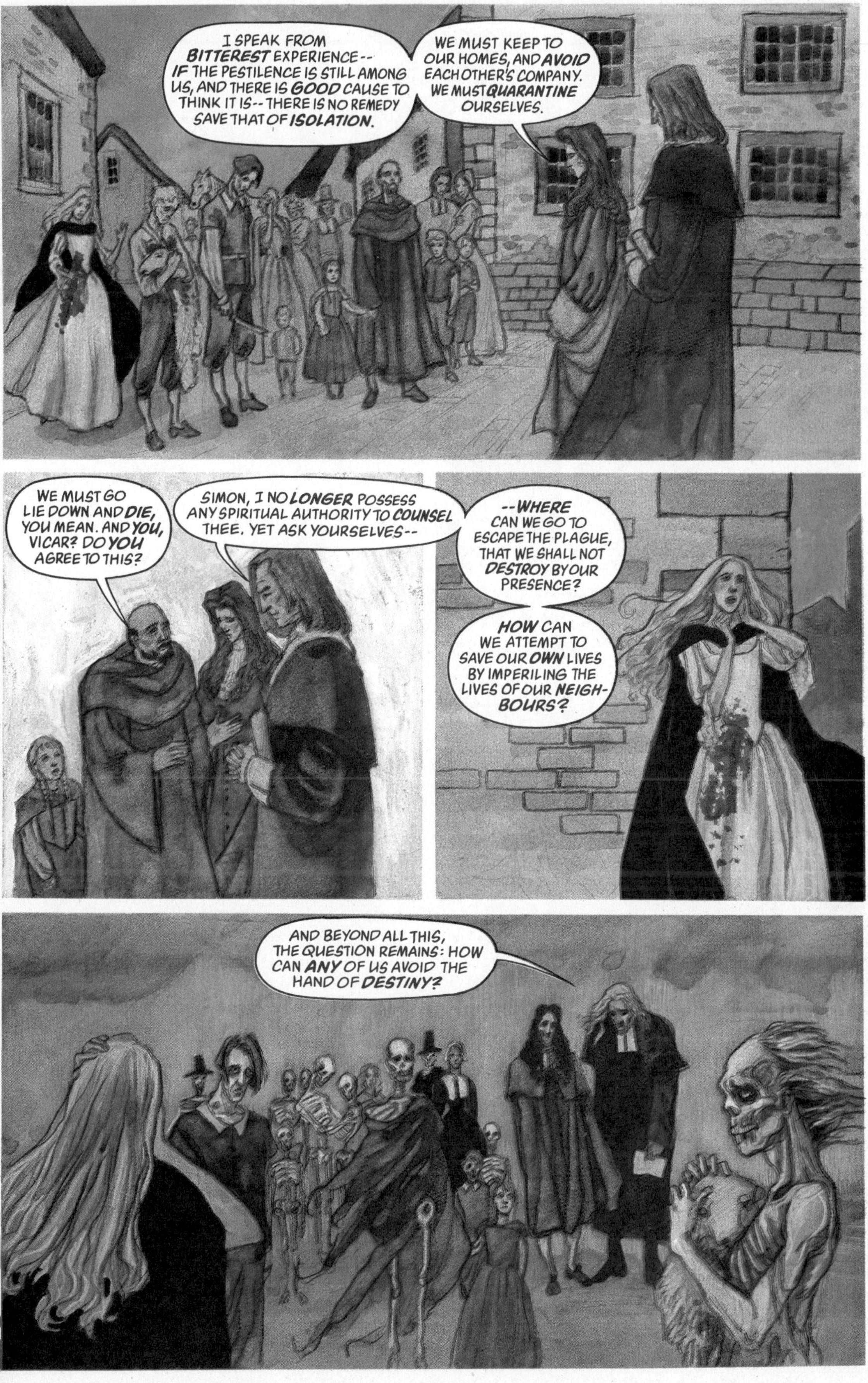
I SPEAK FROM BITTEREST EXPERIENCE-- IF THE PESTILENCE IS STILL AMONG US, AND THERE IS GOOD CAUSE TO THINK IT IS-- THERE IS NO REMEDY SAVE THAT OF ISOLATION.
WE MUST KEEP TO OUR HOMES, AND AVOID EACH OTHER'S COMPANY. WE MUST QUARANTINE OURSELVES.
WE MUST GO LIE DOWN AND DIE, YOU MEAN. AND YOU, VICAR? DO YOU AGREE TO THIS?
SIMON, I NO LONGER POSSESS ANY SPIRITUAL AUTHORITY TO COUNSEL THEE. YET ASK YOURSELVES--
--WHERE CAN WE GO TO ESCAPE THE PLAGUE, THAT WE SHALL NOT DESTROY BY OUR PRESENCE?
HOW CAN WE ATTEMPT TO SAVE OUR OWN LIVES BY IMPERILING THE LIVES OF OUR NEIGH-BOURS?
AND BEYOND ALL THIS, THE QUESTION REMAINS: HOW CAN ANY OF US AVOID THE HAND OF DESTINY?

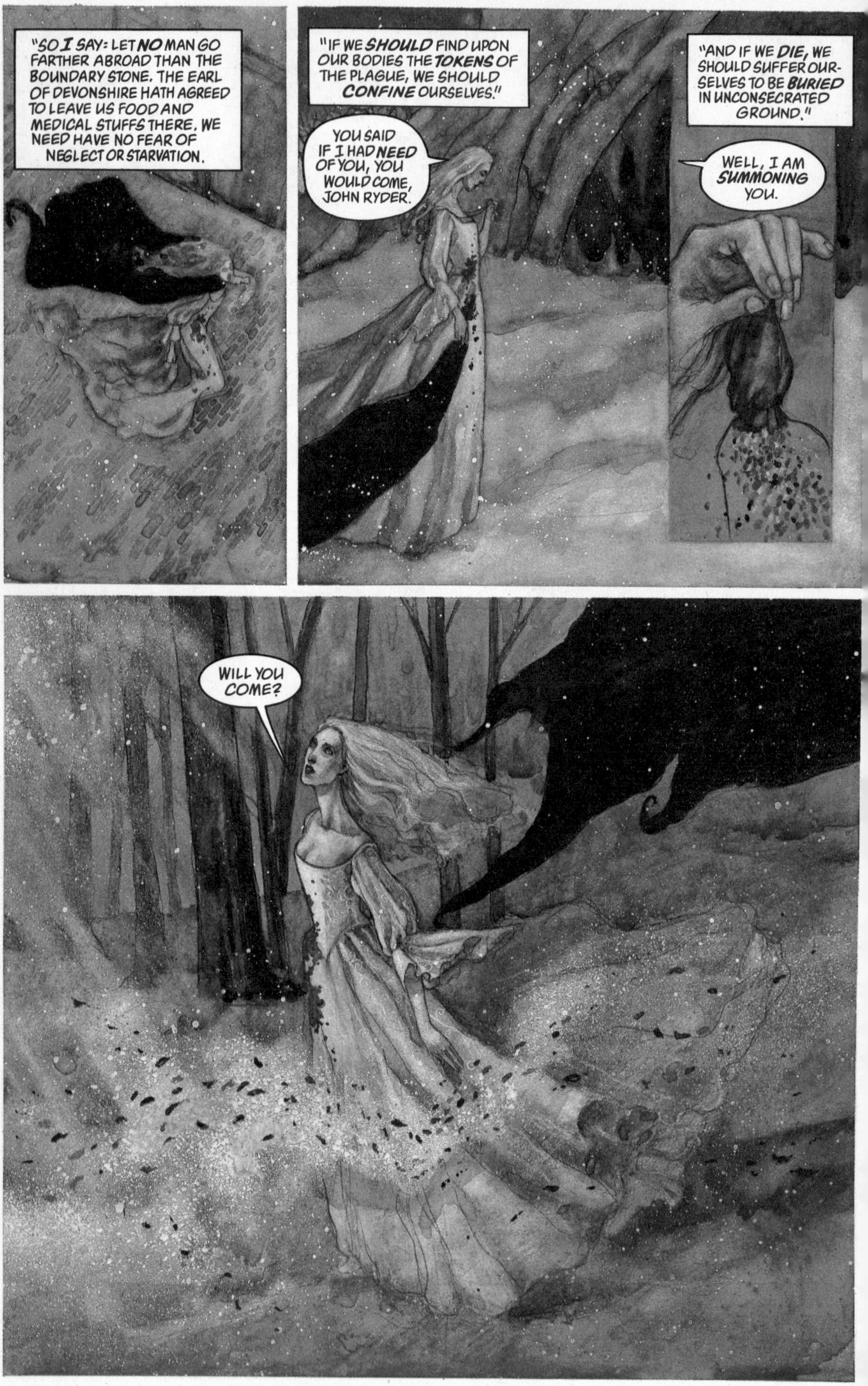
"SO I SAY: LET NO MAN GO FARTHER ABROAD THAN THE BOUNDARY STONE. THE EARL OF DEVONSHIRE HATH AGREED TO LEAVE US FOOD AND MEDICAL STUFFS THERE. WE NEED HAVE NO FEAR OF NEGLECT OR STARVATION.
"IF WE SHOULD FIND UPON OUR BODIES THE TOKENS OF THE PLAGUE, WE SHOULD CONFINE OURSELVES."
YOU SAID IF I HAD NEED OF YOU, YOU WOULD COME, JOHN RYDER.
"AND IF WE DIE, WE SHOULD SUFFER OURSELVES TO BE BURIED IN UNCONSECRATED GROUND."
WELL, I AM SUMMONING YOU.
WILL YOU COME?

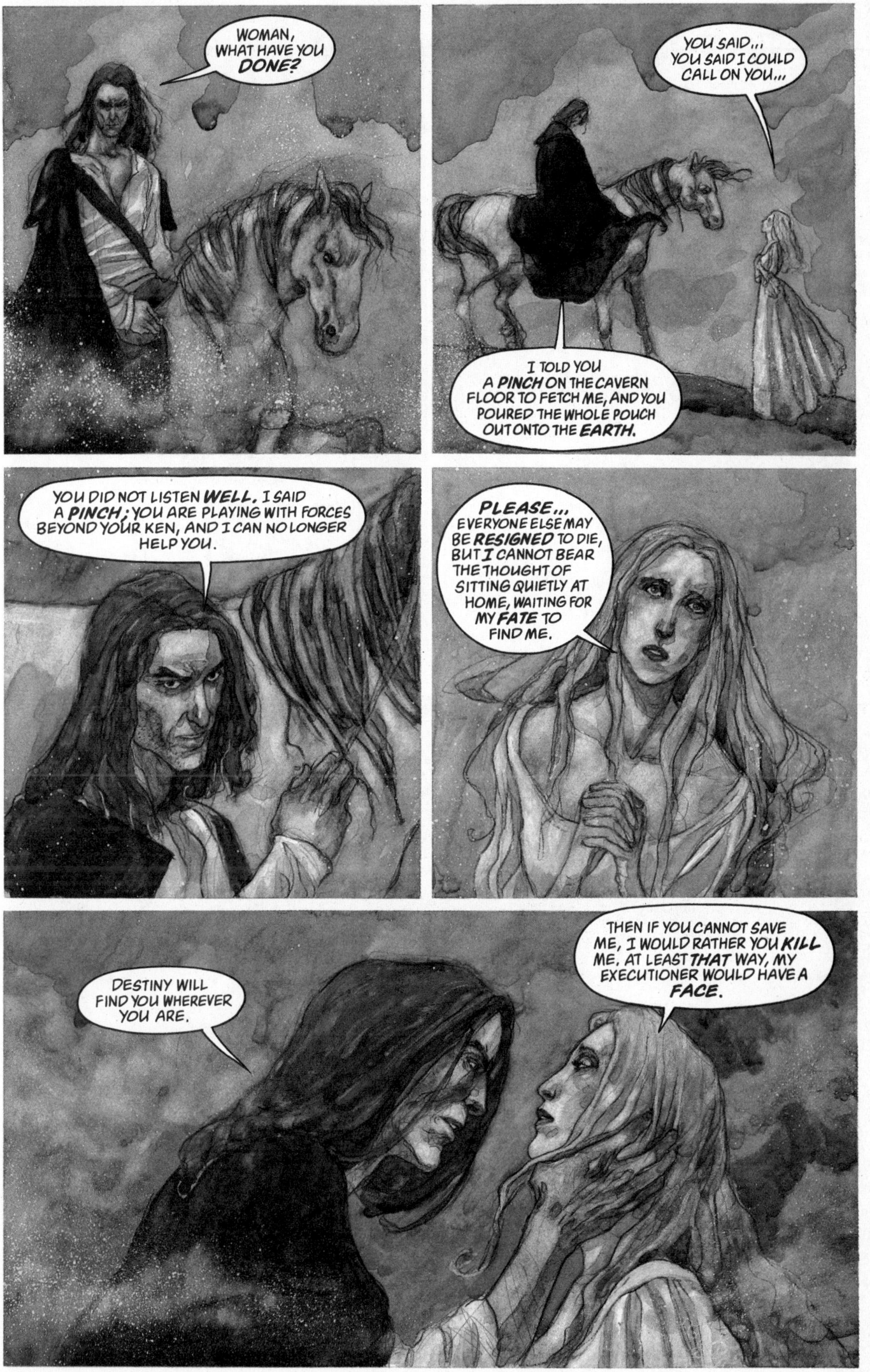
WOMAN, WHAT HAVE YOU DONE?
YOU SAID... YOU SAID I COULD CALL ON YOU...
I TOLD YOU A PINCH ON THE CAVERN FLOOR TO FETCH ME, AND YOU POURED THE WHOLE POUCH OUT ONTO THE EARTH.
YOU DID NOT LISTEN WELL. I SAID A PINCH; YOU ARE PLAYING WITH FORCES BEYOND YOUR KEN, AND I CAN NO LONGER HELP YOU.
PLEASE... EVERYONE ELSE MAY BE RESIGNED TO DIE, BUT I CANNOT BEAR THE THOUGHT OF SITTING QUIETLY AT HOME, WAITING FOR MY FATE TO FIND ME.
DESTINY WILL FIND YOU WHEREVER YOU ARE.
THEN IF YOU CANNOT SAVE ME, I WOULD RATHER YOU KILL ME. AT LEAST THAT WAY, MY EXECUTIONER WOULD HAVE A FACE.

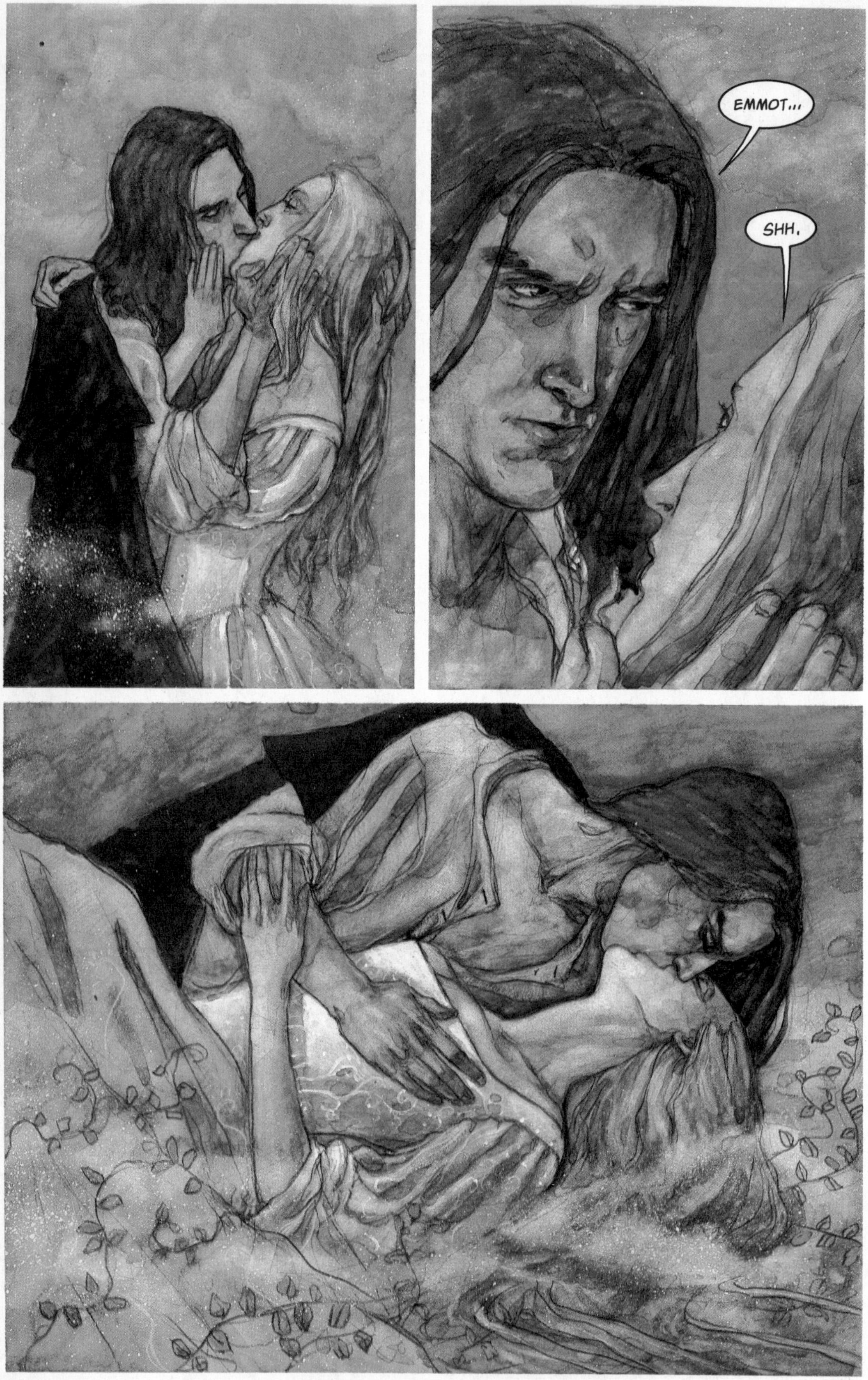
EMMOT...
SHH.

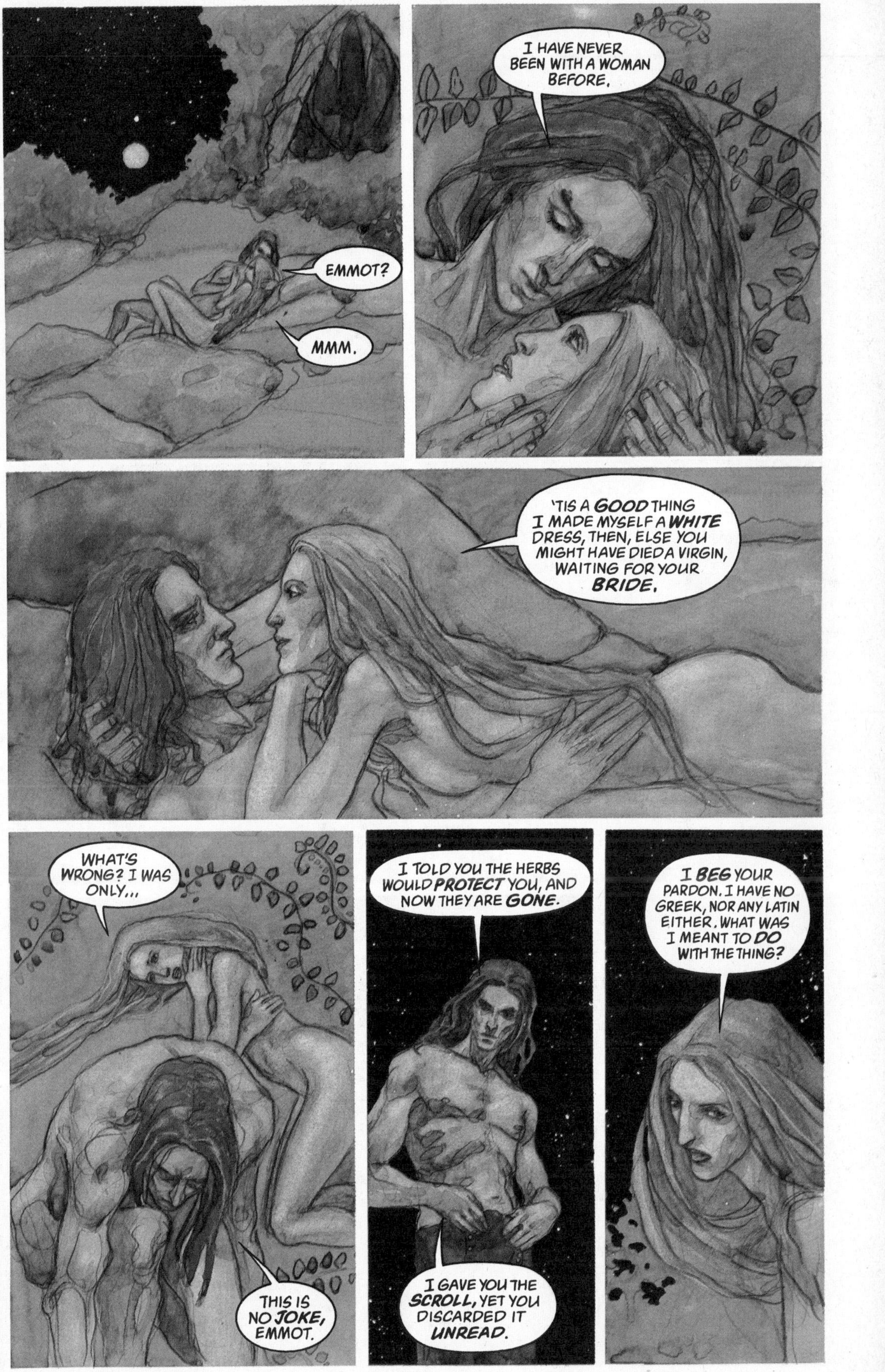
EMMOT?
MMM.
I HAVE NEVER BEEN WITH A WOMAN BEFORE.
'TIS A GOOD THING I MADE MYSELF A WHITE DRESS, THEN, ELSE YOU MIGHT HAVE DIED A VIRGIN, WAITING FOR YOUR BRIDE.
WHAT'S WRONG? I WAS ONLY...
THIS IS NO JOKE, EMMOT.
I TOLD YOU THE HERBS WOULD PROTECT YOU, AND NOW THEY ARE GONE.
I GAVE YOU THE SCROLL, YET YOU DISCARDED IT UNREAD.
I BEG YOUR PARDON. I HAVE NO GREEK, NOR ANY LATIN EITHER. WHAT WAS I MEANT TO DO WITH THE THING?

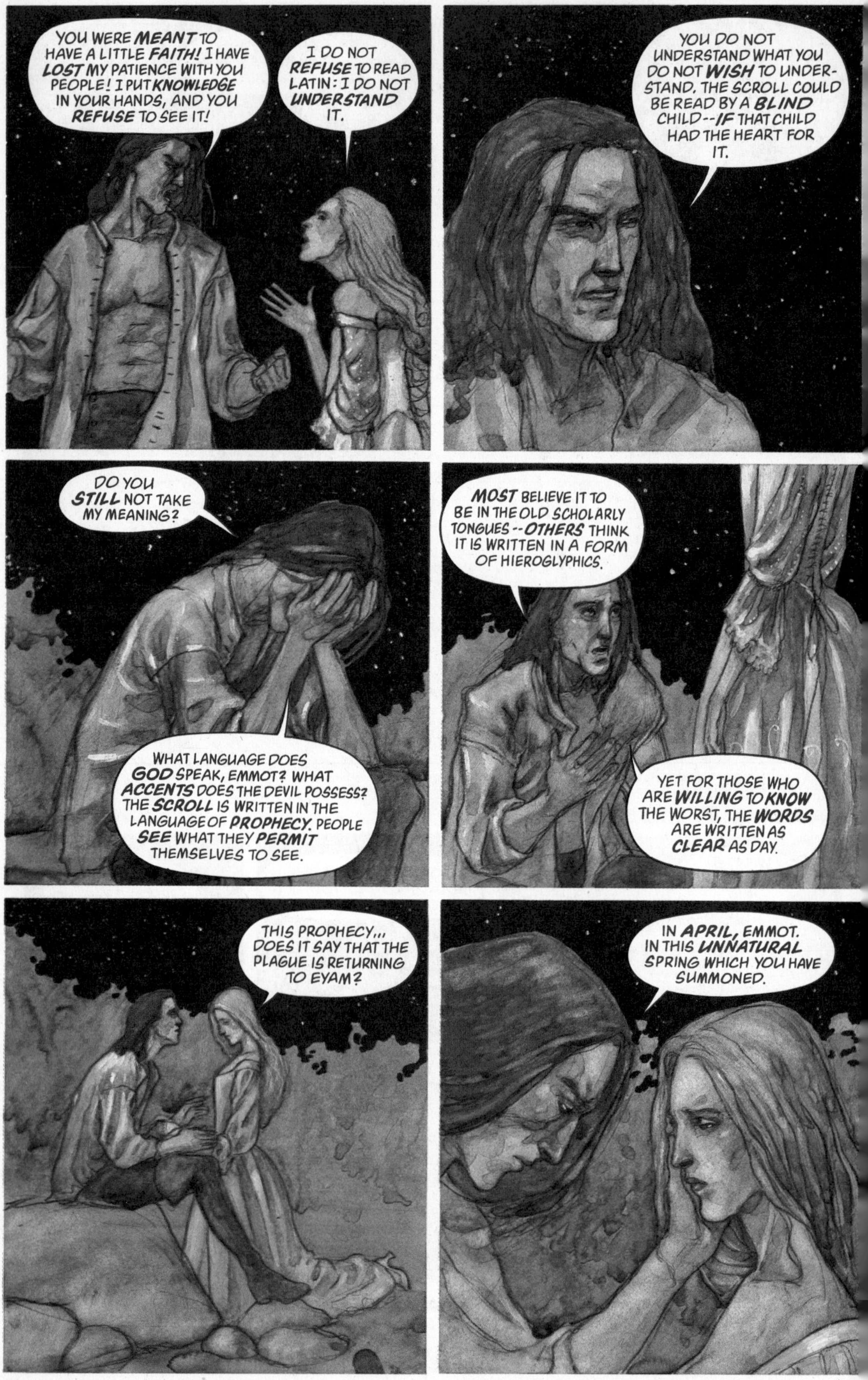
YOU WERE MEANT TO HAVE A LITTLE FAITH! I HAVE LOST MY PATIENCE WITH YOU PEOPLE! I PUT KNOWLEDGE IN YOUR HANDS, AND YOU REFUSE TO SEE IT!
I DO NOT REFUSE TO READ LATIN: I DO NOT UNDERSTAND IT.
YOU DO NOT UNDERSTAND WHAT YOU DO NOT WISH TO UNDER-STAND. THE SCROLL COULD BE READ BY A BLIND CHILD--IF THAT CHILD HAD THE HEART FOR IT.
DO YOU STILL NOT TAKE MY MEANING?
WHAT LANGUAGE DOES GOD SPEAK, EMMOT? WHAT ACCENTS DOES THE DEVIL POSSESS? THE SCROLL IS WRITTEN IN THE LANGUAGE OF PROPHECY. PEOPLE SEE WHAT THEY PERMIT THEMSELVES TO SEE.
MOST BELIEVE IT TO BE IN THE OLD SCHOLARLY TONGUES--OTHERS THINK IT IS WRITTEN IN A FORM OF HIEROGLYPHICS.
YET FOR THOSE WHO ARE WILLING TO KNOW THE WORST, THE WORDS ARE WRITTEN AS CLEAR AS DAY.
THIS PROPHECY... DOES IT SAY THAT THE PLAGUE IS RETURNING TO EYAM?
IN APRIL, EMMOT. IN THIS UNNATURAL SPRING WHICH YOU HAVE SUMMONED.

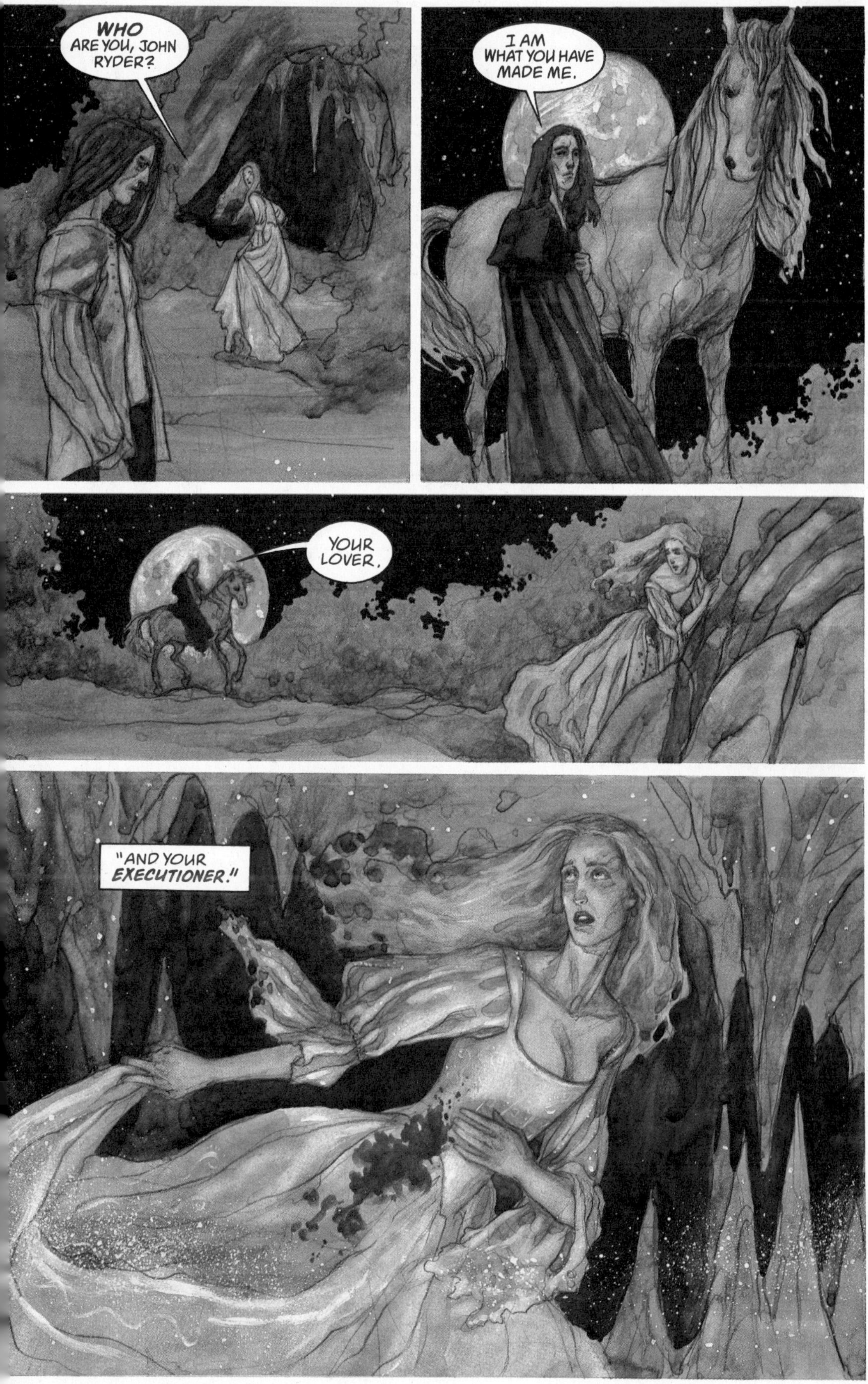
WHO ARE YOU, JOHN RYDER?
I AM WHAT YOU HAVE MADE ME.
YOUR LOVER.
"AND YOUR EXECUTIONER."

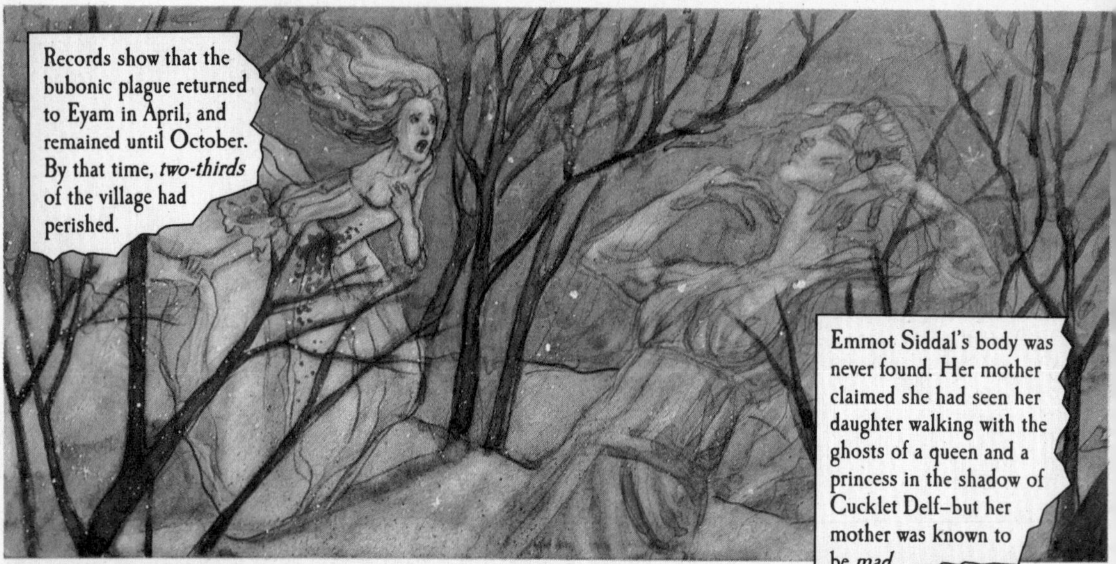
Records show that the bubonic plague returned to Eyam in April, and remained until October. By that time, *two-thirds* of the village had perished.
Emmot Siddal's body was never found. Her mother claimed she had seen her daughter walking with the ghosts of a queen and a princess in the shadow of Cucklet Delf–but her mother was known to be *mad*.

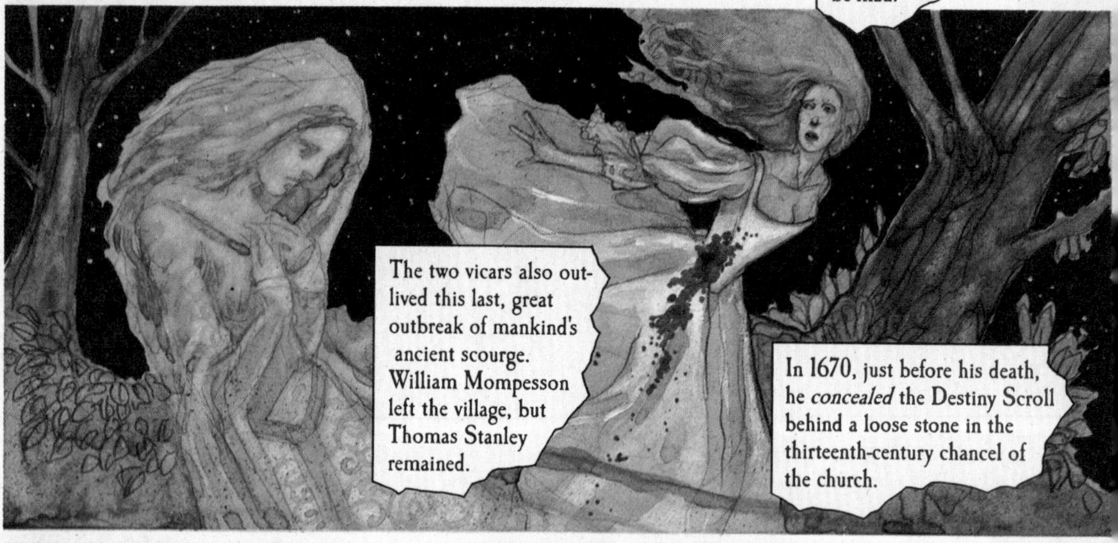
The two vicars also outlived this last, great outbreak of mankind's ancient scourge. William Mompesson left the village, but Thomas Stanley remained.
In 1670, just before his death, he *concealed* the Destiny Scroll behind a loose stone in the thirteenth-century chancel of the church.

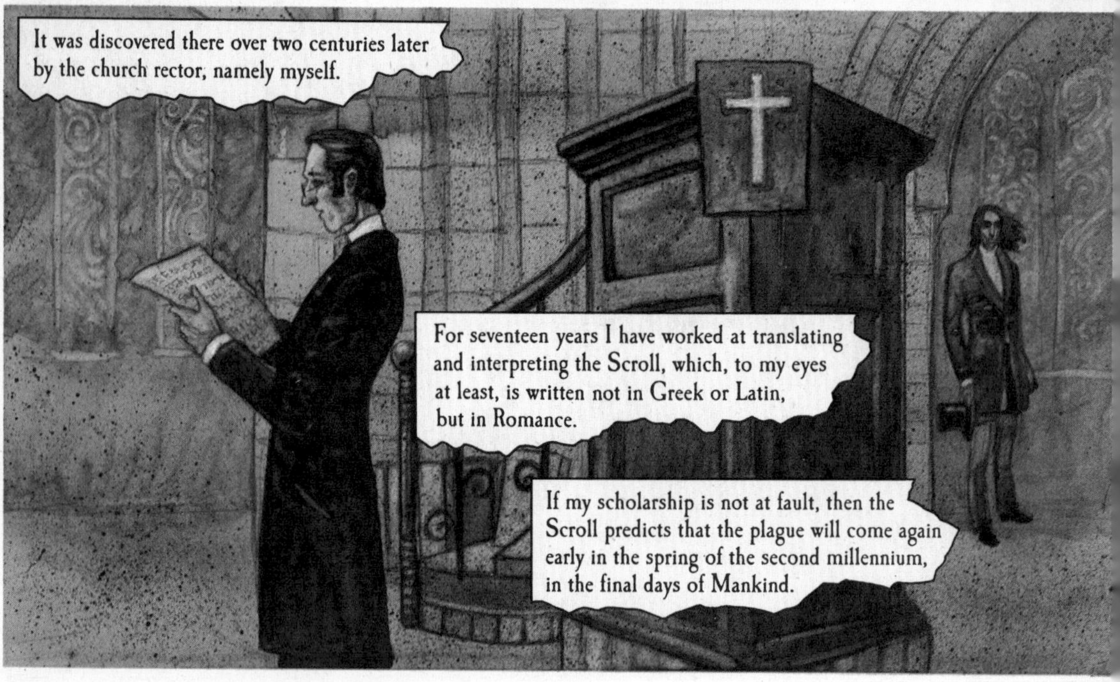
It was discovered there over two centuries later by the church rector, namely myself.
For seventeen years I have worked at translating and interpreting the Scroll, which, to my eyes at least, is written not in Greek or Latin, but in Romance.
If my scholarship is not at fault, then the Scroll predicts that the plague will come again early in the spring of the second millennium, in the final days of Mankind.

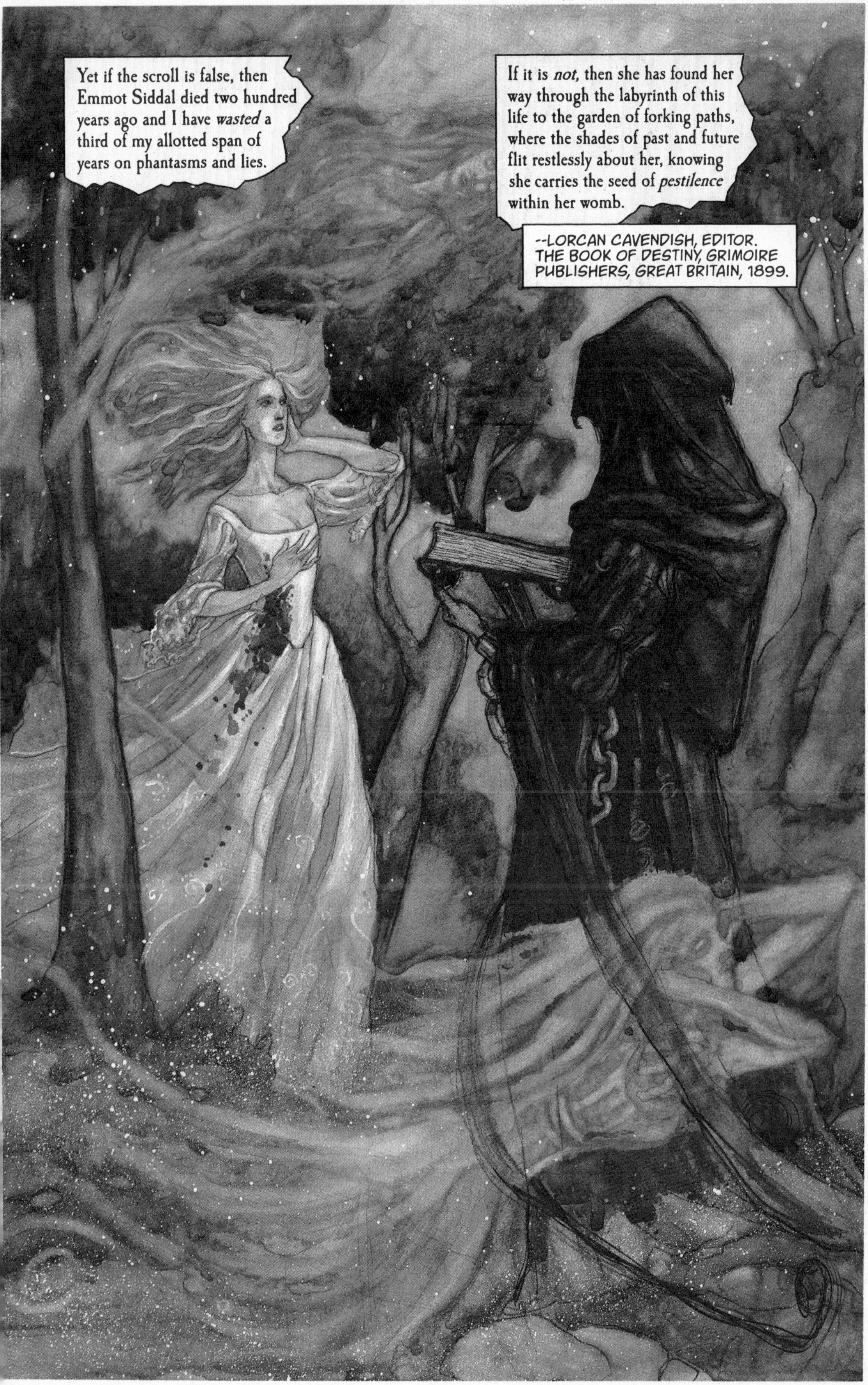
Yet if the scroll is false, then Emmot Siddal died two hundred years ago and I have *wasted* a third of my allotted span of years on phantasms and lies.
If it is *not,* then she has found her way through the labyrinth of this life to the garden of forking paths, where the shades of past and future flit restlessly about her, knowing she carries the seed of *pestilence* within her womb.
--LORCAN CAVENDISH, EDITOR. THE BOOK OF DESTINY, GRIMOIRE PUBLISHERS, GREAT BRITAIN, 1899.

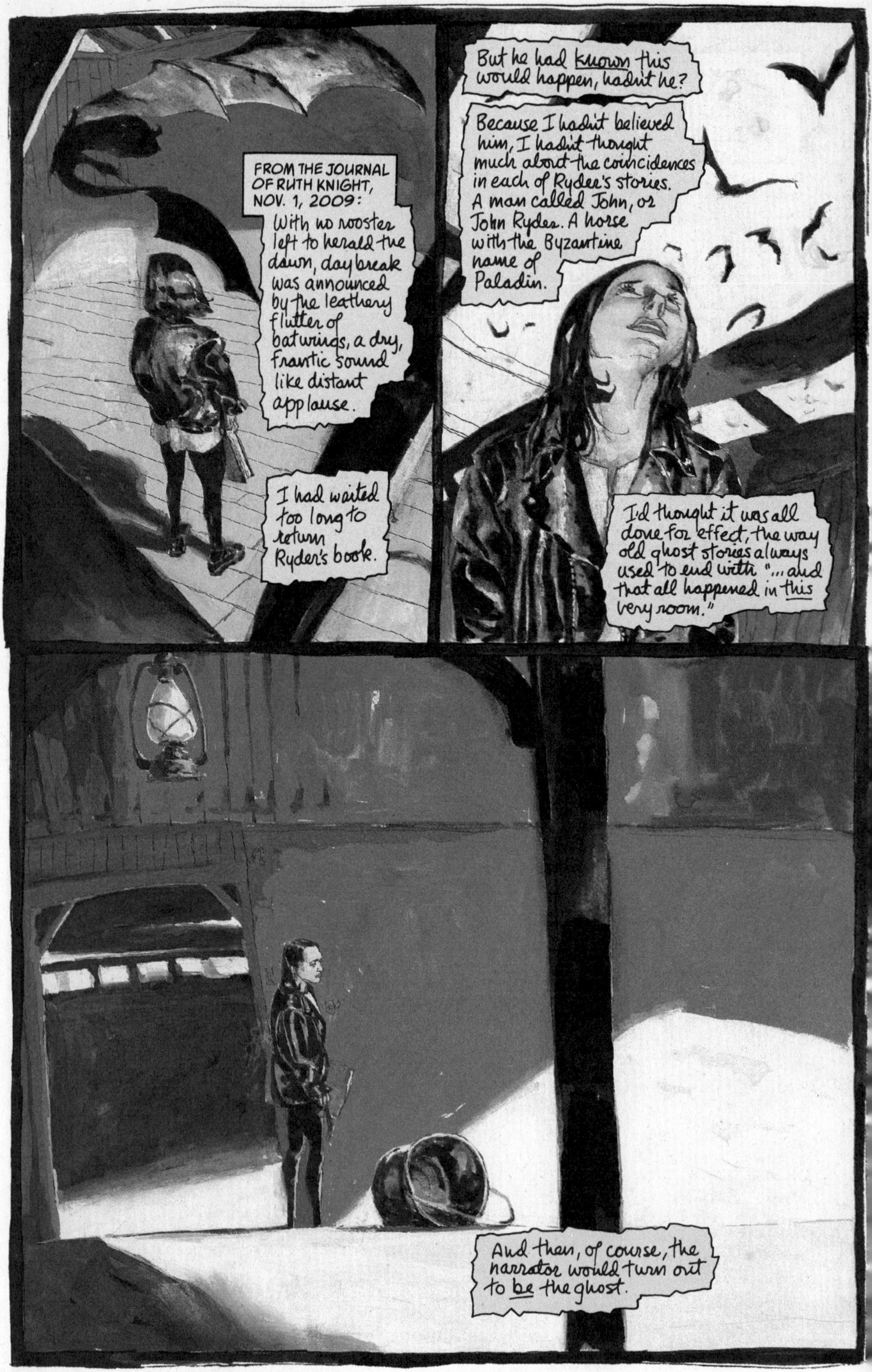
FROM THE JOURNAL OF RUTH KNIGHT, NOV. 1, 2009:
With no rooster left to herald the dawn, daybreak was announced by the leathery flutter of batwings, a dry, frantic sound like distant applause.
I had waited too long to return Ryder's book.
But he had known this would happen, hadn't he?
Because I hadn't believed him, I hadn't thought much about the coincidences in each of Ryder's stories. A man called John, or John Ryder. A horse with the Byzantine name of Paladin.
I'd thought it was all done for effect, the way old ghost stories always used to end with "...and that all happened in this very room."
And then, of course, the narrator would turn out to be the ghost.

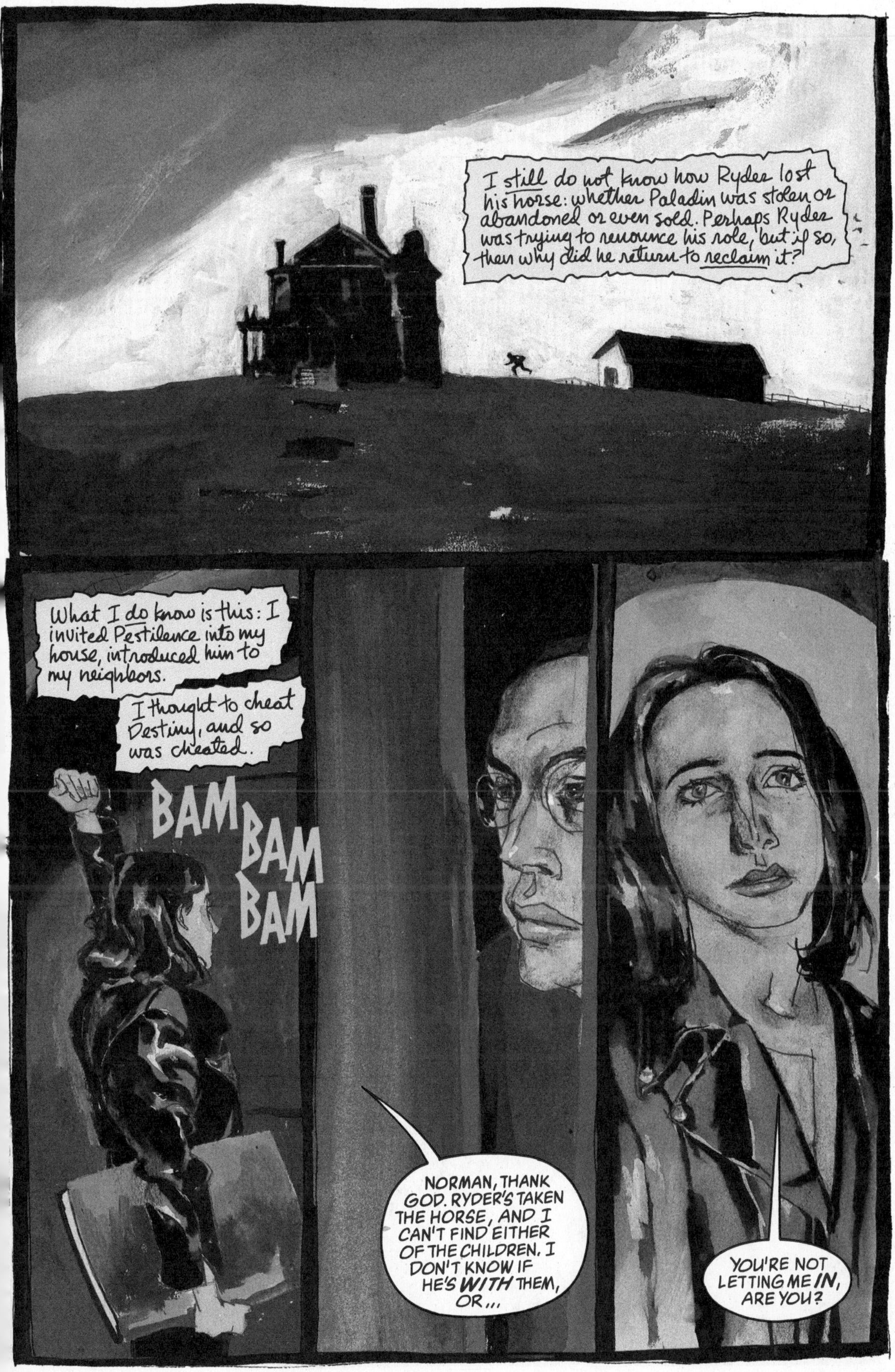
I still do not know how Ryder lost his horse: whether Paladin was stolen or abandoned or even sold. Perhaps Ryder was trying to renounce his role, but if so, then why did he return to reclaim it?
What I do know is this: I invited Pestilence into my house, introduced him to my neighbors.
I thought to cheat Destiny, and so was cheated.
BAM BAM BAM
NORMAN, THANK GOD. RYDER'S TAKEN THE HORSE, AND I CAN'T FIND EITHER OF THE CHILDREN. I DON'T KNOW IF HE'S WITH THEM, OR...
YOU'RE NOT LETTING ME IN, ARE YOU?

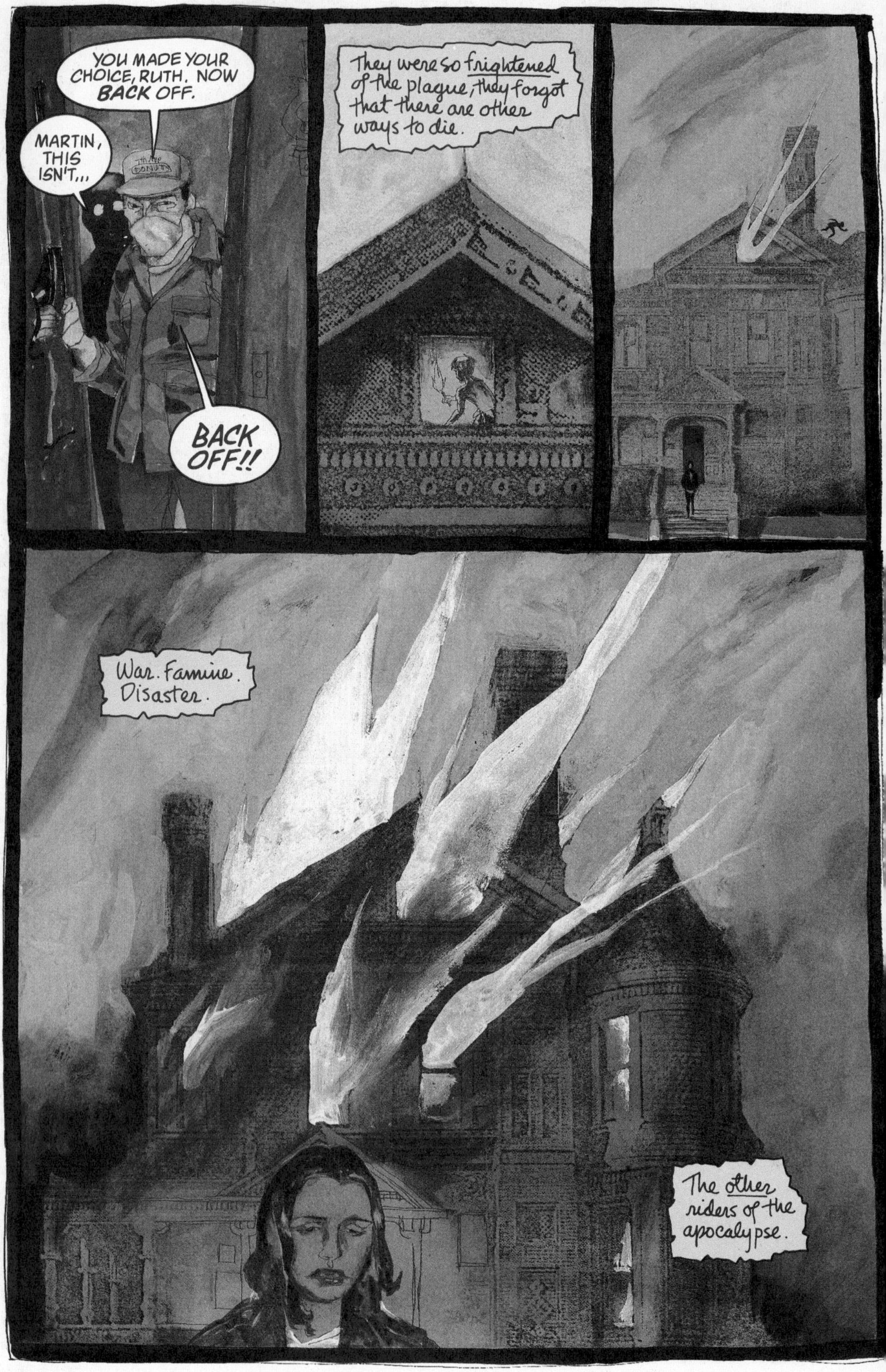
YOU MADE YOUR CHOICE, RUTH. NOW BACK OFF.
MARTIN, THIS ISN'T...
BACK OFF!!
They were so frightened of the plague, they forgot that there are other ways to die.
War. Famine. Disaster.
The other riders of the apocalypse.

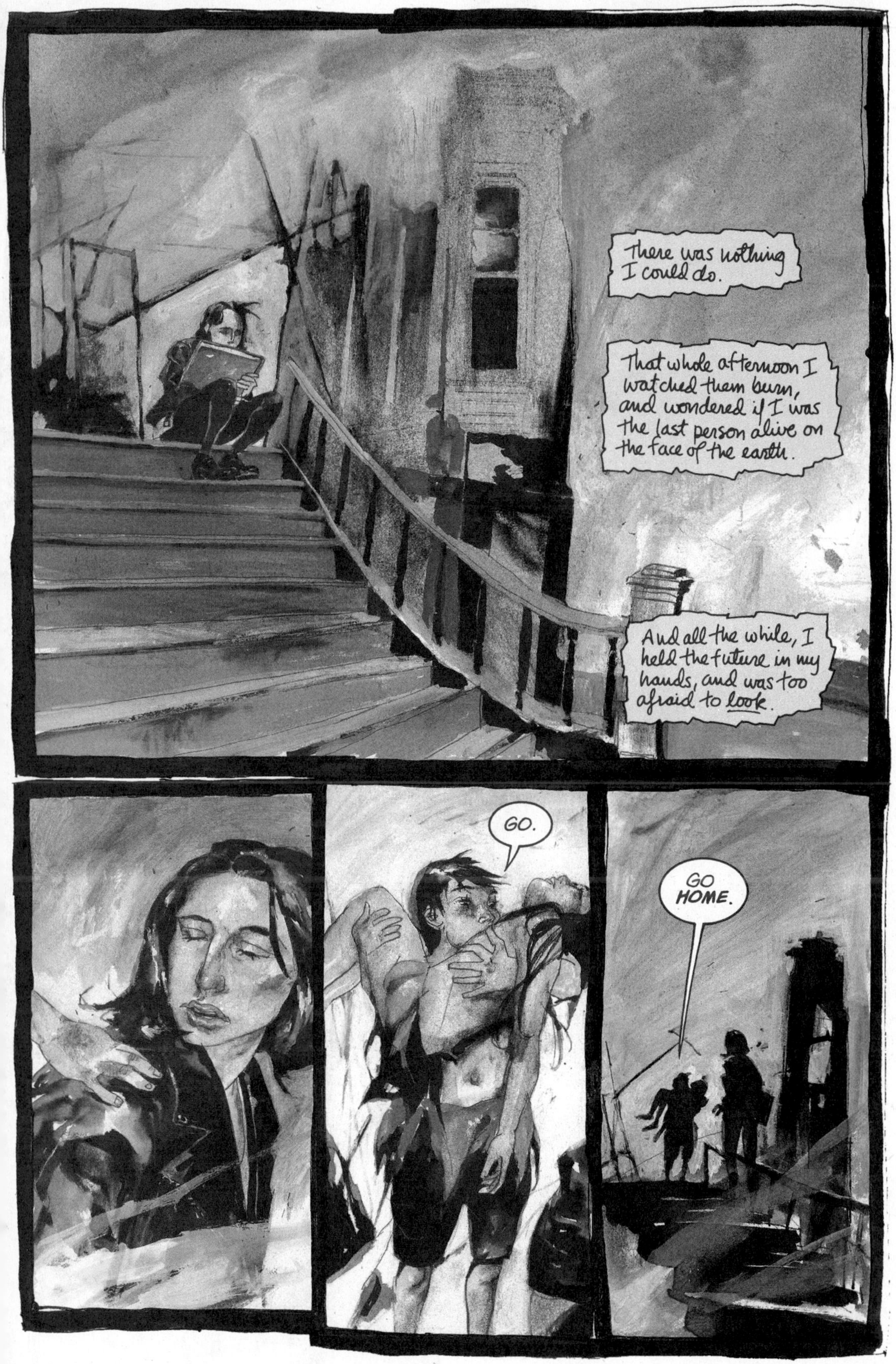
There was nothing I could do.
That whole afternoon I watched them burn, and wondered if I was the last person alive on the face of the earth.
And all the while, I held the future in my hands, and was too afraid to look.
GO.
GO HOME.

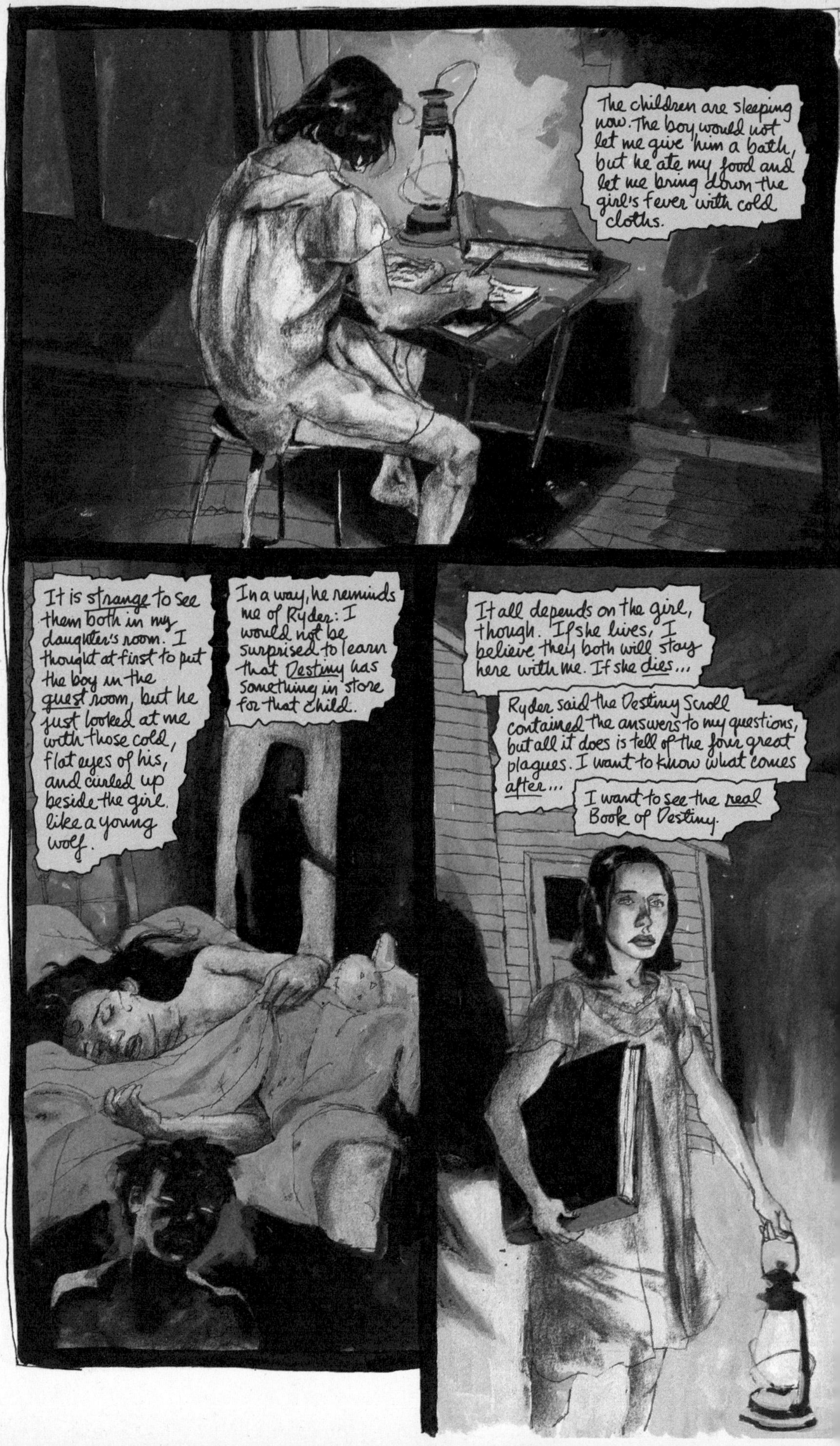
The children are sleeping now. The boy would not let me give him a bath, but he ate my food and let me bring down the girl's fever with cold cloths.
It is strange to see them both in my daughter's room. I thought at first to put the boy in the guest room, but he just looked at me with those cold, flat eyes of his, and curled up beside the girl like a young wolf.
In a way, he reminds me of Ryder: I would not be surprised to learn that Destiny has something in store for that child.
It all depends on the girl, though. If she lives, I believe they both will stay here with me. If she dies...
Ryder said the Destiny Scroll contained the answers to my questions, but all it does is tell of the four great plagues. I want to know what comes after...
I want to see the real Book of Destiny.

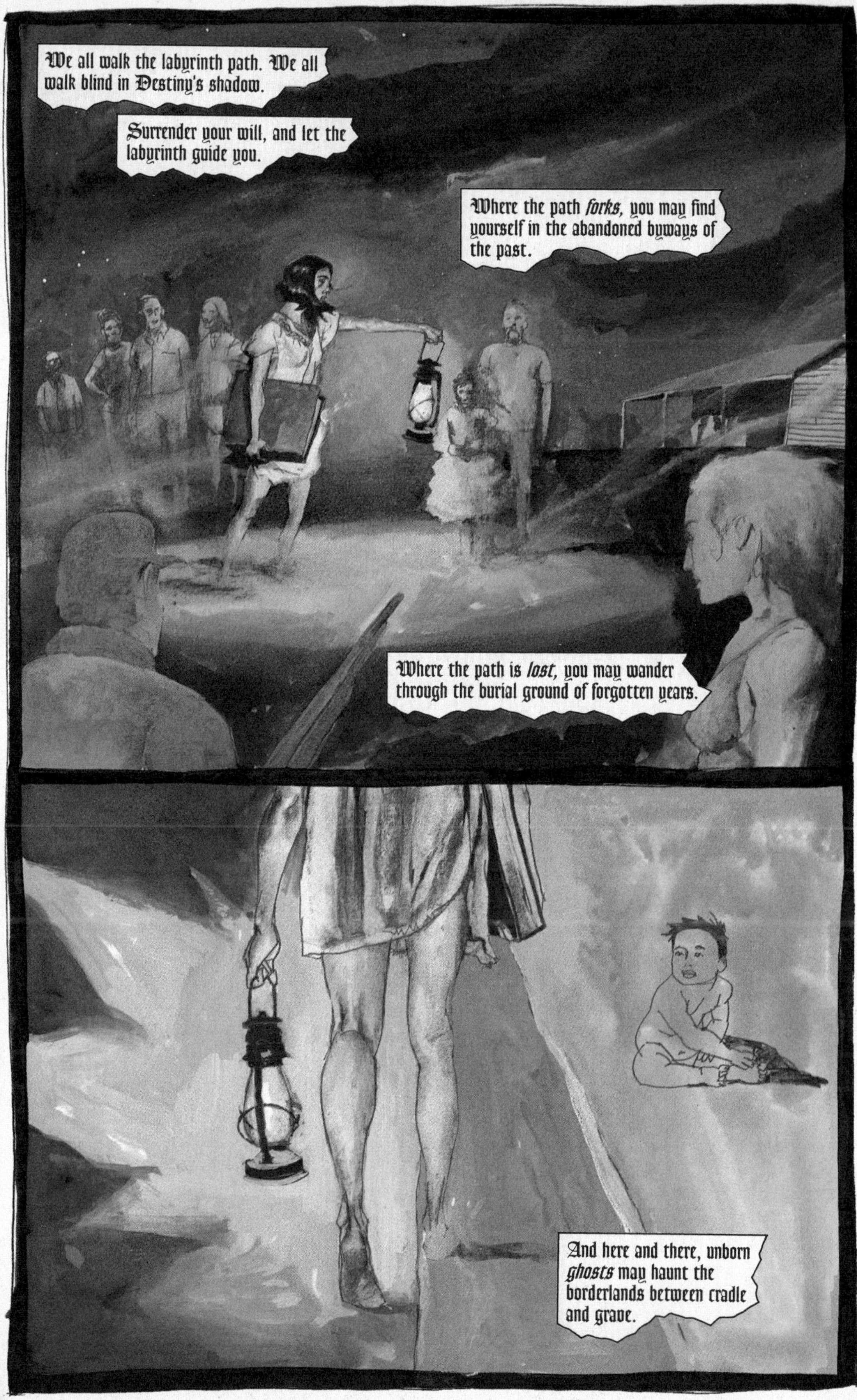
We all walk the labyrinth path. We all walk blind in Destiny's shadow.
Surrender your will, and let the labyrinth guide you.
Where the path *forks,* you may find yourself in the abandoned byways of the past.
Where the path is *lost,* you may wander through the burial ground of forgotten years.
And here and there, unborn *ghosts* may haunt the borderlands between cradle and grave.

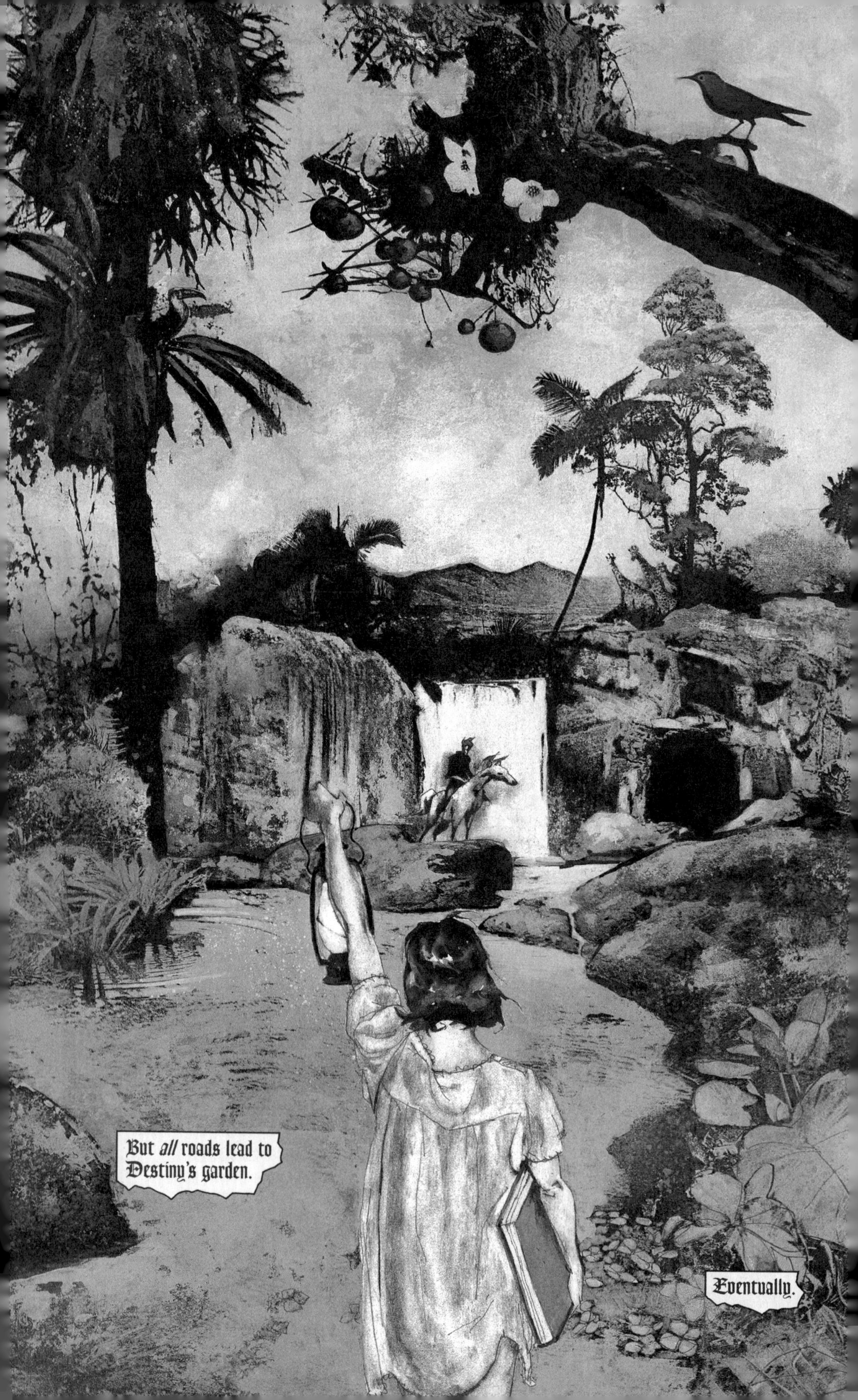
But all roads lead to Destiny's garden.
Eventually.

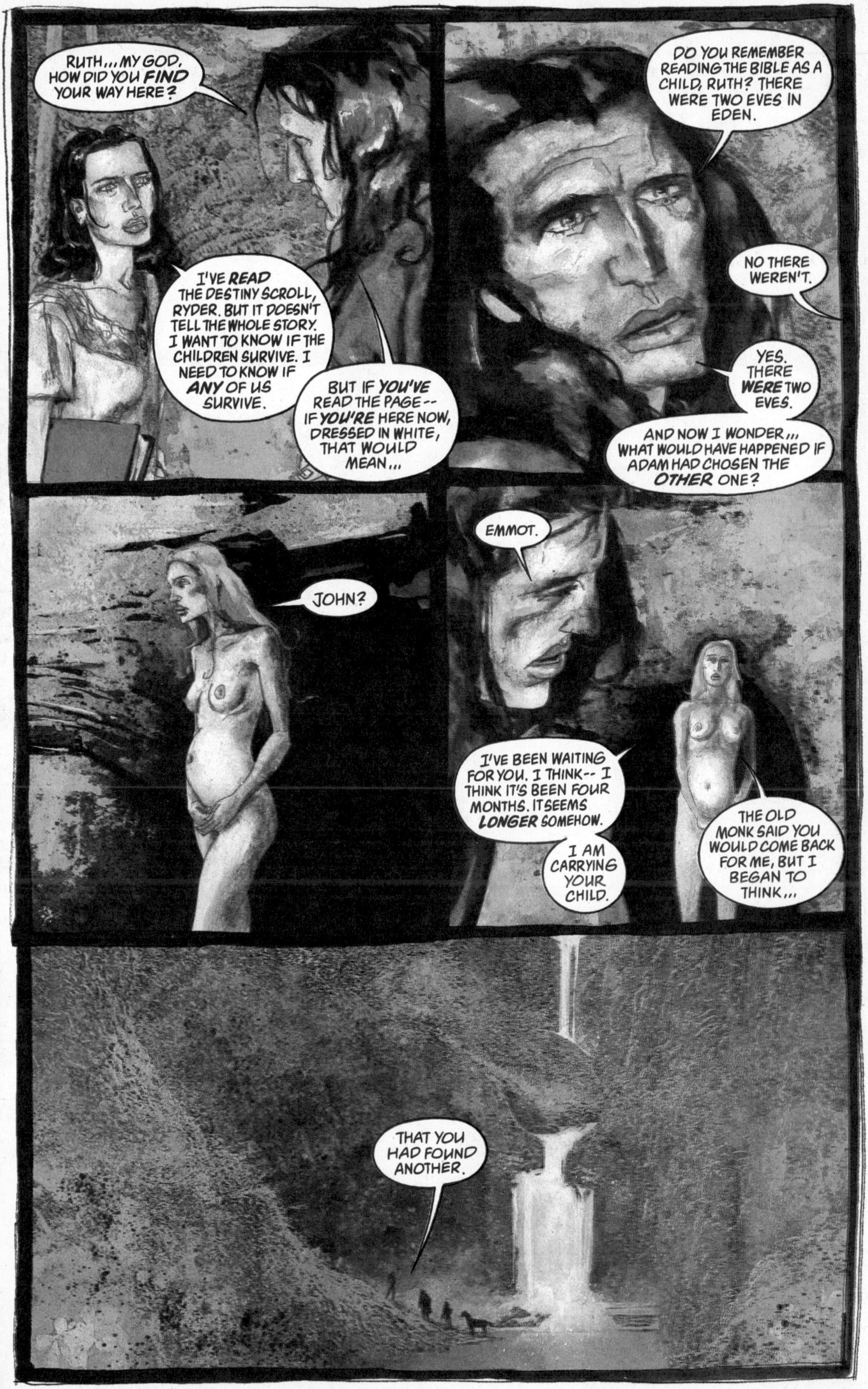
RUTH... MY GOD, HOW DID YOU FIND YOUR WAY HERE?
I'VE READ THE DESTINY SCROLL, RYDER. BUT IT DOESN'T TELL THE WHOLE STORY. I WANT TO KNOW IF THE CHILDREN SURVIVE. I NEED TO KNOW IF ANY OF US SURVIVE.
BUT IF YOU'VE READ THE PAGE -- IF YOU'RE HERE NOW, DRESSED IN WHITE, THAT WOULD MEAN...
DO YOU REMEMBER READING THE BIBLE AS A CHILD, RUTH? THERE WERE TWO EVES IN EDEN.
NO THERE WEREN'T.
YES. THERE WERE TWO EVES.
AND NOW I WONDER... WHAT WOULD HAVE HAPPENED IF ADAM HAD CHOSEN THE OTHER ONE?
JOHN?
EMMOT.
I'VE BEEN WAITING FOR YOU. I THINK-- I THINK IT'S BEEN FOUR MONTHS. IT SEEMS LONGER SOMEHOW.
I AM CARRYING YOUR CHILD.
THE OLD MONK SAID YOU WOULD COME BACK FOR ME, BUT I BEGAN TO THINK...
THAT YOU HAD FOUND ANOTHER.

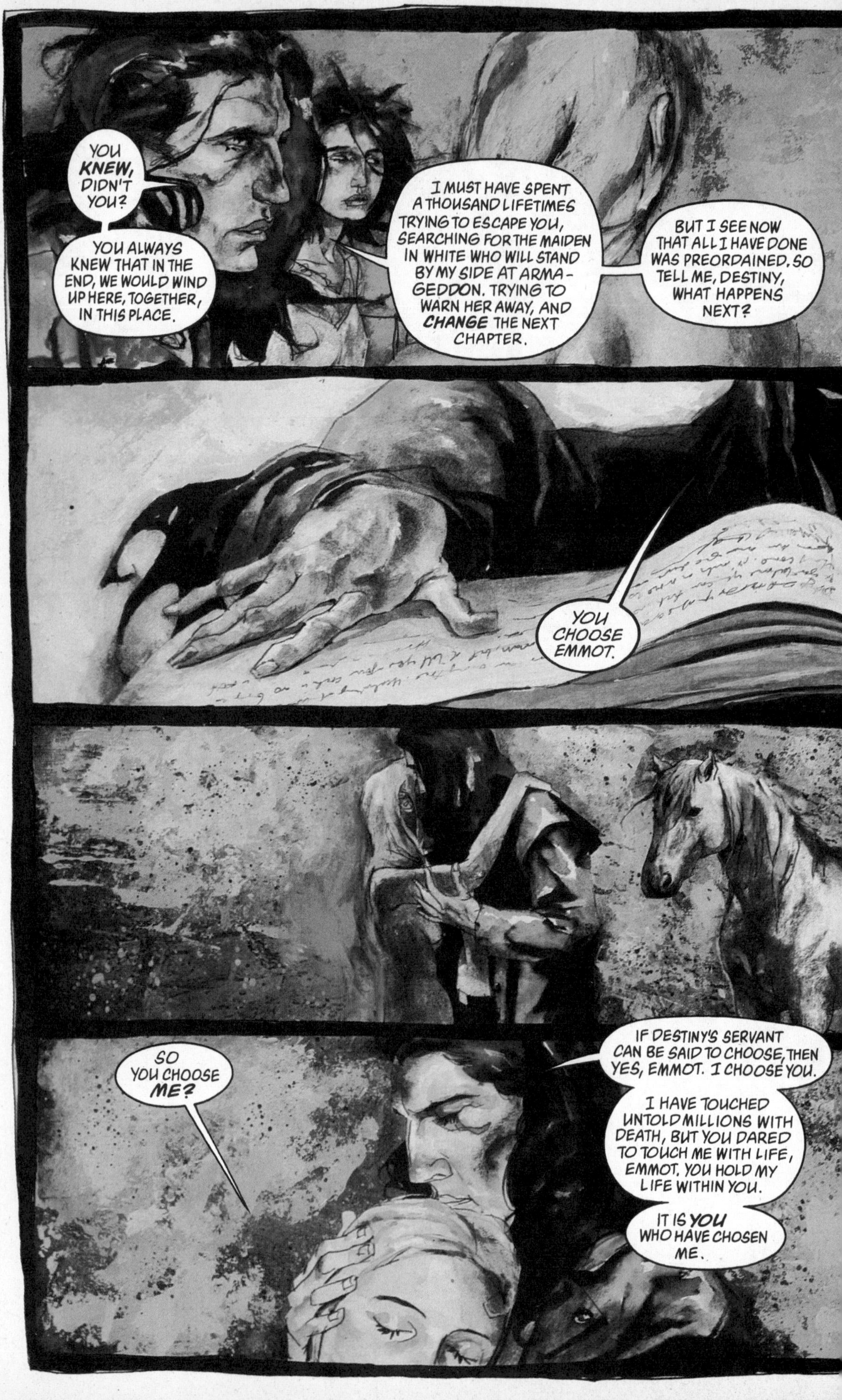
YOU KNEW, DIDN'T YOU?
YOU ALWAYS KNEW THAT IN THE END, WE WOULD WIND UP HERE, TOGETHER, IN THIS PLACE.
I MUST HAVE SPENT A THOUSAND LIFETIMES TRYING TO ESCAPE YOU, SEARCHING FOR THE MAIDEN IN WHITE WHO WILL STAND BY MY SIDE AT ARMA-GEDDON. TRYING TO WARN HER AWAY, AND CHANGE THE NEXT CHAPTER.
BUT I SEE NOW THAT ALL I HAVE DONE WAS PREORDAINED. SO TELL ME, DESTINY, WHAT HAPPENS NEXT?
YOU CHOOSE EMMOT.
SO YOU CHOOSE ME?
IF DESTINY'S SERVANT CAN BE SAID TO CHOOSE, THEN YES, EMMOT. I CHOOSE YOU.
I HAVE TOUCHED UNTOLD MILLIONS WITH DEATH, BUT YOU DARED TO TOUCH ME WITH LIFE, EMMOT. YOU HOLD MY LIFE WITHIN YOU.
IT IS YOU WHO HAVE CHOSEN ME.

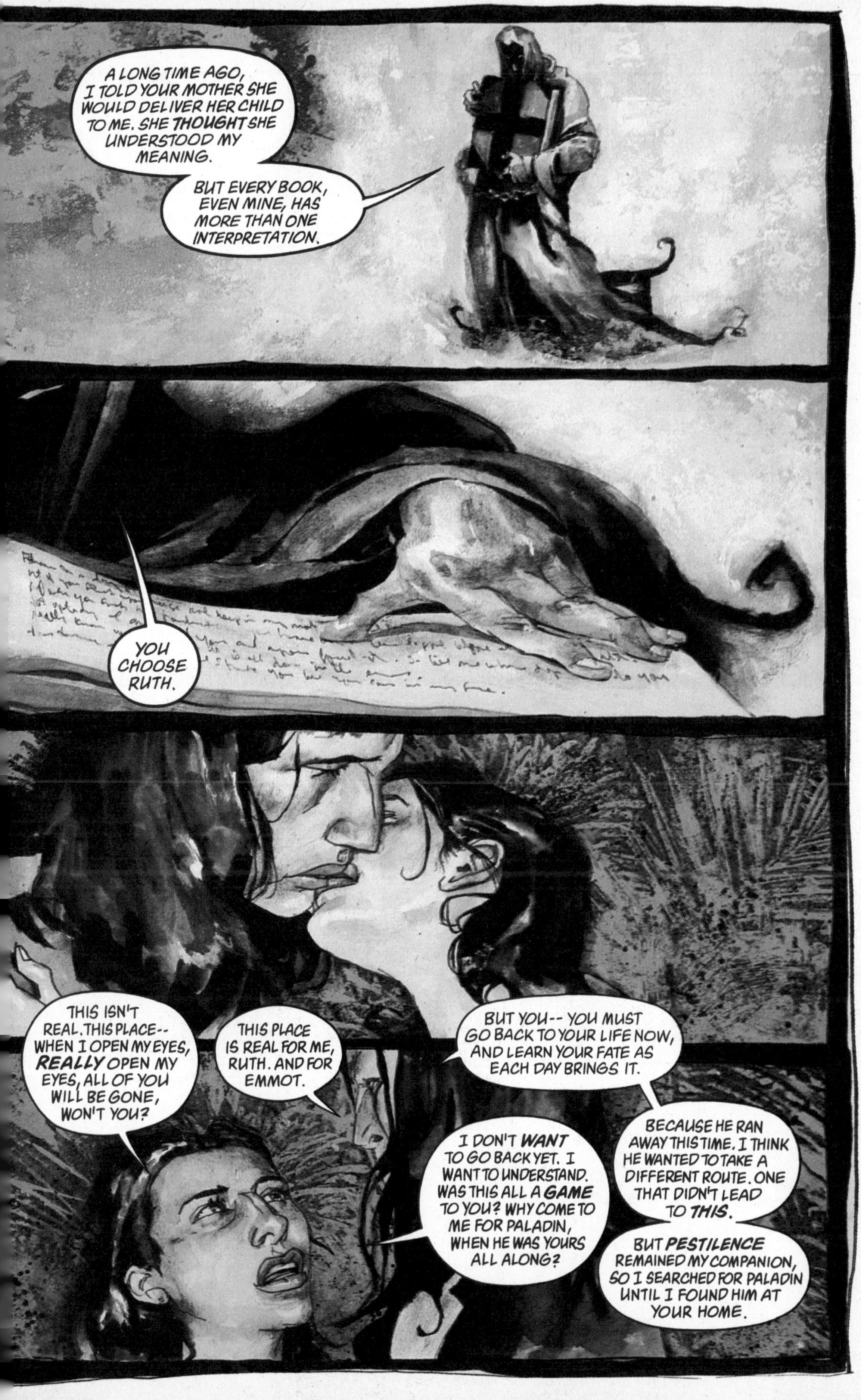
A LONG TIME AGO, I TOLD YOUR MOTHER SHE WOULD DELIVER HER CHILD TO ME. SHE **THOUGHT** SHE UNDERSTOOD MY MEANING.
BUT EVERY BOOK, EVEN MINE, HAS MORE THAN ONE INTERPRETATION.
YOU CHOOSE RUTH.
THIS ISN'T REAL. THIS PLACE-- WHEN I OPEN MY EYES, ***REALLY*** OPEN MY EYES, ALL OF YOU WILL BE GONE, WON'T YOU?
THIS PLACE IS REAL FOR ME, RUTH. AND FOR EMMOT.
BUT YOU-- YOU MUST GO BACK TO YOUR LIFE NOW, AND LEARN YOUR FATE AS EACH DAY BRINGS IT.
I DON'T ***WANT*** TO GO BACK YET. I WANT TO UNDERSTAND. WAS THIS ALL A ***GAME*** TO YOU? WHY COME TO ME FOR PALADIN, WHEN HE WAS YOURS ALL ALONG?
BECAUSE HE RAN AWAY THIS TIME. I THINK HE WANTED TO TAKE A DIFFERENT ROUTE. ONE THAT DIDN'T LEAD TO ***THIS***.
BUT ***PESTILENCE*** REMAINED MY COMPANION, SO I SEARCHED FOR PALADIN UNTIL I FOUND HIM AT YOUR HOME.

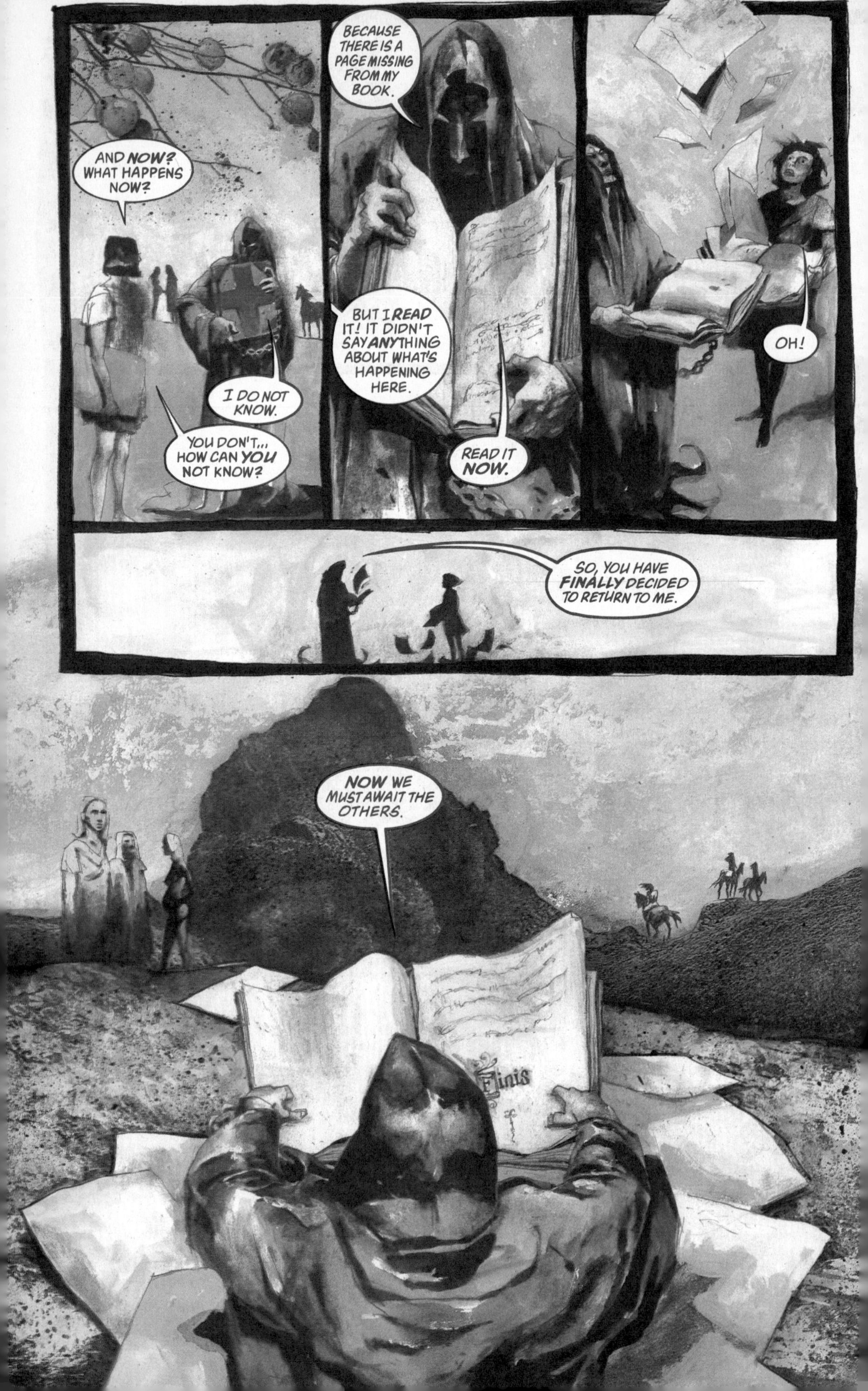
AND NOW? WHAT HAPPENS NOW?
I DO NOT KNOW.
YOU DON'T... HOW CAN YOU NOT KNOW?
BECAUSE THERE IS A PAGE MISSING FROM MY BOOK.
BUT I READ IT! IT DIDN'T SAY ANYTHING ABOUT WHAT'S HAPPENING HERE.
READ IT NOW.
OH!
SO, YOU HAVE FINALLY DECIDED TO RETURN TO ME.
NOW WE MUST AWAIT THE OTHERS.
Finis

Look for these other Vertigo books:

All VERTIGO backlist books are suggested for mature readers

Graphic Novels

DOG MOON
Robert Hunter/Timothy Truman

KILL YOUR BOYFRIEND
Grant Morrison/
Philip Bond/D'Israeli

MENZ INSANA
Christopher Fowler/John Bolton

MERCY
J.M. DeMatteis/Paul Johnson

MR. PUNCH
Neil Gaiman/Dave McKean

MYSTERY PLAY
Grant Morrison/John J Muth

TELL ME, DARK
Karl Edward Wagner/
Kent Williams/John Ney Rieber

TOXIC GUMBO
Lydia Lunch/Ted McKeever

VEILS
Pat McGreal/Stephen John
Phillips/Jose Villarrubia/
Rebecca Guay

WHY I HATE SATURN
Kyle Baker

YOU ARE HERE
Kyle Baker

Collections

BLACK ORCHID
Neil Gaiman/Dave McKean

THE BOOKS OF FAERIE
Bronwyn Carlton/
John Ney Rieber/Peter Gross

THE BOOKS OF MAGIC
Neil Gaiman/John Bolton/
Scott Hampton/Charles Vess/
Paul Johnson

**THE BOOKS OF MAGIC:
BINDINGS**
John Ney Rieber/Gary Amaro/
Peter Gross

**THE BOOKS OF MAGIC:
SUMMONINGS**
Rieber/Gross/Snejbjerg/Amaro/
Giordano

**THE BOOKS OF MAGIC:
RECKONINGS**
John Ney Rieber/Peter
Snejbjerg/Peter Gross/
John Ridgway

**THE BOOKS OF MAGIC:
TRANSFORMATIONS**
John Ney Rieber/Peter Gross

**BOOKS OF MAGIC: GIRL IN
THE BOX**
John Ney Rieber/Peter Gross/
Peter Snejbjerg

BREATHTAKER
Mark Wheatley/Marc Hempel

**THE COMPLEAT
MOONSHADOW**
J.M. DeMatteis/Jon J Muth

**DEATH: THE HIGH COST OF
LIVING**
Neil Gaiman/Chris Bachalo/
Mark Buckingham

**DEATH: THE TIME OF
YOUR LIFE**
Neil Gaiman/Chris Bachalo/
Mark Buckingham/Mark Pennington

**DOOM PATROL: CRAWLING
FROM THE WRECKAGE**
Grant Morrison/Richard Case/
various

**THE DREAMING: BEYOND
THE SHORES OF NIGHT**
Various writers and artists

**THE DREAMING: THROUGH
THE GATES OF HORN
AND IVORY**
Various writers and artists

ENIGMA
Peter Milligan/Duncan Fegredo

HELLBLAZER: ORIGINAL SINS
Jamie Delano/John Ridgway/
various

**HELLBLAZER: DANGEROUS
HABITS**
Garth Ennis/William Simpson/
various

**HELLBLAZER: FEAR AND
LOATHING**
Garth Ennis/Steve Dillon

HELLBLAZER: TAINTED LOVE
Garth Ennis/Steve Dillon

**HELLBLAZER: DAMNATION'S
FLAME**
Garth Ennis/Steve Dillon/
William Simpson/Peter Snejbjerg

HOUSE OF SECRETS:
FOUNDATION
Steven T. Seagle/Teddy Kristiansen

THE INVISIBLES: SAY YOU
WANT A REVOLUTION
Grant Morrison/Steve Yeowell/
Jill Thompson/Dennis Cramer

THE INVISIBLES:
BLOODY HELL IN AMERICA
Grant Morrison/Phil Jimenez/
John Stokes

THE INVISIBLES: COUNTING
TO NONE
Grant Morrison/Phil Jimenez/
John Stokes

NEIL GAIMAN &
CHARLES VESS' STARDUST
Neil Gaiman/Charles Vess

NEVADA
Steve Gerber/Phil Winslade/
Steve Leialoha/Dick Giordano

PREACHER: GONE TO TEXAS
Garth Ennis/Steve Dillon

PREACHER: UNTIL THE END
OF THE WORLD
Garth Ennis/Steve Dillon

PREACHER:
PROUD AMERICANS
Garth Ennis/Steve Dillon

PREACHER: ANCIENT
HISTORY
Garth Ennis/Steve Pugh/
Carlos Ezquerra/Richard Case

PREACHER: DIXIE FRIED
Garth Ennis/Steve Dillon

PREACHER: WAR IN THE SUN
Garth Ennis/Steve Dillon/
Peter Snejbjerg

THE SYSTEM
Peter Kuper

TERMINAL CITY
Dean Motter/Michael Lark

TRANSMETROPOLITAN:
BACK ON THE STREET
Warren Ellis/Darick Robertson/
various

TRANSMETROPOLITAN:
LUST FOR LIFE
Warren Ellis/Darick Robertson

TRUE FAITH
Garth Ennis/Warren Pleece

UNCLE SAM
Steve Darnall/Alex Ross

UNKNOWN SOLDIER
Garth Ennis/Kilian Plunkett

V FOR VENDETTA
Alan Moore/David Lloyd

VAMPS
Elaine Lee/William Simpson

WITCHCRAFT
James Robinson/Peter Snejbjerg/
Michael Zulli/Steve Yeowell/
Teddy Kristiansen

☞ The Sandman Library

THE SANDMAN: PRELUDES &
NOCTURNES
Neil Gaiman/Sam Kieth/
Mike Dringenberg/Malcolm Jones III

THE SANDMAN: THE DOLL'S
HOUSE
Neil Gaiman/Mike Dringenberg/
Malcolm Jones III/Chris Bachalo/
Michael Zulli/Steve Parkhouse

THE SANDMAN: DREAM
COUNTRY
Neil Gaiman/Kelley Jones/
Charles Vess/Colleen Doran/
Malcolm Jones III

THE SANDMAN: SEASON OF
MISTS
Neil Gaiman/Kelley Jones/
Mike Dringenberg/Malcolm Jones III/
various

THE SANDMAN: A GAME
OF YOU
Neil Gaiman/Shawn McManus/
various

THE SANDMAN: FABLES AND
REFLECTIONS
Neil Gaiman/various artists

THE SANDMAN: BRIEF LIVES
Neil Gaiman/Jill Thompson/
Vince Locke

THE SANDMAN:
WORLDS' END
Neil Gaiman/various artists

THE SANDMAN: THE KINDLY
ONES
Neil Gaiman/Marc Hempel/
Richard Case/various

THE SANDMAN: THE WAKE
Neil Gaiman/Michael Zulli/
Jon J Muth/Charles Vess

DUST COVERS—
THE COLLECTED SANDMAN
COVERS 1989-1997
Dave McKean/Neil Gaiman

☞For the nearest comics
shop carrying collected
editions and monthly titles
from DC Comics,
call 1-888-COMIC BOOK.